VANCOUVER

CAROLYN B. HELLER

CONTENTS

MAPS

10 TOP
EXPERIENCES

DISCOVER
VANCOUVER

Vancouver cuts a dramatic urban figure. Set on Pacific coastal inlets with forested mountains beyond, it's frequently named one of the world's most livable cities. When you stroll along the waterfront, or through rainforest parks where evergreens reach the sky, it's easy to see why. Steel-and-glass towers grow like cedars on the downtown peninsula, but in green Vancouver, you're never far from a beach, a mountain, or a public park.

When the sun shines (and even when it doesn't), Vancouverites are outdoors, running or cycling on the seaside paths, kayaking local waters, or sipping a pour-over coffee or local craft beer in a sidewalk café. And unlike in many North American cities, where the city center empties out when the office workers go home, many Vancouver residents live and work downtown, keeping the streets active from early morning into the night.

Home to roughly two million people, Vancouver looks to the Pacific Rim. More than 40 percent of the metro area's population is of Asian descent, influencing everything from art and urban design to food. Vancouver boasts the best Chinese cuisine outside China.

The aboriginal people who've lived on this continent for thousands of years have also made their mark on the city. Vancouver has several museums, galleries, and other attractions where you can explore First Nations culture. An extensive collection of native art at the airport welcomes visitors to the region.

Vancouver is a convenient starting point for trips along the British Columbia coast, north to the mountain resort of Whistler or across the Strait of Georgia to B.C.'s capital city of Victoria. There's much to explore in this part of the world, and it all starts here.

1 **Stanley Park:** The rainforest meets the city in this 1,000-acre parkland, which is crisscrossed with walking trails (page 62).

2 **Dr. Sun Yat-Sen Classical Chinese Garden:** This Chinatown oasis was the first authentic Ming Dynasty garden built outside of China (page 64).

3 **Granville Island Public Market:** Nibble away the day on charcuterie, cheeses, pastries, fudge, and other treats (page 71).

4 **Museum of Anthropology:** This striking modern museum illuminates the culture of British Columbia's aboriginal peoples and traditional cultures from around the world (page 76).

5 **Chinese Food:** More than half the population is of Asian descent in Richmond, where you can dig into some of the best Chinese food in North America (page 120).

6 **Craft Breweries:** A growing number of craft breweries and micro-distilleries welcome visitors for sampling and sipping (page 82).

>>>

^
^
^

7 **Grouse Mountain:** Ride the tram up this North Shore peak for mountaintop hiking trails, a wildlife refuge, and spectacular views (page 87).

8 **Outdoor Adventures:** You don't have to venture far from the city center to experience the rainforest, the mountains, or the sea, whether on a hiking trail, a ski run, or a paddling route (page 166).

9 **Aboriginal Culture:** Stay in Canada's first aboriginal arts hotel, sample traditional foods at a First Nations bistro, paddle a dugout canoe, and shop for works by contemporary native artists (page 23).

>>>

10 **Day Trip to Victoria:** Ferry across the Strait of Georgia for a day trip to visit world-class Butchart Gardens, take afternoon tea at the grand Fairmont Empress Hotel, or go whale-watching (page 200).

EXPLORE
VANCOUVER

THE BEST OF VANCOUVER

In just a few days, you can experience the best of Vancouver, combining outdoor activities, cultural explorations, and time for strolling, snacking, and sipping. Vancouver's public transit system makes it easy to get around without a car; this itinerary includes tips for the most convenient transit options.

>DAY 1:
DOWNTOWN AND
GRANVILLE ISLAND

Get your first glance of the city and orient yourself with the 360-degree view from the observation platform at the **Vancouver Lookout** downtown. Save your ticket to return later for the nighttime views.

Catch bus 50 on Granville Street to **Granville Island.** Browse the stalls and stop for a morning snack in the **Granville Island Public Market,** before checking out the galleries and shops in the **Net Loft,** on **Railspur Alley,** and throughout the island. Don't miss the museum-quality aboriginal art at the **Eagle Spirit Gallery.**

downtown Vancouver

BEST VIEWS

Vancouver is a city of amazing views, so keep your camera handy.

CANADA PLACE
The white sails of Canada Place are one of Vancouver's most recognizable landmarks. Follow the walkway for up-close views, with the water and mountains beyond (page 58).

VANCOUVER LOOKOUT
From this downtown tower, you have 360-degree vistas across the city, overlooking Stanley Park, Gastown, and other districts. It's a good place to get oriented (page 59).

STANLEY PARK
Follow the Seawall around Stanley Park for views across Burrard Inlet to the city skyline and North Shore mountains. At one point, you'll pass under the Lions Gate Bridge, which makes a dramatic photo backdrop (page 62).

OLYMPIC VILLAGE
Stop along False Creek near the Olympic Village to snap photos of city landmarks, including Science World and B.C. Place stadium. You'll have good views of the downtown skyline (page 69).

GROUSE MOUNTAIN
On a clear day, the vistas from the top of Grouse Mountain stretch north toward Howe Sound, over Burrard Inlet, and across metropolitan Vancouver (page 87).

LIGHTHOUSE PARK
Located on the North Shore, this West Vancouver park offers beautiful views across the water toward downtown (page 167).

For lunch, return to the Public Market or sit down for a more leisurely meal, highlighting Canadian products, at **Edible Canada Bistro.**

To start your afternoon on an active note, rent a kayak or a stand-up paddleboard at **Eco-marine Paddlesports Centre** and spend an hour paddling around the island. Back on land, refresh yourself with a sake sampling at the **Artisan Sake Maker** or a craft cocktail made from the small-batch spirits at **Liberty Distilling** before catching the bus back downtown.

Your next stop is the **Bill Reid Gallery of Northwest Coast Art,** which shows works by a noted First Nations artist. Nearby, you can wander the exhibits at the **Vancouver Art Gallery,** making sure to see paintings by B.C.'s renowned Emily Carr.

Siwash Rock, Stanley Park

In the late afternoon, rent a bike and take a leisurely ride along the **Seawall** in **Stanley Park,** stopping to see the **totem poles at Brockton Point,** then pedal past landmark **Siwash Rock.** Pause to rest at **English Bay Beach,** which is also one of Vancouver's best spots to watch the sun set over the ocean. Across the street from the beach, smile at *A-maze-ing Laughter,* a public art piece comprising 14 grinning bronze figures.

Have dinner downtown, perhaps the imaginative contemporary fare at **Royal Dinette** or a creative pizza at **Nightingale,** then return to the **Vancouver Lookout** to gaze over the city's twinkling lights.

>DAY 2:
UBC, GASTOWN, AND CHINATOWN

Enjoy breakfast at **Forage** or **Medina Café** before exploring more of the city's cultural highlights.

From Granville Street, catch bus 4 or 14 west to the **University of British Columbia** and the **Museum of Anthropology.** This first-rate museum has a particularly strong collection of First Nations art, including an awe-inspiring gallery of totem poles. After exploring the museum, take a walk through the serene **Nitobe Japanese Garden** nearby.

When you're finished on campus, take bus 4 back toward Kitsilano for lunch on West 4th Avenue: Thai food at **Maenam** or French bistro fare at **Au Comptoir.** Check out the 4th Avenue shops before stopping for dessert at **Beaucoup Bakery & Café** or a shot of rich hot chocolate from **Chocolate Arts.**

Bus 4 or 7 will take you from Kits to Gastown. Walk along Water Street, watch the **Gastown Steam Clock** toot its steam whistle, and stop into several of the First Nations art galleries, like **Hill's Native Art.**

Continue into **Chinatown** for a late-afternoon tour of the **Dr. Sun Yat-Sen Classical Chinese Garden,** the only authentic Ming Dynasty garden outside China.

Stay in Chinatown for dinner. Try the unusual combination of Italian and Japanese elements at speakeasy-style **Kissa Tanto** or share modern Canadian plates at

Juniper Kitchen & Bar. After your meal, have a drink at the **Keefer Bar,** or take a cab back downtown for a nightcap at **Uva Wine & Cocktail Bar** or elegant **Prohibition Lounge.**

>DAY 3:
THE NORTH SHORE

Today, you're exploring the mountains and rainforests on Vancouver's North Shore. Catch the free shuttle from **Canada Place** to **Grouse Mountain.** If you're up for a challenge, walk up the **Grouse Grind,** a trail nicknamed "Mother Nature's Stairmaster." But there's no shame in taking the **Skyride;** it's North America's largest tram system. At the top, laugh at the lumberjack show, explore the wildlife refuge, and go for a short hike. The views are spectacular on a clear day.

Come down the mountain, and at the Grouse entrance, catch bus 236 to the **Capilano Suspension Bridge.** This 450-foot (137-meter) span swings over a canyon high above the Capilano River. If you're feeling brave, follow the **Cliffwalk,** a series of boardwalks cantilevered over the rushing river. Do you dare

Dr. Sun Yat-Sen Classical Chinese Garden

stand on the glass platform and look down (way down!)?

Get back on bus 236 to **Lonsdale Quay.** Stop for a drink, with views of the city skyline, at **Pier 7 Restaurant & Bar,** a short walk from the quay. Then take the **SeaBus** across the Burrard Inlet to Waterfront Station downtown.

Have dinner in Gastown, where **L'Abbatoir** serves French-accented west coast fare on the site of Vancouver's first jail or stylish **Chambar** combines flavors of North Africa and Belgium with local ingredients.

With More Time

DAY 4: RICHMOND

Ride the Canada Line to spend a day in Vancouver's "new Chinatown" in the city of Richmond. First up: dim sum in the Golden Village along No. 3 Road. At Golden Paramount Seafood Restaurant, choose from a mix of traditional and modern Hong Kong-style plates, or at Su Hang Restaurant, try Shanghai-style dim sum.

After you've eaten, catch bus 403 southbound along No. 3 Road to the International Buddhist Temple, one of the largest Chinese Buddhist temples in North America. Visitors are welcome to tour the gardens and the peaceful temple complex.

From the temple, head to the village of Steveston, an active fishing port where the Asian communities have historic roots. Visiting the Gulf of Georgia Cannery National Historic Site or the Britannia Shipyards National Historic Site will introduce you to the area's multicultural history. Walk along the wharf, where fishing boats sell their fresh catch. Pajo's on the pier makes first-rate fish–and-chips.

Bus 402, 407, or 410 will take you back to the Golden Village, where you can browse the Asian shops at Aberdeen Centre.

If you're in town on a Friday, Saturday, or Sunday between mid-May and mid-October, take the Canada Line to Bridgeport Station for the Richmond Night Market. Graze your way through this Asian-style festival of street foods from China, Taiwan, Japan, and more. Return downtown on the Canada Line.

DAY 5: CAMBIE CORRIDOR AND EAST VANCOUVER

From downtown, take bus 17 to VanDusen Botanical Garden and spend your morning strolling among the blossoms. When you're ready to eat, hop on a northbound bus 17 for lunch at Salmon n' Bannock, a modern aboriginal bistro.

Continue east on Broadway to the Cambie Corridor to browse the neighborhood's boutiques. There's a cluster of shops near Main and Broadway, and more clothing and accessories purveyors on Main between 20th and 30th Avenues (if you don't want to walk, bus 3 can take you along Main Street).

When you're done shopping, it's time for a beer crawl to try the city's craft breweries. Both 33 Acres Brewing and Brassneck Brewery are a short walk from the intersection of Broadway and Main.

For a more serious exploration of Vancouver's microbrewery scene, head for the Commercial Drive and East Village neighborhoods. Parallel 49 Brewing Company has a large tasting room that's a popular neighborhood gathering spot. To sample some spirits, visit Odd Society Spirits, a small-batch distillery in a former motorcycle garage. To get here from Broadway and Main, take bus 99 eastbound on Broadway to Commercial Drive, then change to bus 20 going north and get off on Hastings Street.

When you've tasted your fill, bus 4 or 7 (on Powell St.) or bus 14 or 16 (on Hastings St.) will bring you back downtown for dinner at lively Guu Garden (a Japanese *izakaya*) or at Boulevard Kitchen & Oyster Bar for local seafood in a stylish setting.

VANCOUVER WITH KIDS

With so many outdoor attractions, cool ways to get around the city, and kid-friendly restaurants, Vancouver is a fantastic destination for families. Whether you're exploring a rainforest park, riding a ferry, or following the Dumpling Trail, Vancouver serves up plenty of family-focused fun. Tip: Always ask about special family rates or discounts when you're buying tickets to any sights or attractions.

> DAY 1: STANLEY PARK

Pack a picnic lunch and spend the day in **Stanley Park,** Vancouver's rainforest green space at the end of the downtown peninsula. Visit the **Vancouver Aquarium Marine Science Centre** first (it's less crowded in the mornings), then enjoy your picnic near Lost Lagoon.

After lunch, **rent bikes** to explore more of the park; there are several rental shops just outside the park's West Georgia Street entrance. Follow the **Seawall** to see the majestic **totem poles at Brockton Point,** stop to cool off in the splash park near Lumberman's Arch, and let the kids play in the sand or go for a swim at **Second Beach,** where there's a large pool, restrooms, and snack bar.

For dinner, try one of the Asian restaurants downtown. Most kids enjoy watching the dumpling makers at work at **Dinesty Dumpling House,** or you can dig into Japanese-style hot dogs at **Japadog.**

Science World

BEST PEOPLE-WATCHING

Many of the city's top people-watching locales are beaches and walkways. For more urban people-spotting, head for Gastown, Yaletown, or Granville Island.

THE SEAWALL

Stroll the Seawall in Yaletown, the West End, or near the Olympic Village, particularly on a weekend afternoon or summer evening. You'll have plenty of company (page 58).

GRANVILLE ISLAND

Sit outside along the water behind the **Granville Island Public Market** to survey an endless parade of tourists hopping on and off the tiny False Creek ferries, locals taking a break from shopping, and kayakers out for some exercise (page 71).

YALETOWN

Bars and restaurants with outdoor seating line Hamilton and Mainland Streets. Try **WildTale Coastal Grill,** where you can spot well-dressed millennials out for an evening and yoga mat-toting residents on their way home from the studio (page 105).

GASTOWN

Watch the world go by from the always-packed patio at **Chill Winston,** opposite the Gassy Jack statue in Maple Tree Square (page 128).

ENGLISH BAY BEACH

On the downtown peninsula near Stanley Park, this curve of sand attracts local seniors, gay couples, hordes of visitors, and pretty much anyone who wants to enjoy the views across the water. It's especially busy at sunset (page 154).

KITSILANO BEACH

Serious beach volleyball enthusiasts, families with kids, groups of UBC students, and sunbathers congregate at busy Kits Beach (page 159).

>**DAY 2:**
GRANVILLE ISLAND AND FALSE CREEK

Buy a day pass for the Aquabus ferry, so you can hop on and off these cute little boats as you travel around Granville Island and False Creek. Take the Aquabus to **Science World** and spend the morning exploring the hands-on exhibits. When it's time for lunch, cruise over to **Granville Island,** where there are plenty of family-friendly food options in the **Granville Island Public Market.**

Don't miss the **Kids Market,** with its kid-approved shops and indoor playground. Check out **Sea Village,** too, to let the kids imagine what it would be like to live on a houseboat. When you're done exploring the island, **rent kayaks** for an excursion along False Creek.

Have an early dinner at **Go Fish** (it's a short stroll along the waterfront from Granville Island), then catch the Aquabus to Yaletown for dessert at **Bella Gelateria Yaletown.**

>**DAY 3:**
CANADA PLACE AND THE NORTH SHORE

Start your day at **Canada Place** with a virtual flight across the country at **FlyOver Canada.** You even feel the spray as you soar (virtually) over Niagara Falls.

In front of Canada Place, catch the free shuttle to **Grouse Mountain.** Ride the **Skyride** tram to the top, where you can visit the grizzly bears at the **Grouse Mountain Refuge for Endangered Wildlife,** watch the falcons soar at the **Birds in Motion** demonstration, and get some chuckles at the **Lumberjack Show.** Go for a hike, and have lunch overlooking the city and water below.

Your next stop is the **Capilano Suspension Bridge** (from the

Grouse Mountain entrance, take bus 236 down Capilano Road). Give the kids a thrill as they look from the bridge to the canyon way below. Explore the **Treetops Adventure,** too, where you follow a network of gently swaying wooden bridges to eight treehouse platforms in the forest. When you're ready to go back downtown, catch the free shuttle.

For supper, let the kids play with the jukeboxes at retro diner **The Templeton** or slurp up a bowl of ramen at **Hokkaido Ramen Santouka.** The Korean shaved ice dessert called *bingsoo,* served at **Snowy Village Dessert Café,** makes a fun after-dinner treat.

>DAY 4:
UBC AND POINT GREY

Today, you'll tour the museums on the **University of British Columbia** campus, check out another rainforest park, and then have time to relax at **Jericho Beach.**

From downtown, catch any UBC-bound bus to the campus bus loop. Walk over to the **Museum of Anthropology,** where there's a fantastic collection of First Nations totem poles and other artifacts. Another short walk takes you to the **Beaty Biodiversity Museum,** which has more than two million specimens of bugs, fish, plants, and fossils that the kids can explore, as well as a massive blue whale skeleton. One more campus attraction, located at the **UBC Botanical Garden,** is the **Greenheart TreeWalk,** a network of aerial bridges that takes you high into the rainforest canopy.

Catch bus 99 to Point Grey Village (get off at W. 10th Ave. at

Canada Place

Sasamat St.), where you can have a sandwich and a sweet at **Mix the Bakery.** After you've refueled, walk south to West 16th Avenue, where you can go for a stroll in the rainforest at **Pacific Spirit Regional Park,** which has more than 40 miles (70 kilometers) of hiking trails. The trails are fairly well marked, but the park is large, so you'll need to pay attention to your route.

If the kids aren't too tired, you can walk down to the **Jericho Sailing Centre** (it's 1.25 miles, or two kilometers, straight down Trimble Street); if you'd rather go by bus, it's fastest to take bus 25 or 33 on 16th Avenue back to the UBC Bus Loop, then change to bus 84, which will drop you on West 4th Avenue just above the beach. Have dinner overlooking the sand at **The Galley Patio and Grill,** go for a **sunset kayak paddle,** or simply sit on the beach and watch the sunset. When you're ready to go back downtown, take bus 4 from West 4th Avenue.

>DAY 5:
RICHMOND

Plan a **whale-watching cruise** today. Several operators run trips from **Steveston Village** in the

BEST FOR ROMANCE

Visiting Vancouver with a special some-one? Start by cycling around Stanley Park on a bicycle built for two or pad-dling around Granville Island in a tan-dem kayak. Then check out these other romantic spots.

SIP
Have a drink at **Reflections Lounge** (page 125), hidden on the fourth floor of the Rosewood Hotel Georgia, or sink into the leather chairs at posh **Bacchus Lounge** (page 126) to enjoy your cocktails with live piano music.

EAT
For dinner, **Hawksworth Restaurant** (page 94) always wows for its setting and service, while **West** (page 112), on South Granville Street, serves first-rate contemporary fare appropriate for any special occasion. Book a table at sunset overlooking False Creek at **Ancora Waterfront Dining and Patio** (page 104), and enjoy both the views and the distinctive Peruvian-Japanese dishes. If you consider oysters to be an aphrodisiac, or if you simply crave fresh seafood, reserve your spot for two at **Boulevard Kitchen & Oyster Bar** (page 95).

TREAT
Share two scoops of Vancouver's best gelato at downtown's **Bella Gelateria** (page 99). Detour to Gastown to in-dulge in a lemon chèvre brownie or other decadent sweet at **Purebread** (page 103). Book a chocolate high tea for two at Kitsilano's **Chocolate Arts** (page 110).

SLEEP
When you're ready to call it a day, Yaletown's boutique **Opus Hotel Vancouver** (page 194) will appeal to contemporary couples, while the **Wedgewood Hotel & Spa** (page 190) is a good choice for more traditional ro-mantics. The deluxe **Fairmont Pacific Rim** (page 188) will pamper any pairs, particularly if you book a couple's treat-ment in the posh Willow Spring Spa.

suburb of **Richmond,** and most will include transportation from downtown. Spend the morning on the water looking for orcas, sea lions, and other aquatic life. Back on land, check out the fish-ing boats and vendors along the wharf, and stop for a fish-and-chips lunch at **Pajo's.**

Richmond is the center of Vancouver's Asian community, so instead of heading straight back downtown, catch bus 402, 407, or 410 from Steveston to Rich-mond's **Golden Village,** where you can choose from countless Chi-nese restaurants for dinner. The kids might enjoy mapping out their route along Richmond's **Dumpling Trail** (get a map at www.visitrich-mondbc.com) or choosing from the long list of bubble teas at **Pearl Castle Café.** If you're in town on a weekend between mid-May and mid-October, wrap up your day at the **Richmond Night Market,** where there's plenty of Asian food to sample, before catching the Canada Line back downtown.

A DAY OUTDOORS

From spring through fall, head for the North Shore to enjoy a day outdoors. Although it's possible to do this excursion by public transport, it's easier if you have a car.

fruit tarts, Granville Island Public Market

>MORNING: DEEP COVE

Start your day of adventure by assembling a picnic for lunch outdoors. Make a quick shopping stop at the **Granville Island Public Market.** Then go east from downtown, and cross the Second Narrows Bridge to the North Shore.

Begin your visit to the scenic waterfront village of **Deep Cove** with a freshly made treat from local institution **Honey Donuts.** When you've sated your sweet tooth, rent a **kayak** for a leisurely paddle between the forests and mountains of **Indian Arm fjord.** If you'd rather go with a guide, **Deep Cove Kayaks** offers kayak tours, including a three-hour **Deep Cove Explorer** route that's suitable for novice and more advanced paddlers alike.

>AFTERNOON: LYNN CANYON AND GROUSE MOUNTAIN

Back on shore, it's a short drive to **Lynn Canyon Park,** which has a **suspension bridge** that was built back in 1912—and it's free. Find a shady spot to enjoy your picnic lunch. When you're done eating, follow a forested hiking trail to one of the popular swimming areas and go for a dip.

Late in the afternoon, you'll still have time for a visit to **Grouse Mountain.** Take the **Skyride** up the mountain, or if you have energy to spare, hike up the famous **Grouse Grind** trail. Nicknamed "Mother Nature's Stairmaster," it's essentially a mountain staircase with an elevation gain of 2,800 feet (850 meters). However you get to the top, there's plenty to do when you arrive: Go **zip-lining,** watch one of the wildlife shows, or try out a **paragliding** adventure.

zip-lining at Grouse Mountain

ABORIGINAL CULTURE

Aboriginal people have lived in western Canada for more than 10,000 years. For many visitors, the opportunity to explore this traditional culture and its present-day manifestations is a highlight.

Here are just a few of the numerous places where native culture remains strong. Another valuable resource for visitors interested in First Nations culture is the **Aboriginal Tourism Association of British Columbia** (604/921-1070 or 877/266-2822, www.aboriginalbc.com).

BILL REID GALLERY OF NORTHWEST COAST ART
Dedicated to the work of Haida First Nations artist Bill Reid, this gallery showcases Reid's sculptures, carvings, and jewelry (page 59).

TALKING TREES WALK
Several First Nations made their traditional home in Vancouver's Stanley Park. Tour Stanley Park with an aboriginal guide to learn more about the park's aboriginal heritage (page 62).

Squamish Lil'Wat Cultural Centre

MUSEUM OF ANTHROPOLOGY
This excellent museum illuminates the culture of British Columbia's aboriginal peoples and traditional cultures from around the world (page 76).

SALMON N' BANNOCK RESTAURANT
This contemporary aboriginal bistro uses traditional ingredients in its elk burgers, game sausages, and bison tenderloin. They serve plenty of salmon and bannock (a native bread), too (page 113).

SKWACHÀYS LODGE
Stay at Canada's first aboriginal arts and culture hotel, where works by First Nations artists adorn the one-of-a-kind guest rooms (page 193).

SQUAMISH LIL'WAT CULTURAL CENTRE
In Whistler, learn about the history and present-day culture of the region's First Nations communities at this modern gallery (page 262).

When you're ready to relax, have a drink in the lounge overlooking the city.

❯EVENING: SUNSET ON THE BEACH

Return to Vancouver in time to watch the sunset from **English Bay Beach.** Ready for dinner? Stroll along Denman Street for tapas at **España Restaurant,** walk up Robson Street for farm-to-table fare

at **Forage,** or go for high-end sushi overlooking Canada Place at **Miku.**

Wrap up your day downtown with drinks at all-Canadian gastropub **Timber,** where Caesars (Canada's version of a Bloody Mary) are a signature, or head over to Granville Island for an always-entertaining improv show at **Vancouver Theatre Sports League.** Then get a good night's sleep; with this active day, you've earned it.

VANCOUVER'S ASIAN CULTURE

>MORNING: CHINATOWN

Get a sweet start to your day in Gastown with coffee and a treat from **Purebread,** or pair your caffeine with an avocado toast at **Nelson the Seagull.** Walk from Gastown to **Chinatown,** then spend the rest of your morning at the peaceful **Dr. Sun Yat-Sen Classical Chinese Garden.** Take a guided tour to learn more about the garden's construction and rest up on a bench overlooking the koi pond.

>AFTERNOON: RICHMOND AND STEVESTON

Catch bus 23, Davie, outside the Chinese Garden at the corner of Keefer and Columbia Streets, and change to the Canada Line (Richmond branch) at Yaletown/Roundhouse station. You're heading for the suburb of **Richmond** for a dim sum lunch in the **Golden Village,** which is full of Asian restaurants and shopping malls. Good dim sum options include **Golden Paramount Seafood Restaurant** and **Empire Seafood Restaurant.** Both are a short walk from the Canada Line's Richmond-Brighouse Station.

After you've eaten, continue south to the fishing port of **Steveston.** Bus 402, 407, or 410 can bring you to Steveston Village from outside the Richmond-Brighouse Station on Number 3 Road.

Take a walk on the wharf, check out the fish vendors, then learn about the Asian, European, and First Nations workers who once staffed the **Gulf of Georgia Cannery** or the **Britannia Shipyards,** which are both now National Historic Sites. If you have time when you've finished your Steveston visit, detour to the peaceful **International Buddhist Temple,** one of the largest traditional temples in North America.

>EVENING: DINNER IN RICHMOND

Return to the Golden Village on Number 3 Road to sit down for dinner at one of Richmond's hundreds of Chinese eateries. If you're a spicy food fan, go Hunan-style at **Bushuair Restaurant** or sample the Sichuan cuisine at **New Spicy Chili Restaurant.** For milder fare, **Bamboo Grove** is an excellent upscale Cantonese option. Alternatively, graze your way through the Asian food stalls at the **Richmond Night Market,** near the Bridgeport Canada Line station.

Take the Canada Line back to downtown Vancouver for a nightcap at a Japanese *izakaya* like **Guu Garden,** or at **The Keefer Bar,** an Asian-inspired lounge in Chinatown. Or if you're ready for a late-night snack, stop for a unique-to-Vancouver Japanese-style hot dog at **Japadog.**

PLANNING YOUR TRIP

WHEN TO GO

High season in Vancouver and Victoria runs from May through October, when the weather is generally warm and relatively dry. **July and August** are the region's peak travel months, with the sunny, temperate conditions balancing out the big crowds and high prices. In summer, the comfortable daytime temperatures rarely rise above 75°F (24°C), and the sun doesn't set until after 9pm.

Prices may be somewhat more moderate in spring (April through June) and fall (September through October), although you can expect more rain than in midsummer.

During the winter months of November through February, prices are lowest; except during the Christmas/New Year's holidays, accommodations can drop to half of their summertime rates. The cultural calendar is full with theater, music, and other arts events, and you can ski on the local mountains or just two hours away at Whistler-Blackcomb. Daytime temperatures in the city average 43-46°F (6-8°C) during the winter. The trade-off is that winter is the rainy season, with rain—sometimes quite heavy—and clouds most days. Snow typically falls only at higher elevations,

springtime blossoms on Main Street

although it occasionally snows in the city.

ENTRY REQUIREMENTS

Visitors to Canada must have a valid **passport**. U.S. citizens entering Canada by land can use a **NEXUS** card or **U.S. Passport Card** instead, but note that these documents aren't valid for air travel.

Depending on your country of origin, you may also need either a **visitor visa** or an **Electronic Travel Authorization (eTA)**. See more information in the "Essentials" chapter of this guide, and check with Citizenship and Immigration Canada (www.cic.gc.ca) to confirm what documents you require.

TRANSPORTATION

Vancouver International Airport is south of downtown in the suburb of Richmond. The **Canada Line** subway stops right at the airport and can take you downtown in just 25 minutes.

Visitors arriving by train or bus come into **Pacific Central Station** on the edge of Chinatown. Cabs typically wait outside the station. To get downtown, you can also catch the **SkyTrain** from Main Street Station, which is one block from the train and bus depot.

Vancouver has a very good public transit system, with subway lines, buses, and ferries that can take you almost everywhere around the city. You don't need a car to explore most city attractions. A car is useful, though not essential, for excursions around the North Shore mountains or up the Sea-to-Sky Highway to Whistler. You can get to Victoria from Vancouver without a car on the **BC Ferries Connector,** a combination bus-ferry-bus route.

DAILY REMINDERS

- **Monday:** From mid-May until early September, most Vancouver attractions stay open every day, but some museums close on Monday, particularly during the winter months. Monday can be a good day to visit Granville Island or tour Stanley Park, which can both be extremely crowded on weekends.

- **Tuesday:** On Tuesday evening, admission to the Vancouver Art Gallery is by donation.

- **Thursday:** In Kitsilano, the Museum of Vancouver and the Vancouver Maritime Museum both stay open late on Thursday, closing at 8pm. The Museum of Anthropology is open until 9pm, and evening tickets are discounted.

- **Friday:** The Richmond Night Market operates on Friday, Saturday, and Sunday evenings from mid-May through the middle of October.

- **Saturday:** The West End Farmers Market is open on Saturday from late May until late October. The UBC Farm Market is also open Saturday from June to October.

- **Sunday:** The Vancouver Art Gallery runs free drop-in art activities for kids on Sunday afternoons. The Kitsilano Farmers Market sells fresh produce and baked goods on Sunday from early May through late October.

RESERVATIONS

If you're traveling in the summer, particularly in July and August, book your **hotel reservations** in advance. Car reservations are recommended on **BC Ferries** trips between Vancouver and Victoria in the summer as well.

Many Vancouver restaurants

samples from Japadog on a Vancouver Foodie Tour

fill up with advance reservations, particularly on Friday and Saturday nights. Book a weekend table at least a few of days ahead of time; most local eateries take reservations online. Don't despair if you can't get a reservation, though, since many spots save room for walk-ins, too.

PASSES AND DISCOUNTS

Many Vancouver attractions offer discounted admission for seniors (age 65 and up), students, and families, typically including two adults and up to two children.

If you're going to visit several attractions on the University of British Columbia campus, the **UBC Museums and Gardens Pass** (adults $33, seniors, students, and children $28) can save you money. It includes admission to the Museum of Anthropology, Nitobe Japanese Garden, UBC Botanical Garden, and Beaty Biodiversity Museum, as well as a 10 percent discount on the Greenheart TreeWalk. Purchase the pass at any of the participating attractions.

GUIDED TOURS

Several companies offer Vancouver city tours or explorations of particular neighborhoods, including **Tours by Locals** (www.tours-bylocals.com) and **Context Travel** (www.contexttravel.com). For a guided tour by bike, contact **Cycle City Tours** (http://cyclevancouver.com) or **Vancouver Bike Tours** (http://biketourvancouver.com).

A unique way to tour the city is with **Vancouver Photowalks** (www.vancouverphotowalks.ca), which offers guided photography tours of Stanley Park, Gastown, and other districts.

Vancouver Foodie Tours (http://foodietours.ca) runs several excellent and entertaining food tours, including an eating tour of Granville Island and an exploration of the city's food truck scene. **Off**

the Eaten Track (http://offtheeat-entracktours.ca) offers local food walks in Main Street and Railtown (east of Gastown), as well as an East Village brunch tour.

Want to forage in the rainforest for wild edibles or learn to catch your own crab? Contact **Swallow Tail Culinary Adventures** (http://www.swallowtail.ca), which also organizes pop-up dinners and other food events. **Vancouver Brewery Tours** (http://vancouverbrewery-tours.com) runs regular tasting tours of the city's craft breweries.

The nonprofit **Vancouver Heritage Foundation** (www.vancouverheritagefoundation.org) offers periodic walking tours of different Vancouver neighborhoods, focusing on the architecture and history of each community. Other options for architecture buffs are the Architectural Walking Tours that the **Architectural Institute of BC** (http://aibc.ca) runs throughout July and August.

CALENDAR OF EVENTS

JANUARY TO MARCH

Dozens of restaurants offer special menus, and you can join in food events, from chef dinners and wine-tastings to food tours, during **Dine Out Vancouver** (www.dineoutvancouver.com, Jan.), the city's annual celebration of dining that has grown into one of Canada's largest food and drink festivals.

With its large Asian population, Vancouver hosts plenty of festivities to mark the **Lunar New Year** (Jan.-Feb.), including parades, lion dances, music, fireworks, and other special events held in Chinatown and throughout Richmond.

WHAT'S NEW?

- **A Changing Chinatown:** Cool cafés, restaurants, shops, and condos are remaking this traditional district. You can still find markets with bins of gai lan (Chinese broccoli) and winter melon piled high, and bakeries selling puffy sweet buns, but you're equally likely to linger over a cappuccino or dig into eclectic small plates in a cool neighborhood hangout.

- **New Destinations for Art Lovers:** The **Vancouver Art Gallery** has unveiled plans for its new downtown home, although as this guide went to press, construction had yet to begin. Near Lonsdale Quay, the **Polygon Gallery** will give art aficionados a new reason to visit North Vancouver. The striking, modern **Audain Art Museum** amped up Whistler's art scene when it opened in 2016.

- **Distilleries and Craft Breweries:** Recent changes in local alcohol laws have paved the way for new distilleries and microbreweries, which have opened throughout Vancouver and Victoria. So many craft breweries have set up shop in the East Van neighborhood that the area has earned the nickname "Yeast Van."

- **Eating in the East:** A growing number of restaurants are opening on Vancouver's East Side, so for local dining, go east—to Main Street, East Hastings, and Commercial Drive.

APRIL TO JUNE

A good introduction to the region's growing microbrewery scene, the annual **Vancouver Craft Beer Week** (http://vancouvercraftbeerweek.com, May-June) includes tasting events and other activities that showcase small brewers and their products.

With nearly two weeks of concerts around the city, from big-name big-ticket shows to free music in the park, the **TD**

Vancouver International Jazz Festival (www.coastaljazz.ca, June-July) has tunes for any jazz, Latin, funk, and world music lover.

the annual Celebration of Light over English Bay

JULY TO AUGUST

Vancouver celebrates Canada's birthday, **Canada Day** (www.canadaplace.ca, July 1), with a parade, outdoor concerts, and celebratory fireworks over Burrard Inlet. Canada Place is the center of the festivities.

It's not just folk music at the long-established **Vancouver Folk Festival** (http://thefestival.bc.ca, July). This musical extravaganza draws world beat, roots, blues, and yes, folk musicians from across Canada and around the world to Jericho Beach for three days of always-eclectic music on multiple outdoor stages. It's great fun for all ages.

Fireworks displays over English Bay bring thousands of Vancouverites and visitors out for the **Celebration of Light** (http://hondacelebrationoflight.com, July-Aug.) that takes place over several summer evenings. The best viewing spots are at English Bay Beach, but you can see them from Kitsilano Beach and other points around False Creek.

The **Vancouver Pride Festival** (http://vancouverpride.ca, July-Aug.) features more than 20 events celebrating the city's large gay, lesbian, bisexual, and transgender community, culminating in a festive parade through the downtown streets.

SEPTEMBER TO DECEMBER

For two weeks, the **Vancouver Fringe Festival** (www.vancouverfringe.com, Sept.) takes over Granville Island and other stages around town with innovative, quirky, and often surprising theater, comedy, puppetry, and storytelling performances.

The VanDusen Botanical Garden marks the holiday season with its annual **Festival of Lights** (http://vandusengarden.org, Dec.), illuminating its garden paths with thousands of sparkling lights.

NEIGHBORHOODS

Downtown and
the West End

Map 1

Downtown is a vibrant mix of residential and commercial development, dotted with pocket parks and green spaces. Visitors and locals
walk and bike the Seawall and play at the beach.

Apartment buildings, historic houses, and a few modern towers line the **leafy streets** of the West End, bounded by English Bay,

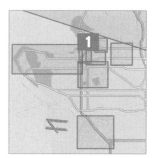

Stanley Park, the Burrard Inlet, and
downtown. Most of the city's **hotels** are located downtown or in the
West End, as are plenty of **dining** and
drinking spots. Robson is a major
shopping street, Granville Street is
the center of Vancouver's nightclub
district, and the city's LGBTQ community congregates in the bars and
cafés along Davie.

TOP SIGHTS
- Bill Reid Gallery of Northwest Coast Art (page 59)

TOP RESTAURANTS
- Nightingale (page 94)
- Guu Garden (page 96)

TOP NIGHTLIFE
- LIFT Bar & Grill (page 125)
- Prohibition Lounge (page 125)
- Reflections Lounge (page 125)

TOP SPORTS AND ACTIVITIES
- English Bay Beach (page 154)

TOP SHOPS
- Hudson's Bay (page 172)

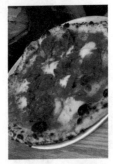

TOP HOTELS
- Fairmont Pacific Rim (page 188)
- Rosewood Hotel Georgia (page 188)
- Burrard Hotel (page 191)
- Listel Hotel (page 191)

GETTING THERE AND AROUND
- SkyTrain lines: Canada Line, Expo Line
- SkyTrain stops: Waterfront (Canada, Expo Lines); Vancouver City Centre (Canada Line); Burrard, Granville (Expo Line)
- Bus lines: 5, 6, 19, 23

DOWNTOWN AND WEST END WALK

TOTAL DISTANCE: 2.5 miles (4 kilometers)
TOTAL WALKING TIME: 1 hour

This walking tour takes you from Canada Place on the Burrard Inlet side of downtown, through the city to English Bay, passing numerous landmarks, artworks, and places to eat. You can do this walk anytime, but if you start in the early afternoon, you can wrap up your stroll at west-facing English Bay Beach as the sun is shining over the sea.

1 Begin your walk at **Canada Place,** the waterfront landmark with its billowing white sails. Follow the Seawall path one block toward the Vancouver Convention Centre's west building, and note the building's living roof. Keeping the water on your right side, continue along the Seawall behind the convention center, passing *The Drop*, a 20-meter (65-foot) bright blue raindrop sculpture that a Berlin-based art collective created in 2009.

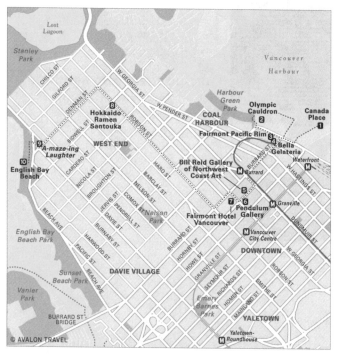

Canada Place

2 At the back of the convention center, after watching the floatplanes taking off and landing on the harbor, turn left up the stairs
to Jack Poole Plaza. Look for *Digital Orca* (2009), by Vancouver artist
Douglas Coupland, a sculpture of a whale that appears to be breaching
toward the sky. Also on the plaza is the **Olympic Cauldron,** which was lit
when Vancouver hosted the 2010 Winter Olympic Games.

3 Turn left (east) onto Canada Place, then in one block, turn right
(south) onto Burrard Street. Walk one more block to the corner
of Burrard and Cordova, and look up. Wrapping around the exterior of
the **Fairmont Pacific Rim** are the words, "Lying on top of a building the
clouds looked no nearer than when I was lying on the street." It's an art
installation by New York artist Liam Gillick.

4 Ready for refreshments? In front of the Fairmont, stop for gelato
or sorbetto at **Bella Gelateria.**

5 When you've finished your treats, continue walking south on busy
Burrard Street, away from the water. After three blocks, turn
left (east) onto Dunsmuir Street and take your first right (south) onto
Hornby Street. In the middle of the block is the **Bill Reid Gallery of
Northwest Coast Art,** one of the best places downtown to explore ab-
original art. Allow about an hour to walk through the gallery.

6 Exit the gallery and turn right (south) on Hornby. In one block, at
the corner of Hornby and Georgia Streets, cross the street and go
into the HSBC Building (885 W. Georgia St.). Why stop at a bank office?

Olympic Cauldron

In the lobby is a massive, swinging stainless steel pendulum, an art piece called *Broken Column* (1987) by Alan Storey. The building's air circulation system powers its movement. Also in the lobby, the free **Pendulum Gallery** mounts small changing art exhibitions.

7 Diagonally across Hornby and Georgia Streets is the landmark **Fairmont Hotel Vancouver,** built in 1939. Duck into the lobby for a quick look, and then exit the building, turning left (south) onto Burrard Street.

8 In one block, cross Burrard and turn right (west) onto Robson Street. Robson is one of downtown's main shopping streets, and while many of the stores are international chains, it's still a lively district. This retail route gradually gives way to restaurants, primarily noodle shops, Korean eateries, and other Asian spots. If you'd like to pause for lunch, line up for a bowl of *tokusen toroniku* ramen at **Hokkaido Ramen Santouka,** on Robson six blocks from Burrard.

Fairmont Hotel Vancouver

9 After your meal, continue on Robson for one more block, and turn left (south) onto Denman Street. You're now in the heart

English Bay Beach

of the West End, with more small food spots and neighborhood shops along Denman. Stay on Denman for six blocks to Morton Park, where you'll spot 14 grinning bronze figures. That's *A-maze-ing Laughter,* the popular public art piece by Chinese artist Yue Minjun.

10 Cross Beach Avenue to **English Bay Beach,** where you can sit in the sand and do some people-watching, resting up from your downtown explorations.

Gastown and Chinatown   Map 2

Gastown, which centers on Water and Cordova Streets between Richards and Main Streets, is one of the city's oldest neighborhoods, with brick and stone buildings dating to the early 1900s. Beyond its historic facades, Gastown is known for its **stylish boutiques** and **aboriginal art galleries.**

The ornate **Millennium Gate** on Pender Street marks the entrance to Vancouver's fast-changing Chinatown. Though a few traditional herbalists, tea shops, and produce markets remain, more and more **hip eateries** are moving in. Many of Vancouver's most **innovative restaurants** have opened here.

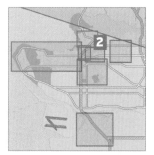

TOP SIGHTS
- Dr. Sun Yat-Sen Classical Chinese Garden (page 64)

TOP RESTAURANTS
- Chambar (page 100)
- L'Abbatoir (page 100)

TOP NIGHTLIFE
- The Pourhouse (page 127)

TOP ARTS AND CULTURE
- Coastal Peoples Fine Arts Gallery (page 139)
- Hill's Native Art (page 139)

TOP SHOPS
- Lululemon Lab (page 175)
- John Fluevog (page 175)

TOP HOTELS
- Skwachàys Lodge (page 193)

GETTING THERE AND AROUND
- SkyTrain lines: Expo Line
- SkyTrain stops: Waterfront, Stadium-Chinatown
- Bus lines: 4, 7, 14, 16, 20, 22, 23

GASTOWN AND CHINATOWN WALK

TOTAL DISTANCE: 1.8 miles (3 kilometers)
TOTAL WALKING TIME: 45 minutes

This walk takes you through two of Vancouver's oldest neighborhoods. Begin with lunch, stop to explore aboriginal art galleries, the city's serene Chinese garden, and the unusual Police Museum, and then wrap up your afternoon with cocktails in Gastown.

1 Fuel up for your walk with lunch at **Chambar,** adjacent to the Stadium-Chinatown SkyTrain station. In a heritage brick building on Beatty Street, this restaurant creatively mixes flavors of Belgium and North Africa with local ingredients.

2 After lunch, turn right out of the restaurant, following Beatty Street one block to Pender Street. Turn right onto Pender, and go east two blocks. On the left side of Pender, stop at the **Urban Aboriginal Fair Trade Gallery,** inside Skwachàys Lodge, Canada's first aboriginal arts hotel, for a look at their works by native artists. As you leave, notice the large aboriginal sculpture atop the hotel building.

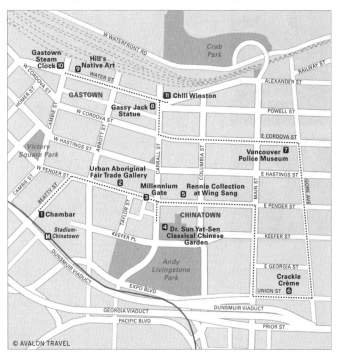

© AVALON TRAVEL

3 Turn left out of the gallery, cross under the ornate **Millennium Gate,** which marks the entrance to Chinatown, and walk one more block east on Pender.

4 At Carrall Street, turn right, walk half a block, and turn left at the garden wall to find the entrance to the **Dr. Sun Yat-Sen Classical Chinese Garden.** It's worth stopping to tour this peaceful retreat, the first authentic Ming Dynasty garden created outside of China.

5 From the garden, retrace your steps back north toward Pender Street and turn east (right) to find the **Rennie Collection at Wing Sang,** a private art museum. The brick building that houses the museum, constructed in 1889, is the oldest structure remaining in Chinatown.

6 Continue one block east on Pender to Main Street and turn right. As you walk south on Main, notice Chinatown's mix of new condos and old-time shops. Stay on Main three blocks, then turn left onto Union Street. Midway down the block is **Crackle Crème,** a café that specializes in crème brûlée.

7 After your break, turn left out of the café, and in half a block, turn north (left) onto Gore Avenue. Follow Gore five blocks north. At Cordova Street, turn left to find the entrance to the **Vancouver Police Museum** on your left. The exhibits at this museum, in the former city morgue, detail Vancouver's seamier side.

8 When you leave the museum, turn left onto Cordova, take the first right onto Main, and in one block, turn left onto Powell Street, which will take you toward Gastown. Follow Powell Street two blocks west to Maple Leaf Square, where Water, Alexander, Powell, and Carrall Streets meet. Stop for a photo at the **statue of Gassy Jack,** the British sailor for whom Gastown is named.

9 Continue west on Water Street, the main street in Gastown, where several galleries specialize in works by aboriginal artists. A block and a half west of Maple Leaf Square is **Hill's Native Art,** which has one of the city's largest collections of First Nations arts and crafts.

10 Take a right out of Hill's, and just across Cambie Street (at the corner of Water), you'll see the **Gastown Steam Clock,** which toots its whistle every quarter hour.

11 Ready for a drink? Retrace your steps two blocks east on Water Street to Maple Leaf Square, where you can wrap up your walk with a cocktail on the patio at **Chill Winston.**

Yaletown and False Creek Map 3

Yaletown's renovated brick warehouses, once part of an industrial district, today house a chic mix of restaurants, boutiques, and **drinking spots.** Browse the **fashionable shops,** meet for cocktails on streetside patios, and dine on local seafood in the **upscale restaurants.** The city's sports arenas, including the home ice of the **Vancouver Canucks,** are also nearby.

False Creek is home to **Science World,** the family-friendly science museum in a geodesic dome. Also here is the **Olympic Village,** where athletes stayed during the 2010 Winter Games, now a complex of pubs, cafés, and condos. South of False Creek is an emerging district of **craft breweries** and **beer-centric pubs,** perfect for a day of strolling and sipping.

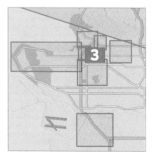

TOP SIGHTS
- Science World (page 68)

TOP RESTAURANTS
- Ancora Waterfront Dining
  and Patio (page 104)

TOP NIGHTLIFE
- 33 Acres Brewing (page 128)
- Tap & Barrel (page 129)
- Opus Bar (page 130)

TOP SPORTS AND ACTIVITIES
- Vancouver Canucks (page 156)

TOP SHOPS
- Fine Finds Boutique (page 177)

TOP HOTELS
- Opus Hotel Vancouver (page 194)

GETTING THERE AND AROUND
- SkyTrain lines: Canada Line, Expo Line
- SkyTrain stops: Yaletown-Roundhouse, Olympic Village (Canada); Stadium-Chinatown, Main Street-Science World (Expo)
- Bus lines: 3, 6, 19, 23, 50, 84
- Ferries: Aquabus, False Creek

FALSE CREEK WALK

TOTAL DISTANCE: 2.6 miles (4.25 kilometers)
TOTAL WALKING TIME: 1.5 hours

On this excursion, which includes a combination of walking and ferry-hopping, you'll start and end in Yaletown. In between, you'll explore the Olympic Village, the emerging arts district known as "The Flats," and the False Creek waterfront. Stop along the way to sample some craft beer.

1 Start your stroll with coffee and pastries at Yaletown's **Small Victory Bakery.** When you're ready to wander, exit the bakery, turning left on Homer Street, and take an immediate left onto Helmcken Street. Follow Helmcken two blocks down the hill, and turn right onto Mainland Street, checking out the neighborhood's restored warehouse buildings. In one block, at Davie Street, turn left to walk south toward the waterfront.

2 In two blocks, at the corner of Davie and Pacific Boulevard, stop for a quick look at the **Engine 374 Pavilion** to see the locomotive that pulled the first transcontinental passenger train into Vancouver in 1887.

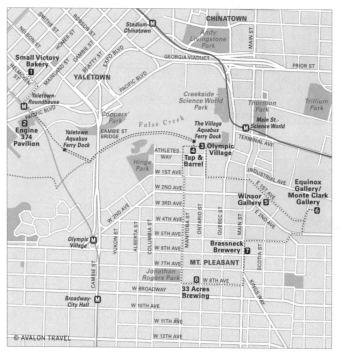

Continue south on Davie Street one more block to False Creek and the Aquabus ferry dock, where colorful ferries shuttle across False Creek, which British naval officer and explorer George Henry Richards is credited with naming. In 1859, Richards traveled up what he thought was a creek in search of coal deposits but discovered that this "False Creek" was actually an inlet of the Pacific Ocean. Board the ferry headed east to The Village.

3 When you get off the ferry, explore the cluster of contemporary buildings in front of you: the **Olympic Village,** also known as the Village at False Creek. The neighborhood's buildings, which housed athletes during the 2010 Olympic Games, have been converted into condominiums, and the district has several brewpubs, cafés, public art pieces, and a community center.

4 If you're ready for a break, nab a patio seat at **Tap & Barrel,** where they've got a long list of B.C. beer and wines on tap and great views of the city skyline.

5 From the Olympic Village, you'll detour away from the water to explore an emerging arts district called The Flats. Walk south through the plaza on Salt Street, past the massive sculptures *The Birds*, and continue two blocks to West 1st Avenue. Turn left onto 1st, and go three blocks east, crossing Main Street. Look for the **Winsor Gallery** on your right; stop and see what's on view in this contemporary art gallery.

6 Leaving the gallery, turn right to continue east on 1st Avenue. In two blocks, when 1st comes to a T at Thornton Street, turn left to check out two more art spaces, **Equinox Gallery** and **Monte Clark Gallery,** both in the same brightly painted building among the warehouses at the foot of Thornton.

7 Retrace your steps up Thornton Street, turning right onto 1st Avenue, then taking the next left onto Scotia Street. Cross busy 2nd Avenue, then continue south up the hill on Scotia for three blocks, turning right onto 5th Avenue. Follow 5th one block west to Main Street, turn left onto Main, and you'll find your next stop, **Brassneck Brewery,** where you can do a tasting of their small-batch beer.

8 Turn left out of the brewery onto Main and walk two blocks south. At 8th Avenue, turn right, walk two more blocks, and you'll see **33 Acres Brewing** on your right. Stop for another beer tasting and a snack, too. To get back to the ferry, turn right onto 8th Avenue and take the first right onto Manitoba Street. Follow Manitoba 10 blocks north, back to the Olympic Village. Pause to take photos of the city skyline and Science World's dome before boarding the Aquabus to return to the Yaletown docks.

Granville Island

Map 4

This former industrial district, across False Creek from downtown, is one of Vancouver's most popular attractions. Technically a peninsula, the 38-acre island is home to more than 300 businesses, including **art galleries** and **theaters,** as well as the popular **Granville Island Public Market.** A few industrial elements remain, including Ocean Concrete, whose brightly painted cement trucks chug around the island.

The island and the Public Market get packed with visitors in the afternoons and on weekends, especially on sunny summer days. Take a ferry from downtown, cycle, or walk onto the island, rather than driving, if you can.

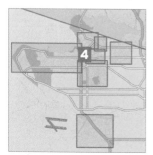

TOP SIGHTS

- Granville Island Public Market (page 71)
- Railspur Alley (page 72)

TOP ARTS AND CULTURE

- Eagle Spirit Gallery (page 141)
- Federation of Canadian Artists Gallery (page 141)
- Vancouver Theatre Sports League (page 143)

TOP SHOPS

- The Umbrella Shop (page 179)

GETTING THERE AND AROUND

- Bus lines: 50
- Ferries: Aquabus, False Creek Ferries

Kitsilano and UBC   Map 5

Kitsilano has a **great beach,** several **museums** in waterfront Vanier Park, and lots of **shops** and restaurants, particularly along **West 4th Avenue,** between Burrard and Balsam Streets.

On the city's far west side, surrounded by forests and sea, the University of British Columbia (UBC) is worth visiting for its stellar **Museum of Anthropology,** and for several gardens and smaller museums. Also on campus are a modern **concert hall** and the only working farm within the city of Vancouver.

Point Grey, between the university and Kitsilano, is a leafy residential area with family-friendly **sandy beaches** along its northern shore. **Pacific Spirit Regional Park,** Vancouver's largest park, is also located here.

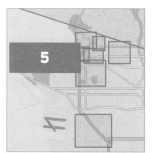

TOP SIGHTS

- Museum of Vancouver (page 74)
- Museum of Anthropology (page 76)
- Nitobe Japanese Garden (page 77)

TOP RESTAURANTS

- Maenam (page 109)
- Chocolate Arts (page 110)

TOP ARTS AND CULTURE

- Chan Centre for the Performing Arts (page 144)

TOP SPORTS AND ACTIVITIES

- Kitsilano Beach (page 159)
- Kitsilano Pool (page 159)
- Jericho Beach (page 160)
- Pacific Spirit Regional Park (page 162)

TOP SHOPS

- Kidsbooks (page 181)
- Les Amis du Fromage (page 181)
- Wanderlust (page 182)

GETTING THERE AND AROUND

- Bus lines: 2, 4, 7 (Kitsilano); 4, 14, 84, 99 (UBC and Point Grey)
- Ferries: Aquabus, False Creek Ferries

Cambie Corridor

Map 6

Cambie Street runs between downtown Vancouver and the Fraser River, bisecting the city's east and west sides. The notable **VanDusen Botanical Garden** is located off Cambie, and to the west, the South Granville district boasts **high-end art galleries.**

To the east, browse **funky Main Street** for its **vintage clothing shops, independent fashion boutiques,** and **locavore restaurants.** You can always discover something new in this fast-changing neighborhood.

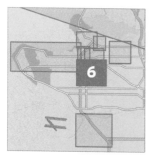

TOP SIGHTS

- VanDusen Botanical Garden (page 80)

TOP RESTAURANTS

- West (page 112)
- The Acorn (page 115)

TOP ARTS AND CULTURE

- Bau-Xi Gallery (page 145)
- Douglas Reynolds Gallery (page 145)

TOP SHOPS

- Barefoot Contessa (page 182)
- Front and Company (page 182)

GETTING THERE AND AROUND

- SkyTrain lines: Canada Line
- SkyTrain stops: Broadway-City Hall, King Edward
- Bus lines: 3, 9, 10, 15, 17, 99

Commercial Drive

Map 7

Funky Commercial Drive runs north-south through the city's East Side. Once the heart of Vancouver's Italian community, the neighborhood is now home to a diverse collection of residents. Along The Drive, you'll find **pubs, cafés,** and a multicultural mix of casual places to eat.

The up-and-coming **East Village** district is along East Hastings Street, between Victoria Drive and Renfrew Street. Nearby, Powell Street is the center of Vancouver's booming **craft brewery** scene.

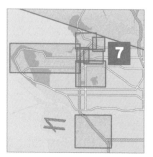

TOP SIGHTS

- Parallel 49 Brewing Company (page 81)
- Odd Society Spirits (page 82)

TOP RESTAURANTS

- The Pie Shoppe (page 117)

TOP NIGHTLIFE

- Storm Crow Tavern (page 133)

TOP ARTS AND CULTURE

- Vancouver East Cultural Centre (page 147)

GETTING THERE AND AROUND

- SkyTrain lines: Expo Line, Millennium Line
- SkyTrain stops: Commercial-Broadway (Expo, Millennium); VCC-Clark (Millennium)
- Bus lines: 4, 7, 14, 16, 20, 135

Richmond

Map 8

Vancouver is now considered the most Asian metropolis outside Asia. Many of its Asian residents have settled in Richmond, a city of more than 200,000 on Vancouver's southern boundaries, where more than half the population is of Asian descent, with most from China, Taiwan, or Hong Kong.

Richmond has several multicultural attractions to explore, including two popular **night markets** and some of the best **Chinese restaurants** in North America. The city's waterfront Steveston Village was important in the region's fishing history and still houses a bustling fish market and numerous seafood restaurants. It's also a departure point for **whale-watching** cruises.

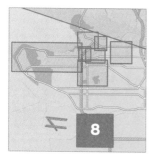

TOP SIGHTS
- Richmond Night Market (page 84)

TOP RESTAURANTS
- Bamboo Grove (page 118)
- New Spicy Chili Restaurant (page 118)
- Hao's Lamb Restaurant (page 119)
- Golden Paramount Seafood Restaurant (page 119)

GETTING THERE AND AROUND
- SkyTrain lines: Canada Line (Richmond-Brig-house branch)
- SkyTrain stops: Aberdeen, Lansdowne, Richmond-Brighouse

The North Shore

Map 9

Ready to get outdoors? Across the Burrard Inlet, the North Shore mountains provide the backdrop for the waterfront cities of North Vancouver and West Vancouver. In any season, you can find plenty of adventures here, whether you're swinging across the Capilano Suspension Bridge, exploring the rainforest in **Lighthouse Park,** or **kayaking** in Deep Cove. Visit **Grouse Mountain** to learn about local wildlife, climb "Mother Nature's Stairmaster," or head down the ski trails. Several other peaks offer **hiking, snowshoeing,** and **skiing**—all a short trip from the city center.

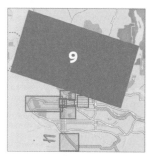

TOP SIGHTS

- Grouse Mountain (page 87)
- Capilano Suspension Bridge (page 89)

TOP SPORTS AND ACTIVITIES

- Deep Cove Kayaks (page 165)
- The Grouse Grind (page 165)
- Lighthouse Park (page 167)

GETTING THERE AND AROUND

- Ferries: SeaBus
- Bus lines: 228, 229, 230, 236, 241, 246, 250, 257

SIGHTS

How to enjoy Vancouver: Wander through the rainforest. Explore diverse cultures. Pair museum visits with hiking or kayaking, and check out the booming craft beer scene.

Gastown Steam Clock

Explore the outdoors in Stanley Park downtown, in blooming botanical gardens, and at the North Shore peaks. For art and food, there's Granville Island, home to galleries, breweries and distilleries, and the lively Public Market.

For cultural explorations, visit the stellar Museum of Anthropology and the Bill Reid Gallery of Northwest Coast Art, which illuminate the region's aboriginal traditions. Dive deep into the city's Asian culture at the Dr. Sun Yat-Sen Classical Chinese Garden or the Richmond Night Market.

There's plenty for kids, too: a family-friendly science center, aquarium, and hands-on museums, ferries and gondolas, and forested trails. On Granville Island, youngsters even have their own Kids Market.

Vancouver is compact enough that you can head for the North Shore, the University of British Columbia, Richmond, or other neighborhoods on the region's extensive public transit system. You can walk or cycle through this green, waterfront city, too.

HIGHLIGHTS

✪ **MOST RENOWNED ABORIGINAL ART:** The **Bill Reid Gallery of Northwest Coast Art** is dedicated to the life and work of notable aboriginal artist Bill Reid (page 59).

✪ **MOST ZEN URBAN ESCAPE:** Tour **Dr. Sun Yat-Sen Classical Chinese Garden,** the first authentic Ming Dynasty garden outside China (page 64).

✪ **BEST MUSEUM FOR KIDS:** Take the youngsters to **Science World,** inside a geodesic dome on the banks of False Creek (page 68).

✪ **MOST PHOTOGENIC FOOD DESTINATION:** You'll have plenty of fodder for your Instagram feed at the **Granville Island Public Market** (page 71).

✪ **BEST HIDDEN ART SPOT:** Find your way to narrow **Railspur Alley,** where you can chat with artists at work in their studios (page 72).

✪ **BEST WAY TO TIME TRAVEL:** The hands-on **Museum of Vancouver** takes you through the city's past (page 74).

✪ **BEST PLACE TO EXPLORE ABORIGINAL CULTURE:** The **Museum of Anthropology** houses one of the world's top collections of First Peoples' art, including massive cedar canoes, elaborate carvings, and towering totem poles (page 76).

✪ **QUICKEST TRIP TO JAPAN:** Stroll among the flowers, waterfalls, and koi ponds in the serene **Nitobe Japanese Garden** (page 77).

✪ **BEST PLACE TO STOP AND SMELL THE FLOWERS:** Among the 250,000 plants at the peaceful **VanDusen Botanical Garden,** the city seems far away (page 80).

✪ **BEST PLACE TO START (OR END) A CRAFT BEER CRAWL:** **Parallel 49 Brewing Company** is both a tasting hall and a spirited neighborhood gathering place (page 81).

✪ **BEST SPOT TO SAMPLE LOCAL SPIRITS: Odd Society Spirits** makes small-batch vodka, gin, and a "moonshine" whiskey that you can sip in their fun and funky lounge (page 82).

✪ **LARGEST NIGHT MARKET:** The lively **Richmond Night Market** sells everything from kebabs and bubble tea to cell phone cases. It's also an amazing Asian food adventure (page 84).

✪ **TOP MOUNTAIN ESCAPE:** For zip-lining, paragliding, skiing, and snowboarding, head for **Grouse Mountain** (page 87).

✪ **BEST PLACE TO SWING OVER A GORGE:** The **Capilano Suspension Bridge** sways high above the Capilano River (page 89).

Downtown and the West End

Map 1

Canada Place

Among Vancouver's most famous downtown landmarks is Canada Place, its billowing white sails recalling a ship ready to set off to sea. Canada Place does have a seafaring function; the building, with its five 90-foot (27-meter) white sails made of Teflon-coated fiberglass, houses the city's cruise ship terminal. Also inside are the east wing of the Vancouver Convention Centre, the Pan Pacific Hotel Vancouver, and several tourist attractions.

Canada Place

The coolest reason to visit Canada Place is FlyOver Canada (604/620-8455, www.flyovercanada.com; 10am-9pm daily, adults $27, seniors, students, and ages 13-18 $21, ages 12 and under $17), a multimedia simulated flight ride that has you swoop and soar across the country, flying over Arctic peaks, past Toronto's CN Tower, and across the Canadian Rockies. You even feel the spray as you hover above Niagara Falls, and at one point, the northern lights spread out around you. The FlyOver Canada experience lasts about 30 minutes; the flight itself is just eight minutes long. Tickets are discounted if you buy them online in advance.

While you're at Canada Place, follow the Canadian Trail, a walkway along the building's west promenade. Check out interpretive panels about Canada's ten provinces and three territories while enjoying the views of Stanley Park, Burrard Inlet, and the North Shore mountains. You'll frequently see massive cruise ships at the docks from spring through fall.

MAP 1: 999 Canada Pl., 604/665-9000, www.canadaplace.ca

Olympic Cauldron

When Vancouver hosted the 2010 Winter Olympic Games, the candelabra-like Olympic Cauldron burned brightly. The 33-foot-tall (10-meter) landmark, comprising four diagonal columns leaning together, stands next to the Vancouver Convention Centre's west building, near the Coal Harbour waterfront downtown—although it's now lit only for special events.

MAP 1: Jack Poole Plaza, foot of Thurlow St.

The Seawall

Snaking along the waterfront on both sides of the downtown peninsula, extending around Stanley Park, through the West End and Yaletown, and along False Creek to Granville Island, Kitsilano Beach, and beyond, the Seawall is Vancouver's most popular walking, running, and cycling path. The first sections of the Seawall were built in Stanley Park, beginning in 1917. Now, this 17.5-mile (28-kilometer) pathway, officially called the Seaside Greenway, may be the world's longest uninterrupted waterfront path.

The majority of the Seawall is paved, although in a few areas, it's made of packed gravel. In most places, too, the Seawall is divided, with pedestrians routed to one side and cyclists, skaters, and anything with wheels on the other; watch for the signs to stay on the proper side, particularly when the pathway is busy.

MAP 1: On the waterfront from Canada Place to Stanley Park, English Bay, Yaletown, and along False Creek to Granville Island, Kitsilano, and the city's west side

Vancouver Lookout

Ride the glass elevator to the top of this observation tower for views across the city, Stanley Park, the waterfront, and the North Shore mountains. Although many downtown buildings now dwarf this 30-story tower, which opened in 1977, it's a good place to get oriented. Admission includes a 20-minute tour highlighting local sights as you circle the observation platform, which offers a 360-degree view. Even if you don't follow a tour, you can ask the guides to point out particular locations and landmarks.

Lookout tickets are good all day, so you can check out the daytime views, then return to see the sunset or watch the evening lights twinkle.

MAP 1: 555 W. Hastings St., 604/689-0421, www.vancouverlookout.com; 8:30am-10:30pm daily May-Sept., 9am-9pm daily Oct.-Apr.; adults $18, seniors $15, students and ages 13-18 $13, ages 6-12 $10

✪ Bill Reid Gallery of Northwest Coast Art

The Bill Reid Gallery of Northwest Coast Art, which you enter through

The Seawall follows the waterfront in downtown Vancouver.

a courtyard in the Cathedral Place complex off Hornby Street, is dedicated to British Columbia artist Bill Reid's life and work. Born to a Haida First Nations mother and a European father, Reid created more than 1,500 sculptures, carvings, and pieces of jewelry, most of which explore Haida traditions. Among the highlights on display are Reid's *Mythic Messengers*, a 28-foot (8.5-meter) bronze frieze; more than 40 pieces of his gold and silver jewelry; and several of Reid's works that the Canadian government featured on Canada's $20 bill.

With exhibits both in its main high-ceilinged exhibition space and on an art deco-style mezzanine, the downtown gallery also showcases other First Nations art, including a full-size totem pole carved by James Hart of Haida Gwaii, and hosts changing exhibits of aboriginal art of the Northwest Coast region. Stop into the gift shop for First Nations prints, jewelry, and other artwork.

MAP 1: 639 Hornby St., 604/682-3455, www.billreidgallery.ca; 10am-5pm daily late May-early Sept., 11am-5pm Wed.-Sun. early Sept.-late May; adults $11, seniors and students $8, ages 13-17 $6

Vancouver Art Gallery

The permanent collection at the Vancouver Art Gallery includes more than 10,000 artworks, emphasizing artists from western Canada, including aboriginal artists, photographers, and artists with connections to the Pacific Rim region. The gallery has a particularly strong collection of works by British Columbia-born Emily Carr, one of Canada's most important early-20th-century painters. Carr is known for her paintings of B.C.'s landscapes and its indigenous people.

Hosting changing exhibitions throughout the year, the gallery is housed in the former 1906 court building designed by architect Francis M. Rattenbury (who also designed Victoria's Parliament Building). Noted B.C. modern architect Arthur Erickson incorporated the stone courthouse into the expanded gallery that was completed in 1983. Built around a grand rotunda, the art gallery has exhibit spaces on four levels.

The gallery offers guided tours (hours vary Thurs. and Sat.-Sun.; free with museum admission). The one-hour Survey Tours give an introduction to the current exhibits, while 30-minute Hot Spot tours focus on particular artworks. The gallery also runs programs for kids and families on Sunday afternoons that range from child-focused exhibit tours to hands-on art workshops.

The Vancouver Art Gallery has announced plans to relocate to a new building, designed by Herzog & de Meuron Architects, which will be constructed at West Georgia and Cambie Streets. Work on the new facility is slated to begin in 2017.

If you stand across Robson Street from the art gallery and look up toward the roof of the original courthouse building, you'll spot two pieces of public art. One work is simply a line of text across the top of the building: *Placed Upon the Horizon (Casting Shadows)*—which is also the name of the piece, created in 1990 by American artist Lawrence Weiner.

The other, *Four Boats Stranded: Red and Yellow, Black and White,* by Vancouver-born artist Ken Lum, includes four fiberglass ships perched on the corners of the roof that represent the city's history: a First Nations longboat (red); English explorer

George Vancouver's ship (white); the *Komagata Maru*, which carried Indian immigrants who were not allowed to disembark in Vancouver (black); and a cargo ship that brought migrants from China's Fujian Province (yellow).

The peaceful Gallery Café (604/688-2233, www.thegallerycafe.ca) serves salads, *panini,* quiche, and wine on a shaded patio.

MAP 1: 750 Hornby St., 604/662-4719, www.vanartgallery.bc.ca; 10am-5pm Wed.-Mon., 10am-9pm Tues.; adults $24, seniors and students $18, ages 6-12 $6.50 (by donation 5pm-9pm Tues.)

Vancouver Central Library

The Vancouver Central Library is both an architectural landmark and a hub of information, art, and events. Designed by Israeli Canadian architect Moshe Safdie and opened in 1995, the building has a distinctive curved shape, modeled after Rome's Colosseum. Before you even get to the books, you can have coffee or a snack in one of several cafés in the library's light and airy interior atrium.

The library regularly hosts events, like lectures, author talks, and movie screenings, most of which are free. In front of the library, near the corner of Homer and Robson Streets, is a public art piece, *The Words Don't Fit The Picture,* a neon sign by Vancouver artist Ron Terada.

MAP 1: 350 W. Georgia St., 604/331-3603, www.vpl.ca; 10am-9pm Mon.-Thurs., 10am-6pm Fri.-Sat., 11am-6pm Sun.; free

Roedde House Museum

Vancouver wasn't always the steel-and-glass city it is today. Go back to the Victorian era at the Roedde House Museum, in an 1893 Queen Anne revival-style home. Outfitted with period furnishings, the 11-room West End manor belonged to Gustav Roedde, the city's first bookbinder, and his family. Admission includes a guided tour, where you learn about day-to-day life at the turn of the 19th century. The Sunday afternoon tour ($8) includes tea and cookies, and on the second Sunday of the month, you can stay for a classical concert (4pm; adults $15, seniors and students $12). There's a jazz concert the second Thursday of the month (7pm; adults $15, seniors and students $12).

MAP 1: 1415 Barclay St., 604/684-7040, www.roeddehouse.org; 1pm-4pm Tues.-Fri. and Sun.; adults and ages 12 and over $5

A-maze-ing Laughter

One of Vancouver's most popular public art pieces, *A-maze-ing Laughter,* by Beijing-based contemporary artist Yue Minjun, is composed of 14 larger-than-life bronze figures, with over-size grins dominating their equally oversized faces. Though the 8.5-foot-tall (2.6-meter) statues appear to be chortling hysterically, the artist has said that these smiling faces actually mask the misery of life in China's post-Tiananmen Square era. The artwork faces English Bay in the West End.

MAP 1: Morton Park, Denman St. at Davie St.

STANLEY PARK

A dense rainforest at the end of the downtown peninsula, Stanley Park is a green refuge, incorporating First Nations culture and heritage, woodland and waterfront trails, the city's aquarium, and spectacular urban and harbor views.

SIGHTS

The **Seawall,** a 5.5-mile (9-kilometer) walking and cycling path, circles the perimeter of Stanley Park and passes many of the park's attractions. You can also follow the park's outer edge by car along Stanley Park Drive. It's also worth exploring the park's interior trails, many of which pass through old-growth rainforest.

Among Stanley Park's highlights are the **totem poles at Brockton Point** and **Siwash Rock,** an offshore rock formation that figures in First Nations legends. A family-friendly stop is the **Vancouver Aquarium Marine Science Centre** (845 Avison Way, 604/659-3474, www.vanaqua.org; 9:30am-6pm daily July-early Sept., 10am-5pm daily early Sept.-June; adults $36, seniors and students $27, ages 4-12 $21), which is Canada's largest aquarium.

On a finger of land jutting into the harbor on Stanley Park's east side, the red and white **Brockton Point Lighthouse** was built in 1914. The Seawall travels under the lighthouse, through archways that support the lighthouse tower.

From **Prospect Point,** the highest spot in Stanley Park, you have great views of the Burrard Inlet, the North Shore mountains, and the **Lions Gate Bridge,** one of the world's longest suspension bridges.

A giant western red cedar, roughly 800 years old, is one of Stanley Park's best-known landmarks and the source of much controversy. Known as the **Hollow Tree,** the massive cedar on the park's west side stopped growing in the 1800s and was essentially a 42-foot-tall (13-meter) tree stump. A 2006 windstorm damaged the tree, causing it to lean precipitously. The historic tree was eventually stabilized with a steel core and a foundation of underground steel "roots." The tree is along Stanley Park Drive, north of Third Beach.

TOURS

The park has a long and rich First Nations heritage. Several First Nations, including the Burrard, Musqueam, and Squamish people, made their home in the park for several thousand years. To learn more about the park's aboriginal connections, take the 90-minute guided **Talking Trees Walk** with First Nations' owned **Talaysay Tours** (604/628-8555 or 800/605-4643, www.talaysay.com; 10am and 12:30pm daily May-Sept.; adults $35, ages 4-18 $28).

One option for getting around Stanley Park is on a trolley tour. The **Vancouver Trolley Company** (604/801-5515 or 888/451-5581, http://vancouvertrolley.com) runs a year-round **hop-on hop-off tour** (one-day pass adults $45, seniors and ages 13-18 $42, ages 4-12 $28) that takes visitors to eight stops within the park and to 27 other locations throughout the city. From late June through early September, the company also operates the **Stanley Park Shuttle** (11am-6pm daily late June-early Sept.; adults, seniors, and ages 13-18 $10, ages 4-12 $5), a narrated ride that makes 15 stops within the park.

BEACHES

Along the Seawall on the west side of Stanley Park, you can swim or sun at busy **Second Beach.** This sandy cove is also a pretty spot to watch the sunset. There's a seasonal snack bar and a children's playground near the beach. **Third Beach** at Ferguson Point on the west side of Stanley Park is a quiet stretch of sand with views toward the North Shore.

WATER SPORTS

A unique way to explore Stanley Park is from the water. Rent a kayak from **Ecomarine Paddlesports Centre** (1700 Beach Ave., 604/689-7575 or 888/425-2925, www.ecomarine. com; 10am-dusk Mon.-Fri., 9am-dusk Sat.-Sun. late May-early Sept.) on the beach at English Bay, paddle past Second and Third Beaches, and see Siwash Rock from the water. If you don't want to navigate the route on your own, take their 2.5-hour **guided kayaking tour** (9:30am Thurs. and Sat., June-early Sept., $69 pp).

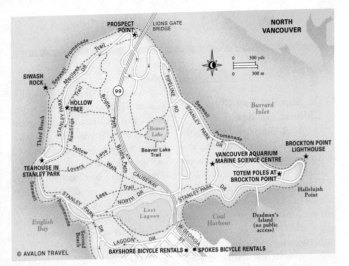

HIKING

Some of the park's interior trails include **Tatlow Walk,** which cuts across the southwest corner of the park, between Third Beach and the north side of Lost Lagoon; **Rawlings Trail,** open to cyclists and pedestrians, which parallels Park Drive on the west side of the park and takes you past the Hollow Tree; and the **Beaver Lake Trail,** which circles the lake of the same name near the center of the park.

The City of Vancouver publishes a Stanley Park trail map on its website (http://vancouver.ca). Don't hike alone on these interior trails, as they can be surprisingly secluded even when the Seawall and beaches are busy.

CYCLING

Vancouver's most popular cycling route runs along the **Seawall,** and the most scenic section of the Seawall is the 5.5-mile (9-kilometer) loop around Stanley Park. The paved path passes many landmarks, including the totem poles at Brockton Point, Prospect Point, and Siwash Rock.

The **Mobi bike share program** (778/655-1800, www.mobibikes.ca) has a number of locations that are convenient to Stanley Park. You can also rent bikes from several West End shops, just outside the park's boundaries:

- **Spokes Bicycle Rentals** (1798 W. Georgia St., 604/688-5141, www.spokesbicyclerentals.com; 9am-5:30pm daily; starting at $8-17/hour)

- **Bayshore Bicycle Rentals** (745 Denman St., 604/688-2453, www.bayshorebikerentals.ca; 9am-dusk daily; starting at $6-14/hour, 2-hour minimum)

- **English Bay Bike Rentals** (1754 Davie St., 604/568-8490, www.englishbaybikerentals.com; 9am-6:30pm daily; starting at $9-$15/hour, electric bikes $18/hour)

PRACTICALITIES

All of the **parking lots** are fee-based ($3.25/hour Apr.-Sept., $2.25/per hour Oct.-Mar.). If you purchase a daily pass, you can use it at any parking lot within the park. You can enter Stanley Park on two sides: from West Georgia Street, near Coal Harbour, or from English Bay, near the intersection of Denman and Davie Streets.

Just above Third Beach, the **Teahouse in Stanley Park** (Ferguson Point, Stanley Park, 604/669-3281, www.vancouverdine.com) serves a crowd-pleasing menu of west coast favorites, from smoked salmon and Pacific sablefish to burgers and steaks. The patio is particularly lovely on a sunny day or at sunset.

✪ Dr. Sun Yat-Sen Classical Chinese Garden

From the building tiles to the pathway pebbles, all the components of the Dr. Sun Yat-Sen Classical Chinese Garden came from China, as did the 52 master craftsmen who arrived from Suzhou in 1985 to construct the first authentic Ming Dynasty garden outside China. Named for the Chinese revolutionary leader and politician who is considered a father of modern China, the garden was built for the Expo '86 world's fair to promote understanding between Chinese and western cultures.

The garden is compact, encompassing just one-third of an acre (1,200 square meters). As traditional Chinese garden design dictates, it's built with a balance of four elements: rocks, water, plants, and architecture. The garden contains several pavilions, with elaborately scalloped roofs, lattice screens, and red columns; one of these structures, the Jade Water Pavilion, appears to float atop a pond. Wheelchair-accessible walkways meander between fish ponds and fountains, and around limestone outcroppings, bamboo groves, and native pine trees. The garden's covered paths provide shelter on rainy days.

Take one of the informative 45-minute garden tours (included with admission) to learn more about the peaceful garden's design and construction. From mid-June through

Dr. Sun Yat-Sen Classical Chinese Garden

August, tours start on the hour 10am to 4pm, with an additional tour at 5:30pm (tour times vary the rest of the year). After your tour, you're free to wander the garden or simply linger in the serene setting.

Adjacent to the garden is the free city-run **Dr. Sun Yat-Sen Park**, which local architects Joe Wai and Donald Vaughan designed at the same time that the garden was constructed. While lacking the classical garden's Chinese pedigree, this smaller park is still a pretty spot to sit. Head for the shaded pagoda and watch the fish swim past.

MAP 2: 578 Carrall St., 604/662-3207, www.vancouverchinesegarden.com; 10am-6pm daily May-mid-June and Sept., 9:30am-7pm daily mid-June-Aug., 10am-4:30pm daily Oct., 10am-4:30pm Tues.-Sun. Nov.-Apr.; adults $14, seniors $11, students and children age 6 and over $10

NEARBY:

- Make an advance reservation to tour the large private art collection of the **Rennie Collection at Wing Sang** (page 65).
- Linger over modern Canadian bites and a cocktail at **Juniper Kitchen & Bar** (page 100).
- Stop into **Juke** for crispy, juicy fried chicken (page 102).
- Browse the kitchenware at **Ming Wo**, which was established back in 1917 (page 176).

Rennie Collection at Wing Sang

Vancouver real estate marketer Bob Rennie has assembled one of Canada's largest private collections of contemporary art. At the Rennie Collection at Wing Sang, a private museum in Chinatown's oldest structure, the 1889 Wing Sang Building, you can see changing exhibitions of these works by both established and emerging international artists.

To visit, you must reserve a spot on a free 50-minute guided tour, offered several times a week, typically Wednesday, Thursday, and Saturday. Book in advance on the gallery website; the gallery doesn't allow walk-in visitors.

The docents walk tour groups through the multilevel gallery's current exhibit, introducing you to the artist and providing background both about the Rennie Collection's holdings, which include works by approximately 200 artists, and about the building itself. Originally a two-story brick Victorian, the Wing Sang Building belonged to Chinese Canadian businessman Yip Sang. Sang expanded the building, adding a third floor in 1901, and in 1912, he constructed a six-story brick building across the alley, with an elevated passageway connecting the two structures. His family—three wives and 23 children—lived in this adjacent building.

Tours end in the rooftop sculpture garden, which has views across Chinatown. Installed on the building's facade above the garden is British artist Martin Creed's 2008 neon sculpture, *Work No. 851: EVERYTHING IS GOING TO BE ALRIGHT*. This string

Rennie Collection at Wing Sang

of text is illuminated at night, making it visible throughout the neighborhood. Rennie selected this work as a symbol of optimism for the future of Vancouver's Chinatown.

MAP 2: 51 E. Pender St., 604/682-2088, www.renniecollection.org; by guided tour only, hours vary; free

Millennium Gate

Topped with three staggered gold roofs, the three-story Millennium Gate welcomes visitors to Vancouver's Chinatown. Erected in 2002, this ornamental gateway spans Pender Street near the International Village mall, a half-block east of Abbott Street. The Chinese characters on the gate's east side exhort visitors to "remember the past and look forward to the future."

MAP 2: E. Pender St. at Taylor Way

Vancouver Police Museum

If you're curious about some of shiny Vancouver's darker moments, plan a visit to the Vancouver Police Museum, where the exhibits about policing, criminology, and various misdeeds are housed in the 1932 former city morgue and autopsy facility.

The museum's holdings include more than 20,000 artifacts, photos, and documents about crime and police work in the city, from the region's early days to the present. In the Sins gallery, you can check out the collection of counterfeit money, illegal drugs, and weapons, all confiscated from criminals. The True Crime gallery exhibits photos and evidence from notorious regional crimes, many of which remain unsolved. You can also visit the autopsy suite, last used in 1980 but still looking ready for its next casualty, which has a collection of preserved human organs. Some people may find the graphic exhibits rather creepy; the museum may not be appropriate for younger children.

The museum runs two two-hour Sins of the City Walking Tours (May-Oct., adults $20, seniors, students, and ages 16-18 $16), where you can explore the underbelly of Gastown and Chinatown. The Red Light Rendezvous Tour tells you about the neighborhoods' brothels and the women who ran them, while on the Vice, Dice, and Opium Pipes Tour, you walk the beat of a 1920s cop, on the lookout for gambling dens, bootlegging joints, and other nefarious activity. Check the museum website or phone for tour times. While kids are allowed in the police museum at their parents' discretion, the minimum age for the walking tours is 16.

The Vancouver Police Museum is located east of Gastown, on the edge of Chinatown. Buses 4 and 7 from downtown stop nearby.

MAP 2: 240 E. Cordova St., 604/665-3346, www.vancouverpolicemuseum.ca; 9am-5pm Tues.-Sat.; adults $12, seniors and students $10, ages 6-18 $8

Gassy Jack Statue

At Maple Tree Square is a statue of Gassy Jack, a fast-talking British sailor and riverboat pilot turned saloonkeeper, from whom Vancouver's

THE EVOLUTION OF CHINATOWN

In 1858, gold was discovered along British Columbia's Fraser River. Among the miners and adventurers who flocked to the province for this emerging gold rush were a number of Chinese settlers. Many came north from California, while others arrived directly from China, primarily from Guangdong Province and the country's southern regions.

Throughout the late 1800s, Chinese immigrants continued to arrive in B.C., including thousands who found work building the Canadian Pacific Railway. Others worked in the canneries in Steveston, or in the logging or mining industries. By the 1890s, more than 1,000 Chinese people had settled in Vancouver's Chinatown, clustered on what is now Pender Street, between Carrall and Columbia Streets. By 1911, Vancouver's Chinatown was the largest in Canada.

In 1923, Chinese immigration came to an abrupt halt, when the Canadian government passed the Chinese Immigration Act—often called the Chinese Exclusion Act—which effectively stopped any additional Chinese immigrants from settling in Canada. This lack of new residents, combined with the Great Depression of the 1930s, sent the neighborhood into decline.

The population of Vancouver's Chinatown ebbed and flowed during the second half of the 1900s. Beginning in the 1980s, many new Chinese residents arrived in the Vancouver area, first from Hong Kong and more recently from Taiwan and mainland China. Most of these newcomers, many of whom were more well-to-do than earlier immigrants, avoided settling in the aging Chinatown, preferring to locate throughout the city or in Richmond, the suburb to the south that has become something of a "new Chinatown."

Some of Chinatown's signature produce markets, herbalists, tea shops, bakeries, and Chinese restaurants still remain, with bins piled high with ginseng, winter melons, and *yu choy* (greens), or display cases filled with tea leaves, coconut buns, and various herbal remedies. In recent years, however, many apartment and condominium buildings have sprouted up, and chic restaurants, cafés, and bars have opened, making it a newly vibrant destination for eating and drinking. While many applaud these businesses and the increased life that they're bringing to Chinatown streets, some residents are expressing concern at the pace and extent of the neighborhood's changes.

With its mix of historic and modern, Vancouver's Chinatown remains an exciting district to explore, but the neighborhood will undoubtedly continue to evolve.

historic Gastown district got its name. In 1867, Captain John Deighton, nicknamed "Gassy Jack" for his habit of telling tall tales, promised local millworkers that he'd serve them drinks if they'd build him a saloon on the shores of Burrard Inlet. The motivated millworkers constructed the bar in just one day, and the fledgling Gastown neighborhood took its title from Deighton's "Gassy" nickname. Artist Vern Simpson crafted the copper statue of the hat-wearing Deighton, who is standing atop a barrel. A gift to the city, the statue was installed in 1970.

MAP 2: Maple Tree Square, intersection of Alexander, Carrall, Water, and Powell Sts.

Gastown Steam Clock

Sure, it's touristy, but you'll still find yourself in front of this local icon, waiting for it to toot its steam whistle every 15 minutes. The historic-looking Gastown Steam Clock actually dates back only to 1977, when area businesses commissioned clockmaker Ray Saunders to create the clock as part of the neighborhood's revitalization. Saunders based his clock on an 1875 design; it draws power from the city's underground steam heating system (and from three electric motors). Weighing over two tons, with steam whistles above its dial, the clock stands 16 feet (five meters) tall.

MAP 2: Water St., at Cambie St.

Woodward's Building

Charles Woodward started his career as a grocer in Ontario before opening a shop in Vancouver in the late 1800s. In 1903, he moved the original location of Woodward's Department Store to Gastown. Woodward's sold clothing for men, women, and children; housewares; and food. Growing to occupy most of a city block, the store developed into a prime Vancouver shopping destination. On its roof was a tower crowned with a red neon "W" that became a city landmark and is visible to this day.

In 1992, Woodward's declared bankruptcy. It wasn't until 2006 that the former store was converted into a mixed-use complex, combining residential, commercial, and arts spaces. **MAP 2:** Hastings and Abbott Sts.

Catfe

For cat lovers only: Vancouver's first cat café is part coffee shop and part foster home for felines. Catfe, inside the International Village mall on the edge of Chinatown, has partnered with the B.C. SPCA, bringing in 8-12 adoptable cats every week. Visitors can pet and play with the animals while enjoying a coffee or light snack. The café allows only 16 guests at one time, for visits of up to one hour. In each time slot, 10 spots can be reserved online; book up to four weeks in advance on their website. The remaining spots are available for walk-ins.

MAP 2: International Village, 88 W. Pender St., #2035, 778/379-0060, www. catfe.ca; 11am-8pm Sun.-Wed., 5pm-9pm Thurs., 11am-9pm Fri.-Sat.; $5 with any café purchase, $8 without purchase

Yaletown and False Creek Map 3

✪ Science World

What's that dome thing? Kids may want to check out the distinctive geodesic dome (constructed for the Expo '86 world's fair) that houses Vancouver's cool science museum, even before they venture inside. Clad in aluminum and illuminated at night with nearly 400 lights, the 155-foot-tall dome looks like a colossal shiny golf ball, shimmering on the edge of False Creek.

Officially called Science World at Telus World of Science, the museum is full of hands-on exhibits about the human body, natural world, light and sound, puzzles and illusions, and more. The BodyWorks exhibit helps kids explore what's inside of them and where they came from, while in

the Eureka! Gallery they can walk on an oversize piano, try to capture their shadows, or launch a parachute. The littlest visitors have their own Kidspace, designed for children under age six, stocked with giant building blocks, water features, and games for exploring light and color. Live science shows and demonstrations take place throughout the day, entertaining (and educating) with fire, electricity, balloons, and other science themes—even grossology ("the impolite science of the human body"). A rotating selection of films plays on the five-story-tall screen in the immersive OMNIMAX Theatre ($6).

Outside in Ken Spencer Science Park, you can explore more interactive exhibits about the local environment and issues of sustainability. The park even has its own chicken coop.

MAP 3: 1455 Quebec St., 604/443-7440, www.scienceworld.ca, subway: Main Street-Science World; 10am-5pm Mon.-Fri., 10am-6pm Sat.-Sun. Apr.-late June, 10am-8pm Thurs., 10am-6pm Fri.-Wed. late June-early Sept., 10am-5pm Tues.-Fri., 10am-6pm Sat.-Mar.; adults $24, seniors and students $19, ages 3-12 $16

Olympic Village

On the south side of False Creek, a new neighborhood developed thanks to the 2010 Winter Olympic Games. The residential buildings where athletes lived during the Games have been transformed into the Olympic Village, also known as the Village at False Creek, comprising stylish condominiums, brewpubs, cafés, a community center, and several public art pieces. Look for *The Birds* in the Southeast False Creek Plaza, two 18-foot-tall (5.5-meter) sparrows crafted by Vancouver artist Myfanwy MacLeod. The Olympic Village provides a great vantage point for skyline photos.

MAP 3: Bounded by Ontario St., Athletes Way, Columbia St., and W. 1st Ave.; subway: Olympic Village or Main Street-Science World

B.C. Place and the B.C. Sports Hall of Fame

The odd-looking structure along False Creek that resembles a giant spaceship is B.C. Place, a sports and concert arena. Major League Soccer's Vancouver Whitecaps (www.whitecapsfc.com) play here, as do the Canadian Football League's B.C. Lions (www.bclions.com). Built in 1983, the arena has hosted the Expo '86 opening ceremonies, the opening and closing ceremonies of the 2010 Olympic Games, the FIFA Women's World Cup Canada 2015, as

Science World, on Vancouver's False Creek

well as concerts by Michael Jackson, The Rolling Stones, Madonna, Paul McCartney, Taylor Swift, and many other performers.

Inside B.C. Place, the **B.C. Sports Hall of Fame** (Beatty St. at Robson St., Gate A, 604/687-5520, www.bc-sportshalloffame.com; 10am-5pm daily; adults $15, seniors, students, and ages 6-17 $12) highlights regional sports history and offers interactive games where kids (and accompanying adults) can test their athletic prowess. Exhibits feature topics like Vancouver's 2010 Winter Olympics, women and ab-original sports figures, and a Hall of Champions showcasing B.C. athletes.

You can also book the All Access Experience ($20), which includes a B.C. Place tour along with access to the Hall of Fame. Tours visit the field, media room, premium boxes, and (when available) the locker rooms. The All Access Experience tours are offered on specific dates, so check ahead for availability.

If you're attending an event at B.C. Place within two weeks of your visit to the Sports Hall of Fame, show your event ticket stub to get 50 percent off your Hall of Fame admission.

Outside the arena, near the intersection of Robson and Beatty Streets, is the **Terry Fox Memorial**, a series of four progressively larger sculptures by Vancouver artist Douglas Coupland. The memorial honors Fox, the B.C. man who embarked on a cross-Canada run in 1980 to raise money for cancer research after losing his own leg to the disease.
MAP 3: 777 Pacific Blvd., 604/669-2300, www.bcplacestadium.com; subway: Stadium-Chinatown

Engine 374 Pavilion
The Canadian Pacific Railway completed its cross-Canada train route in 1885, when rail workers drove the last spike of the transcontinental railroad into the ground at Craigellachie, near the town of Revelstoke, in eastern British Columbia. A year and a half later, on May 23, 1887, the first trans-continental passenger train rolled into Vancouver, pulled by Engine 374.

This historic locomotive is now on view at the Engine 374 Pavilion, next to the Yaletown-Roundhouse Community Centre. Posing next to the engine makes a fun photo op for rail enthusiasts of all ages.

The Engine 374 Pavilion is typically open every day, but hours vary, as the staff are all volunteers. Call to make sure they're open before making a special trip.
MAP 3: 181 Roundhouse Mews, 604/713-1800, http://roundhouse.ca; subway: Yaletown-Roundhouse; hours vary; free

Long Table Distillery
Vancouver's first micro-distillery produces several varieties of gin and vodka in their 80-gallon (300-liter) copper-pot still. Long Table Distillery also makes small batches of seasonal spirits, like Akvavit or Amaro, so stop by their Yaletown tasting room to see what's brewing. In the 28-seat space, with a polished wood bar and a wall of windows into the distilling room, you can choose a flight of three spirits ($6); the staff can explain what you're drinking and how it's made. They also host popular Gin & Tonic Fridays (4pm-9pm) and Cocktail Saturdays (3pm-9pm), when they offer custom cocktails, and you can purchase snacks from food trucks parked out front.
MAP 3: 1451 Hornby St., 604/266-0177, http://longtabledistillery.com; 1pm-6pm Wed.-Thurs., 1pm-9pm Fri.-Sat.

THE ISLAND THE OLYMPICS BUILT

Before hosting the 2010 Winter Olympic Games, Vancouver embarked on numerous building projects: the Canada Line subway connecting downtown and the airport, the Olympic Cauldron on the Coal Harbour waterfront, and the former Athletes Village on the shores of False Creek, which housed competitors during the Games and is now the fashionable Olympic Village district.

Yet one of the Olympics' most unusual legacies may be an artificial island. To build the Athletes Village, developers excavated a vast amount of rocks, sand, and gravel. More than 2 million cubic feet (60,000 cubic meters) of this excavated material was used to construct tiny **Habitat Island**, along Southeast False Creek.

Now city-owned parkland, Habitat Island has more than 200 native trees, shrubs, flowers, and grasses, and, as befits its name, it provides a habitat for birds, crabs, starfish, and other land and sea creatures.

Habitat Island is located on the False Creek waterfront, near the foot of Columbia Street, east of the Cambie Bridge. A rock pathway leads onto the island from the Seawall path. You can wander over to the island for a stroll or a picnic. Or simply explore the island that the Olympics built.

Granville Island   Map 4

TOP EXPERIENCE

✪ Granville Island Public Market

The island's main attraction is the year-round indoor Granville Island Public Market. It's a food lover's heaven, where artistically arranged fruits garnish the produce stalls, and you can nibble away the day on charcuterie, cheeses, pastries, fudge, and other treats. While food vendors predominate among the nearly 50 stands, some stalls sell jewelry, leather goods, and other locally made crafts. There's no particular order to the merchandise, though, so plan to wander, browse, and snack.

Granville Island was once known as "Industrial Island" for the sawmills, factories, and other businesses that operated here. The buildings that house the market were converted from their former industrial uses in the 1970s.

Start at **Blue Parrot Espresso Bar** (604/688-5127, www.blueparrotcoffee.com) for java with a water view.

Sample the unexpectedly addictive **salmon candy** (cured, salty-sweet fish snacks) at any of the seafood counters, or line up with the locals for housemade charcuterie at **Oyama Sausage** (604/327-7407, www.oyamasausage.ca) or nut-studded grape loaves at **Terra Breads Bakery Café** (604/685-3102, www.terrabreads.com). You might hope that the kids won't notice longtime favorite **Lee's Donuts** (604/685-4021), at least until it's time for dessert.

In summer, the **Granville Island**

fresh fish, Granville Island Public Market

Farmers Market (10am-3pm Thurs. June-Sept.) sets up once a week in front of the Public Market, bringing more local farmers and artisans to the island. At any time, musicians and other entertainers might perform outside the market.

You can pick up picnic fixings or prepared foods in the Public Market and eat outdoors behind the market building. If it's too crowded there, take your picnic to the opposite end of the island and enjoy it on the grass overlooking the water in Ron Basford Park.

For a behind-the-scenes look at the Public Market, book the two-hour Granville Island Market Tour with Vancouver Foodie Tours (http://foodietours.ca; 10:30am daily mid-May-mid-Sept., 10:30am Thurs.-Sun. mid-Sept.-mid-May; $54-58). You'll learn the stories of many of the vendors and their products and sample 20 different foods and drinks.

The Public Market is located along False Creek, facing the downtown skyline. As you walk onto the island on Anderson Street, continue till the road forks, then bear left; the market will be one block ahead. The market is busiest on weekend afternoons, especially when the weather is nice.

MAP 4: 1689 Johnston St., 604/666-6655; http://granvilleisland.com; 9am-7pm daily; free

NEARBY:

- Eat your way across the country at Edible Canada Bistro (page 107).
- Check out the local music scene at the Backstage Lounge (page 131).
- Browse museum-quality aboriginal art at Eagle Spirit Gallery (page 141).
- Kayak around the island with

Ecomarine Paddlesports Centre (page 158).

- Find almost anything you'd wear on your head at the Granville Island Hat Shop (page 178).

✪ Railspur Alley

Explore this pedestrian-only cobblestone lane near the center of Granville Island for its artist studios and shops. Go inside the petite studios, where many of the artists welcome you to watch and chat while they work. Look for textile weavers, leather crafters, woodworkers, and even a sake maker in the lane's low buildings.

MAP 4: Between Cartwright St. and Old Bridge St.

Liberty Distilling

Liberty Distilling brews small batches of vodka, gin, and whiskey in their 140- and 220-liter (36- and 58-gallon) copper-pot stills. Sample their handcrafted products in the cocktail lounge with its elaborately carved bar. Listen for the sound of a steam whistle announcing the start of happy hour (3pm-6pm Mon.-Thurs.). On weekends, Liberty offers a tour (11:30am and 1:30pm Sat.-Sun.; $10) of their facilities, where you can learn about the processes of mashing, fermenting, and distilling—with samples, of course. Tours are limited to

Granville Island's Railspur Alley

10 people, so make a reservation to ensure your spot.

MAP 4: 1494 Old Bridge St., 604/558-1998, www.thelibertydistillery.com; 11am-8pm daily

Artisan Sake Maker

At the tiny shop that houses Artisan Sake Maker, Vancouver's only local producer of Japanese rice wine, step up to the counter where the staff explain how sake is brewed. They offer tastings of a single sake ($2) or samples of three types ($5). In business since 2007, the company that Japan-born sake maker

Learn how rice wine is brewed at the Artisan Sake Maker.

Masa Shiroki founded brews several varieties of sake, including sparkling sakes. Shiroki works with local farmers to grow the rice for his sakes here in British Columbia.

MAP 4: 1339 Railspur Alley, 604/685-7253, www.artisansakemaker.com; 11:30am-6pm daily

Sea Village

Sea Village is a community of colorful floating homes, each set on its own dock on False Creek. They're private residences, but you can look at the area from the walkway above and imagine what it would be like to live here on the water. The entrance to Sea Village is off Johnston Street, just west of the Granville Island Hotel.

MAP 4: Off Johnston St., near intersection with Cartwright St.

Kids Market

On Granville Island, youngsters have their own marketplace, the multilevel Kids Market, a family-friendly mini-mall where two dozen cute shops sell toys, games, candy, and clothing. Note the children's-only doorway at the entrance, then walk around to the back of the bright yellow building and notice the painted eyes looking down at you from a mural above. The kids can run around in the Adventure Zone, an indoor playground, or outside in the splash park (late May-early Sept.).

MAP 4: 1496 Cartwright St., 604/689-8447, www.kidsmarket.ca; 10am-6pm daily; free

Granville Island Brewing

Granville Island Brewing started producing craft beers back in 1984. They make a wide variety of beers, including their Island Lager and English Bay Pale Ale, but good choices to try at the brewery are the more limited small batch series, with brews like the Belgian-style Saison, Kellerbier Unfiltered, and West Coast Pale Ale.

Although most of their beer is now made in other locations, you can take the 30-minute **tour** (noon, 2pm, and 4pm daily; $10) of the original island brewery, which provides an education in beer making. The tour wraps up with five-ounce samples of three of their beers. You can also have a drink in their taproom, or pick up beer to go, along with brewery-themed merchandise, in their retail store (10am-8pm daily).

MAP 4: 1441 Cartwright St., 604/687-2739, www.gib.ca; noon-8pm daily

Kitsilano   Map 5

✪ Museum of Vancouver

Though its building resembles a flying saucer that might have landed in Kitsilano's Vanier Park, this city museum's unique structure, created by architect Gerald Hamilton, was actually designed to recall a traditional hat of the Haida First Nations people. Inside the Museum of Vancouver, the exhibition spaces are no less distinctive.

The permanent galleries take you through Vancouver's past, from its aboriginal heritage to early settlement days to the hippie era of the 1960s, with participatory activities that bring the city's history to life. Listen to recordings of First Nations people

Museum of Vancouver

discussing their families, punch up some tunes on the 1950s jukebox, or dress for the Summer of Love in macramé. The sometimes-controversial temporary exhibitions explore social phenomena from happiness to sex. The museum hosts lectures, workshops, and social events that are as engaging as the exhibits themselves; check the calendar on their website for details.

The **Vanier Park Explore Pass** (adults $37, seniors, students, and ages 5-18 $30) includes admission to the Museum of Vancouver and the adjacent H. R. MacMillan Space Centre, as well as the nearby Vancouver Maritime Museum.

It's a half-mile (0.9-kilometer) walk along the Seawall from Kitsilano Beach to the museum; from Granville Island, it's just over a mile (1.8 kilometers) along the water and through Vanier Park. Either route is a lovely seaside stroll. To reach the museum by bus, take bus 2 from Burrard Street downtown into Kitsilano; get off at the corner of Cornwall Avenue and Chestnut Streets, where it's a short walk toward the water to the museum. Or take **False Creek Ferries** (604/684-7781, www.granvilleislandferries.bc.ca) to Vanier Park from Granville Island or downtown.

MAP 5: 1100 Chestnut St., 604/736-4411, www.museumofvancouver.ca; 10am-5pm Sun.-Wed., 10am-8pm Thurs., 10am-9pm Fri.-Sat.; adults $18, seniors and students $15, ages 5-18 $8

H. R. MacMillan Space Centre

In the same building as the Museum of Vancouver, the H. R. MacMillan Space Centre, the city's planetarium, has galleries of space exhibits to explore and astronomy (and other space-themed) shows throughout the day. Presentations might let you experience "A Day in Space," explore "Seven Wonders of the Universe," or take a virtual expedition by "Surfing the Solar System."

The Space Centre's **Gordon MacMillan Southam Observatory** (604/738-2855; Fri.-Sat. early July-early Sept., Sat. only early Sept.-early July; adults $13, seniors and students $10, ages 5-11 $8) is also open for a planetarium show (7:30pm and 9pm) and guided stargazing (8pm-midnight) through the half-meter telescope. If you come only for the stargazing, admission is by donation.

MAP 5: 1100 Chestnut St., 604/738-7827, www.spacecentre.ca; 10am-5pm daily late June-early Sept., 10am-3pm Mon.-Fri., 10am-5pm Sat., noon-5pm Sun. early Sept.-late June, adults $18, seniors and ages 12-18 $15, ages 5-11 $13

Vancouver Maritime Museum

Built in B.C. in the 1920s, the historic Arctic-exploring schooner *St. Roch* is now the centerpiece of the family-friendly Vancouver Maritime Museum, an A-frame building on the waterfront in Vanier Park. The *St. Roch* was the first to sail the Northwest Passage from west to east and the first to circumnavigate North America, when it traveled from Vancouver to Halifax via the Panama Canal in 1950.

Climb aboard the *St. Roch* and learn more about its Arctic adventures. You can clamber around the wooden decks, explore the ship's compact cabins, and even get behind the captain's wheel, as you discover the boat's story. The museum has other hands-on exhibits designed for kids, from piloting a submersible to talking with a model shipbuilder while he works, as well as changing exhibitions about the Pacific Northwest and Arctic maritime history.

Outside the museum is a 100-foot (30-meter) totem pole that Kwakwaka'wakw First Nations artist Mungo Martin carved to mark British Columbia's centennial in 1958.

To get to the museum, take bus 2 from Burrard Street downtown to the corner of Cornwall Avenue and Chestnut Street in Kitsilano. Or take **False Creek Ferries** (604/684-7781, www.granvilleislandferries.bc.ca) to Vanier Park from Granville Island or downtown.

MAP 5: 1905 Ogden St., 604/257-8300, www.vancouvermaritimemuseum.com; 10am-5pm Fri.-Wed., 10am-8pm Thurs. late

Vancouver Maritime Museum in Kitsilano

May-early Sept., 10am-5pm Tues.-Wed. and Fri.-Sat., 10am-8pm Thurs., noon-5pm Sun. early Sept.-late May; adults $11, seniors, students, and ages 6-18 $8.50 (by donation 5pm-8pm Thurs.)

UBC and Point Grey   Map 5

TOP EXPERIENCE

✪ Museum of Anthropology

To explore the culture of British Columbia's aboriginal peoples and traditional cultures from around the world, don't miss the striking Museum of Anthropology on the University of British Columbia campus, which houses one of the world's top collections of Northwest Coast First Peoples' art.

Canadian modernist architect Arthur Erickson, known for his innovative concrete and glass structures, designed the 80,000-square-foot (7,400-square-meter) museum, which opened in 1976. Inside, the Great Hall, with 50-foot-tall (15-meter) windows, provides a dramatic home for the immense totem poles, traditional canoes, and elaborate carvings. The museum also houses the world's largest

collection of works by noted Haida First Nations artist Bill Reid, including his massive cedar sculpture, *The Raven and the First Men*, which depicts a creation legend in which the Raven coaxes tiny humans out of a clamshell and into the world.

The museum's Multiversity Galleries display thousands of objects from different cultures, along with audio, video, and photos that provide context and additional information about these materials and the communities they come from. The museum also mounts temporary exhibitions on world arts and culture, from contemporary Arab art to Peruvian silver and works by present-day indigenous artists.

Choose from several daily gallery tours, included with museum admission. There's a 60-minute overview tour that walks you through the museum's highlights (11am and 2pm daily, additional tour 6pm Thurs.), 30-minute "guide's choice" tours that illustrate a particular theme or exhibit (1pm and 3:30pm daily), and tours of the temporary exhibits (check the website or call for schedules).

Behind the museum is an outdoor sculpture complex with memorial and mortuary totem poles, dating from the early 1950s to the present, as well as a Haida house that Bill Reid constructed.

To reach the museum by public transit, take any UBC-bound bus (including buses 4 or 14 from downtown) to the last stop at the UBC bus loop. From there, you can walk to the museum in 10-15 minutes, or transfer to shuttle bus C18, which stops in front of the museum. By car, it's about 25 minutes from downtown to the museum, which has a public parking lot.

MAP 5: 6393 NW Marine Dr., 604/822-5087, http://moa.ubc.ca; 10am-9pm Thurs., 10am-5pm Fri.-Wed. mid-May-mid-Oct., 10am-9pm Thurs., 10am-5pm Fri.-Sun. and Tues.-Wed. mid-Oct.-mid-May; adults $18, seniors, students, and children $16 ($10 5pm-9pm Thurs.)

NEARBY:

- Stroll among the flowers and koi ponds of the serene Nitobe Japanese Garden (page 77).
- Explore the natural world, from a blue whale skeleton to tiny fossils, at the Beaty Biodiversity Museum (page 78).
- Dine alongside UBC professors at Sage Bistro (page 111).
- Check out the modern art collection at the Morris and Helen Belkin Art Gallery (page 144).

totem pole at the Museum of Anthropology

✪ Nitobe Japanese Garden

You could be in Japan as you stroll among the flowers, waterfalls, and koi ponds at the serene Nitobe Japanese Garden, one of the most authentic traditional Japanese gardens in North America. Several stone lanterns decorate the paths; another feature is the Island of Eternity, a collection of rocks shaped like a turtle, which symbolizes longevity. Many of the plants, from azaleas and irises to maple and cherry trees, came from Japan. The garden is particularly scenic in April and May, when the cherry blossoms bloom.

The 2.5-acre (one-hectare) garden is named for Dr. Inazo Nitobe, a professor, author, and advocate for East-West relations who served as Japan's representative to the League of Nations in the 1920s. The garden's 77-log bridge symbolizes Nitobe's goal of being "a bridge over the Pacific." The garden features five other bridges that crisscross its streams. For an extra fee, participate in a traditional Japanese tea ceremony (May-Sept., $10) in the garden's teahouse, a classical structure in which you pass through exterior and interior gardens before entering the tearoom itself. Ceremonies are held on the last Saturday of the month on the hour from 11am to 3pm. Reservations are recommended; call 604/939-7749 to reserve.

The garden is a short walk from the Museum of Anthropology. From the UBC bus loop, you can walk or take shuttle bus C18.

MAP 5: 1895 Lower Mall, 604/822-6038, www.botanicalgarden.ubc.ca; 11am-5:30pm daily mid-Mar.-Oct.; 10am-2pm Mon.-Fri. Nov.-mid-Mar.; adults $7, seniors and students $5.50, ages 5-12 $4 (by donation Nov.-mid-Mar.)

Beaty Biodiversity Museum

An 85-foot (26-meter) blue whale skeleton, the largest on display in Canada, greets visitors to the Beaty Biodiversity Museum, a modern natural history gallery. The museum has more than two million specimens of bugs, fish, plants, fossils, and more, many of which come from B.C. and the surrounding regions. In this family-friendly museum, many of the items are set at kids' eye level for youngsters to check out; in the interactive Discovery Lab, children can learn to use a microscope, compare different types of fossils, and participate in other hands-on activities.

At 10:30am most weekdays, a museum staffer leads a 30-minute hands-on presentation about specific specimens. The museum also offers 30-minute tours (11:30am and 3pm daily) highlighting particular aspects of the collections.

The museum is near the center of the UBC campus, a short walk from the UBC bus loop.

MAP 5: 2212 Main Mall, 604/827-4955, www.beatymuseum.ubc.ca; 10am-5pm Tues.-Sun.; adults $14, seniors, students, and children ages 13-17 $12, ages 5-12 $10

UBC Botanical Garden

A garden of native B.C. plants, a woodland garden, a traditional Asian garden: These are just a few groupings of the more than 50,000 trees and plants that thrive at the 70-acre (28-hectare) UBC Botanical Garden, where walking paths wend through the woods and grounds.

Explore the B.C. Rainforest Garden, with its tall western red cedars, several varieties of maple trees, and bushes of blackberries, blueberries, and huckleberries. In the Alpine Garden, you can travel the world of mountain-region plants, grouped geographically, while in the Food Garden, you can check out vegetables, fruits, and herbs that grow locally. The David C. Lam Asian Garden blossoms with rhododendrons, magnolias, dogwood, hydrangeas, lilies, and other plants native to China, Korea, Japan, and the Himalayas that also thrive in Vancouver's temperate climate. The garden's two oldest trees, Douglas firs that are more 400 years old, are also in the Asian Garden.

The Botanical Garden is on the south side of the UBC campus. By public transit, take any UBC-bound bus (including buses 4 and 14 from downtown) to the last stop at the UBC bus loop; transfer to shuttle bus C20, which stops in front of the garden. By car, it's about 25 minutes from downtown to the gardens, which have a public parking lot.

MAP 5: 6804 SW Marine Dr., 604/822-4208, www.botanicalgarden. ubc.ca; 9:30am-4:30pm daily; adults $9, seniors $7, ages 5-12 $5 (by donation Nov.-mid-Mar.)

Greenheart TreeWalk

Greenheart TreeWalk

An adventurous way to explore the UBC Botanical Garden is on the Greenheart TreeWalk, a 1,000-foot (310-meter) aerial trail system that takes you high into the rainforest canopy. Cross a series of swinging bridges to eight increasingly higher viewing platforms mounted among the Douglas firs, cedars, and other lofty trees. The tallest platform is 75 feet (23 meters) above the forest floor. To protect the trees, the platforms were constructed without using nails or bolts; a cable tension system suspends them from the tree trunks.

Explore the walkway on your own or on a 45-minute guided tour, included with your walkway ticket, where your guide tells you about the surrounding second-growth forest. Though the area was once logged, many trees are more than a century old. You'll also learn how First Nations use various trees and plants, from carving canoes to traditional medicine. Each tour can accommodate up to 20 people.

The Greenheart TreeWalk is located within the UBC Botanical Garden. From the garden's main entrance, follow the signs to the TreeWalk. Your TreeWalk ticket lets you explore the rest of the botanical gardens, too.

MAP 5: 6804 SW Marine Dr., 604/822-4208, www.botanicalgarden.ubc. ca; 10am-4:30pm daily Apr.-Oct.; adults $20, seniors $15, ages 5-12 $10; admission to UBC Botanical Garden included

UBC Farm Market

The University of British Columbia operates a 60-acre (24-hectare) organic farm on the south side of the campus. You can purchase produce grown onsite at the weekly UBC Farm Market, held Saturday mornings on the farm grounds. The market also sells produce from other local growers, including indigenous farmers, plus baked goods, locally made honey, soaps, prepared foods, and crafts. The farm is a good place for kids, too, who can explore the fields and see what's growing.

During the Saturday market, you can take a 30-minute family-friendly farm tour (11am Sat. June-Oct.; free). Reservations aren't required for the farm tours; meet at the farm about five minutes in advance.

From the UBC bus loop in the

center of campus, catch shuttle bus C18 or C20 to the farm. Get off on Ross Drive at Birney Avenue.

MAP 5: 3461 Ross Dr., 604/822-5092, http://ubcfarm.ubc.ca; 9am-1pm Sat. June-Oct.

Cambie Corridor
Map 6

✪ VanDusen Botanical Garden

Wander the plant world without leaving Vancouver at the 55-acre (22-hectare) VanDusen Botanical Garden. With more than 250,000 plants from around the globe, the garden contains varieties native to the Pacific Northwest, other parts of Canada, and the Himalayas, the Mediterranean, and South America. Different flowers and plants are highlights at different times of year, like cherry trees and dogwood in the spring, roses and lilies in summer, colorful trees in the autumn, and evergreens in winter. You can find your way through an Elizabethan maze, too. A one-hour guided tour (10:30am and 2pm Wed., 2pm Thurs.-Tues. Apr.-mid-Oct., 1pm Sun. mid-Oct.-Mar.) helps you explore what's growing.

From downtown, bus 17 for Oak Street stops at West 37th Avenue at the garden entrance.

MAP 6: 5251 Oak St., 604/257-8335, www.vandusengarden.org; 9am-8:30pm daily June-Aug., 10am-6pm daily Sept., 10am-5pm daily Oct. and Mar., 10am-4pm daily Nov. and Feb., 10am-3pm daily Dec.-Jan., 9am-7pm daily Apr., 9am-8pm daily May; adults $12, seniors and ages 13-18 $9, ages 3-12 $6 (discounted admission Oct.-Mar.)

Queen Elizabeth Park

At Queen Elizabeth Park, at the highest point in Vancouver, you can explore several gardens, have a picnic on its manicured grounds, or take photos of the city skyline and mountains.

In a geodesic dome near the center of the park, the Bloedel Conservatory (604/873-7000, www.vancouver.ca; 9am-8pm Mon.-Fri., 10am-8pm Sat.-Sun. May-early Sept., 10am-5pm daily early Sept.-Apr., adults $7, seniors and students $5, ages 3-12 $4) houses three different ecosystems, including a tropical rainforest, subtropical rainforest, and desert environment, with native plants and more than 200 free-flying birds. It's a warm destination for a cold or rainy day. Also in the park are tennis courts, a pitch-and-putt golf course, and a lawn bowling field.

To get to the park by public transit, take the Canada Line to King Edward station. Then either transfer to bus 15 southbound on Cambie Street to West 33rd Avenue, or walk south on Cambie Street to the park entrance. Follow the

Bloedel Conservatory, Queen Elizabeth Park

trails through the trees or walk along the park road to reach the conservatory; it's a short but uphill climb.

MAP 6: 4600 Cambie St., www.vancouver. ca; dawn-dusk daily

Commercial Drive

Map 7

✪ Parallel 49 Brewing Company

The tasting room at Parallel 49 Brewing Company, one of the more established East Side breweries, is a beer tasting hall, a small-plates restaurant, and a spirited neighborhood gathering place. Three of the brewery's founders grew up nearby in East Van. These days, the company is known for the Gypsy Tears Ruby Ale, the Tricycle Grapefruit Radler (blended from lager and red grapefruit juice), and a changing array of seasonal brews. Stop in for a tasting flight to see what's on tap.

MAP 7: 1950 Triumph St., 604/558-2739, http://parallel49brewing.com; 11am-11pm daily

Callister Brewing

Billing themselves as "Canada's first collaborative brewery," Callister Brewing not only sells and serves their own beer in their East Side tasting room, but every year they also team up with three additional brewers who use the facilities in Callister's red stucco brewery to make their own beers. Along with Callister's own Resolution Dark Saison, Old Robyn English Strong, and 1 Hop Mind Pale Ale, you can sample these partners' creations in the tasting room. Four-ounce samplers start at $2 each. The tasting room is teeny, with a long communal table and a few stools at the counter, so you're likely to strike up a conversation with fellow beer aficionados.

MAP 7: 1338 Franklin St., 604/569-2739, www.callisterbrewing.com; 2pm-9pm Mon.-Thurs., 2pm-10pm Fri., 1pm-10pm Sat., 1pm-9pm Sun.

Doan's Craft Brewing Company

Family-run Doan's Craft Brewing Company operates a tiny café-style tasting room and compact brewery in a converted East Side house, where local artist Ola Volo decorated one wall with an intricate black-and-white mural; her work appears on Doan's labels, too. Try their Rye India Pale Ale or the German-style Kolsch. The 5.5-ounce samplers are $2. Because the petite space measures just 450 square feet (42 square meters), sitting and sipping at the communal table here feels like you're relaxing in a friend's living room.

MAP 7: 1830 Powell St., 604/559-0415, http://doanscraftbrewing.com; 2pm-9pm Mon.-Thurs., 2pm-11pm Fri., noon-11pm Sat., noon-9pm Sun.

Powell Street Craft Brewery

A husband and wife team manages Powell Street Craft Brewery in a small East Side warehouse on busy Powell Street. Old Jalopy Pale Ale and Ode to Citra (also a pale ale) are two of their well-regarded brews. Try a glass or a flight in their tasting room, where you can perch at a blond-wood bar-height table and look through the window into the brewery. Glasses start at $1.75

CRAFT BREWERIES

Vancouver's first microbreweries launched back in the 1980s, but more recent changes in B.C.'s provincial liquor laws paved the way for a craft brewery boom that has been growing exponentially since 2010.

Two East Side neighborhoods have become the center of Vancouver's craft brewery scene. The city's eastern districts are locally known as "East Van," but the increasing number of microbreweries in this area has earned it the nickname "Yeast Van."

One center of local craft beer production is in the Mount Pleasant neighborhood, around Main Street between 2nd and 8th Avenues, a short walk from the Olympic Village. Several breweries with tasting rooms are within walking distance of each other, and there's a congregation of art galleries in the area, too.

the tasting room at Callister Brewing

Even more craft breweries have set up shop farther east, between Hastings and Powell Streets, east of Clark Drive. This partly industrial, partly residential neighborhood isn't the most picturesque, but with lots of excellent beer to sample, it's perfect for a brewery crawl. Most brewery tasting rooms here open around midday or early afternoon and remain open into the evening.

Many of Vancouver's craft breweries are too small for formal tours. However, some do offer regularly scheduled tours, and at others, staff will be happy to show you around if you call ahead.

If you want to learn more about the brewing process and the local beer industry, another option is to take a tour with **Vancouver Brewery Tours** (604/318-2280, http://vancouverbrewerytours.com; $70-90). Each of their three-hour excursions visits three different breweries. Their website details the tour schedule and which breweries each tour visits on which day.

The drinking age in British Columbia is 19, and you may be asked to show identification to verify your age. Cheers!

for a five-ounce sampler; a flight of four is $6.10.

MAP 7: 1357 Powell St., 604/558-2537, www.powellbeer.com; 2pm-8pm Mon., 2pm-9pm Tues.-Thurs., noon-10pm Fri.-Sat., noon-8pm Sun.

✪ Odd Society Spirits

Standing out amid the East Side beer makers, Odd Society Spirits is a small batch distillery housed in a former motorcycle garage, where they make their signature East Van Vodka, along with gin and a "moonshine" whiskey. Tasting flights (three samples for $7) and mixed drinks are available in their front room, an old-time cocktail lounge with marble-top tables and a long bar. In the lounge, floor-to-ceiling windows showcase the distilling room in back, which you can visit if you drop in on weekend afternoons for a free distillery tour. On these informal visits, you'll learn about the distilling process and how they use their two 92-gallon (350-liter) German-made copper-pot stills and their 15-foot (4.5-meter) "vodka column," which removes impurities from the vodka.

MAP 7: 1725 Powell St., 604/559-6745, www.oddsocietyspirits.com; 1pm-10pm Thurs., 1pm-11pm Fri.-Sat., 1pm-6pm Sun.; tours 4pm Sat.-Sun.

Monument for East Vancouver

This illuminated cross with the words "EAST VAN" nested inside isn't a religious symbol. Rather, it's a public art piece, *Monument for East Vancouver*, created by Vancouver-born artist Ken Lum.

Lum has written that the inspiration for the 57-foot (17-meter) sculpture, which lights up after dark, came from a graffiti symbol that circulated throughout the city's East Side as early as the 1940s. Its origin is unknown, although Lum notes that it may derive from the large Catholic community that lived in the area at that time, when many Italian, Greek, and Eastern European immigrants settled in East Van.

East Vancouver was once considered the poorer cousin to the city's well-to-do West Side neighborhoods. As real estate prices have escalated across the region, however, East Van has lost some of its working-class image, but Lum's artwork has become a symbol of local pride for many East Siders. Look for images of this "monument" on T-shirts around town.

MAP 7: Intersection of Clark Dr. and E. 6th Ave.

✪ Richmond Night Market

From spring through fall, Richmond's two weekend night markets are packed with visitors enjoying the Asian food stalls, quirky shopping opportunities, and general carnival atmosphere. Visiting these outdoor Richmond events is like traveling to a night market or festival in Asia, but without the jet lag.

Don't have dinner before you go, since there's plenty to sample: grilled kebabs, squid on a stick, bubble waffles, handmade tofu pudding, and many other Asian-style snacks; most dishes cost $5 or less. Vendors also sell inexpensive cell phone cases, socks, electronic gadgets, and more.

The largest night market in North America, drawing thousands of visitors every weekend, the Richmond Night Market has nearly 300 vendors, including row upon row of snack sellers offering up all manner of Asian savories and sweets. During the evening, the aisles between the outdoor booths, set up in a vast parking lot, get increasingly jammed with hungry patrons looking for their next bite; most dishes are small and easy to share. The market has some tables and benches, but many visitors eat on the go, as they wend through the market aisles or try to find an uncrowded corner to stand.

Lines at the entrance gate can be lengthy. If you're visiting with a group, or if you plan to visit more than once, purchase a $20 pass that includes seven admissions. You can use them all at once or at any time during the season. Passholders enter through a separate gate that bypasses the main queue.

The Richmond Night Market is the easiest of the two Vancouver-area night markets to reach by public transit. Take the Canada Line from downtown to Bridgeport Station. From there, it's a 15-minute walk to the market. Just follow the crowds.

MAP 8: 8351 River Rd., 604/244-8448, www.richmondnightmarket.com; 7pm-midnight Fri.-Sat., 7pm-11pm Sun. mid-May-mid-Oct.; adults $3.75, seniors and kids under 10 free

International Summer Night Market

Richmond's second night market, the International Summer Night Market, has a similar lively mix of food stalls and other vendors. With about 60 outdoor booths, both food vendors and other retailers, it's smaller than the always-packed Richmond Night Market, which can make it a little less overwhelming and more family-friendly. The market also hosts a nightly light show.

Take the Canada Line from downtown to Bridgeport Station, where you can catch a free shuttle to the market, which is located in a parking lot behind the Home Depot.

MAP 8: 12631 Vulcan Way, 604/278-8000, www.summernightmarket.com; 7pm-midnight Fri.-Sun. May-mid-Sept.

Golden Village and Aberdeen Centre

The Richmond branch of the Canada Line follows No. 3 Road through the district known as the Golden

RICHMOND

Village, the region's new Chinatown. You'll know you've arrived when the Chinese-language signs outnumber those in English, and Asian restaurants, markets, and shops line the strip malls and surrounding streets.

A good place to start exploring is Aberdeen Centre, a glitzy Hong Kong-style shopping mall, with shops selling tea, electronics, clothing, Asian-language books, and more. Hunt for all kinds of quirky (but useful) housewares and gadgets at Daiso (604/295-6601, www.daiso-canada.com; 9:30am-9pm daily), the local branch of a Japanese discount chain; at the Richmond location, most products cost just $2. On the mall's third floor, stop for excellent Cantonese, Sichuanese, Taiwanese, Japanese, and Korean fare in the busy food court.

Aberdeen Centre has several good sit-down restaurants, too, including Fisherman's Terrace Seafood Restaurant (604/303-9739; dim sum 10am-3pm daily, dinner 5:30pm-10pm daily; dim sum $4-15, mains $15-35) for dim sum, Chef Hung Taiwanese Beef Noodle (604/295-9357, www.chefhungnoodle.com; 11am-9pm Sun.-Thurs., 11am-9:30pm Fri.-Sat.; $8-13) for Taiwanese noodle soup, and Guu Richmond (604/295-6612, www.guu-izakaya.com; 11:30am-4pm and 5pm-9pm Mon.-Thurs., 11:30am-4pm and 5pm-8pm Fri.-Sat.; $5-13), a branch of Vancouver's popular Japanese *izakaya* minichain.

Aberdeen Centre is one block from the Canada Line's Aberdeen Station, at the corner of Cambie Road and Hazelbridge Way.

MAP 8: Aberdeen Centre, 4151 Hazelbridge Way, 604/270-1234, www.aberdeencentre.com; 11am-7pm Sun.-Wed., 11am-9pm Thurs.-Sat.

Richmond Night Market

INTERNATIONAL BUDDHIST TEMPLE

Richmond's International Buddhist Temple

To explore another aspect of Richmond's Asian culture, detour to the **International Buddhist Temple** (9160 Steveston Hwy., 604/274-2822, www.buddhisttemple.ca; 9:30am-5:30pm daily; free), one of the largest Chinese Buddhist temples in North America.

A serene traditional Chinese garden with two fountains acts as the gateway to the temple complex. As you enter the main courtyard, on your right is the **Seven Buddha Hall**, where the gold Avalokitesvara Bodhisattva stands, with its thousand arms and thousand eyes.

Continue through the courtyard and up the stairs to the gold-roofed **Main Gracious Hall**, constructed in 1983, where a massive gold Buddha dominates, flanked by several towering statues. Behind the main temple, the **Thousand Buddha Hall** is filled with miniatures of the deity. On the lower level, the vegetarian restaurant, **Zen Kitchen**, serves lunch between 11:30am and 3pm.

At the back of the complex, the Meditation Hall, another gold-roofed structure, is used primarily for meditation classes and lectures. The temple offers weekly two-hour **classes on Buddhism and meditation** in English at 9am on Saturday that are open to visitors.

To reach the temple by public transit from downtown Vancouver, take the Canada Line to Bridgeport Station, then transfer to bus 403, Three Road. After the bus turns east onto Steveston Highway, get off at Mortfield Gate, in front of the temple complex. If you're making other stops in Richmond's Golden Village en route to or from the temple, you can board bus 403 along No. 3 Road outside the Aberdeen, Lansdowne, or Richmond-Brighouse stations.

Richmond Olympic Experience

Want to swish down an Olympic bobsled track, pilot a race car, or test your mettle on a ski jump? At the Richmond Olympic Experience, aka "The ROX," an interactive Olympic sports museum, you can try out simulators of several Olympic and Paralympic events. Among the activities, which are best suited for older kids and adults, there are games to test your reaction time and see how high you can jump; you can also pretend to be a sports broadcaster reporting on the Olympic Games. For Olympic trivia buffs, the multimedia exhibits have thousands of facts about the Games through the decades. Actual Olympic medals and torches are on display, too.

The ROX is located inside the **Richmond Olympic Oval**, a sports facility that was a venue for the 2010 Winter Olympic Games. Most exhibits are on the third floor. On the main level, you can watch an eight-minute film about pursuing Olympic dreams. Stop on the second floor to see another small exhibition space that includes *Athlete*, a fascinating photograph by Howard Schatz that portrays the "ideal" male and female body types for a wide variety of sports: a jockey next to a sumo wrestler next to a football player, a boxer next to a gymnast next to a shot-putter, and many more.

Slide down a virtual Olympic bobsled track at the Richmond Olympic Experience.

To reach The ROX by public transit from Vancouver, take the Canada Line (Richmond branch) to Richmond-Brighouse Station. Change to bus C94, which stops directly in front of the Richmond Olympic Oval. The C94 currently runs only every 35 minutes and there's no service on Sunday, so check the schedule online (www.translink.ca) before you set out.

You can also walk along a riverfront path to The ROX from the Canada Line's Aberdeen Station. After exiting the station, walk one block west on Cambie Road to River Road. Turn left (south) onto the path that hugs the Fraser River. From here, it's 1.25 miles (two kilometers) to the Olympic Experience.

MAP 8: 6111 River Rd., Richmond, 778/296-1400, http://therox.ca; 10am-5pm Tues.-Sun.; adults $17, seniors and ages 13-18 $13, ages 6-12 $11

The North Shore   Map 9

✪ Grouse Mountain

Open for wildlife adventures, walks in the woods, and many other activities from spring through fall, and for skiing and snowboarding in winter, Grouse Mountain lets you experience the mountains less than 40 minutes from downtown. On a clear day in any season, you can look out over the peaks and across the Burrard Inlet to the city skyline.

Take the Skyride (8:45am-10pm Mon.-Fri., 8:15am-10pm Sat.-Sun.), North America's largest tram system, to the Peak Chalet, where you can watch a film about the region's wildlife at the Theatre in the Sky or take in the corny but entertaining 45-minute Lumberjack Show (noon, 2:30pm, and 4:30pm daily late May-mid-Oct.), complete with log rolling, tree climbing, and ax throwing. The Birds in Motion demonstration (1:30pm, 3:30pm, and 5:30pm daily late May-late Sept.) shows off the skills of eagles, falcons, and other birds of prey, while at the Grouse Mountain Refuge for Endangered Wildlife you can learn more about bears, wolves, owls, and other creatures.

Several self-guided walking trails through the evergreen forests start near the Peak Chalet, or you can take a 45-minute guided eco-walk (late May-Sept.) that departs several times a day to learn more about local geology, animals, and plants.

The basic access tickets, called the Alpine Experience (adults $45, seniors $41, ages 13-18 $26, ages 5-12 $16), are available year-round and give you access to the Skyride, Theatre in the Sky, Lumberjack Show, Birds in Motion, wildlife refuge, and walking trails. To go higher up on the mountain, where the views are even more expansive, purchase a Peak Experience ticket (late May-Oct., adults $49, seniors $45, ages 13-18 $30, ages 5-12 $16), which adds a ride on the Peak Chairlift. The Ultimate Experience (late May-mid-Oct., adults $59, seniors $55, ages 13-18 $40, ages 5-12 $16) includes a visit to The Eye of the Wind, a mountaintop wind turbine. Separate lift tickets are required for skiing and snowboarding.

To incorporate more adventures into your Grouse visit, go zip-lining across the peaks ($75-115, including a Peak Experience ticket) or try paragliding (late June-Sept., $229, includes Peak Experience ticket if booked in advance). Early risers can have breakfast with the bears (8:30am Sat.-Sun. late Mar.-late June and mid-Sept.-mid-Oct., 8:30am daily late June-mid-Sept., adults $65, seniors $60, ages 13-18 $45, ages 5-12 $35, includes Alpine Experience ticket) at the wildlife refuge, a popular activity for families.

Looking for a challenge? An alternative to riding the Skyride to the Peak Chalet is to hike the Grouse Grind, a 1.8-mile (2.9-kilometer) trek up a forested mountain staircase, where you gain an elevation of 2,800 feet (850 meters). The trail isn't technically difficult, but you're climbing 2,830 steps,

Grouse Mountain views

so it's a workout. Hikers are allowed to walk uphill only and return to the parking area on the Skyride (one-way $10).

In winter, Grouse Mountain has 26 runs for downhill skiing and snowboarding, 14 of which are open at night (you can buy night tickets that are valid 4pm-10pm). It's the only North Shore ski destination that's easily accessible by public transportation. While many of the trails are relatively gentle, more advanced skiers should head for the Blueberry Bowl, where you can access more challenging runs from the Olympic Express and Peak Chairs. If you've arrived in Vancouver without proper winter clothes, you can rent jackets, snow pants, helmets, and gloves, as well as ski and snowboard gear. Lift tickets (full-day/night adults $61/48, seniors ages 13-18 $45/40, ages 5-12 $25/22, ages 0-4 free) include access to the Alpine Experience activities along with the ski and snowboard runs.

Other winter activities include snowshoeing on four groomed trails or ice-skating on the mountaintop rink. For these activities, if you're not already buying a lift ticket to ski or snowboard, you need to purchase an Alpine Experience Pass.

The mountain's fine dining restaurant, The Observatory (604/998-5045, www.observatoryrestaurant.ca; 5pm-10pm daily), in the Peak Chalet, serves seafood, steak, and other west coast fare. Make your dinner reservation in advance to obtain a complimentary Alpine Experience ticket for each member of your party. There are several casual eateries and snack shops on the mountain as well.

You don't need a car to get to Grouse Mountain. From May through early October, a free shuttle departs from Canada Place every 30 minutes from 9am to 5:30pm (no 2pm departure) and returns from the mountain every 30 minutes from 9:30am to 6:30pm (no 1:30pm departure). Year-round, you can take public transit between downtown and Grouse; take the SeaBus from Waterfront Station to Lonsdale Quay and change to bus 236 for Grouse Mountain, which will drop you at the mountain's base.

MAP 9: 6400 Nancy Greene Way, North Vancouver, 604/980-9311, www.grousemountain.com; 9am-10pm daily

NEARBY:

- Get your thrills swaying high above the ground on the Capilano Suspension Bridge (page 89).
- Work up a sweat by hiking up The Grouse Grind, known as "Mother Nature's stairmaster" (page 165).

✪ Capilano Suspension Bridge

Built in 1889, the 450-foot (137-meter) Capilano Suspension Bridge sways 230 feet (70 meters) above the Capilano River in a rainforest park. And yes, it does swing!

Before you cross the bridge, follow the Cliffwalk, a series of boardwalks and stairways cantilevered out over the river. If you're feeling brave, stand on the glass platform and look down (way down!) into the canyon where the river rushes below.

After you've made your way over the suspension bridge, explore the Treetops Adventure, a 700-foot (213-meter) network of gently swaying wooden bridges linking eight treehouse platforms. Many of the surrounding Douglas firs are up to 300 feet (90 meters) tall. Back on the ground, gentle walking trails lead through the rainforest.

Particularly in the summer high season, the least crowded times to visit the bridge are before 11am or after 3pm. Take a free shuttle to the suspension bridge from several locations downtown. Call or check the website for seasonal schedules. By public transportation, take the SeaBus from Waterfront Station to Lonsdale Quay and change to bus 236 for Grouse

Mountain. Get off at Ridgewood Avenue, a block from the bridge park. MAP 9: 3735 Capilano Rd., 604/985-7474, www.capbridge.com; 8:30am-8pm daily late May-early Sept., 9am-6pm daily early Sept.-mid-Oct., 9am-5pm daily mid-Oct.-late Nov., 11am-9pm daily late Nov.-early Jan., 9am-5pm daily early Jan.-mid-Mar., 9am-6pm daily mid-Mar.-late Apr., 9am-7pm daily late Apr.-late May; adults $40, seniors $37, students $33, ages 13-16 $27, ages 6-12 $14

Lynn Canyon Park

The 617-acre (250-hectare) Lynn Canyon Park is a little farther from downtown than the Capilano bridge, but it has its own suspension bridge built back in 1912—and it's free.

Hiking trails wend through the park, including the 30 Foot Pool Trail and the Twin Falls Trail, which both lead to popular swimming areas (bring your bathing suit); both trails are easy and are 0.6 mile (1 kilometer) long, starting from the suspension bridge. The Ecology Centre (3663 Park Rd., North Vancouver, 604/990-3755, www.lynncanyonecologycentre.ca, 10am-5pm daily June-Sept., 10am-5pm Mon.-Fri., noon-4pm Sat. Sun. Oct.-May, donation $2) has kid-friendly exhibits about the region's plants and animals.

To get to the park by public transit, take the SeaBus from Waterfront Station to Lonsdale Quay, then change to bus 228 for Lynn Valley. The bus will drop you off about a 15-minute walk from the park entrance. MAP 9: Park Rd., North Vancouver, www.lynncanyon.ca; 7am-9pm daily summer, 7am-7pm daily spring and fall, 7am-6pm daily winter; free

Lonsdale Quay

A food and shopping complex overlooking the water adjacent to the

treetop trekking at the Capilano Suspension Bridge

SeaBus terminal in North Vancouver, Lonsdale Quay is like a small-scale Granville Island Public Market. Vendors sell fruit, vegetables, seafood, sandwiches, and other prepared foods. **Green Leaf Brewing** (604/984-8409, www.greenleafbrew.com) makes craft beer; the **Artisan Wine Shop** (604/264-4008, www.artisanwineshop.ca) does complimentary wine-tastings.

A new contemporary art museum, the **Polygon Gallery,** is slated to open in November 2017 on the waterfront at the foot of Lonsdale Street, just east of Lonsdale Quay. It will be the new home for **Presentation House Gallery** (604/986-1351, http://presentationhousegallery.org), which has exhibited works by Vancouver and international photographers over the past 30 years.

The easiest way to get to Lonsdale Quay from downtown Vancouver is to take the SeaBus from Waterfront Station, a 12-minute ride.

MAP 9: 123 Carrie Cates Court, North Vancouver, 604/985-6261, www.lonsdalequay.com; 9am-7pm daily

Horseshoe Bay

The seaside village of Horseshoe Bay, 12.5 miles (20 kilometers) northwest of downtown Vancouver, is a departure point for BC Ferries' routes to Bowen Island, Nanaimo (on Vancouver Island), and the Sunshine Coast. It's a pretty spot for a picnic by the shore or for a quick break when you're driving between Vancouver and Whistler.

Another reason to visit Horseshoe Bay is to take a two-hour **Sea Safari** from Sewall's Marina (6409 Bay St., West Vancouver, 604/921-3474, www.sewellsmarina.com; 11am, 1:30pm, and 4pm Apr.-Oct.; adults $87, seniors and ages 13-18 $77, ages 5-12 $57). These scenic guided wildlife cruises in 30-foot (10-meter) Zodiac-style boats take you through the waters of Howe Sound, where you'll spot seals and a variety of seabirds. The company offers a shuttle ($18 pp round-trip) from downtown Vancouver hotels.

By public transit from downtown Vancouver to Horseshoe Bay, catch bus 257 (Vancouver/Horseshoe Bay Express), along West Georgia Street, which takes you to the Horseshoe Bay Ferry Terminal in 45 minutes. The ferry terminal is in the village.

You can generally make the drive from downtown to Horseshoe Bay in 30-35 minutes. Allow extra time if you're catching a ferry, since traffic congestion can cause delays. Returning to the city can take longer, too, since traffic often backs up on the West Vancouver side of the Lions Gate Bridge entrance.

MAP 9: Off Highway 1 West, West Vancouver

RESTAURANTS

What should you eat in Vancouver? As in any major North American city, Vancouver restaurants span the globe, serving meals that take cues from Italy, France, Spain, China, Japan, and more. But here's what Vancouver does best.

Vancouver is known for seafood, particularly salmon, halibut, oysters, and spot prawns, caught in regional waters. The city's restaurants have embraced the "eat local" movement, so look for seasonal produce and locally raised meats. With a large Asian population, Vancouver has some of the best Chinese food in North America, as well as good Japanese and Korean fare. Vancouverites say, only half in jest, that the city has a sushi bar on every corner. Many non-Asian restaurants incorporate Pacific Rim influences in their dishes.

Son-in-Law Egg at
Yaletown's House Special

Vancouver's most innovative restaurants are in Gastown, Chinatown, and along Main Street. In the West End, you'll find a concentration of noodle shops, *izakayas,* and other Asian eateries. For the region's top Chinese food, head to the suburb of Richmond, which has hundreds of Asian dining spots, both large and small.

British Columbia wines, from the Okanagan Valley or Vancouver Island, are good accompaniments to most Vancouver meals, as are regionally brewed craft beers. Plenty of bartenders have adopted an "eat local" philosophy, too, incorporating locally grown herbs, house-made bitters, and other fresh ingredients into creative cocktails and alcohol-free drinks.

HIGHLIGHTS

✪ **MOST GLAM PIZZA SPOT: Nightingale** serves gourmet pizzas in a buzzing dining room (page 94).

✪ **LIVELIEST JAPANESE RESTAURANT: Guu Garden** is a spirited spot for Japanese tapas, even before they break out the sake (page 96).

✪ **BEST GLOBAL JOURNEY:** From waffles in the morning to *moules frites* at night, **Chambar** takes you from Belgium to North Africa (page 100).

✪ **BEST REASON TO GO TO JAIL: L'Abbatoir** is located on the site of Vancouver's first prison (page 100).

✪ **MOST IMAGINATIVE CUISINE COUPLING:** At **Kissa Tanto,** the chef draws on Japanese and Italian flavors to craft creative dishes (page 101).

✪ **BEST SEAFOOD WITH A VIEW: Ancora Waterfront Dining and Patio** is one of the city's most scenic restaurants (page 104).

✪ **TOP THAI: Maenam** impresses with its modern cuisine and contemporary cocktails (page 109).

✪ **WHERE CHOCOLATE LOVERS FIND BLISS:** The chocolate is rich, dark, and homemade at **Chocolate Arts** (page 110).

✪ **WHERE TO WOO A WINE LOVER:** The lengthy wine list makes **West** the oenophile's choice (page 112).

✪ **WHERE TO TAKE YOUR FAVORITE VEGETARIAN:** At **The Acorn,** you'll find interesting plant-based fare (page 115).

✪ **BEST PIE: The Pie Shoppe** bakes up delicious sweet things in a crust (page 117).

✪ **TOP CANTONESE DINING:** High-end **Bamboo Grove** has an elaborate menu emphasizing fresh seafood (page 118).

✪ **BEST PLACE TO SET YOUR MOUTH ON FIRE:** For fiery Chinese fare, plan a meal at **New Spicy Chili Restaurant** (page 118).

✪ **WHERE TO EAT LAMB, AND LOTS OF IT: Hao's Lamb Restaurant** uses every part of the sheep (page 119).

✪ **BEST DIM SUM: Golden Paramount Seafood Restaurant** prepares traditional and innovative dim sum (page 119).

PRICE KEY

$ Entrées less than CAN$15

$ $ Entrées CAN$15-25

$ $ $ Entrées more than CAN$25

Downtown and the West End

Map 1

MODERN CANADIAN
Hawksworth Restaurant $$$

In a chandelier-bedecked space at the Rosewood Hotel Georgia downtown, sophisticated Hawksworth Restaurant attracts expense-account diners, couples celebrating occasions, and gourmets savoring a fine meal with solicitous service. From the foie gras to *wagyu* flank steak to lobster with Korean rice cakes, it's all about the luxe ingredients in the regionally influenced contemporary fare. If the dinner prices are too rich, splurge on a leisurely lunch or a light bites at the bar.

MAP 1: 801 W. Georgia St., 604/673-7000, www.hawksworthrestaurant.com; 6:30am-10:30am, 11:30am-2pm, and 5pm-10pm Mon.-Thurs., 6:30am-10:30am, 11:30am-2pm, and 5pm-11pm Fri., 7am-2pm and 5pm-11pm Sat., 7am-2pm and 5pm-10pm Sun.

✪ Nightingale $$

Owned by chef David Hawksworth of the high-end Hawksworth Restaurant, Nightingale sings a slightly less formal song, though you still get the chef's trademark glamour in the buzzing two-level dining room downtown. The lengthy menu pairs sharing plates and pizzas, teaming up dishes like octopus with capers and fermented chili, maitake mushrooms tossed with pecorino-brown butter and hazelnuts, and fried chicken with preserved lemon yogurt, with straightforward (like cherry tomatoes, basil, and *fior di latte*) and wilder (like braised beef, kale, and gorgonzola) pies. To drink?

Their own "Nighting-ale," from a local craft brewery.

MAP 1: 1017 W. Hastings St., 604/695-9500, https://hawknightingale.com; 11am-midnight daily

vibrant vegetables at Nightingale

Forage $$

The kitchen team at Forage, the contemporary dining room at the Listel Hotel in the West End, sources ingredients from local farmers, fisherfolk, and, yes, foragers, and crafts them into locavore plates to share. Snack on bison jerky as you sip one of the B.C. craft beers or wines on tap. Then graze on kale salad with caramelized apples, corn risotto, or seared tuna with mushroom "soil." Centered around a large U-shaped bar, and furnished with lots of natural wood, the restaurant is a good choice for breakfast or brunch, too.

MAP 1: 1300 Robson St., 604/661-1400, www.foragevancouver.com; 6:30am-10am and 5pm-late Mon.-Fri., 7am-2pm and 5pm-late Sat.-Sun.

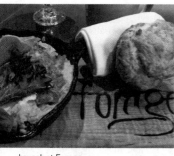
brunch at Forage

mushrooms, or lingcod and clams with nori and *dashi* highlight local seafood in refined Asian-accented preparations. You could stop in for a glass of bubbly and fresh oysters at the long marble bar, too. Boulevard shares its space with the Sutton Place Hotel downtown.

MAP 1: 845 Burrard St., 604/642-2900, www.boulevardvancouver.ca; 6:30am-11pm daily

Royal Dinette $$

Styled like a Parisian brasserie, Royal Dinette is a lively spot for inventive farm-to-table dining downtown. Start with a local craft beer or a fun cocktail, like the "Burning Man" (house-made *kombucha* spiked with your choice of vodka, gin, rum, pisco or *cachaça*). The kitchen makes its pasta fresh daily, creating dishes like squid ink bucatini with sea urchin butter or celeriac ravioli with Asian pears. With options that might include heirloom carrots with sprouted wheat and crème fraîche, or brussels sprouts with pickled garlic, vegetables get special treatment. And how do you choose from smoked salmon with kohlrabi and caramelized whey, or rhubarb-braised short ribs? Find some willing dining companions and share.

MAP 1: 905 Dunsmuir St., 604/974-8077, https://royaldinette.ca; 11:30am-2pm and 4:30pm-10pm pm Mon.-Fri., 5pm-10pm Sat.

SEAFOOD
Boulevard Kitchen & Oyster Bar $$$

Sink into a cream-colored banquette at elegant Boulevard Kitchen & Oyster Bar, where the service is polished and dishes like citrus-cured *hama-chi*, roasted sablefish with grilled

YEW Seafood + Bar $$$

The menus change with the seasons at YEW Seafood & Bar, in the Four Seasons Hotel Vancouver downtown, but you'll always find a variety of options from the sea, perhaps wild salmon with watercress and leeks, a Niçoise salad with fresh albacore, or a traditional bouillabaisse. It's a stylish setting for a business lunch, festive dinner, or drinks with seafood small plates. Surprisingly, YEW also offers an upscale vegan menu.

MAP 1: 791 W. Georgia St., 604/692-4939, www.yewseafood.com; 7am-2:30pm and 5pm-10pm daily

CHINESE
Dinesty Dumpling House $$

Watch the dumpling makers at work at Dinesty Dumpling House, and that's what you should order, too: Shanghai-style soup dumplings, pan-fried pork buns, and steamed vegetable and egg dumplings. Handmade noodles, fresh greens with garlic, and the unusual omelet with pickles are also tasty choices in this bustling West End eatery, where the tables are packed in tightly. They also have several locations in Richmond.

MAP 1: 1719 Robson St., 604/669-7769, www.dinesty.ca; 11am-3pm and 5pm-10pm Mon.-Fri., 11am-10pm Sat.-Sun.

Peaceful Restaurant $$

Visit this simple and friendly local chainlet for northern Chinese dishes, including hand-pulled noodles, lamb, and dumplings. Try the mustard seed salad (carrots, celery, and vermicelli in a mustardy dressing), the Xinjiang cumin lamb, or the "cat ear" stir-fried noodles, shaped like orecchiette and tossed with vegetables and pork. Peaceful Restaurant has several other locations across town.

MAP 1: 602 Seymour St., 604/313-1333, www.peacefulrestaurant.com; 11am-9:30pm Sun.-Thurs., 11am-10pm Fri.-Sat.

JAPANESE

✪ Guu Garden $$

Part of a local minichain of *izakayas*, lively Guu Garden serves Japanese tapas designed to share, like grilled black cod cheeks, crispy cauliflower *karaage*, and sashimi-style tuna *tataki*, to pair with sake, *shochu*, or Japanese beer. Guu is on the top floor of a downtown complex with a similarly named eatery on the main level, so be sure to go upstairs.

MAP 1: 888 Nelson St., 604/899-0855, www.guu-izakaya.com/garden; 11:30am-2:30pm and 5:30pm-midnight Mon.-Thurs., 11:30am-2:30pm and 5:30pm-12:30am Fri., noon-3pm and 5:30pm-12:30am Sat., noon-3pm and 5:30pm-midnight Sun.

Hokkaido Ramen Santouka $

In the West End, there are ramen shops on seemingly every corner. At Hokkaido Ramen Santouka, the local outpost of a Japan-based noodle shop chain, the signature dish is *tokusen toroniku* ramen, a rich, almost creamy soup made from pork cheek meat. This ramen revelation is worth the inevitable queue, but lingering in this cramped space is discouraged, so diners slurp and move on. There's another location on Broadway near Cambie Street.

MAP 1: 1690 Robson St., 604/681-8121, www.santouka.co.jp; 11am-11pm daily

sushi at Guu Garden

Miku $$$

For sushi with a water view, visit Miku, an upscale Japanese dining room opposite Canada Place downtown. They're known for *aburi sushi,* fresh fish seared with a blowtorch, but any of their raw fish options should please *nigiri* and *maki* lovers. The waterside location and the solicitous service make a meal here feel like a classy night out.

MAP 1: 200 Granville St., 604/568-3900, www.mikurestaurant.com; 11:30am-3pm and 5pm-10:30pm daily

Japadog $

A unique-to-Vancouver mash-up of hot dogs and Japanese flavors, fast-casual Japadog concocts their signature sausages, like the *kurobuta*

VANCOUVER'S FOOD TRUCKS

The Kaboom Box, one of downtown Vancouver's food trucks

Vancouver's growing fleet of **food trucks** park downtown, purveying a global gamut of meals to go. A cluster of trucks sets up shop around the Vancouver Art Gallery along Howe and Hornby Streets, some park near the Queen Elizabeth Theatre on Cambie and Georgia Streets, while others locate closer to the waterfront along Burrard and Thurlow Streets. Most operate 11am or 11:30am to 2:30pm or 3pm.

The best way to find what trucks are where is with the **Vancouver Street Food app** (http://streetfoodapp.com/vancouver), which also lists truck locations online. Some favorites include:

- **Mom's Grilled Cheese** (Howe St. at Robson St. and W. Cordova St. at Hornby St., http://momsgrilledcheesetruck.com) for, as you'd expect, grilled cheese sandwiches

- **Le Tigre Cuisine** (check their Twitter feed @LeTigreTruck for locations, www.letigrecuisine.ca) for Asian-fusion fare, including kick-ass fried rice

- **The Kaboom Box** (Granville St. at W. Georgia St., www.thekaboombox.com) for hot smoked salmon sandwiches

- **Yolk's Breakfast Street Meet Truck** (Burrard St. at W. Pender St., http://yolks.ca; generally 8am-2pm Mon.-Fri.) for free-range egg sandwiches and fresh beignets

- **Aussie Pie Guy** (check website for locations, www.aussiepieguy.com) for handheld Australian-style meat or vegetable pies

pork *terimayo,* sauced with teriyaki, mayonnaise, and seaweed, at a diminutive downtown counter-service restaurant and at two downtown food trucks.
MAP 1: 530 Robson St., 604/569-1158, www.japadog.com; 10am-10pm Mon.-Thurs., 10am-midnight Fri.-Sat., 10am-9pm Sun.

FRENCH
Le Crocodile $$$

Classic French cuisine never goes out of style at Le Crocodile, a longstanding downtown favorite, where standards from *la belle France* are updated with west coast ingredients. Grilled salmon sauced with a saffron velouté, locally raised duck breast served with foie gras in an apple cider reduction, and rack of lamb with a mustard sabayon are just some of the menu offerings. Expect white table-cloths and polished service, appropriate for a business lunch or a special night out.

MAP 1: 909 Burrard St., Ste. 100, 604/669-4298, http://lecrocodilerestaurant.com; 11:30am-2:30pm and 5:30pm-10pm Mon.-Thurs., 11:30am-2:30pm and 5:30pm-10:30pm Fri., 5:30pm-10:30pm Sat.

smoked meat sandwich and fries at Timber

SPANISH
España Restaurant $$

At España Restaurant, a narrow store-front tapas bar in the West End, you could almost be in Spain, though here, some of the Spanish classics, like sautéed padron peppers, fried anchovies, or paella, might be made with Pacific Northwest ingredients. To drink, try a sherry flight or choose from the list of Spanish wines by the glass. The restaurant is tiny, and they don't take reservations, so don't be in a rush to sit down—just relax, you're (almost) in Spain!

MAP 1: 1118 Denman St., 604/558-4040, www.espanarestaurant.ca; 5pm-late daily

BREAKFAST AND BRUNCH
Medina Café $

Expect a queue at cheerful window-lined Medina Café, which is known for its sugar-studded Liège waffles (check out the waffle case on the dark wood counter) and for its North African-influenced brunch fare downtown. Try the tagine, a flavorful vegetable stew topped with poached eggs, merguez sausage, and preserved lemon.

MAP 1: 780 Richards St., 604/879-3114, www.medinacafe.com; 8am-3pm Mon.-Fri., 9am-3pm Sat.-Sun.

GASTROPUBS
Timber $$

From the deep-fried cheese curds, ketchup chips, bison burgers, and mushroom poutine to the BeaverTail-like fried dough or the gooey butter tart, Timber, the all-Canadian gastropub at the West End's Listel Hotel, serves fun updates on classic Canuck comfort food. The beer list trends toward local craft labels, or you can choose from several types of Caesars, Canada's version of a Bloody Mary, made with Clamato juice. The TVs are tuned to hockey, of course.

MAP 1: 300 Robson St., 604/661-2166, http://timbervancouver.com; noon-midnight Mon.-Wed., noon-1am Thurs.-Fri., 11am-1am Sat., 11am-midnight Sun.

DINERS
The Templeton $

Retro diner The Templeton, complete with tabletop jukeboxes and soda-fountain stools, has morphed into a cool purveyor of comfort foods among the downtown bars on the Granville strip. Dig into hearty plates of pan-cakes, creative omelets, or burgers, which you can pair with coffee or "big people drinks" (craft beer, local wines, and cocktails). Save room for an ice cream sundae or old-fashioned banana split.

MAP 1: 1087 Granville St., 604/685-4612, http://thetempleton.ca; 9am-11pm Mon.-Wed., 9am-1am Thurs.-Sun.

QUICK BITES
Meat and Bread $

Pull up a stool at the communal table in this downtown sandwich shop catering to the weekday lunch crowd. The signature sandwich at Meat and Bread is the hearty porchetta topped with salsa verde and crackling, but the simple menu typically includes several other varieties, perhaps roast chicken with pickled daikon and lemongrass-ginger sauce or an Indian-seasoned veggie sandwich packed with roast cauliflower, yams, and crispy chickpeas. A soup and a salad, which change daily, are the only accompaniments. There's a branch in Gastown, too.

MAP 1: 1033 W. Pender St., http://meatandbread.ca; 11am-4pm Mon.-Fri.

Tractor Foods $

For a light and quick lunch of salads, soups, and sandwiches near Canada Place downtown, plow a path to cafeteria-style Tractor Foods. Salads come in small portions, so you can build your own salad plate; you can choose half or whole sandwiches, with options like grilled chicken, arugula, and pear or albacore tuna with pesto aioli. They have additional outlets in Kitsilano and the Olympic Village.

MAP 1: 335 Burrard St., 604/979-0500, www.tractorfoods.com; 7am-10:30am Mon.-Fri. and 11am-9pm daily

DESSERT
Bella Gelateria $

When a gelato maker is obsessive about fresh ingredients and traditional Italian techniques, naturally he

and his team make Vancouver's best gelato. Find it downtown at tiny Bella Gelateria, near the Fairmont Pacific Rim hotel. Expect a line, particularly on warm summer nights.

MAP 1: 1001 W. Cordova St., 604/569-1010, http://bellagelateria.com; 11am-10pm Sun.-Thurs., 11am-11pm Fri.-Sat.

Snowy Village Dessert Café $

This West End dessert shop, a branch of an Asia-based chain, specializes in a creamy Korean shaved ice dessert called *bingsoo*. Order at the counter, where you top a melt-in-your-mouth mound of shaved ice with *injeolmi* (chewy sweet mochi-like rice cakes, piled with red beans and dusted with nutty soybean powder), green tea, Oreos, or fruit. Pull up a stool at one of the green tables to enjoy your treat; overflowing with toppings, they're too large to eat on the go. Snowy Village also makes *taiyaki*, fish-shaped waffles filled with red beans, sweet potatoes, custard, or nutella. There's another location in Richmond.

MAP 1: 1696 Robson St., 778/379-3884, http://snowyvillages.ca; 3pm-10pm Mon.-Thurs., 1pm-11:30pm Fri.-Sat., 1pm-10:30pm Sun.

FARMERS MARKETS
West End Farmers Market $

The West End Farmers Market purveys produce, baked goods, and prepared foods on Saturday from late May through late October. There's always a line for the sweets at Purebread, and local cheesemaker Little Qualicum Cheeseworks frequently offers samples. Eli's Serious Sausage, Yolk's Breakfast, and Feastro-The Rolling Bistro (which specializes in local seafood) are among the several food trucks that regularly park here, and there's usually a musician or two performing during market hours. Local distillers or craft breweries, like 33 Acres, offer tastings and sell their brews as well.

MAP 1: Comox St. at Thurlow St., www.eatlocal.org; 9am-2pm Sat. late May-late Oct.

COFFEE AND TEA
Caffè Artigiano $

Local Italian-style coffee chain Caffè Artigiano has several downtown branches, including this convenient location just off Robson Street, opposite the Vancouver Art Gallery. Come for the carefully prepared coffee, which they source from small producers around the world. The baristas here frequently win local competitions for their latte art. To pair with your drinks, they offer a small selection of pastries and sandwiches. There are three other center-city locations, as well as a branch in Yaletown.

MAP 1: 763 Hornby St., 604/694-7737, www.caffeartigiano.com; 5:30am-9pm Mon.-Fri., 6am-9pm Sat., 6am-8pm Sun.

Gastown and Chinatown Map 2

MODERN CANADIAN
✪ Chambar $$$

Combining tastes of North Africa and Belgium with local ingredients, Chambar pleases patrons all day in a window-lined rehabbed warehouse. Kick off your morning with a waffle studded with pearl sugar or breakfast paella topped with spicy sausage and a fried egg. Later, you might sup on Haida Gwaii halibut with sea asparagus or venison with fresh pasta and blue cheese. *Moules frites* (mussels with french fries) are a specialty.

MAP 2: 568 Beatty St., 604/879-7119, www.chambar.com; 8am-3pm and 5pm-late daily

✪ L'Abbatoir $$$

On the site of Vancouver's first jail, transformed into a multilevel space with exposed brick and polished woods, Gastown's L'Abbatoir detains diners with creative cocktails (how about an avocado gimlet with herb-infused gin, schnapps, avocado, and lime?) and a changing menu of west coast plates. Meat eaters might bite into pan-fried sweetbreads or roast lamb with marinated eggplant, while fish fans might favor baked oysters or charcoal-grilled rockfish with peas, potatoes, and clams. At brunch, order the oversize scone mounded with house-made jam and clotted cream.

MAP 2: 217 Carrall St., 604/568-1701, www.labattoir.ca; 5:30pm-10pm Mon.-Thurs., 5:30pm-10:30pm Fri., 10am-2pm and 5:30pm-10:30pm Sat., 10am-2pm and 5:30pm-10pm Sun.

Juniper Kitchen & Bar $$

From the sleek back-lit gray bar to the distillery-inspired copper light fixtures, this high-ceilinged Chinatown room emphasizes cocktails along with its modern Canadian fare. As the "juniper" name suggests, there's a long list of gin and tonics, although local breweries and cideries are also well-represented. Share one of the charcuterie boards—they offer a changing selection of house-made seafood and meat options—or sample lamb and nettle pierogi, cider-braised mussels, or grilled arctic char with purple potatoes.

MAP 2: 185 Keefer St., 604/681-1695, www.junipervancouver.com; 4pm-late daily

ASIAN
Bao Bei Chinese Brasserie $$

At Bao Bei Chinese Brasserie, many of the menu items, from *mantou* (steamed buns) to fried rice, would be at home in a traditional Chinatown kitchen, but this modern lounge and eatery isn't your grandmother's Chinese restaurant. The buns are stuffed with pork belly and sweet peanuts, the fried rice is amped up with clams and salted halibut, and other dishes, like wok-charred octopus with mustard-root gnocchi, start in Asia but wander the world. To drink? Clever cocktails, like Cheung Po the Kid, which blends rum, Dubonnet, pomegranate molasses, and house-made Chinese plum bitters.

MAP 2: 163 Keefer St., 604/688-0876, www.bao-bei.ca; 5:30pm-midnight Mon.-Sat., 5:30pm-11pm Sun.

Pidgin $$

Dan dan "noodles" (made with kohlrabi instead of pasta), octopus glazed with miso and tamarind, or steak with wakame caponata are just a few of the Asian-inspired dishes that might grace your light wood table at this Gastown dining and drinking spot. Order a few plates to share and pair with drinks like the Tiki Tiki Tom Tom, a blend of cognac, carrot orange curaçao, maraschino, lemon, and bitters.

MAP 2: 350 Carrall St., 604/620-9400, www.pidginvancouver.com; 5pm-midnight Mon.-Sat., 6pm-midnight Sun.

JAPANESE
Taishoken Ramen $

The owners of Tsuki Sushi Bar run a busy Japanese noodle shop next door, Taishoken Ramen, where the specialty, in addition to bowls of hot noodle soup, is *tsukemen*, noodles served with a separate dipping broth.

MAP 2: 515 Abbott St., 778/737-3805; 11:30am-4pm and 5pm-9:30pm daily

Tsuki Sushi Bar $

Located opposite the International Village mall, casual Tsuki Sushi Bar does one thing and does it well: preparing fresh sushi and sashimi. See what's on special, or try their *chirashi* bowl, an assortment of raw fish on rice.

MAP 2: 509 Abbott St., 604/558-3805, http://tsukisushibar.ca; 11:30am-2:30pm and 5pm-9:30pm Mon.-Fri., noon-3pm and 4:30pm-9pm Sat.

JAPANESE-ITALIAN
✪ Kissa Tanto $$

This intriguing mash-up of Japanese and Italian flavors, run by the same team that operates nearby Bao Bei Chinese Brasserie, is set in a classy second-floor Chinatown space that draws its design style from 1960s Tokyo jazz cafés. What's Italian-Japanese food, you ask? The fun, adventurous menu might include pasta with pork and sake *kasu* ragu or albacore *crudo* with shiso vinaigrette, olives, and mustard greens. They serve plenty of eclectic cocktails, too.

MAP 2: 263 E. Pender St., 778/379-8078, www.kissatanto.com; 5:30pm-midnight Tues.-Sat.

ITALIAN
Ask for Luigi $$

Why should you Ask for Luigi? Because this highly regarded trattoria serves first-rate handmade pastas along with modern Italian small plates that might include crispy polenta with escargot and watercress or *baccala* (salt cod) fritters. They'll open any bottle of wine on their list if you order two glasses. This small spot doesn't take reservations, so expect a line. To find the restaurant, follow Alexander Street east from Gastown; Luigi is at the corner of Gore Avenue, one block east of Main.

MAP 2: 305 Alexander St., 604/428-2544, www.askforluigi.com; 11:30am-2:30pm and 5:30pm-10:30pm Tues.-Thurs., 11:30am-2:30pm and 5:30pm-11pm Fri., 9:30am-2:30pm and 5:30pm-11pm Sat., 9:30am-2:30pm and 5:30pm-9:30pm Sun.

FRIED CHICKEN
Juke $

This smart-casual Chinatown eatery has a single specialty: crisp and juicy fried chicken that will have you licking your fingers. The kitchen starts with locally raised birds, coats the pieces in a gluten-free batter, and fries them till the skin crackles and the meat is meltingly tender. Add a side or two, like fried brussels sprouts or nutty pork and peanut slaw. The joint is laid-back enough to bring the kids (during the day, you order at the counter), but with local microbrews and a full bar, it's cool enough for the grown-ups.

MAP 2: 182 Keefer St., 604/336-5853, www.jukefriedchicken.com; 11am-11pm daily

BREAKFAST AND BRUNCH
Jam Café $

Lines are common at Jam Café, a relaxed no-reservations import from Victoria, as hungry diners queue for overflowing plates of hearty breakfast and brunch fare. The red velvet

fried chicken at Juke in Chinatown

pancakes are as big as a cake, while savory options include the Charlie Bowl (hash brown potatoes, crumbled biscuit, ham, and cheddar cheese topped with gravy and sunny-side eggs) and the Gravy Coupe (a biscuit piled with fried chicken and eggs slathered with sausage gravy).

MAP 2: 556 Beatty St., 778/379-1992, http://jamcafes.com; 8am-3pm daily

BAKERIES AND CAFÉS
Nelson the Seagull $

A popular destination for Gastown's coffee drinkers, Nelson the Seagull, with classic schoolhouse-style wooden chairs on a historic tile floor, serves light breakfasts (poached eggs, avocado toasts), sandwiches, and salads to pair with your caffeine. They're known for their bread as much as for their coffee.

MAP 2: 315 Carrall St., 604/681-5776, www.nelsontheseagull.com; 8am-5pm Mon.-Fri. 9am-5pm Sat.-Sun.

Purebread $

Vancouverites used to have to drive to Whistler for the decadent pastries and wholesome breads at Purebread. But now Gastown has a Purebread of its own, with drool-inducing treats like freshly baked scones, lemon chèvre brownies, and giant meringues. Enjoy your snack with coffee inside this friendly café, or take your goodies to go.

MAP 2: 159 W. Hastings St., 604/563-8060, www.purebread.ca; 8:30am-5:30pm daily

DESSERT
Crackle Crème $

A café that specializes in crème brûlée? Why, yes, please. Chinatown's Crackle Crème concocts custards in flavors from salted caramel to Asian-inspired matcha. They serve Belgian-style Liège waffles and ice cream, too.

MAP 2: 245 Union St., 778/847-8533, www.cracklecreme.com; noon-10pm Wed.-Sat., noon-9pm Sun.

COFFEE AND TEA
Revolver $

Gastown is Vancouver's coffee central, where hip coffee shops abound. Sip your java among the designers, techies, and laptop-toting cool kids at Revolver, which offers a changing menu of beans from roasters across North America.

MAP 2: 325 Cambie St., 604/558-4444, www.revolvercoffee.ca; 7:30am-6pm Mon.-Fri., 9am-6pm Sat.

Yaletown and False Creek   Map 3

MODERN CANADIAN
Homer Street Café and Bar $$$

Savory rotisserie chicken and other upscale comfort foods draw hearty appetites to Yaletown's Homer Street Café and Bar. Choose from starters like grilled tuna with sweet pepper salsa or bison terrine with pickled cherries. Then, go for the chicken (available in quarter, half, or whole birds), or peruse the daily "fresh sheet" for other seafood, pasta, and meat options. Save room for the peanut butter cookies with Nutella cream, and note the unique architecture; the dining room encompasses space in both a heritage building and a contemporary tower, with ornate tile work, lots of marble, and a shady side-walk patio.

898 Homer St., 604/428-4299, http://homerstreetcafebar.com; 11:30am-10pm Mon.-Thurs., 11:30am-11pm Fri., 10:30am-2:30pm and 5pm-11pm Sat., 10:30am-2:30pm and 5pm-10pm Sun.

SEAFOOD

✪ Ancora Waterfront Dining and Patio $$$

Does chic Ancora Waterfront Dining and Patio have the loveliest outdoor dining space in the city? Its sunny terrace overlooking False Creek in Yaletown is certainly among Vancouver's most scenic waterside dining destinations. Come at sunset or on a sunny day for the best views. On your plate, expect an innovative hybrid of Japanese and Peruvian flavors, crafted from west coast ingredients. Ceviche and sashimi are highlights.

1600 Howe St., 604/681-1164, www.ancoradining.com; noon-2:30pm and 3:30pm-late Mon.-Fri., 5pm-late Sat., 11am-2:30pm and 5pm-late Sun.

Blue Water Café $$$

Busy with business diners and couples celebrating occasions, this long-standing high-end seafood spot in a rehabbed Yaletown warehouse does an excellent job with fresh fish. At Blue Water Café, the chef often spotlights underutilized species—the restaurant hosts an annual "Unsung Heroes" festival, featuring less common sea creatures—so look for seafood that you might not find elsewhere alongside more familiar varieties. A lengthy wine list and well-trained staff make your evening more special.

1095 Hamilton St., 604/688-8078, www.bluewatercafe.net; 5pm-11pm daily

an oyster platter at Fanny Bay Oyster Bar

WildTale Coastal Grill **$$$**

Fresh seafood, simply prepared, is the lure at WildTale Coastal Grill. Start with something from the raw bar, maybe oysters or ceviche, then order the day's fresh catch, with most of the fish options swimming in from Pacific waters. Brunch is a good choice, too, where poached eggs might be stacked with smoked salmon and piled on a potato cake or served atop crisp crab cakes. Inside, where the furnishings are sturdy wood and leather, the well-spaced tables encourage comfortable conversation. On a sunny day, nab a patio seat to watch all of Yaletown go by.

MAP 3: 1079 Mainland St., 604/428-9211, www.wildtale.ca; 11am-midnight Mon.-Sat., 11am-11pm Sun.

Fanny Bay Oyster Bar **$$**

West coast shellfish producer Taylor Shellfish Farms runs Fanny Bay Oyster Bar, which bills itself as the city's first "tide to table" oyster bar. Sit at the long marble counter and watch the shuckers at work while you dig into platters of whatever bivalves are freshest that day; the servers can help you choose from the regularly changing list. Besides oysters, the menu at this smart-casual spot with industrial-style lighting, exposed pipes, and a polished wood floor includes crab cakes, ceviche, fish-and-chips, and other seafood preparations. Near B.C. Place in Yaletown, it's handy for pre- or postgame drinks and snacks.

MAP 3: 762 Cambie St., 778/379-9510, www.fannybayoysters.com; 11am-late Mon.-Fri., 10:30am-late Sat.-Sun.

Rodney's Oyster House **$$**

Bring the gang, raise a glass, and start slurping—oysters, that is—at lively Rodney's Oyster House. This nautical-themed pub-style fish house in Yaletown, outfitted with buoys, model ships, and a pile of fresh oysters on ice at the bar, specializes in simple seafood dishes, from chowders and steamers to the namesake bivalve. To drink, choose from several beers on tap or wines from B.C. and farther afield. There's a second Rodney's in Gastown.

MAP 3: 1228 Hamilton St., 604/609-0080, http://rohvan.com; 11:30am-11pm daily

JAPANESE
Juno Sushi Bistro **$$**

Tiny Juno Sushi Bistro would be right at home in Tokyo, from the friendly greeting (in Japanese) that you get from the staff to the extensive menu of *maki* and *nigiri*. Besides the excellent sushi and sashimi (ask about daily specials), you can order *izakaya*-style small plates like wild salmon *gyoza,* chicken *karaage,* or tempura, along with innovations like yam poutine with teriyaki gravy. The sake list includes several varieties from Vancouver's Artisan Sake Maker on Granville Island. This diminutive dining destination is easy to walk right by; look for it opposite Yaletown's Emery Barnes Park.

MAP 3: 572 Davie St., 604/568-8805, www.junobistro.ca; 4:30pm-10:30pm Mon.-Sat., 4:30pm-9:30pm Sun.

VIETNAMESE
House Special **$$**

A brother-and-sister team runs this modern Vietnamese eatery in a refurbished Yaletown warehouse. House Special, named for the house special *pho* (noodle soup), serves a mix of traditional and more innovative Asian plates that pair well with cocktails and craft beers. Try the spicy-sweet chicken wings, the soft-boiled Son-in-Law Egg in a crispy panko crust, or the fry bread, a sesame bun filled with pork cracklings, duck confit, or sautéed mushrooms.

MAP 3: 1269 Hamilton St., 778/379-2939, www.housespecial.ca; 11:30am-3pm and 5pm-10pm daily

ITALIAN
Giardino $$$

After longtime Vancouver restaurateur Umberto Menghi closed Il Giardino, his classic Italian dining room, many mourned its passing. But never fear: Menghi is back near Yaletown with elegant Tuscan-inspired Giardino, pairing old-world service with updated plates like horseradish-crusted sablefish with lamb ragout or seared venison sauced with a chianti reduction. Don't miss the sweets, like chocolate *fonduta*, a baked chocolate soufflé with chestnut crème anglaise, or almond cannoli served with blood orange sorbet. The dining room could be a refined restaurant in Florence, with its vaulted wood-beamed ceilings, Italian tile work, and European paintings; in summer, sit on the garden patio, hidden behind the restaurant.

MAP 3: 1328 Hornby St., 604/669-2422, www.umberto.com; 11:30am-2pm and 5:30pm-11pm Mon.-Fri., 5:30pm-11pm Sat.

La Pentola $$$

The best way to dine at La Pentola, the fashionable dining room at Yaletown's Opus Hotel, is family-style ($60-75 pp), when the kitchen sends out a procession of contemporary Italian dishes. Even if you opt for a less opulent feast, you can choose from antipasti like braised octopus with fried eggplant, house-made

pastas (perhaps tagliatelle bolognese or *agnolotti* stuffed with duck confit), and mains that might include *branzano* with swiss chard or veal osso buco. Their signature dessert is a sweet-tart lemon cream. With street-level windows bringing in light from two sides and tables well laid out for conversation, La Pentola is also a pleasant spot for brunch or a business meeting.

MAP 3: 350 Davie St., 604/642-0557, www.lapentola.ca; 7am-10pm daily

PIZZA
Bella Gelateria Yaletown $$

Though you wouldn't guess it from the name, the waterside branch of Vancouver's best gelato shop is also a full-fledged Neapolitan-style pizzeria, cooking up creative and traditional pies in their wood-burning oven. Request a seat on the patio overlooking False Creek if you're sitting down for pizza; you can take your gelato or nondairy sorbet for a stroll along the Seawall.

MAP 3: 1089 Marinaside Crescent, 778/737-7890, http://bellagelateria.com; 9am-11pm daily

BAKERIES AND CAFÉS
The Buzz Café and Espresso Bar $

Part art gallery and part coffee shop, The Buzz Café and Espresso Bar sits on a sunny Yaletown corner, inside Harrison Galleries (www.harrisongalleries.com), Vancouver's oldest retail art gallery. Settle into one of the comfy couches or cozy nooks beneath the artworks for baked goods and a cup of coffee or tea. With widely spaced seating, it's a well laid-out place to chat or check your e-mail (there's free Wi-Fi).

FRENCH

Au Comptoir $$$

With its copper bar and copper-rimmed tables, the setting at classic French bistro Au Comptoir declares "Paris." From croissants and omelets in the morning to *croque-monsieur* and house-smoked salmon at midday, continuing with steak frites, bacon-wrapped rabbit with chanterelles, or duck breast paired with an endive tarte tatin in the evenings, the menu would be right at home in La Belle France, too. On a warm day, the windows open to the outdoors, as they might in a traditional Parisian café, to take in the surrounding Kitsilano streetscape.

MAP 5: 2278 W. 4th Ave., 604/569-2278, www.aucomptoir.ca; 8am-10pm Mon. and Wed.-Sat., 8am-9:30pm Sun.

BREAKFAST AND BRUNCH

Café Zen $

Popular with local families, old-favorite Café Zen fuels you up with breakfast classics, like plate-size pancakes or more than a dozen varieties of eggs Benedict, from spinach and mushroom to shrimp and avocado, before you flop down in the sand at nearby Kits Beach. Behind the sunny yellow facade, the hardworking staff keeps your coffee hot, and the long menu also features omelets, crepes, waffles, burgers, and a few sandwiches.

MAP 5: 1631 Yew St., 604/731-4018, www.cafezenonyew.com; 7am-2:30pm Mon.-Thurs., 7am-4pm Fri.-Sun.

BAKERIES AND CAFÉS

✪ Chocolate Arts $

If you like your chocolate rich, dark, and homemade, add Chocolate Arts, near Granville Island, to your itinerary. Along one wall, and in the glass display cases, are handcrafted chocolates in a variety of flavors, where you can assemble a box of bonbons. The chocolate medallions with First Nations motifs make a unique gift.

The other side of the shop is a café, with bright white tables and red chairs. There, try a shot of drinking chocolate, which is very rich and similar to espresso. For a treat, come for Haute Chocolat, a version of afternoon tea, with cocoa, house-made chocolates, petit fours, and other chocolaty pastries.

MAP 5: 1620 W. 3rd Ave., 604/739-0475, www.chocolatearts.com, 10am-6pm Mon.-Sat.

Beaucoup Bakery & Café $

With classic French pastries like croissants or buttery *kouign-amann,* and other baked treats like the kid-pleasing peanut butter sandwich cookies, petite Beaucoup Bakery & Café makes a sweet stop for Kitsilano or South Granville shoppers. It's a short walk from Granville Island, too.

MAP 5: 2150 Fir St., 604/732-4222, www.beaucoupbakery.com; 7am-5pm Tues.-Fri., 8am-5pm Sat.-Sun.

DESSERT

Rain or Shine Ice Cream $

With a fitting name for a sweet shop in a city with changeable weather, Rain or Shine Ice Cream produces ice cream made primarily from locally sourced ingredients, free of chemical additives. Certain flavors, including chocolate, salted caramel, and "cracked mint" (peppermint chocolate chip), are the "keepers," which appear on their regular menu, and you'll also find seasonal varieties like buttered sweet corn and black pepper ice cream or peach bellini sorbet. In addition to this location, with just a couple of tables, they have

MAP 3: 901 Homer St., 604/732-9029, http://thebuzzcafe.net; 7am-6pm Mon.-Fri., 8am-5pm Sat., 9am-5pm Sun.

Small Victory Bakery $

At times, it can seem like a small victory to get a seat at this Yaletown café that's filled with blond wood tables and lots of enticing aromas. At Small Victory Bakery, the coffee is excellent, and the short menu includes pastries, breads, and a few sandwiches. The almond croissants are a special treat.

MAP 3: 1088 Homer St., 604/899-8892, http://smallvictory.ca; 7:30am-6pm Mon.-Fri., 8am-6pm Sat.-Sun.

Terra Breads Bakery Café $

With floor-to-ceiling windows and seats inside and out, cheery Terra Breads Bakery Café in the Olympic Village makes a handy rest stop for coffee and muffins while you're strolling the False Creek Seawall or as a treat for the kids after visiting Science World. Sandwiches, salads, soups, and a range of sweet and savory pastries are available, along with hot and cold drinks, beer, wine, and cider. Terra Breads has other sit-down locations in Kitsilano and off Main Street.

MAP 3: 1605 Manitoba St., 604/877-1183, www.terrabreads.com; 7am-7pm daily

Granville Island   Map 4

MODERN CANADIAN

Edible Canada Bistro $$

Opposite the Public Market, Edible Canada Bistro creates contemporary dishes with ingredients from around British Columbia and across Canada. Though it's always busy with tourists, locals appreciate the Canadian menu, too. At midday, you might try a duck confit sandwich with cherry-onion relish or root vegetable hash with boar bacon and poached eggs. For supper, find plates like maple-glazed pork chops, wild salmon with braised lentils, or bison short ribs. The restaurant regularly partners with Canadian chefs to host special dinners; check the website for upcoming events. Adjacent to the window-lined restaurant, which has an open kitchen and seasonal patio seating, their retail outlet sells Canadian-made gourmet products.

MAP 4: 1596 Johnston St., 604/682-6681, www.ediblecanada.com; 11am-9pm Mon.-Thurs., 11am-10pm Fri., 9am-10pm Sat., 9am-9pm Sun.

SEAFOOD

Go Fish $

Like seafood? Then go fish—at Go Fish, an always busy waterfront take-out shack. Choose fish-and-chips made from cod, salmon, or halibut, or go a little wild with a wild salmon sandwich, an oyster po' boy, or fish tacos. Expect long lines on sunny days. It's a five-minute walk along the seawall from Granville Island; look for the dockside sign that says "Public Fish Sales," and you'll find Go Fish opposite the docks.

MAP 4: 1505 W. 1st Ave., 604/730-5040; 11:30am-6:30pm Tues.-Fri., noon-6:30pm Sat.-Sun.

VIETNAMESE
Chau Veggie Express $

Chau Veggie Express serves Vietnamese-inspired vegetarian and vegan dishes. The short menu at this to-go counter inside the Granville Island Public Market features several soups, fresh spring rolls, and noodle or rice bowls layered with different combinations of vegetables, tofu, and sauces, from vegan "fish" sauce to spicy peanut satay.

MAP 4: Granville Island Public Market, 1689 Johnston St., 778/379-9508, www.chowatchau.ca; 9am-7pm Tues.-Sun.

QUICK BITES
Market Grill $

A takeout stall facing the water at the back of the Granville Island Public Market, the friendly Market Grill cooks up burgers, with beef, chicken, and veggie options. The local favorite is the salmon burgers, with sockeye piled high on a homemade bun. Simple but good, the burgers all come with either thick-cut fries or Caesar salad. Market Grill also serves hot dogs and breakfast options (bacon and eggs, breakfast sandwiches).

MAP 4: Granville Island Public Market, 1689 Johnston St., 604/689-1918; 8am-7pm daily

The Stock Market $

Inside the Granville Island Public Market, the Stock Market prepares three kinds of homemade soup daily. On the rotating menu, one soup is fish-based (like the tasty wild salmon chowder), one is meat-based, and the third is vegetarian. Each bowl is served with a slab of bread and makes for a quick market lunch. Although the stall itself has no seating, you can sit at tables nearby or take your food to a bench outdoors.

MAP 4: Granville Island Public Market, 1689 Johnston St., 604/687-2433, http://thestockmarket.ca; 8am-7pm daily

Kitsilano   Map 5

MODERN CANADIAN
AnnaLena $$$

Though it's named for the chef's grandmothers, there's nothing old-fashioned about AnnaLena, a smart Kitsilano bistro with white walls, black banquettes, and west coast wood trimmings. The modern menu, designed to share, might include kale salad with raw and confit radishes, buttermilk fried chicken with charred shishito peppers, and lamb neck with spaetzle, asparagus, and egg yolk gel. To sip? Local microbrews, B.C. wines, and fun cocktails.

MAP 5: 1809 W. 1st Ave., 778/379-4052, www.annalena.ca; 5pm-late Tues.-Sun.

Bishop's $$$

Chef-owner John Bishop helped pioneer Vancouver's farm-to-table movement long before the 100-mile diet was on the lips of every locavore. At Bishop's namesake classy, white-tablecloth restaurant, adorned with works by local artists, the polished staff can guide you to seasonal suppers that might start with tuna tartare served with pickled garlic scapes or a duck and quail terrine, before continuing with Haida Gwaii halibut paired with roasted cauliflower or heritage pork with clams, corn, and grilled peaches. Finish with a summer berry oat crumble or the Valrhona chocolate terrine topped with espresso ice cream.

MAP 5: 2183 W. 4th Ave., 604/738-2025, www.bishopsonline.com; 5:30pm-11pm Tues.-Sun.

Fable $$$

While the name Fable—"from farm to table"—may be a bit earnest, the kitchen at this Kitsilano eatery has a sense of humor, with starters like an oversize duck meatball that bursts open to sauce the tagliatelle it's served on, and sweets like "Oops, I Dropped the Dessert," a mash-up of rhubarb, vanilla custard, and ice cream. In between are hearty unpretentious plates featuring local seafood, meats, and fresh veggies. Sit at the long counter to watch the chefs at work, or sink into a banquette beneath the exposed brick wall in the dining room.

MAP 5: 1944 W. 4th Ave., 604/732-1322, www.fablekitchen.ca, 11:30am-2pm and 5pm-10pm Mon.-Fri., 10:30am-2pm and 5pm-10pm Sat.-Sun.

Mission $$$

At the front of this sophisticated Kitsilano restaurant, you can settle into the lounge for cocktails and casual plates to share, but to experience what chef-owner Curtis Luk is known for, make a reservation in the narrow, white-walled main dining room. There, you'll indulge in a locally focused multicourse meal, offered in either vegetarian or "omnivore" versions, with optional wine pairings. Your most difficult mission may be to choose between four ($45) or six ($65) courses, where the changing parade of dishes might include squash blossoms with *fromage frais* and saffron potatoes, pork with comp[...] termelon, or humpback sh[...] with tomatoes and almond[...]

MAP 5: 2042 W. 4th Ave., 604/[...] http://missionkits.ca; 5:30pm-10[...] Mon.-Fri., 10:30am-2pm and 5:30pm-midnight Sat., 10:30am-[...] 5:30pm-11pm Sun.

THAI
✪ Maenam $$

Serving modern Thai cuis[...] minimalist Kitsilano space, [...] brightens Vancouver's dark[...] with banana blossom salad, [...] fermented sausage with cris[...] and flavorful curries. If yo[...] decide, go for the six-course[...] menu ($45 pp). Asian-inspire[...] tails, like the *tang kwa luck* (c[...] ber-infused gin, lime, lemon[...] ginger, and Balinese long pepp[...] the alcohol-free house-made g[...] beer pair well with the brightl[...] vored dishes.

MAP 5: 1938 W. 4th Ave., 604/730-55[...] www.maenam.ca, 5pm-10pm Sun.-Mo[...] noon-2pm and 5pm-10pm Tues.-Sat.

VIETNAMESE
Mr. Red Café $

This family-run eatery in Kitsil[...] decked out with bamboo pane[...] and a tropical feel, specializes in di[...] from Hanoi and northern Vietn[...] Recommended choices include [...] turmeric fish with dill, mango s[...] with shrimp, and *pho ga* (chicken [...] dle soup). To drink, try a traditi[...] sweet Vietnamese coffee with c[...] densed milk. The restaurant's or[...] nal location is a smaller storefron[...] the East Side.

MAP 5: 2680 W. Broadway, 604/559-6[...] 11am-9pm daily

a second outlet in Cambie Village that keeps the same hours.

MAP 5: 1926 W. 4th Ave., 604/428-7246, http://rainorshineicecream.com; noon-10pm daily

FARMERS MARKETS
Kitsilano Farmers Market $

Operating on Sunday from spring through fall, the Kitsilano Farmers Market sets up behind the Kitsilano Community Centre with more than 50 vendors selling fresh produce, baked goods, and other local treats. The highlights are freshly made crepes from Creperie La Boheme, croissants from Batard Boulangerie, and locally produced ginger beer from Dickie's Ginger.

MAP 5: Kitsilano Community Centre, 2690 Larch St., 604/879-3276, www.eatlocal.org; 10am-2pm Sun. early May-late Oct.

COFFEE AND TEA
Culprit Coffee $

Take a break from shopping along West 4th Avenue with a cup of coffee and gluten-free baked goods from Culprit Coffee, a cozy neighborhood café. Look for its bright yellow facade and its sunny sidewalk tables.

MAP 5: 2028 Vine St., 604/730-0133, www.culpritcoffee.com; 7:30am-6pm Mon.-Fri., 8:30am-6pm Sat.-Sun.

O5 Tea Bar $

When you step into this serene Asian-style tea salon, you leave the bustle of West 4th Avenue far behind and enter the space of the tea masters. O5 Tea Bar specializes in rare, single origin teas from around the world, the majority of which they purchase directly from the growers. Take a seat at the long bar, made of reclaimed Douglas fir, and linger over a cup of tea, or do a traditional tea tasting. They also have house-brewed kombucha on tap, which you can sip in the shop or take to go.

MAP 5: 2208 W. 4th Ave., 604/558-0500, http://o5tea.com; 10am-10pm daily

UBC and Point Grey   Map 5

MODERN CANADIAN
Sage Bistro $$

One of the more upscale dining options on the UBC Campus, overlooking the gardens with views of the North Shore mountains beyond, Sage Bistro serves weekday lunches in the Leon and Thea Koerner University Centre, a short walk from the Museum of Anthropology. The menu draws on local ingredients whenever possible, in dishes like kale salad with radishes, feta, and sunflower seeds, grilled king oyster mushrooms with warm farro salad, broccolini, and rainbow carrots, or pan-seared halibut paired with warm potato salad. Don't worry, though; while the bistro is popular with university faculty, you won't be graded on whether you finish your meal.

MAP 5: 6331 Crescent Rd., UBC, 604/822-0968, http://sage.ubc.ca; 11:30am-2pm Mon.-Fri.

PUB FARE
The Galley Patio and Grill $$

Overlooking the sea from the second floor of the Jericho Sailing Centre at Jericho Beach, The Galley Patio and

Grill cooks up simple, beach-friendly bites, including burgers, grilled salmon, and sweet potato fries, served on a deck with killer ocean views. Local beer is on tap. If you can't find a seat, take your food outside and picnic. Tip for morning beachcombers: The Galley also serves breakfast.

MAP 5: 1300 Discovery St., 604/222-1331, www.thegalley.ca; 10am-10pm Mon.-Fri., 9am-10pm Sat.-Sun. June-Sept., hours vary Oct.-May

BAKERIES AND CAFÉS
Mix the Bakery $

On your way to or from UBC, stop at Mix the Bakery, a homey Point Grey neighborhood café, for coffee, baked goods, or sandwiches. For breakfast, there's always a selection of muffins, scones, and toast with homemade jam. Among the sandwich choices, look for the Granny Gobbler (smoked turkey, cheddar cheese, spinach, and apple) or a vegetarian option, with grilled zucchini, pan-fried onions, roasted tomatoes, and swiss cheese. Staff set up enticing displays of fruit tarts, cakes, and other pastries along the counter that will perk up your afternoon.

MAP 5: 4430 W. 10th Ave., 604/221-4145, www.mixthebakery.com; 7am-5pm Mon.-Sat., 8am-4pm Sun.

Cambie Corridor　　　Map 6

MODERN CANADIAN
✪ West $$$

A wall of wine sets the sumptuous scene at South Granville's West, where the gracious service and just-inventive-enough cuisine make any meal feel like an occasion. Wild salmon with a morel mushroom crumble, a pork duo of braised cheek and crispy belly, or smoked duck with kale and roasted corn are just some of the locally sourced plates you might encounter. Sweets are special, too, with choices like a raspberry tart with sorrel ice cream or a chocolate tasting plate.

MAP 6: 2881 Granville St., 604/738-8938, www.westrestaurant.com; 11:30am-2:30pm and 5:30pm-10:30pm Mon.-Thurs., 11:30am-2:30pm and 5:30pm-11pm Fri., 10:30am-2:30pm and 5:30pm-11pm Sat., 10:30am-2:30pm and 5:30pm-10:30pm Sun.

Burdock & Co $$

Chef-owner Andrea Carlson runs this relaxed neighborhood bistro, delivering a creative, hyper-local menu to customers seated at Burdock & Co's rustic wooden tables. Dishes like heirloom tomato and melon salad, sea bream crudo with purslane and garlic-shio puree, or salt cod fritters with pickled sea asparagus change with the harvest; the house-made kimchi and the crispy fried chicken with buttermilk mashed potatoes are well-loved staples. The short but distinctive wine list includes bottles from B.C., Oregon, France, Italy, and even Lebanon. Weekend brunch, which might bring mushrooms on toast, tomato baked eggs with feta, and more of that fried chicken, will put you in the mood for some Main Street shopping.

UKRAINIAN CHURCH SUPPERS

Looking to kick off the weekend with something different? On the first Friday of every month since 1995, the **Holy Trinity Ukrainian Orthodox Cathedral** (154 E. 10th Ave., 604/876-4747, http://uocvancouver.com; 5pm-8pm first Fri. of the month) has been hosting a moderately priced family-style supper that's open to all, in the church hall just off Main Street. Dinners feature stick-to-your-ribs classics like pierogi, cabbage rolls, *koubassa* (sausage), and borscht (beet vegetable soup) that church volunteers prepare. The ambience is a cross between a traditional church supper and a hipster hangout, with apron-clad ladies serving from the buffet line, and everyone from kids to seniors sharing the communal tables.

MAP 6: 2702 Main St., 604/879-0077, www.burdockandco.com; 5pm-10pm Mon.-Fri., 10:30am-2pm and 5pm-10pm Sat.-Sun.

Farmer's Apprentice $$$

Imaginative multicourse tasting menus inspired by local products bring adventurous diners to Farmer's Apprentice, a petite South Granville dining room. Lingcod with epazote and radishes? Dry-aged duck with emmer and sea buckthorn? You won't find these creations on any other tables around town. The same team runs the more casual wine and tapas bar, **Grapes and Soda** (1541 W. 6th Ave., 604/336-2456, www.grapesandsoda. ca) next door.

MAP 6: 1535 W. 6th Ave., 604/620-2070, www.farmersapprentice.ca; 5:30pm-10pm Mon.-Fri., 11am-2pm and 5:30pm-10pm Sat.-Sun.

FIRST NATIONS
Salmon n' Bannock $$

If you're keen to explore First Nations cuisine, visit Salmon n' Bannock. This modern aboriginal bistro uses traditional ingredients in its elk burgers, game sausages, and bison tenderloin—and yes, there's plenty of salmon and bannock, a native bread, on the menu, too. Wines come from Nk'Mip Cellars, Canada's first aboriginal-owned winery, based in B.C.'s Okanagan region. Desserts include bannock bread pudding and homemade fruit pies.

MAP 6: 1128 W. Broadway, 604/568-8971, www.salmonandbannock.net; 11:30am-3pm and 5pm-9pm Mon.-Thurs., 11:30am-3pm and 5pm-10pm Fri., 5pm-10pm Sat.

CHINESE
Dynasty Seafood $$

Dynasty Seafood serves some of Vancouver's best dim sum, a sophisticated mix of traditional and creative dumplings, buns, and other small bites. Highlights include lemony baked barbecue pork buns, steamed black truffle dumplings, and sweet sago pudding, a tapioca dessert. The busy second-floor dining room, with views of the downtown skyline and North Shore mountains, is a short walk west of the Broadway/City Hall Canada Line station. Reservations are recommended for dim sum, especially on Saturday and Sunday.

MAP 6: 777 W. Broadway, 604/876-8388, www.dynasty-restaurant.ca; 10am-3pm and 5pm-10:30pm daily

Shao Lin Noodle House $

Watch the noodle makers stretch, pull, and toss their lumps of dough at the Shao Lin Noodle House, a casual eatery near the Broadway/City Hall Canada Line station that specializes in dishes from northern China. Order a bowl of the handmade noodles, of course, choosing from different shapes and adding your choice of meat or vegetable toppings, but don't neglect the steamed or pan-fried dumplings or the side dishes, like diced cucumbers in sesame sauce or the spicy fried green beans.

MAP 6: 656 W. Broadway, 604/873-1618, www.shalinnoodlehouse.com; 11am-9:30pm Sun.-Thurs., 11am-10pm Fri.-Sat.

JAPANESE
Tojo's $$$

Long considered Vancouver's top Japanese dining room, Tojo's, which takes its name from chef-owner Hidekazu Tojo, is known for the high quality of its sushi and sashimi. Chef Tojo first arrived in Vancouver in the early 1970s, when North Americans were not very familiar with Japanese food. Tojo reportedly created a roll made from cooked crabmeat and fresh avocado—widely known today as the California roll. For a special evening, sit at the sushi bar and order *omakase* (chef's choice, $80-150 pp), a parade of traditional and creative dishes. Sip rice wines and order small plates at The Sake Bar, adjacent to the main restaurant, when you don't want a full meal.

MAP 6: 1133 W. Broadway, 604/872-8050, www.tojos.com; 5pm-late Mon.-Sat.

INDIAN
Vij's $$

Celebrated for its innovative riffs on Indian cuisine, Vij's, which became equally famous for its no-reservations waiting lines, relocated in 2015 to a larger space, six blocks from the Broadway/City Hall Canada Line station. The no-bookings policy, and the modern Indian fare, from chickpeas in black cardamom curry to grilled venison atop tamarind-date puree to the signature lamb "Popsicles," remain largely unchanged; a cocktail or a cup of *chai* makes the wait go more smoothly. In summer, you can dig into basmati rice bowls or snacks like *papri* (spiced potatoes and sprouted lentils served with chutneys and wheat crisps) up on the rooftop patio.

MAP 6: 3106 Cambie St., 604/736-6664, www.vijsrestaurant.ca; 5:30pm-10:30pm daily

Rangoli $

Under the same ownership as Vij's, the more casual Rangoli serves interesting Indian dishes in a South Granville café. Many of the choices are vegetarian, like the kale, jackfruit, cauliflower, and potato curry or the chickpeas in fenugreek curry with grilled eggplant, while meat lovers might opt for the spicy pulled pork with sautéed greens or the beef short ribs with pickled vegetables. To drink, try a salty or sweet *lassi* (yogurt drink), which is also available in a dairy-free coconut-mango version.

MAP 6: 1480 W. 11th Ave., 604/736-5711, www.vijsrangoli.ca; 11am-2:30pm and 5pm-11pm Mon., 11am-2:30pm and 5pm-midnight Tues.-Fri., 11am-midnight Sat.-Sun.

LATIN AMERICAN
Chicha $$

This lively storefront just west of Main Street takes you to Peru by way of the Pacific Northwest, incorporating local ingredients into classic Peruvian dishes. Start your sipping with a traditional pisco sour or with the restaurant's nonalcoholic namesake, *chicha morada*, a sweet beverage made from purple corn. Among the sharing-style plates, order one of the ceviches, or opt for a ceviche trio to sample several varieties. Other good choices include

colorful Peruvian fare at Chicha

the addictive *palitas de yuca* (cassava root fries); empanadas filled with butternut squash, corn, kale, and cheese; and any of the *causas*, whipped potatoes topped with seafood or vegetables. For a sweet finish, try the *picarones*, sweet potato and pumpkin doughnuts.

MAP 6: 136 E. Broadway, 604/620-3963, www.chicharestaurant.com; 5pm-11pm Mon.-Thurs., 11:30am-2:30pm and 5pm-midnight Fri., 10:30am-2:30pm and 5pm-midnight Sat., 10:30am-2:30pm and 5pm-11pm Sun.

VEGETARIAN
✪ The Acorn $$

At Vancouver's most innovative vegetarian restaurant, plant-based food shakes off its crunchy-granola reputation with ambitious plates that would enhance any upscale table: kale salad with tempeh and smoked paprika croutons, beer-battered halloumi cheese with zucchini-potato pancakes, or orecchiette with fresh peas and almonds. The dining space isn't much larger than the restaurant's namesake, and they don't take reservations, so you might chill at the bar with a Cock-A-Tail (coconut-infused rum, amaro, lime, and apricot riesling syrup) or a local craft beer.

MAP 6: 3995 Main St., 604/566-9001, www.theacornrestaurant.ca; 5:30pm-10pm Mon.-Thurs., 5:30pm-11pm Fri., 10am-2:30pm and 5:30pm-11pm Sat., 10am-2:30pm and 5:30pm-10pm Sun.

BAKERIES AND CAFÉS
Liberty Bakery $

The homey Liberty Bakery draws its inspiration from Scandinavia, from the white wood walls to the baked goods, like cardamom-scented cinnamon rolls or *pulla*, a Finnish sweet bread, which you can pair with your morning coffee. At lunchtime, choose from open-faced sandwiches, classic grilled cheese, black bean soup, or several salads. This Main Street café is popular with neighborhood families who often pop in for an after-school or weekend treat.

MAP 6: 3699 Main St., 604/709-9999, www.liberty-bakery.com; 8am-6pm Mon.-Fri., 9am-6pm Sat.-Sun.

COFFEE AND TEA
49th Parallel Coffee Roasters $

This airy coffeehouse is perpetually packed with friends catching up over an espresso or freelancers tapping away at their laptops. The shop's popularity is partly because they make Lucky's Donuts fresh throughout the day, in flavors like classic old-fashioned, salted caramel, and white chocolate-matcha. The team at Vancouver-based 49th Parallel Coffee Roasters is serious about their coffee, too, sourcing beans from small producers and brewing top-notch cups. In addition to this Main Street location, they have a branch in Kitsilano.

MAP 6: 2902 Main St., 604/420-4900, http://49thcoffee.com; 7am-10pm Mon.-Sat., 7:30am-10pm Sun.

Gene Coffee Bar $

Notable for its unusual triangular-shaped space as much as for its brews, Gene Coffee Bar is a narrow wedge of a café with two walls of windows where Main Street and Kingsway intersect. Park at one of the long communal tables and soak up the neighborhood scene while you sip your drip coffee, latte, or macchiato. MAP 6: 2404 Main St., 604/568-5501, http://genecoffeebar.com; 7:30am-7pm Mon.-Fri., 8:30am-7pm Sat.-Sun.

Commercial Drive   Map 7

SEAFOOD
Merchant's Oyster Bar $$

This compact corner storefront with seats indoors at their dark wood tables or out on a narrow sidewalk patio is the spot for seafood and other light bites on Commercial Drive. Merchant's Oyster Bar shucks a changing selection of bivalves (ask the obliging staff for the day's features), along with inventive sharing plates like pork terrine with peach mostarda, tuna crudo with sea asparagus, or local crab with tarragon aioli, that you can pair with creative cocktails and craft beer. For something more substantial, you might find tagliatelle with prawns and uni butter or duck with five-spice barbecue sauce. MAP 7: 1590 Commercial Dr., 604/258-0005, www.merchantsoysterbar.ca; 2pm-10pm Mon.-Thurs., 2pm-11pm Fri., 11am-11pm Sat., 11am-10pm Sun.

MIDDLE EASTERN
Jamjar $$

Casual Jamjar serves traditional Lebanese dishes, updated with local ingredients, in a space that mixes pendant lights, white subway tiles, and other industrial elements, with homey wooden tables and jars of their own hummus, dips, and sauces on display. From *fattoush* salad to *makdous* (pickled eggplant stuffed with chili and walnuts) to *makali* (fried cauliflower with pomegranate molasses), plates are designed to share, with lots of vegetarian options. There's a second location in South Granville. MAP 7: 2280 Commercial Dr., 604/252-3957, www.jam-jar.ca; 11:30am-10pm daily

THAI
Kin Kao Thai Kitchen $$

Convenient for a bite before a show at the Vancouver East Cultural Centre or the York Theatre, Kin Kao Thai Kitchen serves Thai dishes with contemporary twists in a modern minimalist space, where you can perch at the counter or line up for seats at one of the light wood tables (it's a small spot). Don't miss the tangy, sour cured pork ribs. Other recommended dishes

pork ribs and salad at Kin Kao Thai Kitchen

include papaya salad, steak salad, or any of the curry dishes. Craft beers from neighborhood breweries are on tap.

MAP 7: 903 Commercial Dr., 604/558-1125, www.kinkao.ca; 5pm-10pm Mon., 11:30am-3pm and 5pm-10pm Tues.-Sat.

DINERS
The Red Wagon $

What brings the all-day breakfast crowds of families, East Side hipsters, and other neighborhood denizens to The Red Wagon, a homey diner in the heart of the East Village? First of all, there are pulled pork pancakes—buttermilk pancakes layered with tender pork and Jack Daniels-laced maple syrup. Beyond this indulgent specialty, the menu starts with eggs, bacon, and other morning classics, but gets creative with Vietnamese-influenced "breakfast *bánh mì*," a vegetarian tofu scramble, and a goat cheese and basil frittata. If you're in more of a lunch mood, opt for a burger, soups, salads, or sandwiches.

MAP 7: 2296 E. Hastings St., 604/568-4565, www.redwagoncafe.com; 8am-3pm Mon.-Tues., 8am-midnight Wed.-Fri., 9am-midnight Sat.-Sun.

QUICK BITES
La Grotta Del Formaggio $

A delicious reason to visit Italian grocer La Grotta Del Formaggio is for the Italian sandwiches that this Commercial Drive shop makes to order. Load up your fresh bread or focaccia with salami, prosciutto, or other cured meats, along with cheeses, peppers, olives, and various condiments. The shop has a couple of seats out on the sidewalk, but a better plan is to take your meal to a nearby park. The shop also sells imported pastas, anchovies, and a large selection of cheeses.

MAP 7: 1791 Commercial Dr., 604/255-3911, www.lgdf.ca; 9am-6pm Mon.-Thurs. and Sat., 9am-7pm Fri., 10am-6pm Sun.

BAKERIES AND CAFÉS
✪ The Pie Shoppe $

The Pie Shoppe turns out a seasonally changing array of sweet things in a crust. The proprietors of this cheerful East Side bakery with a common table and handcrafted pine counter, located down the street from several craft breweries, also run Panoramic Roasting Company, a small batch coffee roaster, and pair their blueberry, nectarine-cardamom, chocolate pecan, or other slices with pour-overs, espressos, and cappuccinos from their own beans. They sell whole pies and savory options, too, but beware: They close early if they run out of pie.

MAP 7: 1875 Powell St., 604/338-6646, http://thepieshoppe.ca; 11am-6pm Wed.-Sun.

COFFEE AND TEA
Prado Café $

A hip Commercial Drive coffee spot that's expanded to several locations across the city, window-lined Prado Café serves its brews in turquoise mugs to clients who settle at the wooden tables to chat or get some work done. Staff use locally roasted 49th Parallel beans and bake their pastries in-house.

MAP 7: 1938 Commercial Dr., 604/255-5537, http://pradocafevancouver. com; 7am-8pm Mon.-Fri., 7am-7pm Sat., 8am-7pm Sun.

Turks Coffee House $

As the first independent coffee bar on Commercial Drive, this coffee shop may claim that they've been "non-conforming since 1992," but Turks Coffee

House conforms to seriously high coffee standards, serving Italian-style brews sourced primarily from small, fair trade, and organic producers. Sip your drip-, pour over-, or espresso-style java at the long communal counter, a sunny window table, or out on the pocket-size sidewalk patio.

MAP 7: 1276 Commercial Dr., 604/255-5805, 6:30am-11pm daily

Richmond

Map 8

CANTONESE
✪ Bamboo Grove $$$

From the front, Bamboo Grove looks like a nearly abandoned, old-time Asian eatery. But go around back, enter through the parking lot, and you'll find a high-end Cantonese restaurant, with white tablecloths, black-suited waiters, and an elaborate menu. Any fresh fish dish would be a good option, as would the eggplant with tiger prawns, the fried rice with cod roe, and the unusual pork stomach with ginkgo soup, a pale, creamy, and rich broth. If you have a big budget and adventurous tastes, try the succulent geoduck clam sautéed with velvety scrambled eggs; check the current price before ordering, as geoduck can often run $50 a pound. Reservations are recommended.

MAP 8: 6920 No. 3 Rd., 604/278-9585; 4:30pm-10:30pm daily; subway: Richmond-Brighouse

HUNAN
Bushuair Restaurant $$

Like spice? Richmond's Bushuair Restaurant prepares the blistering hot cuisine of China's Hunan province. A portrait of Mao, who hailed from Hunan, welcomes patrons to this nondescript strip-mall storefront, where it's all about the food. From the thick menu, which is filled with photos, choose any preparation with smoked bacon or pickled chilies, which give dishes their distinctive Hunan flavors. The whole fish buried in chili peppers is a showstopper.

MAP 8: Empire Centre, 4540 No. 3 Rd., #121, 604/285-3668; 11am-midnight daily; subway: Aberdeen

SHANGHAINESE
Su Hang Restaurant $$

Su Hang Restaurant, in a Richmond strip mall, specializes in dishes from Shanghai and the surrounding regions, from delicate *xiao long bao* (pork-filled soup dumplings) to fresh fish or crab to meaty pork ribs. To sample their signature dish, Hangzhou beggar chicken, order a day in advance. At lunchtime, they serve Shanghai-style dim sum. Make a reservation; the restaurant is small.

MAP 8: 8291 Ackroyd Rd., #100, 604/278-7787, www.suhang.ca; 11am-3pm and 5pm-10pm daily; subway: Lansdowne

SICHUAN
✪ New Spicy Chili Restaurant $$

Many dishes at Richmond's Sichuan-style New Spicy Chili Restaurant incorporate the delectably mouth-numbing Sichuan peppercorns that balance out hot peppers' chili heat. The staff at this relaxed little storefront, tucked into the corner of a minimall, do their best to assist with

rack of lamb at Hao's Lamb Restaurant

recommendations, but if you like spicy fare, you can't go wrong with dishes like the "water-boiled fish" (known here as "tilapia fish with spicy sauce"), kung pao chicken, or the smoked bacon with bamboo shoots (the meat is cured in-house). They do interesting vegetable dishes here as well, including sautéed cauliflower or stir-fried lotus root.

MAP 8: 4200 No. 3 Rd., #160, 604/273-3388; 11:30am-9:30pm Mon.-Thurs., 11:30am-10pm Fri.-Sun.; subway: Aberdeen

XI'AN STYLE
✪ Hao's Lamb Restaurant $$

Sesame flatbread stuffed with sliced lamb, steamed lamb dumplings, creamy lamb soup with hand-pulled noodles, cumin-spiced lamb stir-fry—if you enjoy lamb dishes of many varieties, make tracks to Hao's Lamb Restaurant, which specializes in dishes from western China's Xi'an region. The kitchen uses every part of the sheep (yes, you can even order lamb penis). Accompany your meat with refreshing cold plates, including pickled radishes or garlicky cucumbers, from the display case at the counter or with vegetable options like the crisp and creamy fried eggplant.

MAP 8: 8788 McKim Way, #1180, 604/270-6632; 11am-9:30pm Fri.-Wed.; subway: Aberdeen

DIM SUM
✪ Golden Paramount
Seafood Restaurant $

In an ordinary Richmond strip mall, Golden Paramount Seafood Restaurant is a first-rate spot for Hong Kong-style dim sum. Try the pan-fried oysters, congee (rice porridge), and steamed dumplings filled with pork and crab, or survey what other tables are eating and politely point. Reservations are recommended, particularly on weekends.

MAP 8: 8071 Park Rd., 604/278-0873; 5pm-10pm Wed.-Mon. (dim sum 10:30am-3pm); subway: Richmond-Brighouse

CHINESE FOOD

More than 40 percent of the population in metropolitan Vancouver is of Asian descent. These strong Asian influences permeate the city, from business culture to food. In particular, the Vancouver region has hundreds of Chinese restaurants, many serving high-end cuisine that rivals the fare in Hong Kong, Taipei, and Beijing.

Chinatown, near the city center, was once a vibrant immigrant community. While it still has Chinese markets, bakeries, and restaurants, the best place for traditional Asian meals is Richmond, the region's new Chinatown, where dozens of restaurants serve cuisines from across China.

Whether you're looking for spicy Sichuan or Hunan fare, handmade noodles and dumplings like you'd see in Shanghai, delicately seasoned Cantonese seafood, or the hearty lamb dishes of China's western provinces, you'll find it in Richmond. Cafés serving bubble tea and Taiwanese shaved ice desserts draw a young crowd, while families pack the round tables of countless dim sum houses. Richmond's Alexandra Road, which runs for several blocks east from No. 3 Road, has so many restaurants that it's known locally as **"Food Street."**

jumbo prawns with eggplant at Richmond's Bamboo Grove

The center of Richmond's Asian food scene is the **Golden Village,** along No. 3 Road from Cambie Road south toward Granville Avenue. Most restaurants are located in shopping centers or minimalls, so don't hesitate to explore.

The city even has a **Dumpling Trail** (www.visitrichmondbc.com), which highlights where to eat pot stickers, *xiao long bao* (soup dumplings), and other delectable stuffed dough dishes.

Empire Seafood Restaurant $

For dim sum classics, like *har gow* (delicate steamed shrimp dumplings), *siu mai* (pork and shrimp dumplings topped with fish roe), and barbecue pork buns, Empire Seafood Restaurant is a good choice. Other items to sample include scallop and shrimp dumplings, pan-fried turnip cakes, and steamed egg yolk buns. To find the entrance, head for the second floor of the Richmond complex that also houses a London Drugs store. Arrive before 11am or book ahead for dim sum.

MAP 8: London Plaza, 5951 No. 3 Rd., #200, 604/249-0080, www. empirerestaurant.ca; 5:30pm-10:30pm daily (dim sum 9am-3pm); subway: Richmond-Brighouse

QUICK BITES
The BBT Shop $

Hidden in the parking garage underneath a Richmond grocery superstore, The BBT Shop not only makes tasty bubble tea, but is also known for its eggy bubble waffles, which you can sample plain or with a variety of sweet toppings, including fresh strawberries with whipped cream or matcha ice cream with red beans. One seasonal specialty is the "super mango" version, piled high with mango ice cream, fresh mango, and mango sauce; bring a friend and share. There's another location in the West End.

MAP 8: 4651 No. 3 Rd., 604/285-8833; noon-9:30pm Sun.-Thurs., noon-11:30pm Fri.-Sat.; subway: Aberdeen

RICHMOND

Pearl Castle Café $

Modern Pearl Castle Café has long been a favored destination for young Richmond residents to meet up over bubble tea, from classic milk tea to fresh fruit slush to their own creations. Accompany your drinks with Taiwanese snacks like spiced fried chicken, pork and kimchi fried rice, or thick toast slathered with condensed milk. You'll find a second smaller branch inside the Richmond Centre Mall.

MAP 8: Continental Centre, 3779 Sexsmith Rd., #1128, 604/270-3939, www. pearlcastle.com; 11:30am-1am daily; subway: Aberdeen

Richmond Public Market $

When you need a quick lunch or early supper, wander past the vegetable sellers and other stalls on the main level of the Richmond Public Market and find your way to the second-floor food court. At Xi'an Cuisine, which serves dishes from western China, try a lamb dish with hand-pulled noodles or the pan-fried pot stickers. To drink, get a bubble tea from Peanuts, which also makes a sweet, round waffle-like pastry known as a "car wheel cake," filled with your choice of coconut, peanuts, sweet red beans, even radish. Although not every vendor is open every day, you'll always have several options during the market's regular hours.

MAP 8: 8260 Westminster Hwy., no phone; 10am-8pm daily; subway: Richmond-Brighouse

The North Shore   Map 9

SEAFOOD
Pier 7 Restaurant & Bar $$

Near Lonsdale Quay in North Vancouver, Pier 7 Restaurant & Bar perches over the water with views across Burrard Inlet to the downtown skyline. While the menu emphasizes simple fresh seafood and casual pub fare, the waterfront setting makes the room feel more special. It's a nice spot for sunset drinks, too. The restaurant is a five-minute walk from the SeaBus terminal, so you can start and end your evening with a 12-minute cruise between Waterfront Station and the North Shore.

MAP 9: 25 Wallace Mews, North Vancouver, 604/929-7437, http://pierseven. ca; 11:30am-10pm Mon.-Fri., 10:30am-10pm Sat.-Sun.

PERSIAN
Yaas Grill House $

Vancouver's North Shore has a large Persian community, and one of the best places to sample the food of this region is at Yaas Grill House. This cafeteria-style eatery is not especially atmospheric, but order at the counter, find a seat in the cramped storefront, and the staff will pile your table high with platters of kebabs, stews, and freshly grilled breads that are nearly as large as the tabletops. You'll particularly appreciate the hearty portions if you've been adventuring in the nearby mountains. For dessert, have a piece of classic baklava.

MAP 9: 1629 Lonsdale Ave., North Vancouver, 604/990-9099, http://yaasgrill. com; 11am-10pm daily

seafood plate at Pier 7 Restaurant & Bar

BAKERIES AND CAFÉS
Honey Donuts $

For many Vancouverites, a day kayaking at Deep Cove isn't complete without a stop for an old-fashioned, freshly made doughnut at North Shore institution Honey Donuts. Besides the doughnuts—honey is the classic flavor—you can fuel up with eggs and bacon, hot soup, or a selection of sandwiches.

MAP 9: 4373 Gallant Ave., Deep Cove, North Vancouver, 604/929-4988, http://honeydoughnuts.com; 6am-5pm daily

Savary Island Pie Company $

This West Vancouver café is known for its pies, particularly seasonal fruit varieties, and you can recover from your North Shore outdoor adventures over a cup of coffee and a slice or two. A relaxed neighborhood gathering place, Savary Island Pie Company also serves savory varieties, including chicken potpie and a Quebec-style *tourtière* (meat pie), along with sandwiches, soups, and other pastries.

MAP 9: 1533 Marine Dr., West Vancouver, 604/926-4021, http://savaryislandpiecompany.com; 6am-7pm daily

NIGHTLIFE

Nightlife in Vancouver means meeting up over locally brewed craft beer, a glass of B.C. wine, or a creative cocktail at one of the pubs or lounges around the city.

On a sunny day or mild summer evening, locals and visitors alike crowd the outdoor patios of area watering holes.

Bars, nightclubs, and concert venues line Granville Street in downtown Vancouver, drawing young crowds who want to dance and party. Gastown's historic buildings and Yaletown's converted warehouses host many of the city's popular cocktail lounges and brewpubs. For quieter places to enjoy a cocktail, look to the lounges in Vancouver's downtown hotels.

With Vancouver's craft beer scene growing exponentially, you can find locally produced beer at restaurants and bars all over the city. To sip these brews at their source, visit the East Side neighborhoods—nicknamed "Yeast Van"—that have become the center of the craft brewery boom. Brewery tasting rooms typically open in the early afternoon and remain busy into the evening.

the Opus Bar in Yaletown

The West End is the center of Vancouver's LGBTQ community. Wander along Davie Street, where a brightly painted rainbow crosswalk marks the intersection at Bute Street, to find a variety of gay-friendly pubs and lounges.

Night owls, take note: Vancouver isn't a party-all-night city. Most bars and lounges close at 1am Sunday through Thursday and at 2am or 3am on weekends.

HIGHLIGHTS

⭐ **MOST SCENIC VIEWS:** If you were any closer to the water at **LIFT Bar & Grill,** an upscale waterfront pub overlooking Stanley Park, you'd be swimming (page 125).

⭐ **BEST THEMED NIGHT OUT:** The elegant **Prohibition Lounge** has a Roaring Twenties theme, with music several nights a week (page 125).

⭐ **BEST SECRET DRINKING HIDEAWAY:** Settle around the fire pit for cocktails at posh outdoor **Reflections Lounge,** hidden on the fourth floor of the Rosewood Hotel Georgia (page 125).

⭐ **FRESHEST COCKTAILS:** The talented mixologists at **The Pourhouse** are always creating something new for guests to sip (page 127).

⭐ **WHERE TO PAIR WAFFLES WITH CRAFT BEER:** Beer and waffles? At **33 Acres Brewing,** the weekend waffle brunch draws legions of fans (page 128).

⭐ **WHERE TO HANG OUT ON A BLUE-SKY DAY:** Head to the friendly pub **Tap & Barrel** for B.C. beer and wines on their sunny patio (page 129).

⭐ **COOLEST COCKTAIL LOUNGE:** The **Opus Bar** resembles a trendy living room, where well-dressed young people gather in the curvaceous lounge chairs in front of the fireplace to chat over creative cocktails (page 130).

⭐ **BEST PLACE FOR A GEEKY GOOD TIME:** As "Vancouver's Original Nerd Bar," **Storm Crow Tavern** hosts trivia nights, provides stacks of board games to play, and shows sci-fi (never sports!) on their TVs (page 133).

the Tap & Barrel, overlooking False Creek

Downtown and the West End

Map 1

PUBS

✪ LIFT Bar & Grill

Enjoy one of the best views of Vancouver while you raise your glass at LIFT Bar & Grill, an upscale waterfront pub and Pacific Northwest eatery on Coal Harbour that draws a mix of visitors, local businesspeople, and after-work meet-ups. Look across to Stanley Park as you take your craft beer, B.C. wine, or favorite cocktail on the terrace, where, if you were any closer to the water, you'd be swimming.

MAP 1: 333 Menchions Mews, 604/689-5438, http://liftbarandgrill.com; 11:30am-late Mon.-Fri., 11am-late Sat.-Sun.

Jonnie Fox's Irish Snug

Amid the nightclubs along Granville Street downtown, Jonnie Fox's Irish Snug is a classic Irish pub, where a diverse crowd settles in at the bar or wooden booths for a whiskey or a pint. Irish breakfast (served all day), Yorkshire pudding, and steak and Guinness pie add a Gaelic twist to the otherwise standard pub menu.

MAP 1: 1033 Granville St., 604/685-4946, www.johnniefox.ca; 11:30am-1am Sun.-Thurs., 11:30am-2am Fri.-Sat.

LIVE MUSIC

The Commodore Ballroom

First opened in 1930, The Commodore Ballroom downtown hosts live concerts in its art deco-designed ballroom, featuring performers as diverse as the Tragically Hip, Lady Gaga, and Katy Perry, and drawing crowds of over 900. Its original "sprung" dance floor, which cushioned dancers' feet with a layer of horsehair, was one of the first such floors in North America.

MAP 1: 868 Granville St., 604/739-4550, www.commodoreballroom.com; tickets $20-45

The Roxy

Head to The Roxy, a dark neon-lit club downtown on the Granville strip, when you want to dance. Their rockin' house bands play several nights a week, drawing a young partying crowd; the club accommodates 200-plus people. Sunday is country-and-western night.

MAP 1: 932 Granville St., 604/331-7999, www.roxyvan.com; 8pm-3am daily; cover $5-13

COCKTAIL BARS AND LOUNGES

✪ Prohibition Lounge

Elegant Prohibition Lounge at the Rosewood Hotel Georgia has a Roaring Twenties theme, with music or DJs several nights a week. Wear something stylish when you stop in to sip the daily punch, try an absinthe tasting, or go for a classic cocktail, like the Scofflaw (rye, dry vermouth, lemon, and house-made grenadine) or the Jazz Singer (gin, maraschino, lemon, cherries, and bubbles).

MAP 1: 801 W. Georgia St., 604/673-7089, www.prohibitionrhg.com; 5pm-1am Tues.-Thurs., 5pm-2am Fri.-Sat.

✪ Reflections Lounge

Secreted away on the fourth floor of the Rosewood Hotel Georgia, the posh outdoor Reflections Lounge, where you can sip your wine or classic cocktail on teak couches around a fire pit, brings Los Angeles glamour to downtown Vancouver. Because the lounge is exposed to the elements, it's typically only open April through October.

MAP 1: 801 W. Georgia St., 604/673-7043, www.rosewoodhotels.com; 11:30am-10:30pm daily Apr.-Oct.

Bacchus Lounge

Polished Bacchus Lounge at the Wedgewood Hotel is appropriate for cocktails and quiet conversation with a colleague or a consort. Don a cocktail dress or suit, then sink into the leather chairs or velvet banquettes and listen to the live piano music every evening.

MAP 1: 845 Hornby St., 604/608-5319, www.wedgewoodhotel.com; 2:30pm-midnight Sun.-Wed., 2:30pm-1am Thurs.-Sat.

Gerard Lounge

Styled like an English club room, with dark wood paneling, leather chairs, and oriental rugs, Gerard Lounge at the Sutton Place Hotel has a popular happy hour (3pm to 6pm daily), where the after-work crowd loosens their ties over craft beer flights and discounted highballs. With french fries that are hand cut and crispy chicken wings spiced with sambal chili, the bar snacks go beyond the ordinary.

MAP 1: 845 Burrard St., 604/642-2900, www.suttonplace.com; noon-late daily

Uva Wine & Cocktail Bar

Quiet enough for conversation (except maybe on Saturday evenings when musicians perform live jazz), snug Uva Wine & Cocktail Bar serves creative cocktails, craft beer, and a long list of wines by the glass to a hip crowd. During the day, you can pop in for a coffee, linger with your laptop, or tuck into a plate of pasta. In the evening, arancini, charcuterie plates, or wine-poached mussels make a snack or a light meal.

MAP 1: 900 Seymour St., 604/632-9560, www.uvavancouver.com; 11:30am-2am daily

GAY AND LESBIAN
Celebrities Nightclub

Davie Street, in the West End, is the center of Vancouver's LGBTQ community, where nightspots include Celebrities Nightclub, a frequently packed party-hardy dance club that's open to all, known for its light shows and booming sound system. Stereotype Fridays (9pm-3am) are electronic music nights; Playhouse Saturdays (9pm-3am) get dancers moving with a mix of club hits and house anthems.

MAP 1: 1022 Davie St., 604/681-6180, www.celebritiesnightclub.com; cover varies

Fountainhead Pub

A West End local hangout since 2000, the easygoing Fountainhead Pub is a classic neighborhood bar with a heated patio (especially busy at brunch), a pool table, and room to talk. It's long been a popular spot for the area's gay community, although all are welcome. Cocktails get a little racy with drinks like the Porn Star (blue curacao, Sour Puss raspberry, and cranberry juice) or a Slippery Nipple shooter of Sambucca and Bailey's.

MAP 1: 1025 Davie St., 604/687-2222, www.thefountainheadpub.com; 11am-midnight Sun.-Thurs., 11am-2am Fri.-Sat.

SPORTS BARS

Red Card Sports Bar

Want to watch the hockey game? Red Card Sports Bar downtown has 16 HD TVs and two massive projection screens, so you won't miss any of the action. It's not all hockey either, although Vancouver Canucks' games get priority over football, baseball, and other sports. Beers come from around the world, and to ward off mid-match munchies, choose from Italian classics (pizzas, pastas), burgers, sandwiches, or other comfort food.

MAP 1: 560 Smithe St., 604/602-9570, www.redcardsportsbar.ca; 11:30am-1am Sun.-Thurs., 11:30am-2am Fri.-Sat.

Gastown and Chinatown   Map 2

CRAFT BEER

The Alibi Room

Beer lovers need no excuse to visit The Alibi Room, a low-key Gastown pub with 50 taps of local and imported craft beers. Housed in a century-old building with big curved windows, brick walls, and long communal tables, this laid-back bar draws a diverse crowd, united by their love of microbrews. In summer, you can sit on the narrow streetside patio.

MAP 2: 157 Alexander St., 604/623-3383, www.alibi.ca; 5pm-11:30pm Mon.-Thurs., 5pm-12:30am Fri., 10am-12:30am Sat., 10am-11:30pm Sun.

Six Acres

In Vancouver's oldest brick building, near the Gassy Jack statue, this cozy pub has a rotating selection of local beers (with more options in the bottle) and a menu of creatively comforting small plates. It's a good place to meet up for drinks and conversation.

MAP 2: 203 Carrall St., 604/488-0110, http://sixacres.ca; 11:30am-11:30pm Sun.-Thurs., 11:30am-12:30am Fri.-Sat.

LIVE MUSIC

Guilt & Company

A club within a club, Guilt & Company, on the lower level beneath Chill Winston, has live music most nights. The lineup is eclectic, from swing, reggae, and alt-rock to spoken word and burlesque. Admission for most shows ranges from pay-what-you-can to $20; starting times vary, too, so check their website for details.

MAP 2: 1 Alexander St., 604/288-9575, www.guiltandcompany.com; 8pm-late daily; cover $0-20

COCKTAIL BARS AND LOUNGES

✪ The Pourhouse

With a name like The Pourhouse, you'd expect a joint that serves great cocktails—and you'd be right. The resident mixologists at this upscale Gastown saloon, set in a 1910 building lit with vintage lamps, concoct drinks like the Alamo Flip (a blend of tequila, house-made root beer, chocolate bitters, egg, and cinnamon) and the Old Pal (rye, vermouth, and Campari). Enjoy yours at the 38-foot (11.5-meter) bar, crafted from reclaimed Douglas fir planks.

MAP 2: 162 Water St., 604/568-7022, www.pourhousevancouver.com; 5pm-midnight Sun.-Thurs., 5pm-1am Fri.-Sat.

Chill Winston

On a mild evening, join the crowds for drinks on the patio at Chill Winston, where you have a front-row seat for Gastown's street life. While it's nice enough inside, with brick walls and low lighting, it's buzzing with both locals and tourists outdoors. Cocktails like the Ritual Sacrifice (Victoria gin, Aperol, grapefruit tea, lemon, and peach bitters) stand up to sharing plates that include charcuterie boards, flatbread pizzas, and poutine with Jack Daniels gravy.

MAP 2: 3 Alexander St., 604/288-9575, www.chillwinston.com; 11:30am-midnight daily

The Diamond

A lively speakeasy-style cocktail bar with exposed brick walls and tall windows overlooking Gastown's Maple Leaf Square, The Diamond groups its cocktails by adjective, such as refreshing, proper, and notorious. There's a short menu of sushi, charcuterie, and sandwiches to snack on, too.

MAP 2: 6 Powell St., 604/568-8272, http://di6mond.com; 5:30pm-1am Mon.-Thurs., 5:30pm-2am Fri.-Sat., 5:30pm-midnight Sun.

The Keefer Bar

The Keefer Bar, a swank Chinatown hideout, concocts aromatic cocktails using house-made bitters, teas, and syrups. Join the well-dressed crowd in this dark den, and pair the Opium Sour (bourbon, grapefruit, tamarind, lemon, and poppy-seed tincture) or the Bloody Ming (vodka, guava, lemon, Worcestershire, and Tabasco) with the Asian-inspired small plates.

MAP 2: 135 Keefer St., 604/688-1961, www.thekeeferbar.com; 5pm-1am Sun.-Thurs., 5pm-2am Fri.-Sat.

WINE BARS
Salt Tasting Room

A wine bar hidden in a Gastown alley, tiny Salt Tasting Room offers a long list of wines by the glass that's strong on B.C. labels, along with craft beers, ciders, and a selection of whiskeys. In this warm, inviting room, with solid wooden tables and brick walls, you can pair your drinks with a cheese and charcuterie board, then nibble and sip the night away.

MAP 2: 45 Blood Alley, 604/633-1912, www.salttastingroom.com; 4pm-late daily

Yaletown and False Creek Map 3

CRAFT BEER
✪ 33 Acres Brewing

You can sample a flight or raise a glass at 33 Acres Brewing, which draws a casual hipster crowd to its 60-seat tasting room between Cambie and Main Streets, a sleek white-walled space with shared tables and stools along the counter. Their well-regarded brews include 33 Acres of Sunshine (a blond summer ale) and 33 Acres of Darkness (a malty dark beer). Six-ounce samplers are $2; you can put together a flight of up to four. Food trucks park here regularly, and the weekend waffle brunch has legions of fans.

MAP 3: 15 W. 8th Ave., 604/620-4589, www.33acresbrewing.com; 9am-11pm Mon.-Fri., 10am-11pm Sat.-Sun.

Brassneck Brewery

The communal tables in the compact Main Street tasting room at hip Brassneck Brewery fill up fast, particularly on weekend evenings, with fans of their frequently changing small-batch brews. Perhaps it's not surprising that Brassneck is the craft brewery that other local brewers often recommend. Choose from 8-10 different brews, which might include their signature Brassneck Ale, a straightforward pale ale; the dry-hopped Passive Aggressive pale ale; or Old Bitch, an English bitter. Six-ounce samples are $2.50, a flight of four is $8. There's no kitchen, but food trucks are frequently parked outside.

MAP 3: 2148 Main St., 604/259-7686, www.brassneck.ca; 2pm-11pm Mon.-Fri., noon-11pm Sat.-Sun.

Central City Brew Pub

Known for their Red Racer label, especially the popular IPA, Central City has been making beer at their brewery in the Vancouver suburb of Surrey since 2003. Their brewpub in Yaletown, a roomy warehouse-style space with a long bar, exposed brick walls, and communal wooden tables, showcases Central City's own brews and other local varieties from 40 taps. Close to the sports arenas, it attracts hockey and soccer fans; if you're not headed for the game, you can sip your beer here and watch the match on TV.

MAP 3: 871 Beatty St., 778/379-2489, http://centralcitybrewing.com; 11am-midnight Sun.-Thurs., 11am-1am Fri.-Sat.

PUBS

✪ Tap & Barrel

With a sunny patio facing False Creek lined with their signature red umbrellas, the Olympic Village branch of local pub chain Tap & Barrel is perpetually packed on summer days. Yet, even in winter, you can take in the city views through the oversize windows. They serve a long list of B.C. beer on tap, from producers like 33 Acres, Four Winds, and Whistler Brewing. Order a flight of five ($10.50) to sample a few different options. They've got taps for B.C. wines as well. The comfort food menu amps up basic pub fare with dishes like a PBJ burger (slathered with chipotle peanut butter and bacon jam) and craft beer macaroni and cheese. For an interesting brunch twist, try the pork belly and soft egg pizza. You'll find other Tap & Barrel locations downtown and in North Vancouver. The company also runs smaller Tap Shack pubs (http://tapshack.ca).

MAP 3: 1 Athletes Way, 604/685-2223, www.tapandbarrel.com; 11am-midnight Mon.-Fri., 10am-midnight Sat.-Sun.

Yaletown Brewing Company

The always-busy Yaletown Brewing Company, with a rotating selection of taps, is a lively spot to meet up for a drink or bring the gang for appetizers and a beer. It can get loud inside, so ask for a table on the wraparound patio, where the added benefit is a front row seat for the Yaletown neighborhood scene. Look over the lengthy menu of sandwiches, salads, pizzas, and other pub fare if you need sustenance with your brews.

MAP 3: 1111 Mainland St., 604/681-2739, www.mjg.ca/yaletown; 11:30am-midnight Sun.-Wed., 11:30am-1am Thurs., 11:30am-3am Fri.-Sat.

Yaletown Brewing Company

LIVE MUSIC
Frankie's Jazz Club

A venue for serious jazz fans, Frankie's Jazz Club hosts performances by local and international musicians several nights a week. More casual music sessions, with no cover charge, take place during happy hour, 4pm to 6pm Wednesday through Friday. Sax player Cory Weeds, a longtime fixture on Vancouver's jazz scene, is a frequent performer. Other musicians who've entertained here include Canadian acoustic string ensemble Van Django; Los Angeles-born bassist, singer, and bandleader Katie Thiroux; and New York-based pianist and composer Helen Sung, performing with her quartet.

MAP 3: 765 Beatty St., 778/727-0337, www.coastaljazz.ca; hours vary by performer; cover $15-30

LOUNGES
✪ Opus Bar

In the lobby of Yaletown's hip Opus Hotel Vancouver, the Opus Bar is styled like a trendy living room, where well-dressed young people gather in curvaceous lounge chairs in front of the fireplace to chat over drinks like the Little Chile (pisco, campari, egg white, and orange blossom water) or Room 207 (tequila, Cointreau, Galliano, and citrus). Come at happy hour (3pm-6pm) for discounted drinks and snacks. Earlier in the day (7:30am-1:30pm), you can linger over coffee, pastries, and freshly made waffles.

MAP 3: 322 Davie St., 866/642-6787, http://vancouver.opushotel.com; 7:30am-late daily

Granville Island

Map 4

the patio at Dockside Lounge

CRAFT BEER
Dockside Lounge

At the east end of Granville Island, connected to the Granville Island Hotel, Dockside Brewing Company has been making craft beer since 2001. Among their long-running classics are the Cartwright Pale Ale and Johnston Street Pilsner. For brews with water views, take a seat in their Dockside Lounge, which looks out across False Creek, a perfect spot for drinks on a sunny afternoon. Even if you sit inside, you can check out the vistas through the expansive windows.

MAP 4: Granville Island Hotel, 1253 Johnston St., 604/685-7070, www. docksidevancouver.com; 11:30am-11pm daily

LIVE MUSIC
Backstage Lounge

In the same building as the Granville Island Stage, next to the Public Market, the Backstage Lounge overlooks the water and city skyline. Several nights a week, this cozy pub hosts an eclectic lineup of live music, featuring local artists performing everything from indie rock to world music to open-mic jams.

MAP 4: 1585 Johnston St., 604/687-1354, www.thebackstagelounge.com; 5pm-2am Mon.-Fri., noon-2am Sat., noon-midnight Sun.; cover $7-12

Kitsilano

Map 5

PUBS
Corduroy

Looking for an offbeat way to spend an evening? Corduroy, an eclectic pub near Kitsilano Beach, is best known for its Rock Paper Scissors tournaments that take place on Monday nights, popular with local university students and 20-somethings. Part game night and part comedy show, the fun starts at 10pm, but plan to arrive by 9pm or earlier to nab a seat. If you laugh so hard that you work up an appetite, you can munch on pizzas, tacos, wings, and poutine.

MAP 5: 1943 Cornwall Ave., 604/733-0162, www.corduroyrestaurant.com; 4pm-2am Mon.-Sat., 4pm-midnight Sun.

Local Public Eatery

Although it's not actually local to Vancouver (it's part of a Canada-wide chain), the Local Public Eatery is a lively spot to grab a beer and a bite to eat, with a beach bar vibe. They offer a rotating selection of beer on tap, with a mix of commercial and craft varieties, while the food runs to burgers and other pub fare. The sunny umbrella-lined patio seats opposite Kitsilano Beach are packed with beachgoers and sunseekers all summer.

MAP 5: 2210 Cornwall Ave., 604/734-3589, http://localkits.com; 11am-1am Mon.-Thurs., 11am-2am Fri., 10am-2am Sat., 10am-1am Sun.

The Wolf and Hound

A traditional Irish pub, The Wolf and Hound has a classic wooden bar and pours a proper pint from its changing selection of local and Irish taps. On Thursday, Friday, and Saturday evenings, typically starting around 8:30pm, there's live music, with bands playing folk, Celtic, and other tunes.

MAP 5: 3617 W. Broadway, 604/738-8909, www.wolfandhound.ca; 4pm-midnight Mon., noon-midnight Tues.-Thurs., noon-1am Fri.-Sat., 11am-11pm Sun.

Cambie Corridor Map 6

COCKTAIL BARS AND LOUNGES

The Cascade Room

A comfortable neighborhood lounge with exposed wood beams and a garage door-style front window, The Cascade Room specializes in classic cocktails, from daiquiris, negronis, and margaritas to many variations on the martini. Like any good Main Street watering hole, they serve a selection of local microbrews, too, with a rotating roster of guest taps. You won't go hungry here either, with a cascade of updated pub fare like burgers, mussels and fries, or Scotch eggs sharing the table with larger plates that range from wild salmon to venison chops.

MAP 6: 2616 Main St., 604/709-8650,

www.thecascade.ca; 11am-1am Mon.-Thurs., 11am-2am Fri.-Sat., 11am-midnight Sun.

The Shameful Tiki Room

If you're longing for a holiday in the Polynesian islands or a classic tiki bar, there's no shame in spending an evening at The Shameful Tiki Room, Main Street's homage to kitschy tiki lounges. In the dimly lit space, adorned with palm fronds, masks, and tapa cloth, you can sip a Singapore sling, a zombie, or other vintage cocktail, while grazing on pupus like Hawaiian-style ribs or teriyaki chicken wings.

MAP 6: 4362 Main St., no phone, www.shamefultikiroom.com; 5pm-midnight Sun.-Thurs., 5pm-1am Fri.-Sat.

CRAFT BEER

St. Augustine's

To find out whether your favorite beer is in stock before heading to this easy-going Commercial Drive pub, check the St. Augustine's website, which lists their 60 beer taps and how much of each variety is remaining. The friendly beer-loving staff dispense a vast selection of local craft beer and cider, as well as other brews from the Pacific Northwest and farther afield. Pizzas, burgers, and other bar snacks round out the menu.

MAP 7: 2360 Commercial Dr., 604/569-1911; http://staugustinesvancouver.com; 11am-1am Sun.-Thurs., 11am-2am Fri.-Sat.

PUBS

✪ Storm Crow Tavern

Consider yourself a nerd? Then this Commercial Drive pub, which bills itself as "Vancouver's Original Nerd Bar," is your place. Its walls decorated with ray guns and science fiction photos, Storm Crow Tavern hosts nerd trivia nights (first and third Tuesday of the month), provides stacks of board games to play, and shows sci-fi (never sports!) on their TVs. To pair with locally made craft beer, the nerd-themed munchies run from Romulan Wings of Vengeance (chicken wings) to Patton Oswalt's Sadness Bowl (which involves a mess of french fries, chili, cheese, gravy, and meat) to the Dungeon Master's Sinister Sundae.

the sunny patio at Havana

MAP 7: 1305 Commercial Dr., 604/566-9669, www.stormcrowtavern.com; 11am-1am Mon.-Sat., 11am-midnight Sun.

Havana

Open since 1996, this Commercial Drive fixture is a pub, restaurant, art gallery, and performance space rolled into one. Havana serves Cuban-inspired cocktails and Latin-influenced bar food out on their heated watch-the-world-go-by patio and in their cozy interior. An eclectic musical lineup performs on a small stage several nights a week—comedy, magic, fringe theater, and more.

MAP 7: 1212 Commercial Dr., 604/253-9119, www.havanarestaurant.ca; 10am-11pm Sun.-Thurs., 10am-midnight Fri.-Sat.

La Mezcaleria

The front door of La Mezcaleria proclaims: *"Para Todo Mal Mezcal, Para Todo Bien Tambien"* ("For everything bad, mescal, and for everything good,

snacks at La Mezcaleria

too.") If that's your philosophy, then raise a glass at this lively Mexican pub that pours a large selection of mescal, tequila, and south-of-the-border cocktails. Nibble some ceviche or guacamole while you sip. There's a second location in Gastown.

MAP 7: 1622 Commercial Dr., 604/559-8226, www.lamezcaleria.ca; 5pm-11pm Tues., 11am-11pm Wed.-Thurs., 11am-midnight Fri., 9am-midnight Sat., 9am-11pm Sun.

ARTS AND CULTURE

Vancouver's major cultural institutions include a symphony orchestra, ballet and opera companies, and local repertory theaters, with the majority of these arts organizations performing downtown, on Granville Island, and on the University of British Columbia campus. Throughout the city, smaller venues, like the Vancouver East Cultural Centre near Commercial Drive, host plays, dance performances, concerts, and other productions featuring local, national, and international performers. Special events, including annual jazz, folk music, fringe theater, and film festivals, round out the cultural calendar.

The Vancouver Symphony Orchestra performs at the Orpheum Theatre.

Vancouver's gallery scene is particularly strong on works by aboriginal artists from British Columbia and along North America's west coast. Several Gastown galleries specialize in art by First Nations and Inuit artists, as do galleries on Granville Island and on nearby South Granville Street. For other contemporary art, explore Granville Island or head for The Flats, an emerging arts district centered off East 2nd Avenue, at Main Street.

For local event listings, see the *Georgia Straight* (www.straight.com), the *Vancouver Theatre Guide* (www.gvpta.ca) from the Greater Vancouver Professional Theatre Association, or *Inside Vancouver* (www.insidevancouver.ca). The blog Miss 604 (www.miss604.com) also publishes monthly lists of upcoming events.

HIGHLIGHTS

☀ **HOW TO GET ACQUAINTED WITH ABORIGINAL ART:** Wander through the spacious **Coastal Peoples Fine Arts Gallery,** which specializes in Northwest Coast and Inuit artwork, displaying masks, carvings, jewelry, and more (page 139).

☀ **TOP SHOP FOR ABORIGINAL-THEMED GIFTS:** Hill's Native Art stocks T-shirts, jewelry, and books with aboriginal themes, along with high-quality First Nations art (page 139).

☀ **WHERE TO FIND EAGLES, RAVENS, AND OTHER CREATURES:** The museum-like **Eagle Spirit Gallery** displays high-quality stone carvings, totem poles, masks, and more by First Nations and Inuit artists (page 141).

☀ **BEST VARIETY OF CANADIAN ART:** The **Federation of Canadian Artists Gallery** shows work by its emerging and established member artists from across Canada (page 141).

☀ **BEST WAY TO LAUGH YOURSELF SILLY:** Catch a show from the city's top improv troupe, the **Vancouver Theatre Sports League** (page 143).

☀ **BEST PERFORMANCE SPACE:** The **Chan Centre for the Performing Arts** presents jazz, blues, world music, and orchestral concerts in a curvaceous, modern building (page 144).

☀ **WHERE TO SEE WHAT'S NEW IN CANADIAN ART:** Bau-Xi Gallery regularly shows work by a wide range of Canadian painters, photographers, and other artists (page 145).

☀ **TOP SPOT TO BUY A TOTEM POLE:** The **Douglas Reynolds Gallery** shows and sells museum-worthy First Nations art—even totem poles (page 145).

☀ **MOST OFFBEAT THEATER OFFERINGS:** The **Vancouver East Cultural Centre,** aka "The Cultch," presents eclectic, always-interesting theater, dance, and music events, showcasing local, Canadian, and international performers (page 147).

☀ **BEST REASON TO WEAR A RAINBOW:** The annual **Vancouver Pride Festival** celebrates the city's LGBT community with parties, picnics, and a high-spirited parade (page 150).

Downtown and the West End

Map 1

GALLERIES

Pendulum Gallery

In the lobby of the HSBC Building, this small gallery space mounts different exhibits throughout the year. Recent shows have varied from "The Art of Dr. Seuss," to paintings by Newfoundland artist David Blackwood, to "Canstruction," featuring sculptures made entirely from cans of food; the dismantled creations were donated to the local food bank at the end of the exhibition. Also on view in the atrium-style lobby is a massive, swinging stainless steel pendulum, an art piece called *Broken Column* by Alan Storey, which HSBC Bank commissioned. The building's air circulation system provides the power that keeps the pendulum moving.

MAP 1: 885 W. Georgia St., 604/250-9682, www.pendulumgallery.bc.ca; 9am-6pm Mon.-Wed., 9am-9pm Thurs.-Fri., 9am-5pm Sat.; free

THEATER

Tickets Tonight

Tickets Tonight sells same-day, half-price theater tickets from their counter inside the Tourism Vancouver Visitor Centre near Canada Place downtown. Check the current day's availability by phone, on the website, or via their Twitter feed, @TicketsTonight. You have to buy tickets in person, before noon for matinee performances and 4pm for evening shows. Tickets Tonight also sells full-price advance tickets to many local productions.

MAP 1: Tourism Vancouver Visitor Centre, 210-200 Burrard St., 604/684-2787, www.ticketstonight.ca; 9am-5pm daily

MUSIC

CBC Musical Nooners

Looking for lunchtime entertainment? CBC Musical Nooners is a free summertime concert series that brings pop, blues, folk, and world music performers to the plaza in front of the CBC building downtown for an hour of weekday live music. Bring your lunch, if you'd like.

MAP 1: CBC Plaza, 700 Hamilton St., www.cbc.ca; noon Mon.-Fri. early July-mid-Aug., free

Vancouver Opera

Canada's second largest opera company, the Vancouver Opera stages its productions downtown in the 2,765-seat Queen Elizabeth Theatre (650 Hamilton St.) or at the adjacent Vancouver Playhouse (630 Hamilton St.). Recent shows have included Mozart's *The Marriage of Figaro*, the contemporary opera *Dead Man Walking*, and *Stickboy*, a new work about bullying, with a libretto by Canadian spoken word artist Shane Koyczan. Attend a preview talk, free to all ticketholders, an hour before each performance for an introduction to the show. If you're between the ages of 19 and 34, the Vancouver Opera's Get O.U.T. (Get Opera Under Thirty-Five) program sets aside a limited number of $35 tickets for younger patrons at certain performances.

MAP 1: 604/683-0222, www.vancouveropera.ca; $30-165

Vancouver Symphony Orchestra

Established in 1919, the Vancouver Symphony Orchestra performs 150 concerts every year. Their main venue is the historic Orpheum Theatre (601 Smithe St.) downtown. They also play at the Chan Centre for the Performing Arts (6265 Crescent Rd.) on the UBC Campus and at several other spaces. In addition to traditional classical performances, the orchestra presents pops concerts, a new music festival, events for children, and even movie nights, where the musicians accompany a film. If you're under age 35 or a full-time student, sign up online for the All-Access Pass, which lets you buy up to two $15 tickets to many performances.

MAP 1: 604/876-3434, www.vancouversymphony.ca; $20-95

DANCE
Ballet BC

Vancouver's professional contemporary ballet company, Ballet BC presents several productions a year at the Queen Elizabeth Theatre downtown. The company's repertoire emphasizes works from the late 20th century to the present day, created by choreographers from Canada and around the world. They frequently stage new pieces by B.C.-based choreographers, including Crystal Pite, Wen Wei Wang, and the company's own artistic director, Emily Molnar. They have also collaborated with international choreographers, including Barcelona's Cayetano Soto and Ohad Naharin of Israel's Batsheva Dance Company.

MAP 1: 650 Hamilton St., 855/985-2787, www.balletbc.com; $22-92

DanceHouse

Fans of contemporary and modern dance should check out the offerings from DanceHouse, which brings Canadian and international dance companies to downtown's Vancouver Playhouse stage. They produce several shows each year. In recent seasons, Les Ballets Jazz de Montréal, Brazil's Companhia Urbana de Dança, and Hofesh Shechter from the UK are among the groups that have taken the stage. DanceHouse also presented *Betroffenheit*, a unique dance-theater collaboration between two Vancouver-based organizations, Kidd Pivot Dance and the Electric Company Theatre.

MAP 1: 630 Hamilton St., 604/801-6225, www.dancehouse.ca; $40-80

COMEDY
The Comedy Mix

Stand-up comics perform several nights a week at The Comedy Mix, a cabaret-style comedy club at the Century Plaza Hotel downtown. Among the comedians who've taken the stage here are Charlie Demers (a Vancouver-based performer who's a regular on CBC Radio's *The Debaters*), Maria Bamford (known for her web series *The Maria Bamford Show*), and Al Madrigal, who has appeared on *The Daily Show*. Tuesdays are "ProAm" nights, where aspiring comedians try out their material, while more established performers make you laugh later in the week.

MAP 1: 1015 Burrard St., 604/684-5050, www.thecomedymix.com; shows 8:30pm Tues.-Thurs., 8pm and 10:30pm Fri.-Sat.; $8-20

GALLERIES
✪ Coastal Peoples Fine Arts Gallery

Coastal Peoples Fine Arts Gallery specializes in Northwest Coast and Inuit artwork in their spacious, modern gallery in a brick Gastown building. On view are masks, carvings, and jewelry, with works ranging in price from several hundred to thousands of dollars.
MAP 2: 312 Water St., 604/684-9222, www.coastalpeoples.com; 10am-7pm daily mid-Apr.-mid-Oct., 10am-6pm daily mid-Oct.-mid-Apr.; free

✪ Hill's Native Art

Lloyd and Frances Hill first began showing and selling native art after they acquired the Koksilah General Store on Vancouver Island's east coast in 1946. Their business has grown to several locations, housing one of North America's largest collections of Northwest Coast native art. Three-story Hill's Native Art in Gastown carries a large range of First Nations and Inuit works, from souvenir-style items to fine art. Head for the top floor, where a wall of windows looks out over Water Street, to find high-quality artworks, carvings, and more by noted aboriginal artists. On the lower levels, they carry T-shirts printed with native designs, jewelry, books, cards, and heavy wool Cowichan sweaters.
MAP 2: 165 Water St., 604/685-4249, www.hills.ca; 9am-9pm daily; free

Inuit Gallery of Vancouver

A specialist in Canadian aboriginal art, the Inuit Gallery of Vancouver, which has been operating since 1979, exhibits works by First Nations and Inuit people in their light and open second-floor Gastown space. They showcase an extensive collection of sculpture, carved from stone, alabaster, or bone. They also show drawings, prints, wall hangings, carvings, and jewelry.
MAP 2: 206 Cambie St., 604/688-7323, www.inuit.com; 10am-6pm Mon.-Sat., 11am-5pm Sun.; free

Urban Aboriginal Fair Trade Gallery

On the main floor of Skwachàys Lodge, a boutique aboriginal art hotel, the small Urban Aboriginal Fair Trade Gallery showcases works by Canadian aboriginal artists, including many from British Columbia. The nonprofit Vancouver Native Housing Society owns the gallery, and proceeds from the prints, carvings, and jewelry sold here help support the society's mission to provide affordable urban housing for aboriginal people.
MAP 2: 29 W. Pender St., 604/558-3589, www.urbanaboriginal.org; 10am-4pm Mon.-Fri., 11am-5pm Sat.-Sun.; free

THEATER
Firehall Arts Centre

A venue for diverse theatrical, dance, and musical productions, the 136-seat Firehall Arts Centre is housed in a 1906 former city fire station on the edge of Chinatown. From the exterior, with its brightly painted garage doors, the building still resembles the fire station that it was until the 1970s. The theater produces contemporary works that highlight Canada's multicultural communities, with productions throughout the year by an assortment of companies and performers.

MAP 2: 280 E. Cordova St., 604/689-0926; http://firehallartscentre.ca; tickets $23-33

CINEMA
Movies in the Morgue

The Vancouver Police Museum, located in the former city morgue, presents a monthly film series, Movies in the Morgue, on the second Tuesday of the month September through May. Though the setting may be spooky, they're not all horror films. They do sell out, so book tickets at least a few days in advance on the museum website.

MAP 2: 240 E. Cordova St., 604/665-3346, www.vancouverpolicemuseum.ca; 2nd Tues. of the month Sept.-May; tickets $10

Yaletown and False Creek Map 3

GALLERIES
Contemporary Art Gallery

The Contemporary Art Gallery shows eclectic works by modern artists. Even if you just walk by the small Yaletown exhibit space, check out the windows, where there's often an unusual or thought-provoking display.

MAP 3: 555 Nelson St., 604/681-2700, www.contemporaryartgallery.ca; noon-6pm Tues.-Sun.; suggested donation $5

Equinox Gallery

Several contemporary art galleries cluster in The Flats district, near the intersection of Main Street and East 2nd Avenue, close to the Olympic Village. The largest is the 14,500-square-foot (1,347-square-meter) Equinox Gallery, in a bright orange building that once housed a tractor company, which mounts regular exhibitions of work by established Canadian artists.

MAP 3: 525 Great Northern Way, 604/736-2405, www.equinoxgallery.com; 10am-5pm Tues.-Sat.; free

Monte Clark Gallery

Monte Clark Gallery, in the same former industrial building as the Equinox Gallery, shows work by contemporary Canadian artists. Among the creatives that the gallery represents are Vancouver artist Roy Arden, Toronto-based Scott McFarland, and lighting designer Omer Arbel.

MAP 3: 525 Great Northern Way, 604/730-5000, www.monteclarkgallery. com; 10am-5:30pm Tues.-Sat.; free

Winsor Gallery

Established in 2002 and relocated from the South Granville district in 2012, the Winsor Gallery represents Canadian and international contemporary artists, including Patrick Hughes (known for his "reverspective" optical illusion paintings), sculptor Alexander Calder, and text artist Ben Skinner. Check the gallery website for a calendar of shows and artists' receptions.

MAP 3: 258 E. 1st Ave., 604/681-4870, www.winsorgallery.com; 10am-6pm Tues.-Fri., 10am-5pm Sat.; free

THEATER
Goldcorp Stage at the BMO Theatre Centre

The Arts Club Theatre Company, Vancouver's leading repertory theater, performs on three stages, presenting their more experimental works in the Olympic Village at the Goldcorp Stage at the BMO Theatre Centre. This striking contemporary building features a multistory, glass-walled lobby. Recent productions in the 250-seat theater have included *Peter and the Starcatcher,* a prequel to the Peter Pan story; *Onegin,* a new musical based on the poem by Pushkin and opera by Tchaikovsky; and *As I Lay Dying,* an adaptation of William Faulkner's southern gothic novel.

MAP 3: 162 W. 1st Ave., 604/687-1644, www.artsclub.com; $29-49

DANCE
Scotiabank Dance Centre

A variety of dance events, from ballet and modern to flamenco and Bollywood, take place throughout the year at Scotiabank Dance Centre, a Yaletown theater and rehearsal complex, opened in 2001, with seven studio spaces. The Discover Dance! series includes one-hour lunchtime performances by a varied range of B.C.-based companies, while the Global Dance Connections series showcases contemporary works by local and international performers. Among the recent events are *Sweat Baby Sweat,* a duet by Flemish choreographer Jan Martens; *empty. swimming.pool,* a collaboration between Vancouver-based Tara Cheyenne Friedenberg and Italy's Silvia Gribaudi; and a new work by Vancouver's Wen Wei Dance, led by dancer and choreographer Wen Wei Wang, who formerly performed with Ballet BC.

MAP 3: 677 Davie St., 604/606-6400, www.thedancecentre.ca; $14-36

Granville Island   Map 4

GALLERIES
✪ Eagle Spirit Gallery

The large, museum-like Eagle Spirit Gallery specializes in Northwest Coast native art. Stone carvings, sculptures, totem poles, wood carvings, masks, and paintings by First Nations and Inuit artists are among the original high-quality works on view.

MAP 4: 1803 Maritime Mews, 604/801-5277 or 888/801-5277, www.eaglespiritgallery.com; 11am-5pm Tues.-Sun., free

✪ Federation of Canadian Artists Gallery

Founded in 1941 by several noted Canadian landscape painters from the Group of Seven, the Federation of Canadian Artists now has more than 2,000 members, including both established and emerging artists. In a large corner space at the east end of Cartwright Street, their Granville Island gallery exhibits work by member artists from across Canada.

MAP 4: 1241 Cartwright St., 604/681-2744, www.artists.ca; 10am-4pm Tues.-Fri., 10am-1pm and 1:30pm-4pm Sat.-Sun.; free

the Arts Club Theatre Company's Granville Island Stage

Crafthouse

Crafthouse, located in a cute little house, shows work by members of the Craft Council of British Columbia. Look for pieces in ceramic, glass, wood, textiles, and other media. They stock a large selection of handcrafted jewelry.

MAP 4: 1386 Cartwright St., 604/687-6511, www.craftcouncilbc.ca; 10am-6pm daily May-Aug., 10:30am-5:30pm daily Sept.-Apr.; free

Gallery of B.C. Ceramics

Owned by the nonprofit Potters Guild of British Columbia, the Gallery of B.C. Ceramics displays and sells decorative and functional pottery and ceramic work, including mugs, vases, and wall hangings, in a range of prices. In a metal-clad warehouse-style building, they also host periodic special exhibitions of ceramic art.

MAP 4: 1359 Cartwright St., 604/669-3606, www.bcpotters.com; 10:30am-5:30pm daily Feb.-Dec., 10:30am-5:30pm Tues.-Sun. Jan.; free

THEATER
Arts Club Theatre Company

Vancouver's top repertory theater and the largest theater company in western Canada, the Arts Club Theatre Company performs on three stages around the city. On Granville Island, their shows are held at the Granville Island Stage, next to the Public Market. At this 440-seat venue, the Arts Club produces new plays, contemporary works, and eclectic musicals. Recent productions have included *Mom's the Word* (from a Vancouver-based playwrights' collective), *The Men in White* (by Indian Canadian author Anosh Irani), and *Avenue Q*, the racy puppet musical.

MAP 4: 1585 Johnston St., 604/687-1644, www.artsclub.com; $29-49

Carousel Theatre for Young People

If you're traveling with kids, see what's on stage at Granville Island's Carousel Theatre for Young People, a theater and troupe that produces shows for toddlers through teens. Some productions take place on their own small stage, while others are held in the larger Waterfront Theatre across the street or at other nearby venues; confirm the location when you buy your tickets. Recent productions have included *Sultans of the Street*, by Indo-Canadian playwright Anusree Roy; *A Charlie Brown Christmas*; and *Dr. Seuss' The Cat in the Hat*.

MAP 4: 1411 Cartwright St., 604/669-3410, www.carouseltheatre.ca; adults $25, seniors and students $21, ages 17 and under $12.50

Performance Works

The building that houses Performance Works, a theater space used by a variety of performers and companies, including the Vancouver Fringe Festival in September, was once a machine shop, built in the 1920s. Nowadays, it no longer resembles its industrial origins; the performance area can be configured for auditorium or cabaret-style seating for 150-200 people.

MAP 4: 1218 Cartwright St., 604/687-3020, www.performanceworks.ca; prices vary

Waterfront Theatre

Confusingly, the Waterfront Theatre isn't actually located on the waterfront, but this 224-seat auditorium-style performance space hosts festivals, theater events, and other performances throughout the year. It's a mainstage venue for the annual Vancouver Fringe Festival in September.

MAP 4: 1412 Cartwright St., 604/685-1731, www.waterfronttheatre.ca; prices vary

COMEDY
✪ Vancouver Theatre Sports League

Established in 1980, the popular Vancouver Theatre Sports League performs always-entertaining improv shows at their cabaret-style waterside theater on Granville Island. Among their recent productions are *Firecracker!* with an all-women improv cast; *OK Tinder—Swipe Right Comedy*, a send-up of Vancouver's dating scene; and *Laugh Till Your Face Hurts*, a two-team improv competition. Most shows have mature themes and aren't appropriate for kids. Prices vary depending on the day and time of the show, with the least expensive performances occurring on Sunday, Wednesday, and Thursday evenings. Have a drink before or after the performance in their lounge overlooking False Creek.

MAP 4: 1502 Duranleau St., 604/738-7013, www.vtsl.com; showtimes vary Wed.-Sun.; adults $8-24, seniors and students $8-19

Kitsilano   Map 5

THEATER
Bard on the Beach

From June through September, the Bard on the Beach Shakespeare Festival performs several of Shakespeare's plays under billowing white tents in Kitsilano's Vanier Park. Established in 1990, this professional theater company has a dramatic performance space: The back of the mainstage tent is open to views of the waterfront and North Shore mountains.

MAP 5: Vanier Park, Whyte Ave., 604/739-0559, http://bardonthebeach.org; adults $20-67, ages 6-22 $20-29

UBC and Point Grey   Map 5

GALLERIES
Morris and Helen Belkin Art Gallery

The Morris and Helen Belkin Art Gallery on the UBC campus mounts several exhibitions every year, highlighting Canadian and international contemporary art from the second half of the 20th century to the present. In particular, their shows emphasize Canadian avant-garde artists of the 1960s and '70s, as well as emerging artists. In its boxy modernist building, opened in 1995, the gallery also exhibits works from the 2,500-object University Art Collection, including their significant holdings of collages, drawings, paintings, and prints by British Columbia's Jack Shadbolt. Works by Emily Carr, Lawren Harris (a founding member of the Group of Seven, early 20th-century Canadian landscape artists), and First Nations artist Lawrence Paul Yuxweluptun are also among their collections. The gallery is closed between exhibitions, so call or check the website before making a special trip.

MAP 5: 1825 Main Mall, 604/822-2759, www.belkin.ubc.ca; 10am-5pm Tues.-Fri., noon-5pm Sat.-Sun.; free

THEATER
Frederic Wood Theatre

The well-regarded UBC Theatre Department produces several plays every year with all-student casts in the Frederic Wood Theatre on campus. The season might include works from Shakespeare's era to modern times; recent productions have ranged from Christopher Marlowe's *Edward II* to Caryl Churchill's *Love and Information* and *Les Belles-soeurs* by Quebecois playwright Michel Tremblay. Most performances are held Wednesday through Saturday evenings between late September and April. Admission to the preview show, held the night before each play's official opening, is only $7 per person.

MAP 5: 6354 Crescent Rd., 604/822-2678, http://theatrefilm.ubc.ca; adults $24.50, seniors $16.50, students $11.50, ages 16 and under $5

MUSIC
✪ Chan Centre for the Performing Arts

On the UBC campus, the modern Chan Centre for the Performing Arts hosts jazz, blues, and world music performers, as well as early music and chamber concerts. The wide-ranging events calendar might feature a student musical group one day and an internationally known artist the next, from jazz musician Herbie Hancock to Mongolian throat singers Anda Union and flamenco guitarist Paco Peña. The Vancouver Symphony performs here periodically as well. Opened in 1997, the curvaceous contemporary building, surrounded by evergreens, has a 1,185-seat concert hall and several smaller performance spaces.

MAP 5: 6265 Crescent Rd., 604/822-2697, www.chancentre.com; prices vary

Jericho Folk Club

On Tuesday evenings from May to September, Vancouver folk music fans congregate at the Jericho Sailing Centre in Point Grey, where the Jericho Folk Club presents programs of local or touring musicians performing acoustic music in a casual setting. Doors open at 7:15pm, with an "open stage" segment, typically featuring four performers, each doing 15 minute sets, starting at 8pm. The feature act begins at about 9:15. Check their website for a season calendar.

MAP 5: Jericho Sailing Centre, 1300 Discovery St.; www.jerichofolkclub.ca; Tues. May-Sept., $10

Cambie Corridor Map 6

GALLERIES

⊕ Bau-Xi Gallery

See what's on view at Bau-Xi Gallery, which features regular showings of contemporary fine art in an airy, white South Granville space. Established in 1965, the gallery represents a wide range of Canadian painters, photographers, sculptors, and other artists.

MAP 6: 3045 Granville St., 604/733-7011, www.bau-xi.com; 10am-5:30pm Mon.-Sat., 11am-5:30pm Sun.; free

⊕ Douglas Reynolds Gallery

Stop into Douglas Reynolds Gallery, a white-walled, two-level space in the South Granville district, to explore the museum-quality exhibits of historic and contemporary Northwest Coast First Nations art, from masks, jewelry, and sculpture to totem poles. The gallery shows works by Bill Reid, Robert Davidson, and other notables, along with pieces by emerging native artists.

MAP 6: 2335 Granville St., 604/731-9292, www.douglasreynoldsgallery.com; 10am-6pm Mon.-Sat., noon-5pm Sun.; free

THEATER

Arts Club Theatre Company

Vancouver's top repertory theater and the largest theater company in western Canada, the Arts Club Theatre Company, which was established in 1958, now performs on three stages. Their main stage shows are held at the 650-seat Stanley Industrial Alliance Stage, a historic theater in the South Granville district. The Arts Club began performing here in 1998 and now produces crowd-pleasing musicals, entertaining comedies, and thought-provoking dramas on the Stanley's stage; recent seasons have included *Billy Elliot, Baskerville: A Sherlock Holmes Mystery,* and *Angels in America.*

MAP 6: 2750 Granville St., 604/687-1644, http://artsclub.com; $29-69

The Flame

The Flame is Vancouver's homegrown storytelling series, modeled after the U.S.-based storytelling organization and National Public Radio show, *The Moth.* The Flame hosts monthly storytelling evenings at the Cottage Bistro on Main Street. The 8-10 preselected performers in each show must abide by The Flame's three rules: Stories must be true, about you, and told in "a few" (typically under 10 minutes).

The Flame is held on the first Wednesday of the month September through November and January through June, although schedules occasionally vary, so check the Cottage Bistro website (www.cottage-bistro.com) to confirm. Shows start at 7pm, but arrive before 6:30pm if you want a seat.

AN AIRPORT ART TOUR

Airports aren't normally designed for lingering (at least voluntarily), but the Vancouver International Airport (YVR) has made visitors' time in the terminals more enjoyable by assembling a striking set of artworks. In fact, the airport now houses one of the world's **largest collections of Northwest Coast native art.** Here's a guide to the notable pieces to look for as you begin or end your Vancouver air travels.

If you're arriving from outside Canada, several pieces of art welcome you into the customs hall. At the top of the escalators above the customs area, *Flight (Spindle Whorl)*, by Susan Point, a Coast Salish artist from the Musqueam First Nation, is the world's largest Coast Salish spindle whorl, measuring 15.7 feet (4.8 meters) in diameter. This circular red cedar carving uses traditional images to illustrate flight. Point also carved the two 17-foot-tall (5.2-meter) *Musqueam Welcome Figures* that flank the escalators into the immigration arrivals area.

Travelers arriving on flights from the United States typically walk through the airport's "Pacific Passage," where *Hetux,* a mythological Thunderbird, appears to fly above the walkway. Artist Connie Watts, who is of Nuu-chah-nulth, Gitxsan, and Kwakwaka'wakw ancestry, crafted the piece from powder-coated aluminum and stained birch panels.

One of the airport's most famous sculptures is located between the U.S. and international departure counters. Haida First Nations artist Bill Reid created *The Spirit of Haida Gwaii: The Jade Canoe,* a jade green bronze cast work, in 1994. Behind Reid's work is *The Great Wave,* Lutz Haufschild's glass wall that depicts B.C.'s ocean and coastline.

In the domestic terminal, a contemporary carved and painted 35-foot (10.69-meter) cedar pole, *Celebrating Flight,* by Haida artist Don Yeomans, incorporates LED lights, Chinese characters, and Celtic knots along with its native imagery. On Level 2, also in the domestic terminal, look for *Hugging the World,* a red cedar carving suspended from the ceiling and depicting Eagle and Raven figures, by notable artist Robert Davidson. In the same area is Richard Hunt's *Thunderbird and Killer Whale* and Dempsey Bob's red cedar *Human/Bear Mask.*

So stay alert to your surroundings as you arrive at or depart from YVR. Beyond the typical coffee shops, baggage carousels, and departure gates, there's a world of native art to explore.

MAP 6: 4470 Main St., 604/876-6138; 7pm 1st Wed. Jan.-June and Sept.-Nov.; by donation

COMEDY

The Sunday Service

No, it's not like going to church. Held in the Fox Cabaret, a former adult theater turned alternative club, The Sunday Service, by the comedy group of the same name, is a weekly improv show. The five performers typically mix short improv games with a longer comedic improvisation. Guest comedians occasionally share the stage with the regular troupe.

MAP 6: Fox Cabaret, 2321 Main St., www. thesundayservice.ca; 9pm Sun.; $7

Yuk Yuk's Vancouver Comedy Club

At this local branch of a national chain of comedy venues, you can chuckle through stand-up shows by local and visiting comedians in this 170-seat cabaret-style club. The two weekend evening shows generally run 90 minutes to two hours and include a warm-up host, an opening act, and the featured performer. Wednesday evenings at 8pm are amateur nights, where newer comics can get their start.

MAP 6: 2837 Cambie St., 604/696-9857, www.yukyuks.com; show times vary; $7-20

Commercial Drive — Map 7

THEATER

⊗ Vancouver East Cultural Centre

The Vancouver East Cultural Centre, known locally as "The Cultch," hosts an eclectic season of theater, dance, and musical events, showcasing local, Canadian, and international performers. Among their recent shows are *The Daisy Theatre,* provocative puppetry by Toronto-based Ronnie Burkett and his 40-plus marionettes; *The Elephant Wrestler,* a drama set in present-day India by New Zealand's Indian Ink Theatre Company; and *Empire of the Son,* a solo show written and performed by former CBC radio host Tetsuro Shigematsu. Their main East Side building houses two performance spaces: the 200-seat Historic Theatre and the small black-box Vancity Culture Lab, which can be configured for 72 to 102 seats. Off-site, they also produce shows at the nearby York Theatre.

MAP 7: 1895 Venables St., 604/251-1363, http://thecultch.com; prices vary

York Theatre

The Vancouver East Cultural Centre produces music, dance, theater, and other events at the restored 355-seat York Theatre, down the street from their main building. Built in 1913, the York started life as the Alcazar Theatre, and over the years, it was home to a movie house, the Vancouver Little Theatre Association, a concert venue (Nirvana played here), and an Indian cinema. More recent productions have included *Elbow Room Café: The Musical,* an original musical based on a Vancouver breakfast joint; *Children of God,* a world premiere about an Oji-Cree family, whose children are sent to a residential school in northern Ontario; and a show from storyteller Edgar Oliver, often featured on the U.S. public radio show *The Moth.*

MAP 7: 639 Commercial Dr.; 604/251-1363, http://thecultch.com; prices vary

Festivals and Events

WINTER

Festival of Lights

The VanDusen Botanical Garden marks the holiday season with its annual Festival of Lights, illuminating its garden paths with thousands of sparkling lights. The festival runs from early December until the beginning of January.

Cambie Corridor: VanDusen Botanical Garden, http://vandusengarden.org; Dec.

Dine Out Vancouver

More than 250 restaurants offer special menus, and you can join in food events, from chef dinners and wine-tastings to food tours, during Dine Out Vancouver, the city's annual celebration of dining that has grown into one of Canada's largest food and drink festivals. The festival runs for two and a half weeks from late January into early February. Organizers publish the event schedule and list of participating restaurants on the Dine Out website in the second week of January. Make reservations right away, since many restaurants and events sell out.

Various locations: www.dineoutvancouver.com; Jan.-Feb.

PuSh International Performing Arts Festival

An eclectic selection of theater, music, dance, and multimedia events brighten up the winter nights at the PuSh International Performing Arts Festival, featuring local and international performers. Taking place at theaters and performance spaces across Vancouver, the festival begins in mid-January and runs for three weeks.

Various locations: http://pushfestival.ca; Jan.-Feb.

Lunar New Year

With its large Asian population, Vancouver hosts plenty of festivities to mark the Lunar New Year, including parades, lion dances, music, fireworks, and other special events in Chinatown and throughout Richmond. Chinatown's Spring Festival Parade draws crowds of nearly 100,000 spectators every year, and nearby, the Dr. Sun Yat-Sen Classical Chinese Garden organizes more New Year's festivities. In Richmond, Aberdeen Centre hosts a week of performances and New Year's events, and on the eve of the Lunar New Year itself, many people welcome the coming year at the International Buddhist Temple.

Chinatown and Richmond: www.cbavancouver.ca, http://vancouverchinesegarden.com, and www.visitrichmondbc.com; Jan.-Feb.

Vancouver International Wine Festival

Wine-tastings, seminars, and dinners show off more than 1,500 wines from around the world at the Vancouver International Wine Festival, a week-long event that usually takes place in mid-February. Many events are held downtown at the Vancouver Convention Centre's West Building, but restaurants and other venues host festivities as well.

Various locations: http://vanwinefest.ca; Feb.

Talking Stick Festival

The 10-day Talking Stick Festival, in late February, typically produces more than two dozen theater, dance, storytelling, and music events by aboriginal performers or featuring aboriginal themes. The Roundhouse Community Arts & Recreation Centre (181 Roundhouse Mews) in Yaletown, the Goldcorp Centre for the Arts at Simon Fraser University (Woodward's Building, 149 W. Hastings St.) in Gastown, and the Vancouver East Cultural Centre (1895 Venables St.) near Commercial Drive stage many of the productions.

Various locations: http://fullcircle.ca; Feb.

Chutzpah! Festival

At the monthlong Chutzpah! Festival, which showcases contemporary and traditional Jewish arts and culture, internationally recognized theater artists, dancers, musicians, and comedians perform in a diverse collection of shows from mid-February through mid-March. The Norman Rothstein Theatre at the Jewish Community Centre of Greater Vancouver (950 W. 41st Ave.) is the festival's home base, although events take place at venues around the city.

Various locations: http://chutzpahfestival.com, Feb.-Mar.

SPRING
Vancouver Sun Run

Close to 50,000 runners and walkers take to the streets for the Vancouver Sun Run, a fun-for-all 10K that starts and ends downtown, usually on the third Sunday in April.

Downtown and the West End: www.vancouversun.com/sunrun; Apr.

Vancouver International Children's Festival

Bring the kids to Kitsilano's Vanier Park when the weeklong Vancouver International Children's Festival offers family-friendly concerts, circus performers, crafts, and other activities in late May and early June.

Kitsilano: Vanier Park, Whyte Ave., www.childrensfestival.ca; May-June

Vancouver Craft Beer Week

A good introduction to the region's growing microbrewery scene, the annual Vancouver Craft Beer Week, normally held the last week of May into the first week of June, includes tasting events and other activities that showcase small brewers and their products.

Various locations: http://vancouvercraftbeerweek.com; May-June

SUMMER
TD Vancouver International Jazz Festival

With nearly two weeks of concerts around the city, from big-name big-ticket shows to free music in the park, the TD Vancouver International Jazz Festival has tunes for any jazz, Latin, funk, and world music lover. The festival runs during the last two weeks of June and early July at venues downtown, in Yaletown, on Granville Island, and elsewhere across town, with popular outdoor concerts in Yaletown's David Lam Park (Pacific Blvd. at Drake St.).

Various locations: www.coastaljazz.ca; June-July

Canada Day

Vancouver celebrates Canada's birthday, Canada Day, with a parade, outdoor concerts, and celebratory fireworks over Burrard Inlet. Canada Place is the center of the festivities. The fireworks, which start at 10:30pm, draw big crowds. You'll need tickets to watch from the outdoor Fireworks Viewing Zone (adults $15) at Canada Place, but you can see them anywhere along Burrard Inlet, including Harbour Green Park on the Coal Harbour Seawall and in Stanley Park near the Nine O'Clock Gun, east of the Brockton Point totem poles.

Downtown and the West End: Canada Place, www.canadaplace.ca; July 1

Vancouver Folk Festival

It's not just folk music at the long-established Vancouver Folk Festival. This musical extravaganza draws world beat, roots, blues, and yes, folk musicians from across Canada and around the world to Jericho Beach for three days of always-eclectic music on multiple outdoor stages. Held the third weekend of July, it's great fun for all ages.

UBC and Point Grey: Jericho Beach, http://thefestival.bc.ca; July

Indian Summer Festival

A unique celebration of South Asian, Canadian, and international culture, the Indian Summer Festival serves up two weeks of films, lectures, food

Vancouver Folk Festival at Jericho Beach

events, theater, and other thought-provoking programming in mid-July. SFU's Goldcorp Centre for the Arts (Woodward's Building, 149 W. Hastings St.) in Gastown hosts many events, as do other venues downtown and elsewhere in the city.

Various locations: http://indiansummerfest.ca; July

Celebration of Light

Fireworks displays over English Bay bring thousands of Vancouverites and visitors out for the Celebration of Light that takes place on three summer evenings. The best viewing spots are at English Bay Beach, but you can see them from Kitsilano Beach and other points around False Creek. Held the last week of July and the first week of August on Wednesday and Saturday evenings, the fireworks start at 10pm. Try to arrive no later than 9pm to find a place to sit; many people come early and bring picnic suppers to enjoy before the displays begin.

Downtown and the West End: http://hondacelebrationoflight.com; July-Aug.

✪ Vancouver Pride Festival

The Vancouver Pride Festival features more than 20 events celebrating the city's large gay, lesbian, bisexual, and transgender community. Several days of parties, cruises, picnics, and other celebrations culminate in a festive parade through the downtown streets on the Sunday before B.C. Day (the first Monday in August).

Downtown and the West End: http://vancouverpride.ca; July-Aug.

FALL

Vancouver Fringe Festival

For two weeks in the first half of September, the Vancouver Fringe Festival takes over Granville Island and other stages around town with in-novative, quirky, and often surprising theater, comedy, puppetry, and story-telling performances. The Waterfront Theatre and Performance Works on

Granville Island host some of the larger performances.

Various locations: www.vancouverfringe.com; Sept.

Vancouver International Film Festival

Movie lovers line up at the Vancouver International Film Festival to see the latest releases from Canadian, American, and international filmmakers. Yaletown's Vancity Theatre (1181 Seymour St.) is the festival's main venue, but films are shown at other theaters downtown, in Gastown, and elsewhere around the city. The two-week festival begins in late September and runs until mid-October.

Various locations: www.viff.org; Sept.-Oct.

Vancouver Writers Fest

The Vancouver Writers Fest, a week of readings, lectures, and other literary events, features more than 100 authors from across Canada and abroad. Most of the festival events, held the third week of October, take place on Granville Island.

Granville Island: www.writersfest.bc.ca; Oct.

EAT! Vancouver Food + Cooking Festival

Dinners featuring chefs from across Canada, cooking workshops, a food expo, and lots of other delicious events draw foodies to the week-long EAT! Vancouver Food + Cooking Festival.

Various locations: http://eat-vancouver.com; Oct.-Nov.

Eastside Culture Crawl

East Vancouver artists open their studios to visitors during the popular Eastside Culture Crawl. Whether you're in the market for artwork or just like to browse, most artists are interested in chatting with visitors during this mid-November weekend. Most of the open studios are located between Gastown and Commercial Drive.

Various locations: www.culturecrawl.ca; Nov.

ACTIVITIES

SPORTS AND ACTIVITIES

Ringed with beaches, crisscrossed with walking and biking paths, and dotted with parks large and small, Vancouver is an active city. Locals take every opportunity to get outside—rain or shine.

cyclists in Stanley Park

In downtown Vancouver, wander amid the towering evergreens in Stanley Park, jog or cycle the Seawall path, or simply enjoy the sunset on the beach. You can kayak or go stand-up paddle-boarding on False Creek or from English Bay, Kitsilano, and Jericho Beaches. Whale-watching outfitters make day trips from Granville Island and Richmond's Steveston Wharf.

The North Shore mountains serve up even more recreational opportunities. Hike the Grouse Grind, explore the rainforest at the Capilano or Lynn Canyon Suspension Bridges or at Lighthouse Park, or kayak from scenic Deep Cove. In winter, when it's raining in the city, it can be snowing on the North Shore peaks, where you can ski, snowboard, snowshoe, or go tubing. Winter tires are recommended on the roads that climb up to the mountains from October to April, particularly at Cypress and Mount Seymour.

If your idea of getting sporty is watching the action from the stands, there's still plenty to do. Join the locals cheering on their National Hockey League team, check out the city's professional soccer or football leagues, or bring the family to see the city's minor league baseball team play at historic Nat Bailey Stadium.

HIGHLIGHTS

✪ **BEST PLACE TO GET SANDY DOWNTOWN:** The busiest of the city-center beaches, **English Bay Beach** is a prime spot for people-watching, swimming, or enjoying the sunset (page 154).

✪ **BEST WAY TO BECOME A TRUE CANADIAN:** Do as the locals do and cheer for the **Vancouver Canucks,** the city's National Hockey League team, who take to the ice at Rogers Arena from October through April (page 156).

✪ **SPORTIEST STRETCH OF SAND:** Appealing to volleyball players, swimmers, kayakers, and stand-up paddleboarders, **Kitsilano Beach** is a hub for all sorts of activities (page 159).

✪ **MOST SCENIC SPOT TO SWIM:** For stellar vistas of the ocean, mountains, and city skyline while you splash around, head for **Kitsilano Pool** (page 159).

✪ **BEST BEACH FOR WATER SPORTS AND A BEER:** Besides its quiet curve of sand, **Jericho Beach** has kayak rentals and tours, wind-surfing rentals, and a popular laid-back pub overlooking the sea (page 160).

✪ **WHERE TO WANDER IN THE RAINFOREST:** Explore the many miles of hiking trails that wind between the tall trees, verdant ferns, and mossy rocks of **Pacific Spirit Regional Park,** a dense rainforest that's even larger than Stanley Park (page 162).

✪ **MOST SCENIC PADDLE:** At North Vancouver's **Deep Cove Kayaks,** you can paddle through the forest-lined coves and majestic fjords of Indian Arm (page 165).

✪ **MOTHER NATURE'S STAIRMASTER:** You'll earn bragging rights when you hike **The Grouse Grind,** a trail with 2,830 steps that takes you to the summit of Grouse Mountain (page 165).

✪ **WHERE TO FIND ANCIENT TREES AND SKYLINE VIEWS:** Explore old-growth forests on easy wooded trails at West Vancouver's **Lighthouse Park,** and enjoy spectacular views across the water toward downtown Vancouver (page 167).

Downtown and the West End

Map 1

BEACHES

✪ English Bay Beach

You don't have to leave downtown Vancouver to go to the beach. English Bay Beach, in the West End, is the busiest of the city-center beaches, fun for people-watching, swimming, or enjoying the sunset. A landmark on English Bay is the Inukshuk, made of granite boulders. This type of traditional Inuit sculpture was used as a trail marker or symbol of welcome. Carver Alvin Kanak, of Rankin Inlet, Nunavut, crafted the 20-foot (six-meter) English Bay Inukshuk, which weighs nearly 70,000 pounds (31,500 kilograms).

You can follow the Seawall path from English Bay into Stanley Park or around to Yaletown. In summer, you can rent kayaks and stand-up paddleboards on the beach from Ecomarine Paddlesports Centre (1700 Beach Ave., 604/689-7575 or 888/425-2925, www.ecomarine.com; 10am-dusk Mon.-Fri., 9am-dusk Sat.-Sun. late May-early Sept.).

MAP 1: Beach Ave. at Denman St., http://vancouver.ca; 6am-10pm daily; free

Sunset Beach

As you'd expect from the name, Sunset Beach, along the Seawall near English Bay, is a west-facing beach with sunset views. Near the beach, built into the hillside at the foot of Broughton Street, is the AIDS Memorial, a

English Bay Beach

public art piece installed in 2004. The names of nearly 800 people from British Columbia who died of AIDS are engraved on its rust-oxidized steel panels.

MAP 1: Beach Ave. at Thurlow St.; http://vancouver.ca; 6am-10pm daily; free

ICE-SKATING
Robson Square Ice Rink

From December through February, you can ice-skate right downtown at the Robson Square Ice Rink, under a dome outdoors beneath Robson Square, near the Vancouver Art Gallery. The rink is particularly busy on weekend afternoons, when families take to the ice, and on Friday and Saturday evenings. You can rent skates ($4) if you don't have your own.

MAP 1: 800 Robson St., 604/209-8316, www.robsonsquare.com; 9am-9pm Sun.-Thurs., 9am-11pm Fri.-Sat. Dec.-Feb.; free

Yaletown and False Creek Map 3

PARKS
David Lam Park

Between Yaletown's condo towers and the waterfront, you can sit by the water in the grassy expanse of David Lam Park, named for the Hong Kong-born philanthropist, real estate mogul, and politician who became Canada's first Asian Canadian lieutenant governor. The 10.7-acre (4.34-hectare) park along the Seawall has a playground, tennis and basketball courts, and plenty of space for picnics. The park hosts free outdoor concerts during the annual Vancouver Jazz Festival in late June.

MAP 3: 1300 Pacific Blvd. at Drake St., http://vancouver.ca; 6am-10pm daily; free

KAYAKING AND STAND-UP PADDLEBOARDING
Creekside Kayaks

False Creek is an especially beautiful spot for a late-in-the-day paddle, with views of the city skyline. At the Olympic Village on False Creek, Creekside Kayaks rents kayaks and stand-up paddleboards from spring through fall.

MAP 3: 1 Athletes Way, 604/616-7453, www.creeksidekayaks.ca; 11am-dusk Mon.-Fri., 9am-5pm Sat.-Sun. mid-Apr.-mid-Oct.; single kayak $20/hour, double kayak $35/hour, paddleboard $20/hour

CYCLING
BIKE RENTALS
Bicycle Sports Pacific

Opposite the Burrard Bridge where Yaletown meets the West End, Bicycle Sports Pacific rents seven-speed cruiser or hybrid bikes. You can reserve a rental in advance or simply drop in when you're ready to ride.

MAP 3: 999 Pacific St., 604/682-4537, http://bspbikes.com; 10am-6pm Mon.-Sat., noon-5pm Sun.; $20/2 hours, $40/day

Reckless Bike Stores

Reckless Bike Stores rents city bikes and cruisers along the Seawall in Yaletown. The shop gets busy on summer weekends, so don't be in a rush when picking up or returning your rental. They have another Yaletown location, which also rents electric bikes (starting at $28 for 1.5 hours), and a branch near Granville Island.

MAP 3: 110 Davie St., 604/648-2600, www.reckless.ca; 9:30am-7pm daily; $19/1.5 hours, $40/day

SPECTATOR SPORTS
✪ Vancouver Canucks

Vancouver is wild for hockey, particularly the city's National Hockey League team, the Vancouver Canucks, whose regular season runs from October through April. The Canucks take to the ice at Rogers Arena (604/899-7400, http://rogersarena.com) on False Creek.

Games are always packed with fans wearing blue Canucks jerseys, but in years when the team is playing well, tickets are in particularly high demand. Expect larger crowds when the Canucks face off against their rivals, including the Calgary Flames, Chicago Blackhawks, and Los Angeles Kings.

Rogers Arena has a place in Olympic hockey history, too. In the 2010 Winter Olympics, the Canadian men's team beat their U.S. rivals here in the gold medal game, a 3-2 overtime cliffhanger, and Canada's women's team took gold on the same ice, winning 2-0 over the United States.

Behind-the-scenes tours (10:30am, noon, and 1:30pm Wed.-Sat.; noon, 1:30pm, and 3pm Sun.; adults $12, seniors and students $8, ages 4-12 $6) of Rogers Arena are offered regularly, although access to certain areas of the building, particularly the locker rooms, isn't guaranteed. Check the arena website to confirm tour schedules. Tours are first-come, first served; meet at the Canucks Team Store, located at Gate 6 (Pat Quinn Way at Pacific Boulevard), at least 10-15 minutes before the scheduled tour time.

MAP 3: 800 Griffiths Way, 604/899-7440

or 800/745-3000, http://canucks.nhl.com; Oct.-Apr.; tickets $55-300

B.C. Lions

Curious about how professional Canadian Football differs from its American cousin? Watch the B.C. Lions run the field at B.C. Place (604/669-2300, www.bcplacestadium.com). Both the U.S. and Canadian versions of the sport got their start back in the 1800s, but they've diverged with a few different rules.

The nine-team Canadian Football League (CFL) plays on a longer and wider field than the National Football League (NFL), making passing more important to the game. Canadian teams have 12 players on the field, compared to 11 in the States, and have three downs rather than four to move the ball 10 yards forward. The CFL season begins in July, and the Canadian equivalent of the Super Bowl, called the Gray Cup, is played in late November. While the CFL isn't the mega-business that the sport has become for the NFL, and it pales in comparison to hockey, plenty of orange-shirted B.C. Lions fans turn out for their local team's games.

MAP 3: 777 Pacific Blvd., 604/589-7627, www.bclions.com; July-Nov.; tickets $35-130

Vancouver Whitecaps

Vancouver's professional Major League Soccer team, the Vancouver Whitecaps, also plays at B.C. Place (604/669-2300, www.bcplacestadium.com). The regular season runs March through October. Since many Vancouver youth, both boys and girls, play soccer themselves, families often bring their kids to Whitecaps games.

The Whitecaps played their first match in 1974, in what was then known as the North American Soccer

CYCLING IN THE CITY

cycling near the Olympic Village

Vancouver is becoming one of North America's top bicycling cities. Throughout the metropolitan area, you can pedal along a growing number of urban cycling routes, from downtown bike lanes to the popular **Seawall** route, which circles Stanley Park and follows False Creek through Yaletown, past the Olympic Village, and on to Granville Island, continuing west to the beaches in Kitsilano and Point Grey. Another city cycling path, the **Central Valley Greenway,** takes you through Vancouver's eastern suburbs.

TIPS FOR CYCLING THE SEAWALL
One of the most pleasant ways to explore Vancouver is by bike on the paved, mostly flat Seawall that follows the water around the outside of Stanley Park and along False Creek. To help ensure a safe cycling excursion, keep these tips in mind:

Stay on the cyclist side of the path. In most places, there's a parallel walking path for pedestrians, but at some points, which are clearly marked, the path is shared.

Watch for pedestrians. Many people unwittingly wander onto the cycling path to snap a photo or enjoy the view. Stay alert whenever pedestrians are nearby.

To avoid collisions, **don't stop suddenly** and make sure no one is directly behind you when you slow down, particularly on the Seawall's narrower stretches. And when you do stop, pull off the path to let other cyclists pass.

Wear a helmet. Vancouver law requires all cyclists to wear a bike helmet.

Note that within Stanley Park, while pedestrians can follow the Seawall in either direction, it's one-way for cyclists. Whether you enter the park near English Bay or Coal Harbour, you must **ride only in a counterclockwise direction**, keeping the water on your right side.

BIKE SHARING IN VANCOUVER
The city of Vancouver has a bike-sharing program that enables you to rent a bike at one location and return it at another. For visitors, the easiest way to use the **Mobi bike share system** (778/655-1800, www.mobibikes.ca) is to sign up online for a day pass. For $7.50 per day, you can take an unlimited number of 30-minute rides within a 24-hour period.

After you register online, you'll receive a seven-digit user code that will unlock your bike. Bikes are stationed throughout the downtown area; search the Mobi website for the bikes nearest to you. Helmets, which local laws require cyclists to wear, are available at each rental station.

If you keep the bike for more than a half hour during any ride, you'll pay an extra $5 for each additional 30 minutes, so it's more cost-effective to dock your bike when you stop to sightsee, shop, or eat. You can check out another bike after your stop.

League. In 2011, the Vancouver club launched its first season as a Major League Soccer team.

MAP 3: 777 Pacific Blvd., 604/669-9283, www.whitecapsfc.com; Mar.-Oct.; tickets $30-80

Granville Island   Map 4

PARKS
Ron Basford Park

The grassy green space known as Ron Basford Park occupies a hilly knoll at the eastern end of Granville Island, between the Granville Island Hotel and Performance Works Theatre. Take a break to sit on the lawn and enjoy the views of False Creek and the city skyline. The park's outdoor amphitheater hosts occasional concerts.

The park is named for the Honorable Stanley Ronald Basford, a member of Parliament and cabinet minister. Basford was instrumental in transforming the island into its current lively collection of studios, shops, markets, and theaters, earning him the nickname, "Mr. Granville Island."

MAP 4: Eastern end of Cartwright and Johnston Sts.; dawn-dusk daily

WHALE-WATCHING
Wild Whales Vancouver

Wild Whales Vancouver offers whale-watching trips leaving from Granville Island from spring through fall. Depending on where the whales are swimming on a particular day, the boats will take you from False Creek, into English Bay, and on the Strait of Georgia, heading either for the Gulf Islands or the San Juan Islands in Washington State, on trips lasting from three to seven hours. The on-board guides will help you spot orcas, Pacific gray whales, humpback whales, and minke whales; you might see seals and various birds along the way, too. While environmental regulations limit how close you can get to the whales, you'll usually come near enough to see them swimming and spouting. A telephoto lens will help you get the best photos. Boats typically carry up to 23 passengers and have bathroom facilities.

MAP 4: 1806 Mast Tower Rd., 604/699-2011, www.whalesvancouver.com; mid-Apr.-Oct.; adults $135, seniors and students $110, ages 3-12 $85

KAYAKING AND STAND-UP PADDLEBOARDING
Ecomarine Paddlesports Centre

From the sheltered waters around Granville Island you get great views of the downtown skyline, making it a good spot to set out in a kayak or on a stand-up paddleboard. Ecomarine Paddlesports Centre rents kayaks and stand-up paddleboards and offers guided kayak and SUP tours. Their last rentals on Granville Island go out three hours before sunset; call to confirm seasonal hours. Be alert for boat traffic.

MAP 4: 1668 Duranleau St., 604/689-7575 or 888/425-2925, www.ecomarine.com; 9am-9pm daily late May-July, 9am-8pm daily Aug.-early Sept., 10am-6pm daily early Sept.-late May; paddleboard rental $19-39 for 1-3 hours, kayak rental $39-85 for 2 hours to full day

Vancouver Water Adventures

Vancouver Water Adventures rents kayaks and stand-up paddleboards, offers tours, rents Jet Skis, and teaches SUP yoga classes. In addition to this branch on Granville Island, they have a seasonal rental location on Kitsilano Beach.

MAP 4: 1812 Boatlift Ln., 604/736-5155, www.vancouverwateradventures.com; May-Sept., hours vary by season; paddleboard rental $20-30/hour; kayak rental $25-35/hour

Kitsilano   Map 5

BEACHES
✪ Kitsilano Beach

Popular Kitsilano Beach, aka Kits Beach, is a good swimming and people-watching spot. In summer, serious beach volleyball players flock here, and you can rent kayaks or stand-up paddleboards. Adjacent to the sandy beach is a children's playground, along with public tennis courts and a grassy lawn for lounging and picnicking.

Around the start of the 20th century, Kits Beach, then known as Greer's Beach after one of its first nonnative settlers, was a popular tent camping area, with many holiday-makers making their way across the water from the fashionable West End. While overnight camping is no longer permitted, you can perch on a log or spread your blanket on the sand to watch the beach action.

Bus 2 from Burrard Street downtown stops directly in front of the beach; get off on Cornwall Avenue at Yew Street. From Kits Beach, you can follow the Seawall path east around Vanier Park (popular with kite-flyers and home to the Museum of Vancouver and the Vancouver Maritime Museum) to Granville Island.

MAP 5: Off Cornwall Ave. between Arbutus and Vine Sts.; http://vancouver.ca; 6am-10pm daily; free

SWIMMING
✪ Kitsilano Pool

Kitsilano Pool, next to Kitsilano Beach, is a 450-foot-long (135-meter) outdoor saltwater swimming pool with three waterslides to entertain the kids. As you lounge on the pool deck, you can take in views of the city skyline, the North Shore mountains, and the sea. The pool gets wildly busy, particularly with families; expect lines on hot-weather weekends. Many people pair a swim in the pool with a picnic at the beach. When the original pool opened here in 1931, it was the first saltwater pool in Canada.

MAP 5: 2305 Cornwall Ave., 604/731-0011, www.vancouver.ca; 7am-8:30pm Mon.-Fri., 9am-8:30pm Sat.-Sun. June-early Aug., 7am-7pm or later Mon.-Fri., 9am-7pm or later early Aug.-early Sept.; adults $7, seniors and ages 13-18 $5, ages 3-12 $4

BEACHES
⭐ Jericho Beach

West of Kitsilano, three connected beaches draw families with sandy swimming areas and grassy stretches for picnicking and playing. The easternmost of these Point Grey beaches is Jericho Beach, which is divided into two sections. One section, where Point Grey Road ends just west of Alma Street, has a long crescent of sand, backed by a grass lawn. The other section of the beach is to the west, at the foot of Discovery Street; here there's a smaller sandy beach, a pier where you can often see fisherman at work, and the Jericho Sailing Centre, a public watersports facility where you can go kayaking or windsurfing, or enjoy a burger and a beer in the water-view pub.

You can also cycle along a waterside path that connects Point Grey's beaches. The Seaside Cycling Route continues west from Kitsilano Beach along Point Grey Road and onto a flat gravel pathway along Jericho, Locarno, and Spanish Banks Beaches.

To reach Jericho Beach by public transit from downtown, take bus 4 toward UBC. For the eastern section, get off along West 4th Avenue at Alma Street. Walk north on Alma to Point Grey Road and turn west toward the beach. To the Jericho Sailing Centre and the western area, get off the bus at West 4th Avenue and Northwest Marine Drive. Follow Northwest Marine toward the water, and turn

Jericho Beach

right onto Discovery Street, which leads to the center.

There's a public parking lot ($3.25/hour, $11/day Apr.-Sept., free Oct.-Mar.) adjacent to the Jericho Sailing Centre.

MAP 5: NW Marine Dr. and Discovery St. to Point Grey Rd. and Alma St., http://vancouver.ca; 6am-10pm daily; free

Locarno Beach

A sandy shore with evergreens beyond, Locarno Beach, just west of Jericho, is a city-designated "quiet" beach, which means that amplified music is not allowed. There's plenty of space for sunning, swimming, and picnicking, and the beach has a snack bar and restrooms. Bus 4 between downtown and UBC stops on West 4th Avenue at Trimble Street; walk north on Trimble down the hill to the beach. There's a small free parking area adjacent to the beach. Parking is also permitted along Northwest Marine Drive.

MAP 5: Northwest Marine Dr. at Trimble St, http://vancouver.ca; 6am-10pm daily; free

Spanish Banks Beach

Spanish Banks, the westernmost of the three Point Grey beaches, has sandy stretches, an expansive grassy lawn with picnic tables, an off-leash dog park, and a launch site for kiteboarders. Vancouverites heading for Spanish Banks Beach often suggest, "Let's meet at *The Anchor*," a massive concrete sculpture that B.C. artist Christel Fuoss-Moore created in 1986. Designed to mark the 1791 arrival of Spanish explorer Don José Maria Narvaez, who was reportedly the first European to arrive in this harbor, this anchor-shaped artwork is installed toward the beach's western end. Spanish Banks also has a snack bar, restrooms, and a large free parking area.

Bus 4 between downtown and UBC can drop you on West 4th Avenue at Tolmie Street. It's a steep walk down the hill on Tolmie to the beach. To avoid the hill, you can walk to or from the bus stop at West 4th Avenue and Northwest Marine Drive; it's about a third of a mile (0.5 kilometer) longer, but much flatter.

MAP 5: NW Marine Dr. at Tolmie St., http://vancouver.ca; 6am-10pm daily; free

Wreck Beach

Vancouver's clothing-optional Wreck Beach is located along the shore below the far west end of the UBC campus. Extending nearly five miles (7.8 kilometers), it's among Canada's longest naturist beaches. You don't have to get naked on the sand, but it's considered poor etiquette to gawk.

On temperate days, vendors sell snacks, sandwiches, and crafts at the main section of the beach, near Trail 6—though their schedules can be erratic, so come prepared with your own water and food.

Several trails lead down to Wreck Beach from the campus. From the UBC bus loop, the most direct route is to walk west on University Boulevard to Northwest Marine Drive and look for Trail 6. It's more than 400 steps down to the sand.

Another option is to walk along the shore from Spanish Banks. Wear running shoes or sport sandals that will protect your feet from rocks and logs, and allow at least an hour if you're heading toward the Trail 6 section of the beach.

Do this walk only at low tide, or you can be stranded as the tide comes in.

MAP 5: Off NW Marine Dr., on the west side of the UBC campus, www.wreckbeach. org; dawn-dusk daily; free

KAYAKING

Ecomarine Paddlesports Centre

From their location behind the sailing center at Jericho Beach, Ecomarine Paddlesports Centre rents kayaks and offers guided kayak tours. One popular tour is the guided sunset paddle ($69) offered on Friday evenings from June to early September. On this 2.5-hour tour, you'll explore the shoreline, looking for bald eagles and other birds and even the occasional harbor seal, while enjoying views of the setting sun reflecting off the city skyline. You don't need prior kayaking experience; your guide will provide brief paddling instructions and safety information before you launch. Tour rates include all your gear; reservations are required.

If you're renting a kayak, you can take out a boat until two hours before sunset. To verify specific rental hours, call or check the website.

MAP 5: Jericho Sailing Centre, 1300 Discovery St., 604/689-7575 or 888/425-2925, www.ecomarine.com; 10am-dusk Mon.-Fri., 9am-dusk Sat.-Sun. late May-early Sept.; single kayak rental $39-69 for 2 hours to full day, double kayak rental $52-85 for 2 hours to full day

WINDSURFING

Windsure

If you have experience windsurfing, you can rent a board and related gear from Windsure at Jericho Beach. If you're keen to try windsurfing for the first time, sign up (at least 48 hours in advance) for one of their lessons, such as the 2.5-hour group beginner class. They're generally open daily between April and September, although hours can vary in spring and fall or if the weather is questionable; call before you go to make sure they're open.

MAP 5: Jericho Sailing Centre, 1300 Discovery St., 604/224-0615 or 604/728-7567, http://windsure.com; generally 8:30am-8:30pm daily Apr.-Sept.; rentals $21-23/hour

HIKING

✪ Pacific Spirit Regional Park

Although it's less well known than downtown's Stanley Park, Pacific Spirit Regional Park, in Vancouver's Point Grey neighborhood near the University of British Columbia campus, is actually larger, measuring more than 1,800 acres (760 hectares). More than 40 miles (70 kilometers) of hiking trails wend through this dense rainforest. Most are gentle forest strolls, although some steeper routes lead from the park to Spanish Banks Beach.

You can access several park trails off West 16th Avenue between Discovery Street and Acadia Road; several others start from Chancellor Boulevard west of Blanca Street. Another park entrance is on West 29th Avenue at Camosun Street. Maps are posted at the start of most trails. For an online map, see the website of the Pacific Spirit Park Society (www.pacificspiritparksociety.org).

Don't hike alone here. While you're close to the city, many trails quickly lead deep into the forest and feel quite remote.

MAP 5: Central section bounded by W. 16th Ave., Camosun St., SW Marine Dr., and Binning Rd.; north section between NW Marine Dr. and University Blvd., west of Blanca St. and east of Acadia Rd.; 604/224-5739, www.metrovancouver.org; dawn-dusk daily; free

DUDE CHILLING PARK

Until one day in 2012, Cambie's Guelph Park was just one of Vancouver's many small neighborhood parks. Then, on an otherwise ordinary November day, a sign appeared in a corner of the park. Looking like other official Vancouver Park Board signage, the sign made it seem that the park's name had been changed. The new name? **Dude Chilling Park.**

Local artist Victor Briestensky created and erected the sign in jest, referring to a wooden sculpture, *Reclining Figure* by Michael Dennis, which was installed in the park in 1991. City staff promptly removed Briestensky's fake sign, but not before it circulated widely on social media.

Local media picked up the story, and the community rallied around the artist, submitting a petition with more than 1,500 signatures requesting that the sign be permanently reinstalled. The artist offered to donate the work, and the Park Board agreed to reinstall it as part of the city's public art program.

Officially, the park's name remains Guelph Park. But at the corner of East 8th Avenue and Brunswick Street, where this unique artwork is now installed, it's Dude Chilling Park.

Cambie Corridor   Map 6

SPECTATOR SPORTS
BASEBALL
Vancouver Canadians

The city's minor league baseball team, the Vancouver Canadians, plays June through early September at family-friendly **Nat Bailey Stadium,** a historic outdoor venue built in 1951 near Queen Elizabeth Park. The Canadians are affiliated with Major League Baseball's Toronto Blue Jays. Several nights during the season, the skies light up with postgame fireworks at the stadium; check the website for schedules.

By public transit from downtown, take the Canada Line to King Edward station. From there, you can walk to the stadium in about 15-20 minutes, or catch bus 33 toward 29th Avenue and ride it three stops to Midlothian Avenue at Clancy Loranger Way, opposite the stadium.

MAP 6: 4601 Ontario St., 604/872-5232, www.canadiansbaseball.com; June-early Sept.; adults $14-25, seniors $11

Commercial Drive   Map 7

CYCLING
Central Valley Greenway

A 15-mile (24-kilometer) urban cycling route, the Central Valley Greenway takes you through Vancouver's eastern districts, beginning near Science World and the Olympic Village and continuing east to Commercial Drive and beyond, traveling through the suburbs of Burnaby and New Westminster. Part of the route runs along neighborhood streets, while other sections follow a paved path under or alongside the SkyTrain line. Some of the greenway feels more industrial than "green," while other sections are naturally scenic, particularly the area near **Burnaby Lake Regional Park** (www.burnaby.ca), where you can stop to walk a trail along the lake.

WHALE-WATCHING

Where the Fraser River meets the Pacific Ocean, the village of Steveston has long been a launching point for fishing boats, and it remains among Canada's largest commercial fishing ports. Steveston Harbour is also a departure point for whale-watching tours.

Most whale-watching trips that depart from Steveston head out through the Strait of Georgia toward the Gulf Islands and San Juan Islands, where you'll most often spot orcas. You might see humpback whales, minke whales, or gray whales, as well as sea lions, bald eagles, and other wildlife. Whale-watching excursions run from April through October.

Steveston Seabreeze Adventures (12551 No. 1 Rd., Richmond, 604/272-7200, www.seabreezeadventures.ca; adults $120, seniors and students $100, ages 3-12 $75) operates whale-watching trips and provides a shuttle (round-trip $7.50) from downtown Vancouver hotels. In the spring, they also offer 90-minute **sea lion tours** (Apr.-mid-May; adults $31.50, seniors and students $23.50, kids $18.50) to view migrating California sea lions.

Vancouver Whale Watch (210-12240 2nd Ave., Richmond, 604/274-9565, www.vancouverwhalewatch.com; $130-140) offers whale-watching tours with a shuttle (round-trip $15) between Steveston and several downtown Vancouver hotels.

Also in Steveston are a few cultural attractions. Steveston once had more than 15 salmon canneries lining its waterfront. The largest is now the **Gulf of Georgia Cannery National Historic Site** (12138 4th Ave., Richmond, 604/664-9009, www.gulfofgeorgiacannery.org; 10am-5pm daily; adults $8, seniors $7, ages 6-16 $4). Inside, see what it was like to work the canning line. To see how Steveston's community lived, visit the **Britannia Shipyards National Historic Site** (5180 Westwater Dr., Richmond, 604/718-8050, http://britanniashipyard.ca; 10am-5pm daily May-Sept., noon-5pm Sat.-Sun. Oct.-Apr.; free). This collection of restored homes and shops housed Chinese, Japanese, European, and First Nations people.

To get a bite to eat before heading back downtown, stop by **Pajo's** (12351 3rd Ave., Richmond, 604/272-1588, www.pajos.com; 11am-7pm daily Feb.-Oct.; $8-21), a simple spot known for its fish-and-chips, which you can order with cod, salmon, or halibut.

To reach Steveston by public transit, take the Canada Line to Richmond-Brighouse Station, then change to any Steveston-bound bus (402, 407, or 410).

The Greenway's easternmost point is near the **River Market** (810 Quayside Dr., New Westminster, 604/520-3881, http://rivermarket.ca), where you can take a break at several food stalls like **Longtail Kitchen** (http://longtailkitchen.com) for street food-inspired Thai fare and **Freebird Chicken Shack** (http://freebirdchickens.com) for Asian-flavored roast chicken, served with rice and papaya salad. River Market is one block south of the New Westminster SkyTrain station.

If you don't want to ride the Greenway all the way out of town and back, or if you get tired along the way, you and your bike can board the SkyTrain to return downtown. Bikes are allowed on the Expo and Millennium Lines, except during weekday rush hours: 7am to 9am traveling westbound (toward downtown) and 4pm to 6pm traveling eastbound. **MAP 7:** From Quebec St. near Terminal Ave. to Quayside Dr. in New Westminster; http://vancouver.ca

ICE-SKATING
Richmond Olympic Oval

During the 2010 Winter Olympic Games, the Richmond Olympic Oval hosted the speed-skating events. You can practice your own skating moves on the indoor Olympic-size rink during the Oval's public skating hours. Most skating sessions run 90 minutes, and rentals are available ($3 skates, $2.25 helmets). The Oval also has a large fitness center, a climbing wall, an indoor track, and other activities, which are included in the drop-in prices. Tip for seniors: Admission for ages 60 and over is only $5 between 9am and 2:30pm Monday through Friday. **MAP 8:** 6111 River Rd., Richmond, 778/296-1400; www.richmondoval.ca; hours and days vary seasonally; $16.50 adults, seniors and ages 19-25 $11.50, ages 13-18 $9.25, ages 6-12 $5

KAYAKING AND STAND-UP PADDLEBOARDING
✪ Deep Cove Kayaks

For a water-based excursion just outside the city, head for the North Shore village of **Deep Cove,** where you can explore the scenic 11-mile (18-kilometer) Indian Arm fjord that's ringed with forests, mountains, and rocky shores. Deep Cove Kayaks rents single and double kayaks, as well as stand-up paddleboards and surf skis (open-cockpit kayaks). They offer lessons and run a number of kayak tours, including a **Full Moon Evening tour** (June-Sept., $65), scheduled on the two or three evenings closest to the full moon. Another option is the full-day **Boats, Bikes, & Beers tour** (dates vary, $279 ages 19 and up), which includes a guided kayak excursion, lunch, a cycling tour, and a beer tasting.

To reach Deep Cove by public transit from downtown Vancouver, take bus 211 from Burrard Station (Burrard St. at Dunsmuir). It's a 50- to 60-minute ride. This bus doesn't run early in the mornings or in the evenings. **MAP 9:** 2156 Banbury Rd., Deep Cove, North Vancouver, 604/929-2268, www.deepcovekayak.com; 10am-dusk Sat.-Sun. Mar. weather permitting, 10am-dusk daily Apr., 10am-dusk Mon.-Fri. and 9am-dusk Sat.-Sun. May, 9am-dusk Mon.-Fri. and 8:30am-dusk Sat.-Sun. June, 9am-dusk Mon.-Fri. and 8am-dusk Sat.-Sun. July, 9am-dusk daily Aug., 10am-7pm daily Sept., 10am-6pm daily early-mid-Oct.; rentals $39-109 for 2 hours to full day

HIKING
✪ The Grouse Grind

You can't call yourself a Vancouverite until you've hiked the Grind, or so say the many who've made the trek up Vancouver's best-known trail. Nicknamed "Mother Nature's Stairmaster," the Grouse Grind is only 1.8 miles (2.9 kilometers) long, but it's essentially a mountain staircase that you climb straight up, gaining an

OUTDOOR ADVENTURES

If you love the outdoors, Vancouver is your city—in any season. With its stellar natural setting, you don't have to venture far from the city center to experience the rainforest, the mountains, or the sea, whether on a hiking trail, a ski run, or a paddling route. Even on damp winter days, you'll find locals playing soccer, going for a run, or strolling along the beach, and when the sun shines, it seems like the entire city is outdoors.

kayakers on False Creek

PARKS

Just steps from the downtown skyscrapers, there's **Stanley Park** (page 62), the city's 1,000-acre (400-hectare) green space to explore on foot, by bike, or in a kayak. The **Seawall** (page 58), a walking and cycling path, circles the park's perimeter and continues around downtown's waterfronts, along both the Burrard Inlet and False Creek; with a couple of detours, you can follow this waterside path all the way out to the University of British Columbia campus. There, on the city's west side, is another rainforest park to explore: **Pacific Spirit Regional Park** (page 162).

BEACHES

You can go to the beach right downtown, too, at **English Bay Beach** (page 154) in the West End or in Stanley Park at **Second Beach** or **Third Beach. Kitsilano Beach** (page 159) is one of the city's most popular. Families gravitate to the Point Grey sands at **Jericho Beach** (page 160), **Locarno Beach** (page 161), and **Spanish Banks Beach** (page 161).

WATER SPORTS

Want to get out on the water? Rent a kayak at **Jericho Beach** (page 162) or take a stand-up paddleboard or kayak out on **False Creek** (page 155). Or head to the North Shore to paddle the scenic Indian Arm fjord with a kayak from **Deep Cove Kayaks** (page 165).

THE NORTH SHORE

For more outdoor adventures, the North Shore is your day-trip destination. Go hiking, skiing, or snowshoeing at **Grouse Mountain** (page 87) or **Cypress Mountain** (page 168), explore the walking trails in West Vancouver's waterfront **Lighthouse Park** (page 167), or take a wildlife cruise from **Horseshoe Bay** (page 91).

---

elevation of 2,800 feet (850 meters). Along most of the trail, you're hiking in the forest. The reward comes at the top, with vistas across the city.

Average active hikers can generally complete the Grouse Grind, which has 2,830 steps, in about 90 minutes, but plenty of people need at least two hours.

Hikers are allowed to walk uphill only. To return to the parking area, you ride down on the **Skyride**

(one-way $10), the Grouse Mountain tram. Check the trail status if you're planning a spring or fall hike; there can be snow on the trail even when it's warm in the city.

The mountain runs a free shuttle (May-Sept.) from Canada Place. By public transportation, take the SeaBus from Waterfront Station to Lonsdale Quay and change to bus 236 for Grouse Mountain, which will drop you at the mountain's base.

The Grouse Grind

MAP 9: 6400 Nancy Greene Way, North Vancouver, 604/980-9311, www. grousemountain.com; Skyride $10 one-way

✪ Lighthouse Park

There are beautiful views across the water toward downtown Vancouver from Lighthouse Park, a seaside recreation area in West Vancouver. Perched on a point between Burrard Inlet and Howe Sound, the 185-acre (75-hectare) park has several easy trails through old-growth forests that lead to dramatic lookout points. Some of the park's trees, which include Douglas fir, western hemlock, and western red cedar, are roughly 500 years old and grow as tall as 200 feet (61 meters).

The park's lighthouse, which is a national historic site, is not open to the public. The original lighthouse was built here in 1874, and the current structure dates to 1912. A nearby viewpoint has expansive water vistas. The Beacon Lane trail is the most direct route from the parking area to the lighthouse viewpoint.

On the east side of the park, the Valley of the Giants trail takes you among the towering trees to a lookout at Eagle Point. On the park's west side, follow the Juniper Loop to the Juniper Point Trail, which leads to a viewpoint facing Howe Sound and the Gulf Islands.

Pack a picnic if you plan to stay a while. The park has restrooms but no other services. Lighthouse Park is 12.5 miles (20 kilometers) northwest of downtown Vancouver. By public transit, catch bus 250 (toward Horseshoe Bay) along West Georgia Street and get off on Marine Drive at Beacon Lane. It's a 40- to 45-minute ride. Walk south on Beacon Lane to the park.

MAP 9: Beacon Ln., West Vancouver, 604/925-7275, www.lighthousepark.ca; dawn-dusk daily; free

Cypress Provincial Park

In winter, you can ski, snowboard, cross-country ski, or snowshoe at Cypress Mountain, located within

Cypress Provincial Park. After the snow melts, it's a close-to-the-city hiking destination. Encompassing three peaks—Black Mountain, Mount Strachan, and Hollyburn Mountain—Cypress is known for its spectacular views across Howe Sound, to the Gulf Islands, and toward downtown Vancouver.

A popular trail for day hikers is the Hollyburn Peak Trail, which starts at the Nordic ski area base and gradually ascends 1,300 feet (400 meters) to the top of Hollyburn Mountain. Your reward for hiking this five-mile (eight-kilometer) round-trip trail is expansive vistas over the peaks and forests.

Another option with excellent views over Howe Sound is the shorter trail to the Bowen Lookout, which begins at the alpine ski area base. With an elevation change of 325 feet (100 meters), the trail is three miles (five kilometers) round-trip.

The best time to hike the Cypress area is June or July through October, since snow can cover the trails at higher elevations the rest of the year.

MAP 9: 6000 Cypress Bowl Rd., West Vancouver, 604/926-5612; www. cypressmountain.com; dawn to dusk daily; free

SKIING, SNOWBOARDING, AND SNOWSHOEING

Cypress Mountain

The largest of the North Shore mountains, Cypress Mountain hosted several events during the 2010 Winter Olympics. You can ski and snowboard on the mountain's 53 downhill trails. You can buy tickets for a full day, afternoon only (from 12:30pm-closing), or night (5pm-closing), and you get a discount if you purchase them online in advance. Check the Cypress website on the day you plan to ski or snowboard, since they offer a changing "daily discount" coupon, which might save you money on gear rentals, food in the on-site cafeteria, or purchases in the mountain shop. You can rent equipment and clothing on the mountain, and lessons are offered for both kids and adults.

Cypress has a separate Nordic area with trails for cross-country skiing and snowshoeing. Of the 12 miles (19 kilometers) of cross-country trails, nearly five miles (7.5 kilometers) stay open for night skiing. If you're snowshoeing, unless you're with a guide, you need to be off the trails before sunset (check website for hours). Several guided snowshoe tours are available, from a two-hour introductory tour to an evening excursion that wraps up with chocolate fondue.

Cypress also has a snow tube park, where both adults and kids (ages 6 and up) can slide down six chutes and let a tube tow pull you back up to the top. Tickets are good for two hours of tubing fun.

There is no public transportation to Cypress, but you can catch the Cypress Coach Lines shuttle bus (604/637-7669, http://cypresscoach-lines.com) between the city and the mountain during the winter ski season. Check the website for schedules and pickup/drop-off locations. You can purchase round-trip tickets (adults $23, ages 13-18 $18) from the driver when you board (cash only). On the mountain, you can buy one-way tickets (adults $11, ages 13-18 $8) from the Guest Relations office in the downhill area or from the Nordic area ticket office. Up to two kids (ages 6-12) ride free with a paying adult.

MAP 9: 6000 Cypress Bowl Rd., West Vancouver, 604/926-5612, www.cypressmountain.com; hours and days vary by attraction; downhill: adults $46-69, seniors $30-44, ages 13-18 $37-52, ages 6-12 $24-32, ages 0-5 $6-8; cross-country: adults $18-22, seniors and ages 13-18 $12-14, ages 6-12 $9-11, ages 0-5 $5; snowshoe: adults $10, seniors and ages 13-18 $8, ages 6-12 $5, ages 0-5 $2; snow tube park: $20

Mount Seymour

Family-friendly Mount Seymour, the North Shore's smallest ski area, has five lifts serving 40 downhill runs, with tickets available for a full day, afternoon (2:30pm-10pm), or evening (6pm-10pm) of skiing or snowboarding. It's a good spot for snowshoeing, with easy trails through the forest, and there's a snow tube park, too.

A shuttle bus (one-way $8) can take you between Mount Seymour and the Rupert SkyTrain station in East Vancouver. Buy a ticket from the shuttle driver when you board (cash only). Check the Mount Seymour website for shuttle schedules. From downtown to Rupert station, catch the Expo Line to Commercial/Broadway station, where you change to the Millennium Line for Rupert.

MAP 9: 1700 Mt. Seymour Rd., North Vancouver, 604/986-2261, www.mountseymour.com; downhill trails 10am-10pm Mon.-Fri., 9am-10pm Sat.-Sun. Dec.-Mar., snowshoe and snow tube park hours vary seasonally; downhill: adults $33-56, seniors $25-40, ages 13-18 $27-45, ages 6-12 $15-25, ages 5 and under free; snowshoe: adults $10, seniors and ages 13-18 $9, ages 6-12 $8, ages 5 and under free; snow tube park: $20-22

SHOPS

If you're coming from a major city in the United States, you may be disappointed with the shopping options in Vancouver, since selections are typically smaller

Barefoot Contessa boutique on Main Street

and prices higher than at similar stores south of the border. Of course, if the exchange rate is in your favor, shopping here may be a better value.

Regardless of your home base, products to look for in Vancouver include Canadian-designed clothing, local art, B.C. wines and beer, and local food items. Among the Vancouver-born brands that have gone international are shoe designer John Fluevog and yoga-wear maker Lululemon, which has a local "lab" store selling prototypes and limited edition clothing. Vancouver has a number of well-stocked outdoor stores where you can find outdoor gear for your Canadian travels.

Robson and Granville are the main downtown shopping streets, while a growing number of high-end international brands have opened boutiques on nearby Alberni Street. For local and independent labels, visit Gastown or Yaletown, or browse the storefronts along Main Street or in Kitsilano on West 4th Avenue. There's a group of outdoor gear stores along Broadway between Cambie and Main, and another in Kitsilano.

If you're in the market for art, Gastown and Granville Island are the most art-full neighborhoods, particularly if you're interested in jewelry, crafts, and other works by aboriginal artists. Granville Island is also the top spot to find gifts for foodie friends or to locate your own delicious souvenirs.

HIGHLIGHTS

✪ **MOST HISTORIC SHOPPING DESTINATION:** The Vancouver flagship location of **Hudson's Bay,** Canada's original department store, is in a six-story 1914 building downtown (page 172).

✪ **WHERE TO FIND YOGA WEAR NO ONE ELSE HAS:** **Lululemon Lab,** a concept store for the Vancouver-based yoga-wear maker, sells prototypes and limited edition clothing (page 175).

✪ **MOST UNUSUAL SHOE STORE:** Resembling an art studio more than a shoe store, the shop of Canadian shoemaker **John Fluevog** is a stylish spot for funky footwear (page 175).

✪ **BEST DISCOVERIES:** You never know quite what you'll uncover at **Fine Finds Boutique,** a Yaletown shop stocked with casually stylish women's clothing, hats, jewelry, and handbags (page 177).

✪ **WHERE TO SHOP FOR VANCOUVER'S MOST USEFUL ACCESSORY:** The namesake items at **The Umbrella Shop** are helpful on the city's frequent rainy days—and they're fashionable to boot (page 179).

✪ **BEST BOOKSTORE FOR KIDS AND TEENS:** With a huge selection of books and a bibliophile staff quick with advice, **Kidsbooks** is excellent for browsing (page 181).

✪ **EASIEST WAY TO MAKE FRIENDS WITH CHEESE:** The friendly cheese mongers at **Les Amis du Fromage** will help you pick the perfect wedge (page 181).

✪ **BEST TRAVEL STORE:** Need books, maps, or gear for your travels? Head to well-stocked **Wanderlust** (page 182).

✪ **WHERE TO FIND FRILLY, FLOUNCY FROCKS:** The **Barefoot Contessa** boutique carries "all things lovely," from dresses and blouses to sparkly jewelry (page 182).

✪ **MOST FASHION-FORWARD VINTAGE SHOP:** Stylish shoppers check out **Front and Company** for good-quality vintage clothing (page 182).

SHOPPING DISTRICTS

Robson Street

Vancouver's main downtown shopping district is along Robson Street, between Jervis and Granville Streets. Mid-priced Canadian and international chains predominate; a few small shops sell trinkets and souvenirs. One block north of Robson, on Alberni Street between Burrard and Bute, look for luxury brands like Tiffany and Burberry.

MAP 1: Robson St. between Jervis and Granville Sts.

Granville Street

Department stores, outdoor gear shops, and mid-priced boutiques line Granville Street downtown, in between the nightclubs and tattoo parlors. The Hudson's Bay flagship store is located on Granville.

MAP 1: Granville St. between Davie and Cordova Sts.

Gastown

Visit Gastown for smaller fashion boutiques and clothing by local designers.

MAP 2: Water and Cordova Sts., between Richards and Carrall Sts.

West 4th Avenue

On Vancouver's West Side, the Kitsilano neighborhood mixes North American chains and local boutiques, centered along West 4th Avenue. There's a collection of ski and snowboard gear shops on 4th at Burrard.

MAP 5: W. 4th Ave., between Burrard and Vine Sts.

Main Street

Looking for clothes you won't find at the local mall? Main Street is lined with independent boutiques, many carrying clothing by local and Canadian designers.

MAP 6: Main St., between E. 20th and 30th Aves.

Downtown and the West End

Map 1

DEPARTMENT STORES

✪ Hudson's Bay

The Vancouver flagship location of Hudson's Bay, Canada's original department store, is in a six-story 1914 downtown building, selling clothing and accessories for women, men, and kids, as well as housewares, luggage, and small appliances. One department carries striped Hudson's Bay blankets and other Canadiana. The Hudson's Bay Company opened their first Vancouver store in Gastown in 1887. They subsequently added a branch on Granville Street and then built this store, which has remained its Vancouver base for more than 100 years.

MAP 1: 674 Granville St., 604/681-6211, www.hbc.com; 9:30am-9pm Mon.-Sat., 11am-7pm Sun.

Holt Renfrew

For high-fashion designer clothing, with prices to match, visit Holt Renfrew downtown, built around a gleaming white atrium at the Pacific Centre Mall. You can book an appointment with their personal shoppers to help you navigate the chic designs.

MAP 1: 737 Dunsmuir St., 604/681-3121, www.holtrenfrew.com; 10am-7pm Mon.-Tues., 10am-9pm Wed.-Fri., 10am-8pm Sat., 11am-7pm Sun.

Nordstrom
Seattle-based Nordstrom has a sizable store at Vancouver's Pacific Centre Mall downtown, in a multistory glass-clad space at the corner of Robson and Granville. This high-end department store chain got its start as a shoe retailer and still has a large selection of footwear. The store has three food outlets: Bistro Verde, a contemporary restaurant; Ebar for coffee and smoothies; and Habitant, a wine and cocktail bar.

MAP 1: 799 Robson St., 604/699-2100, www.nordstrom.com; 9:30am-9pm Mon.-Sat., 11am-7pm Sun.

Winners
You can often find deals on designer apparel, other clothing, shoes, and accessories at Winners, a discount department store that carries both men's and women's garments. In addition to their large downtown location, there's a branch near Broadway and Cambie.

MAP 1: 798 Granville St., 604/683-1058, http://winners.ca; 9am-9pm Mon.-Sat., 10am-7pm Sun.

CLOTHING AND ACCESSORIES
Lululemon Athletica
The now-ubiquitous yoga- and workout-wear maker Lululemon Athletica got its start in Vancouver and still has its flagship store downtown, where you'll find yoga pants, running gear, and clothing for other athletic pursuits or for just lounging around

looking cool. There's another location in Kitsilano.

MAP 1: 970 Robson St., 604/681-3118, www.lululemon.com; 10am-9pm Mon.-Sat., 10:30am-7:30pm Sun.

Yoga-wear store Lululemon Athletica was launched in Vancouver.

BOOKS AND STATIONERY
Bookmark
Run by the Friends of the Vancouver Public Library, Bookmark, the gift shop in the library's central branch downtown, carries a small selection of gently used books, along with cards, stationery, T-shirts, and gift items with literary themes. Sales benefit the library and its programs.

MAP 1: 350 W. Georgia St., 604/331-4040, www.friendsofthevpl.ca; 10am-5:30pm Mon.-Fri., noon-5pm Sat.

DESIGN AND GIFTS
Designhouse
Cool furniture, housewares, and other fun design-y stuff, including watches, bags and backpacks, and gift items, fill Designhouse downtown. This sleek Scandinavian-style store

BEST SOUVENIRS

What should you bring home to remember your Vancouver visit? Besides a camera full of photos of this scenic waterfront city, look for the following souvenirs:

- Artwork, jewelry, or other crafts by aboriginal artists

- Locally caught cured salmon, packed for travel

- Clothing from Canadian designers

- B.C. wine or craft beer

- A locally made umbrella

carries packs from Vancouver-based Herschel Supply Company, stainless steel water bottles from S'well, and the "Anna G." corkscrew from Alessi that resembles a smiling woman. The shop shares its space with **Marimekko Vancouver** (604/609-2881, http://marimekkovancouver.com), which stocks brightly patterned clothing, accessories, household items, and fabrics from the Finnish design company.

MAP 1: 851 Homer St., 604/681-2800, http://designhouse.ca; 10:30am-6pm Mon.-Sat., noon-5pm Sun.

SPECIALTY FOOD AND DRINK

Ayoub's Dried Fruits and Nuts

The aroma of freshly roasted nuts may draw you into Ayoub's Dried Fruits and Nuts, which sells in-house roasted almonds, pistachios, cashews, walnuts, and more, attractively displayed in ornate silver tureens. They also carry dried fruits, vegetable chips, Mediterranean spices, and Persian-style pastries and candies. Try their unique lime-and-saffron seasoned nuts. In addition to this West End shop, you'll find this nut vendor in Kitsilano and North Vancouver.

MAP 1: 986 Denman St., 604/732-6887, www.ayoubs.ca; 10am-9pm Mon.-Thurs., 10am-10pm Fri.-Sat., 10am-8pm Sun.

Viti Wine & Lager

Viti Wine & Lager, a compact shop at the Moda Hotel downtown, stocks an extensive selection of B.C. wines, particularly labels from the Okanagan region. They also carry more than 350 types of beer and a large collection of whiskeys. In the coolers lining the walls, they always keep a selection of chilled wine and beer, ready to drink.

MAP 1: 900 Seymour St., 604/683-3806, www.vitiwinelagers.com; 9am-11pm Mon.-Sat., noon-11pm Sun.

CLOTHING AND ACCESSORIES
✪ Lululemon Lab
Operated by the Vancouver-based yoga-wear maker in a warehouse-style Gastown space, Lululemon Lab is a concept store that offers prototypes and other limited edition clothing not carried at the company's regular retail outlets. Watch the designers at work while you browse for unique active and casual wear. The city is also home to several regular Lululemon locations.
MAP 2: 50 Powell St., 604/689-8013, www.lululemonlab.com; 11am-7pm Mon.-Sat., noon-6pm Sun.

Kit and Ace
Ready to upgrade your yoga look? Shannon Wilson, who's married to Lululemon founder Chip Wilson, and J. J. Wilson (Chip's son), founded Kit and Ace, which designs and sells hip men's and women's work-to-weekend clothing made from "technical cashmere" and other luxury fabrics, designed to dress up while still being comfortable. The soft, comfy garments may be too pricey for the gym, but they'd be lovely for the office or a casual evening out. They have a second location in Kitsilano.
MAP 2: 151 Water St., 844/548-6223, www.kitandace.com; 10am-7pm Mon.-Sat., 11am-6pm Sun.

Oak + Fort
Launched in Vancouver, Oak + Fort has a spacious Gastown store purveying stylishly relaxed, moderately priced clothing for men and women, along with jewelry and accessories. Both the monochromatic designs and the airy, high-ceilinged shop have a minimalist, almost Japanese aesthetic, and the well-spaced racks are comfortable for browsing.
MAP 2: 355 Water St., 604/566-9199, www.oakandfort.ca; 11am-7pm Mon.-Wed., 11am-8pm Thurs.-Fri., 10am-7pm Sat., 11am-6pm Sun.

One of a Few
This small but chic boutique in Gastown sells women's clothing from emerging and established designers from around the world. Catering to the young, style-conscious, and well-heeled, One of a Few carries distinctive fashions that you might wear to work or for a night out at an of-the-moment bistro.
MAP 2: 354 Water St., 604/605-0685, www.oneofafew.com; 11am-6pm Mon.-Thurs. and Sat., 11am-7pm Fri., noon-5pm Sun.

Tees.ca
Pop into Tees.ca for funky T-shirts designed by local artists and other creatives. In this tiny storefront, piled high with tees, many have Vancouver motifs and would make fun souvenirs.
MAP 2: 227 Abbott St., www.tees.ca, 11am-6pm Mon.-Sat.; noon-5pm Sun.

SHOES
✪ John Fluevog
Canadian shoemaker John Fluevog started his funky footwear line in Vancouver, offering high-end, unconventional designs for both men and women, many of which feature bright colors and distinctive heel shapes. His two-level Gastown shop, with massive windows and a greenhouse-like

175

ceiling, looks more like an art studio than a shoe store. There's a second Fluevog branch among the Granville Street nightclubs downtown.

MAP 2: 65 Water St., 604/688-6228, www.fluevog.com; 10am-7pm Mon.-Wed. and Sat., 10am-8pm Thurs.-Fri., noon-6pm Sun.

The Paper Hound Bookshop

BOOKS
The Paper Hound Bookshop

The floor-to-ceiling shelves at The Paper Hound Bookshop are crammed with a diverse array of used (and some new) titles, sorted into sometimes quirky categories that range from literature and Eastern enlightenment to "books with folding maps." In this chockablock Gastown shop, kids' books get the same tongue-in-cheek treatment, too, organized into sections from "indomitable orphans" to

"the rodent as hero." If you can't find what you need, ask the helpful bibliophile staffers.

MAP 2: 344 W. Pender St., 604/428-1344, http://paperhound.ca; 10am-7pm Sun.-Thurs., 10am-8pm Fri.-Sat.

HOUSEWARES
Ming Wo

This kitchenware shop was founded in Chinatown back in 1917, and Ming Wo is still jam-packed with anything you might need to prepare or serve a meal, whether you're looking for pots and pans, dishes, utensils and gadgets, aprons, or tableware. They stock a sizable selection of woks, steamers, chopsticks, and other tools for Asian cooking. In addition to this location opposite the Dr. Sun Yat-Sen Classical Chinese Garden, there are branches in Kitsilano and South Granville.

MAP 2: 23 E. Pender St., 604/683-7268, www.mingwo.com; 9am-6pm Mon.-Sat., 11am-5pm Sun.

Örling & Wu

The carefully curated collection of hip housewares draws you into this window-lined storefront in a rehabbed Gastown building, where it's fun to browse for things you didn't know you needed. Örling & Wu carries cards and paper goods, coffee- and tea-making supplies, tableware, soaps and bath products, and even stylish dog collars.

MAP 2: 28 Water St., 604/568-6718, www.orlingandwu.com; 10am-6pm Mon.-Sat., 11am-5pm Sun.

CLOTHING AND ACCESSORIES
✪ Fine Finds Boutique

You'll likely unearth some fine finds at Fine Finds Boutique, a Yaletown shop stocked with casually stylish women's clothing, hats, jewelry, and handbags, mixing local labels and global brands. They carry a large selection of vegan leather wallets, purses, and packs from Canadian maker Matt & Nat, plus cards and gift items, too, all attractively displayed in this window-lined storefront.

MAP 3: 1014 Mainland St., 604/669-8325, http://finefindsboutique.com; 10am-6pm Mon.-Tues., 10am-7pm Wed.-Sat., 11am-5pm Sun.

Global Atomic Designs

Hidden down a narrow corridor in a restored brick building, this surprisingly spacious boutique outfits millennial men and women in everything from funky T-shirts, hoodies, and denim to spangled club wear from Canadian and international designers, like Naked & Famous, Religion, and John Varvatos. In the center of this boutiques to open in Yaletown back in 1998, is a coffee bar where you can pull up a stool and consider your purchases over an espresso and a cookie.

MAP 3: 1144 Mainland St., 604/806-6223, www.globalatomic.com; 11am-7pm daily

Moulé

The staff at family-owned Moulé can help you select from garments that are smart enough to dress up while still doubling as comfy casual wear. Among their women's and men's

clothing lines, they carry several of their own in-house brands, including Rachel Mara, Colter, and Ten62. They also stock jewelry and a small assortment of housewares, and there's even a corner with toys and clothing for the kids. Their roomy Yaletown shop, set in a heritage building with black wood floors and white wood walls, has plenty of space for browsing.

MAP 3: 1062 Homer St., 604/685-1062, http://moulestores.com; 10am-7pm Mon.-Sat., 11am-6pm Sun.

Woo To See You

Inside Woo To See You, a teeny white-walled Yaletown boutique that gets its distinctive name from owner Hans Woo, you'll find jeans, blouses, jackets, and other fashionably casual women's clothing, primarily mid-priced garments from smaller or independent labels. Prepare for winter with handmade hats by Vancouver's Hendrik.Lou, and check out the cases along the wall displaying original jewelry, including Vancouver designer Carli Marie Sita's "famous fingers" series, necklaces inspired by American Sign Language (and other hand gestures). There's another location on Main Street.

MAP 3: 1062 Mainland St., 604/559-1062, https://wootoseeyou.com; 10am-8pm Mon.-Sat., 11am-6pm Sun.

VINTAGE AND SECONDHAND
My Sister's Closet

Shopping at this Yaletown "eco-thrift" boutique supports a good cause. At My Sister's Closet, which the local Battered Women's Support Services organization operates, proceeds from the store's sales help fund violence prevention and intervention services. Allow some time to browse; this corner store is crammed with racks of women's secondhand clothing, from pants to coats to formal wear, along with some jewelry, shoes, bags, and a small selection of men's garments.

MAP 3: 1092 Seymour St., 604/687-0770, www.bwss.org; 10am-6pm Mon.-Thurs., 10am-7pm Fri., 11am-7pm Sat., noon-6pm Sun.

SPECIALTY FOOD AND DRINK

Legacy Liquor Store

British Columbia's largest privately owned liquor store, Legacy Liquor Store, in the Olympic Village, has an excellent selection of B.C. wines from more than 80 wineries around the province. The knowledgeable staff can help you choose, whether you're looking for a gift or for a bottle to sip with your bread-and-cheese picnic. In this 8,600-square-foot (800-square-meter) store, they stock plenty of B.C. craft spirits, and their selection of 1,000-plus beers includes many local microbrews. They hold periodic wine-tastings and other special events; check the website or phone for a schedule.

MAP 3: 1633 Manitoba St., 604/331-7900, http://legacyliquorstore.com; 10am-11pm daily

Granville Island

Map 4

SHOPPING MALLS

Net Loft

Opposite the Public Market is the Net Loft, an indoor minimall in a former warehouse building. Explore its hallways, a warren of tiny shops and art galleries, for gifts and unique souvenirs, from jewelry to kitchenware to hats to aboriginal art.

MAP 4: 1666 Johnston St., no phone; 10am-7pm daily

CLOTHING AND ACCESSORIES

Funk Shui Atelier

In this light and open Railspur Alley studio, the textile artists at Funk Shui Atelier craft handmade hats, scarves, and other wearable or decorative fabric items. You can often watch the artists as they work.

MAP 4: 1375 Railspur Alley, 604/684-5327, www.funkshuifelt.com; 10am-5pm daily

Granville Island Hat Shop

At the Granville Island Hat Shop, inside the Net Loft building, you can find almost anything to wear on your head, for both men and women. Stacks and stacks of hats line the shelves, and the staff can help you find your best style. They craft custom hats and do hat repair and restoration as well.

MAP 4: Net Loft, 1666 Johnston St., 604/683-4280, www.thehatshop.ca; 10am-6pm daily

Little Dream

Little Dream carries an eclectic assortment of locally made fashions, jewelry, and accessories for women in its compact Net Loft shop. Crafted by Vancouver designers, their distinctive clothing, which ranges from casual to more dressy, isn't on the racks at your standard suburban mall.

MAP 4: Net Loft, 1666 Johnston St., 604/683-6930, www.dreamvancouver.com; 10am-7pm daily

Silk Weaving Studio

It's worth hunting for Silk Weaving Studio, hidden in a corrugated metal-clad bungalow near the waterfront, between the Public Market and Ocean Concrete. You can frequently watch the weavers at work, creating hand-woven scarves, shawls, and other garments and textile pieces on their sizable looms.

MAP 4: 1531 Johnston St., 604/687-7455, www.silkweavingstudio.com; 10am-5pm daily

Silk Weaving Studio

DESIGN AND GIFTS
✪ The Umbrella Shop

Even if you're visiting in the sunny summertime, you may want as a souvenir the constant companion of Vancouverites: an umbrella. The Umbrella Shop sells good-quality rain protectors in a broad range of colors and styles, and the helpful staff can explain the benefits of different designs. Besides this branch under the bridge on Granville Island, look for their location on West Pender Street, handy if you get caught in the rain downtown.

MAP 4: 1550 Anderson St., 604/697-0919, www.theumbrellashop.com; 10am-6pm daily

Ainsworth Custom Design

Part metalworking studio (specializing in furniture) and part gift shop, Ainsworth Custom Design carries whimsical one-of-a-kind items from magnets and cards to prints and T-shirts.

MAP 4: 1243 Cartwright St., 604/682-8838, www.ainsworthcustomdesign.com; 10am-6pm Mon.-Fri., noon-6pm Sat., noon-5pm Sun.

Circle Craft Co-Operative

In the Net Loft, spacious Circle Craft Co-Operative is a good place to browse for handmade jewelry, leatherwork, ceramics, and other work by more than 150 B.C. craftspeople, with items attractively displayed on wooden tables and shelves.

MAP 4: Net Loft, 1666 Johnston St., 604/669-8021, www.circlecraft.net; 10am-7pm daily Apr.-Dec., 10am-6pm daily Jan.-Mar.

Granville Island Broom Co.

Harry Potter and his Quidditch team would covet the handmade sweepers from the Granville Island Broom Co. Sisters Mary and Sarah Schwieger, who own the shop, craft brooms using traditional Shaker methods. Check out the "marriage brooms" with their entwined brushes, or the only-in-Canada versions with handles made of hockey sticks.

MAP 4: 1406 Old Bridge St., 604/629-1141, www.broomcompany.com; 10am-6pm daily

Sterling Glassworks

Watch the glassblowers at work at Sterling Glassworks, a glassblowing studio and shop that sells colorful glass pieces of various sizes. If you're interested in learning about glassblowing yourself, ask about their 30- to 60-minute workshops, offered by appointment only, for adults and teens (ages 14 and up).

MAP 4: 1440 Old Bridge St., 604/681-6730, www.sterling-glassworks.com; 10am-6pm Mon.-Sat., 11am-5pm Sun.

Wickaninnish Gallery

The compact Wickaninnish Gallery sells cards, prints, scarves, and other moderately priced items with First Nations designs.

MAP 4: Net Loft, 1666 Johnston St., 604/681-1057, www.wickaninnishgallery. com; 10am-7pm daily

SPECIALTY FOOD AND DRINK

Edible Canada

Looking for a souvenir for a foodie friend or an edible memory from your Vancouver visit? Edible Canada, opposite the Granville Island Public Market and connected to the restaurant of the same name, stocks locally produced salts, jams, vinegars, and more from around British Columbia and across Canada. The shop is decorated with canoes and other Canadiana.

MAP 4: 1596 Johnston St., 604/682-6675, www.ediblecanada.com; 10am-6pm Mon.-Fri., 9am-6pm Sat., 9am-5pm Sun.

Liberty Wine Merchants

A good source of wines from B.C. and elsewhere is Liberty Wine Merchants, near the Granville Island Public Market. The staff can introduce you to the region's wines and advise you about local labels. They have additional locations in the Point Grey neighborhood and on the East Side.

MAP 4: 1660 Johnston St., 604/602-1120, www.libertywinemerchants.com; 9:30am-8pm Mon.-Thurs., 9:30am-9pm Fri., 9am-9pm Sat., 9am-8pm Sun.

Kitsilano   Map 5

CLOTHING AND ACCESSORIES

Two of Hearts

For women's clothing and accessories by emerging Canadian designers, check out Two of Hearts, a friendly boutique in Kitsilano. They carry their own made-in-Vancouver label, Cici, as well as designs from other independent companies, stocking both moderately priced casual clothes and dressier wear. In the center of the shop, look for displays of jewelry.

MAP 5: 1986 W. 4th Ave., 604/428-0998, www.twoofhearts.ca; 11am-6pm Mon. and Wed.-Sat., noon-5pm Sun.

SHOES

Gravity Pope

Kitsilano's Gravity Pope sells upscale style-conscious shoes for men and women, including brands like Camper, Cydwoq, Vans, and their own in-house line. Park yourself on one of the curved banquettes while you see what fits. Their next-door boutique, Gravity Pope Tailored Goods (2203 W. 4th Ave., 604/731-7647, 10am-8pm Mon.-Fri., 11am-7pm Sat., 11am-6pm Sun.), carries high-end women's clothing that ranges from funky to fine, from labels like Comme des Garçons, Naked & Famous, and Alexander Wang.

MAP 5: 2205 W. 4th Ave., 604/731-7673, www.gravitypope.com; 10am-9pm Mon.-Fri., 10am-7pm Sat., 11am-6pm Sun.

BOOKS
✪ Kidsbooks

Kidsbooks is Vancouver's best place to find reading matter for toddlers to teens. The Kitsilano shop stocks a large selection of titles by Canadian authors and books with multicultural themes, plus games, crafts, science projects, and audiobooks. This spacious store has nooks for young readers, middle grades, and teenagers to browse. If you're shopping for a gift or want some suggestions, ask the knowledgeable staff for ideas.

MAP 5: 2557 W. Broadway, 604/738-5335, www.kidsbooks.ca; 9:30am-6pm Mon.-Thurs. and Sat., 9:30am-9pm Fri., 11am-6pm Sun.

Pulp Fiction Books

One of the city's long-established booksellers, Pulp Fiction Books carries both new and used books on their sturdy pine shelves in their Kitsilano location. They also have two shops on the East Side.

MAP 5: 2754 W. Broadway, 604/873-4311, http://pulpfictionbooksvancouver.com; 11am-7pm daily

SPECIALTY FOOD AND DRINK
✪ Les Amis du Fromage

The friendly cheese mongers at Les Amis du Fromage will help you pick the perfect wedge, whether you're looking for locally made brie or a pungent époisses from France. Sampling is encouraged. The Kitsilano storefront, where you can peruse the cheese-filled display cases and coolers, is a short walk from Granville Island; there's a second location on the East Side.

MAP 5: 1752 W. 2nd Ave., 604/732-4218, www.buycheese.com; 9am-6pm Sat.-Wed., 9am-6:30pm Thurs.-Fri.

Les Amis du Fromage

Silk Road Tea

Based in Victoria, local leaf expert Silk Road Tea runs a spacious store in Kitsilano, where you can browse and sample from their extensive inventory of tea, tea-related products, and cosmetics. They also offer tea classes and workshops; check their website or call for details.

MAP 5: 2066 W. 4th Ave., 778/379 8481, www.silkroadteastore.com; 10am-7pm Mon.-Sat., 10am-6pm Sun.

OUTDOOR GEAR
Comor Sports

Near West 4th Avenue at Burrard Street in Kitsilano, several shops sell gear for skiing, snowboarding, surfing, and cycling. Comor Sports is a well-stocked outdoor gear store with a helpful staff. In their large, warehouse-like location, they carry skis, snowboards, winter accessories, and bicycles, as well as clothing for outdoor sports.

MAP 5: 1766 W. 4th Ave., 604/736-7547, www.comorsports.com; 10am-6pm Mon.-Wed. and Sat., 10am-8pm Thurs.-Fri., 11am-5pm Sun.

TRAVEL

✪ Wanderlust

Wander into Wanderlust, a well-stocked Kitsilano travel store, for a large selection of guidebooks, maps, luggage, and other travel gear. One room is full of books, while the second is stocked with useful gadgets and bags of all shapes and sizes. The staff know their stock, whether it's what kind of plug adapter you need or which backpacks fit different body shapes, and they're quick to make recommendations.

MAP 5: 1929 W. 4th Ave., 604/739-2182, www.wanderlustore.com; 10am-7pm Mon.-Fri., 10am-6pm Sat., noon-5pm Sun.

The Travel Bug

The Travel Bug has a cozy nook filled with travel books, and this compact but well-stocked storefront carries luggage, bags, and travel supplies as well. They also host occasional author talks or presentations about travel destinations.

MAP 5: 2865 W. Broadway, 604/737-1122, www.thetravelbug.ca; 10am-6pm Mon.-Sat., noon-5pm Sun.

Cambie Corridor   Map 6

CLOTHING AND ACCESSORIES

✪ Barefoot Contessa

The motto of this Main Street boutique is "all things lovely," and with their stock of frilly, flouncy, feminine styles, it's hard to dispute that claim. At Barefoot Contessa (which has no connection to cooking guru Ina Garten), you can find a perfect dress to wear to a garden party or a flowery frock to brighten a rainy day. Check out their vintage-inspired jewelry and other sparkly baubles. Their second location is on Commercial Drive.

MAP 6: 3715 Main St., 604/879-8175, www.thebarefootcontessa.com; 11am-6pm Mon.-Sat., noon-5pm Sun.

✪ Front and Company

For vintage, designer consignment, and smart new clothing, the fashion-conscious frequent Front and Company. While it can take some hunting to unearth the stylish finds from this jam-packed Main Street shop, the selection of men's and women's garments is generally high quality. They also stock jewelry, handbags, shoes, and fun gift items.

MAP 6: 3772 Main St., 604/879-8431, www.frontandcompany.com; 11am-6:30pm daily

Twigg & Hottie

The three Vancouver designers who founded the Main Street boutique Twigg & Hottie carry their own made-in-Canada We3 label along with clothes, shoes, and accessories by other local creators and international brands that meet their sustainable, ethical ethos. Some of their comfortably fashionable pieces, like the Spanish Banks dress and the Kits Beach cover-up, take their names from local landmarks.

MAP 6: 3671 Main St., 604/879-8595, www.we3.ca; 11am-6pm Mon.-Sat., noon-5pm Sun.

BOOKS AND STATIONERY

Indigo

Canada's largest bookstore chain has a two-level location on the corner of West Broadway and South Granville. Find all types of books, including fiction, travel, food, and titles for kids and teens, by both Canadian and international authors; there's plenty of room for browsing. They carry some gift items, stationery, and magazines as well.

MAP 6: 2505 Granville St., 604/731-7822, www.chapters.indigo.ca; 9am-10pm Mon.-Sat., 10am-10pm Sun.

Vancouver Special

The Regional Assembly of Text

Remember the days when writing meant pen and paper or perhaps a typewriter? Even if you don't, you can journey back to the pre-digital era at The Regional Assembly of Text, a Main Street stationer that stocks cards, journals, and anything to do with correspondence.

Even cooler is their **Letter Writing Club**, held at 7pm on the first Thursday of every month, where you can gather to send notes to your friends and family. The shop provides supplies for this free event; all you need to do is show up and write. Your mom will thank you.

MAP 6: 3934 Main St., 604/877-2247, www.assemblyoftext.com; 11am-6pm Mon.-Sat., noon-5pm Sun.

DESIGN AND GIFTS

Vancouver Special

If you need a retro-styled Bluetooth clock radio, a guide to Canadian cocktails, or vibrantly colored nesting measuring cups, stop into this emporium of cool design stuff. At Vancouver Special on Main Street, you'll find shelves and tables piled with art books, cookbooks, Scandinavian textiles, Japanese ceramics, and a few Vancouver-made objects, as well as a second room with a selection of home furnishings.

The shop shares its name (though not its design) with a type of house built across the city in the 1960s and '70s. Resembling a ranch house atop a box, many of these two-story homes sheltered multigenerational families.

MAP 6: 3612 Main St., 604/568-3673, https://shop.vanspecial.com; 11am-6pm Mon.-Sat., noon-5pm Sun.

OUTDOOR GEAR

MEC

If you need outdoor clothing and equipment, camping supplies, or cycling gear, head for Broadway between Yukon and Main Streets, where you'll find a cluster of outdoor shops. The largest, MEC, as Mountain Equipment Co-op is known, is a Canadian chain stocking their own label and other brands of clothing, backpacks, and gear for hiking, bicycling, rock climbing, kayaking, and other sports. You must be a "member" to purchase anything at MEC; a lifetime membership, which you can include with your first purchase, is $5.

The Vancouver MEC store organizes a variety of events, from free group runs, hikes, and cycles to back-country adventure planning workshops and bike maintenance clinics. Check the website for an event schedule.

MAP 6: 130 W. Broadway, 604/872-7858, www.mec.ca; 10am-7pm Mon.-Wed., 10am-9pm Thurs.-Fri., 9am-6pm Sat., 10am-5pm Sun.

Sports Junkies

Sports Junkies has good deals on new and used sports equipment and clothing for both kids and adults. The jam-packed store, located between Cambie and Main Streets, can feel a little disorganized, but if you take the time to hunt, you can frequently find bargains.

MAP 6: 102 W. Broadway, 604/879-6000, www.sportsjunkies.com; 10am-7pm Mon.-Wed., 10am-8pm Thurs.-Fri., 10am-6pm Sat., 10am-5pm Sun.

Commercial Drive   Map 7

VINTAGE AND SECONDHAND
Still Fabulous

Commercial Drive thrift shop Still Fabulous carries good-quality secondhand women's and men's clothing. It's a small shop, but the packed racks may hold bargains, and your purchases are for a good cause, too. Proceeds from the shop benefit B.C. Children's Hospital and B.C. Women's Hospital. There's another location on Main Street.

MAP 7: 1124 Commercial Dr., 604/620-6110, www.stillfabulousthrift.com; 10am-5pm daily

SPECIALTY FOOD AND DRINK
Gourmet Warehouse

Vancouver's best kitchen supply store is the cavernous East Side Gourmet Warehouse, which carries a vast stock of small appliances, kitchenware, and food items, from spices to snacks to chocolates. If you can eat it or cook with it, they have it, and the accommodating staff can help you find what you need or suggest why you might choose one product over another, whether you're looking for the Pacific Northwest's best dried cherries, Vancouver-made snack crackers, or ingredients for a molecular gastronomy project. They'll make up gift baskets for your foodie friends, and they offer periodic cooking workshops and other events.

MAP 7: 1340 E. Hastings St., 604/253-3022, http://www.gourmetwarehouse.ca; 10am-6pm daily

WHERE TO STAY

Most Vancouver accommodations are on the downtown peninsula, with a few B&Bs and smaller hotels in other parts of the city. Rates peak, and availability is limited, in July and August, so book early if you're planning a summer visit. At other times, especially during the slower winter season, hotel rates drop significantly from the high-season prices listed here.

When you stay **downtown**, you're in the center of everything, close to sights, restaurants, clubs, and theaters. If you prefer a more residential neighborhood that's still convenient to downtown attractions and close to Stanley Park, choose accommodations in the **West End.**

Gastown buzzes late into the night with innovative restaurants and lively bars and lounges; stay here if you love nighttime action. Expect street noise in this neighborhood.

Yaletown is a center of dining and nightlife, so the streets are busy till the wee hours. You're close to the Seawall (great for morning or evening jogs) and most downtown attractions.

Victorian Hotel in Gastown

There's just one hotel on **Granville Island**, but it's located on the waterfront a short stroll from the Public Market. To get downtown, you can hop on a miniferry; just note that ferries don't run late at night.

Kitsilano has a few B&Bs in Victorian-era homes and far more short-term rentals, available from sites like AirBnB.com and VRBO.com. As long as you're near a major thoroughfare, like West 4th Avenue or Broadway, you can catch a bus from Kits to downtown, Granville Island, or UBC.

HIGHLIGHTS

✪ **BEST SPLURGE:** Vancouver's most elegant modern hotel is the **Fairmont Pacific Rim**, a luxurious Asian-influenced tower near the waterfront (page 188).

✪ **BEST HOTEL FOR CLASSIC GLAMOUR:** Originally built in the 1920s, the classy restored **Rosewood Hotel Georgia** has upscale guest rooms, excellent eateries, and stylish lounges (page 188).

✪ **MOST RETRO MOTEL:** The **Burrard Hotel**, an old-time motor hotel downtown, has been converted into a fun retro-chic lodging (page 191).

✪ **MOST ARTISTIC SLEEPING SPOT:** Original contemporary art distinguishes the low-rise **Listel Hotel** with a prime perch on Vancouver's main downtown shopping street (page 191).

✪ **BEST WAY TO SUPPORT THE ARTS WHILE YOU SLEEP:** One-of-a-kind works by First Nations artists adorn the rooms at **Skwachàys Lodge**, Canada's first aboriginal arts hotel (page 193).

✪ **COOLEST HOTEL:** At **Opus Hotel Vancouver**, many of the vibrantly hued rooms have windows into the baths. Don't be shy (page 194)!

PRICE KEY

$	Less than CAN$150 per night
$ $	CAN$150-300 per night
$ $ $	More than CAN$300 per night

Fairmont Pacific Rim

WHERE TO STAY IF...

YOU'RE ONLY HERE FOR A WEEKEND
Stay **downtown,** where you're within walking distance of many attractions, restaurants, bars, and outdoor activities.

YOU LOVE GETTING OUTDOORS IN AN URBAN SETTING
Choose a lodging in the **West End,** and you'll have Stanley Park, the Seawall, and English Bay at your door.

YOU PLAN YOUR DAYS AROUND YOUR NEXT MEAL
Look for accommodations in or near **Gastown** to stay in the center of Vancouver's food and drink scene.

YOU WANT TO EXPERIENCE LIFE AS A LOCAL
Imagine yourself living in Vancouver when you sleep amid the condos and lofts in **Yaletown,** where you're a short stroll from **False Creek** and from plenty of restaurants and bars.

YOU WANT TO FEEL LIKE A STUDENT AGAIN
Stay in dorm-style suites or a hostel on the **UBC** campus.

Budget travelers, take note: On the University of British Columbia campus, close to attractions like the Museum of Anthropology, you can stay in simple hotel-style suites or, from May through mid-August, bunk hostel-style in a residence hall. The downside of campus life? Dining options tend toward student-centered fast food, and you're a 30-minute ride from downtown.

Sleeping in Richmond, where the airport is located, is handy if you're arriving late or have an early flight out, and you'll be in the heart of the Asian dining scene. Choose a hotel near a Canada Line station, and you can get downtown in less than 25 minutes. Since far more attractions are located in Vancouver proper, however, you'll spend more time in transit.

Staying on the North Shore means being close to the mountains and all their outdoor activities. The drawback is that getting downtown means crossing an often-congested bridge (or taking a ferry); touring other parts of the city will be easier if you have a car.

ALTERNATIVE LODGING OPTIONS
Online Lodging Services

Online lodging services like AirBnB.com and VRBO.com are huge in Vancouver, offering listings for apartments on the downtown peninsula and for houses, basement suites, apartments, and condo buildings throughout the rest of the city. Despite the number of offerings, availability can be tight in the peak months of July and August; book early.

Get to know these Canadian real estate terms if you're looking for a short-term rental. A suite is another word for an apartment; a bachelor suite is a studio (one-room) apartment. A strata unit is a condominium, and a parkade is a parking garage. And a "garburator?" That's a garbage disposal.

Camping

Recreational vehicles and other campers should plan to stay outside the city proper; RVs and other large vehicles are not allowed to park on Vancouver streets between 10am and 6pm. The closest private campgrounds are in

West Vancouver at the Capilano River RV Park (www.capilanoriver-rvpark.com), which is almost directly under the Lions Gate Bridge, and in suburban Burnaby at the Cariboo RV Park & Campground (http://bcrvpark.com). RVs can also stay south of the city at the Peace Arch RV Park (www.peacearchrvpark.ca) in Surrey and north of Vancouver at Paradise Valley Campground (http://paradisevalleycampground. net) in Squamish.

Several provincial parks within an easy drive of Vancouver offer a more scenic setting for campers, including Alice Lake Provincial Park (http:// seatoskyparks.com) in Squamish, Cultus Lake Provincial Park (http:// seatoskyparks.com) near Chilliwack east of Vancouver, and Golden Ears Provincial Park (www.env.gov.bc.ca), also east of Vancouver, near the city of Maple Ridge.

Airport Hotels

The posh Fairmont Vancouver Airport Hotel is the only lodging right at the Vancouver International Airport; the lobby sits above the U.S. departures hall. Many other Richmond lodgings advertise themselves as "airport hotels" and provide shuttles for guests. Of these off-airport accommodations, the Pacific Gateway Hotel (3500 Cessna Dr., Richmond, 604/278-1241 or 866/382-3474, www.pacificgateway-hotel.com) is closest to the terminals, a five-minute ride on the hotel's complimentary shuttle.

Downtown and the West End

Map 1

✪ Fairmont Pacific Rim $$$

High-tech, Asian-inspired Fairmont Pacific Rim is one of the city's most luxurious lodgings. Stearns & Foster beds topped with Italian linens, plush robes, and marble baths with soaker tubs make the 377 contemporary guest rooms feel like urban oases. And that's before you open the electronically controlled drapes to check out the city and harbor views, or head for the rooftop to lounge around the secluded swimming pool. When you're ready to venture out, the hotel's bicycle butler can outfit you with two-wheeled transportation, or you can book the complimentary car service for downtown outings. As at all Fairmont properties, Wi-Fi is free to Fairmont President Club members.

MAP 1: 1038 Canada Pl., 604/695-5300 or 877/900-5350, www.fairmont.com

✪ Rosewood Hotel Georgia $$$

Originally built in the 1920s and still channeling that era's glamour, the Rosewood Hotel Georgia downtown has 156 classy guest rooms and suites, done in blues, creams, and chocolate browns with Italian linens and luxe baths with heated floors. Make time to exercise in the indoor salt-water lap pool or the 24-hour fitness center, since the hotel's Hawksworth Restaurant (604/673-7000, www.hawksworthrestaurant.com) is among the city's top special-occasion dining spots and Bel Café (604/673-7000, http://belcafe.com) is an upscale place for pastries. Room service is available around the clock, and when you need to venture out, the hotel's car service can chauffeur you around town.

MAP 1: 801 W. Georgia St., 604/682-5566 or 888/767-3966, www.rosewoodhotels.com

Rosewood Hotel Georgia

Fairmont Hotel Vancouver $$$

At the oldest of the Fairmont chain's downtown properties, the green copper roof and stone gargoyles of the 1939 Fairmont Hotel Vancouver make it a recognizable landmark amid the city's glass-and-steel towers. The least expensive of the 556 English manor-style guest rooms are small, but all come with modern amenities such as air-conditioning and flat-screen TVs, as well as the classic Fairmont service. For free Wi-Fi, sign up for Fairmont's complimentary frequent-stay program. The indoor pool is in a window-lined greenhouse space, and on the lower level, Absolute Spa at the Fairmont (604/684-2772, www.absolutespa.com) caters to men, although women are welcome.

MAP 1: 900 W. Georgia St., 604/684-3131 or 866/540-4452, www.fairmont.com

Four Seasons Hotel Vancouver $$$

Though it fades into the urban cityscape, surrounded by newer and flashier towers, the Four Seasons Hotel Vancouver is a discreetly deluxe downtown property. Spread over 28 floors, its 372 traditionally decorated rooms and suites have down pillows and fluffy duvets, dark wood furnishings, flat-screen TVs, and free Wi-Fi; pick a room on the 20th floor or above for peekaboo mountain views. A hotel highlight is the private fourth-floor deck, with an indoor-outdoor pool and fitness facility facing the garden terrace. On the lobby level, Yew Seafood + Bar (604/692-4939, www.yewseafood.com) draws fish lovers with its emphasis on regional seafood.

MAP 1: 791 W. Georgia St., 604/689-9333 or 866/223-9333, www.fourseasons.com

Loden Hotel $$$

Health-conscious travelers should check out the WanderFIT program at the Loden Hotel. These guided hiking, cycling, and trail running adventures let you keep active as you explore the city. You can also tool around on complimentary electric bikes, work out in the window-lined gym, or tune into the 24-hour yoga channel in your room, which comes with a yoga mat. The 77 guest rooms in this skinny 15-story West End boutique lodging have earth-tone furnishings, dark granite baths, and floor-to-ceiling windows. Recover from all this activity with a drink or a meal at Tableau Bar Bistro (604/639-8692, http://tableaubarbistro.com), which serves updated French classics.

Loden Hotel

MAP 1: 1177 Melville St., 604/669-5060 or 877/225-6336, http://theloden.com

Pan Pacific Hotel Vancouver $$$

Above the cruise ship terminal at Canada Place downtown, the 23-story Pan Pacific Hotel Vancouver is especially convenient if you're starting or ending your Vancouver stay on a boat, though even landlubbers appreciate the panoramic views of the harbor and North Shore mountains. Enjoy the vistas from the heated saltwater pool and from many of the 503 nautical-style guest rooms, outfitted with padded white-leather headboards, white duvets trimmed with navy piping, and maple furniture. Have a drink in the Coal Harbour Bar or the Patio Terrace for more sea-to-sky views.

MAP 1: 999 Canada Pl., 604/662-8111 or 800/663-1515, www.panpacific.com

Wedgewood Hotel & Spa $$$

You don't hear much buzz about the Wedgewood Hotel & Spa, but guests at this fashionable downtown hideaway seem to like it that way. The 83 traditional rooms and suites feature deluxe amenities like plush robes and slippers, twice-daily housekeeping, and homemade bedtime cookies. You can work out in the up-to-date fitness facility and relax in the eucalyptus steam room; there's also a full-service spa. Elegant Bacchus Restaurant and Lounge (604/608-5319) serves French-accented cuisine with west coast ingredients, as well as a weekend afternoon tea (2pm-4pm Sat.-Sun.).

MAP 1: 845 Hornby St., 604/689-7777 or 800/663-0666, www.wedgewoodhotel.com

West End Guest House $$$

This colorfully painted 1906 Victorian on a quiet residential block is just a short stroll from Robson Street. It's a classic B&B, where guests mingle over afternoon sherry and sit down around the dining table for a full hot breakfast. Owners Paul Wylie and David Birch have lined the hallways with historic Vancouver photos and furnished the eight guest rooms, all with Wi-Fi, TVs, and en suite baths, with antiques and period pieces, though the updated linens and upholstery give them a more contemporary feel. Bonus: The inn offers free parking for guests.

MAP 1: 1362 Haro St., 604/681-2889, www.westendguesthouse.com

✪ Burrard Hotel $$

Built in 1956, the four-story Burrard Hotel is an old-time motor hotel gone glam. The best feature of this retro-chic mid-century-modern lodging downtown is the courtyard garden, with palm trees and a fire pit, hidden from the surrounding city hum. The 72 guest rooms are small (baths are particularly petite), but they're well designed with espresso makers, mini-fridges, and flat-screen TVs. Rates include Wi-Fi, North American phone calls, a pass to a nearby health club, and use of the hotel's bicycles. Off the lobby, Elysian Coffee (http://elysiancoffee.com) serves drip coffee and espresso drinks (from beans they roast in-house), a selection of teas, avocado toast, and pastries.

MAP 1: 1100 Burrard St., 604/681-2331 or 800/663-0366, www.theburrard.com

Burrard Hotel

✪ Listel Hotel $$

Original artworks adorn the lobby, corridors, and guest rooms at the low-rise 129-room Listel Hotel on Vancouver's main downtown shopping street. The "museum" rooms feature works by First Nations artists, while staff from a local gallery decorated the eclectic "gallery" rooms. The retro-designed standard units on the second floor are simpler but less expensive. You can work out in the small fitness center or request a complimentary pass to a nearby health club. Overall, the hotel is a comfortable and classy choice. On-site restaurant Forage (604/661-1400, www.foragevancouver.com), which emphasizes B.C. ingredients, is a bonus. The Listel charges an additional 6 percent fee to cover Wi-Fi and North American phone calls.

MAP 1: 1300 Robson St., 604/684-8461 or 800/663-5491, www.thelistelhotel.com

Barclay House B&B $$

Each of the six guest rooms at the Barclay House B&B, in a yellow 1904 Victorian home in the midst of urban Vancouver, is decorated differently. The bay-windowed turquoise-accented Beach room has a queen bed and a cozy sitting area, while the Peak room, under the eaves on the top floor, has skylights and a claw-foot tub. Guests can mingle in the lounge or games room, both furnished with a mix of contemporary and antique pieces. Rates at this West End inn include parking, Wi-Fi, and a full breakfast.

MAP 1: 1351 Barclay St., 604/605-1351 or 800/971-1351, www.barclayhouse.com

Blue Horizon Hotel $$

Built in the 1960s, the Blue Horizon Hotel was Vancouver's first high-rise.

These days, all 214 rooms in this skinny 31-story downtown tower are corner units, with private balconies and city views, as well as flat-screen TVs, minifridges, Keurig coffeemakers, air-conditioning, and free Wi-Fi. The family suites on the 29th floor have a separate living room with a queen bed and double sofa bed, as well as a king bedroom. Other amenities include an indoor lap pool, a hot tub, and a sauna. Prices rise as you get higher in the building.

MAP 1: 1225 Robson St., 604/688-1411 or 800/663-1333, www.bluehorizonhotel.com

Century Plaza Hotel & Spa $$

The apartment-style Century Plaza Hotel & Spa isn't fancy, but the studio and one-bedroom units have kitchen facilities and free Wi-Fi. Outside the busy summer season, you can often find good deals here. The 240-room hotel has a fitness center, indoor pool, and a branch of the local Absolute Spa chain, and you're just a short stroll from most downtown attractions.

MAP 1: 1015 Burrard St., 604/687-0575 or 800/663-1818, www.century-plaza.com

Moda Hotel $$

In a restored 1908 building downtown, the boutique Moda Hotel has 67 cozy rooms. The smallest measure just 150 square feet (14 square meters), while standard doubles are 300-350 square feet (28-32 square meters), but they're smartly designed, with red accents, updated baths, air-conditioning, and free Wi-Fi and North American phone calls. You don't have to go far to eat and drink: Uva Wine & Cocktail Bar (604/632-9560, www.uvavancouver.

com), Red Card Sports Bar (604/689-4460, www.redcardsportsbar.ca), and Cibo Trattoria (604/602-9570, www.cibotrattoria.com) are all on the lobby level.

MAP 1: 900 Seymour St., 604/683-4251 or 877/683-5522, www.modahotel.ca

Sunset Inn and Suites $$

On a residential West End block, steps from lively Davie Street, the Sunset Inn and Suites, in a 1970s former apartment building, has 50 unpretentious studios and one-bedroom units (with sofa beds), all with full kitchens and handy features like multiple outlets and USB ports by the beds. Rates include lots of extras: Wi-Fi, a light continental breakfast, and free parking. The cheapest units overlook the back alley; the priciest have views toward False Creek. The tiny fitness room has just three cardio machines, but get outdoors: you're a short stroll from the Seawall.

MAP 1: 1111 Burnaby St., 604/688-2474, http://sunsetinn.com

Sylvia Hotel $$

Sure, the ivy-covered Sylvia Hotel, constructed as a West End apartment building in 1912, is a little old-fashioned. But all 120 units, from basic queens and kings to larger family suites, have free Wi-Fi and flat-screen TVs; some have kitchens, and the best rooms have million-dollar views of English Bay. Even if your room doesn't, you can walk out the front door to the beach, Stanley Park, and plenty of dining spots.

MAP 1: 1154 Gilford St., 604/681-9321 or 877/681-9321, www.sylviahotel.com

✪ Skwachàys Lodge $$

At Skwachàys Lodge, Canada's first aboriginal arts and culture hotel, aboriginal artists worked with hotel designers to craft 18 distinctive guest rooms in an early-20th-century brick Victorian. In the Poem Suite, poems and pencil drawings dance across walls; in the Moon Suite, artists painted a golden moon face on the ceiling watching over the bed below. An aboriginal-owned company created the hotel's bath products; Wi-Fi and both local and international calls are included in the rates. Guests can participate in sweat lodge or smudging ceremonies with an aboriginal elder, with advance reservations. An added benefit: Hotel profits help subsidize housing for First Nations artists.

MAP 2: 31 W. Pender St., 604/687-3589 or 888/998-0797, http://skwachays.com

Delta Vancouver Suites $$

Managed by Marriott, this 23-story tower caters to business travelers, but with separate sitting and sleeping areas, many of the 225 all-suite rooms at the Delta Vancouver Suites accommodate families, too. Minifridges, coffeemakers, flat-screen TVs, and Wi-Fi are standard, and the floor-to-ceiling windows make rooms feel larger.

MAP 2: 550 W. Hastings St., 604/689-8188, www.marriott.com

Victorian Hotel $$

The 47-room Victorian Hotel is a European-style boutique property in two brick buildings, dating to 1898

Skwachàys Lodge

and 1908. While the least expensive rooms are tiny and share hallway baths, others are more spacious and have private baths. All tastefully mix period pieces and modern furnishings, with pillow-top mattresses, robes, flat-screen TVs, and iPod docks. Rates include Wi-Fi and continental breakfast.

MAP 2: 514 Homer St., 604/681-6369, www.victorianhotel.ca

Yaletown and False Creek Map 3

✪ Opus Hotel Vancouver $$$

A clear contender for the title of "Vancouver's coolest hotel," the boutique Opus Hotel Vancouver outfitted its 96 guest rooms in eye-popping lime greens, magentas, purples, and vibrant oranges. Many of the spacious baths have a window into the bedroom, while in others, bath windows face outside (don't be shy!). Rooms aren't huge, though they come with high-tech toys like flat-screen TVs, Keurig coffeemakers, and iPads that you can use throughout your stay (with free Wi-Fi, of course). Staff greet guests with a complimentary glass of sparkling wine; to get around town, book the hotel's complimentary car service or borrow a gratis mountain bike.

MAP 3: 322 Davie St., 866/642-6787, http://vancouver.opushotel.com

Hotel BLU $$

This contemporary 75-room lodging sits at the foot of Robson Street, within shouting distance of B.C. Place, and at Hotel BLU, there's plenty to keep you active: an indoor pool with a courtyard patio, 24-hour fitness room, morning runs with a personal trainer, and complimentary bicycles. Guest rooms are technology-friendly, with tablet computers, free Wi-Fi, handy USB ports, and plenty of electrical outlets. Other amenities include minifridges, microwaves, tea-kettles, and one-cup espresso makers, and many of the modern bathrooms have glass walls into the showers. The building also has a self-service guest laundry.

MAP 3: 177 Robson St., 604/620-6200 or 855/284-2091, www.hotelbluvancouver.com

YWCA Hotel Vancouver $

One of Vancouver's best options for travelers on a budget is the modern YWCA Hotel Vancouver. The 155 rooms range from basic singles with either a hall bath or a semiprivate bath (shared between two rooms) or doubles with hall, semiprivate, or private facilities to larger units that accommodate three to five people. All have air-conditioning, flat-screen TVs, minifridges, and free Wi-Fi. Guests can prep meals in one of the three common kitchens or grab a snack in the lobby café.

MAP 3: 733 Beatty St., 604/895-5830 or 800/663-1424, www.ywcavan.org

Granville Island

Map 4

Granville Island Hotel $$$

To stay right on Granville Island, book a room at the waterfront Granville Island Hotel. The 82 guest rooms and suites are all furnished differently; the nicest ones take advantage of the island location with balconies and water views. Wi-Fi is included, and the hotel has a small fitness room—but for a more interesting workout, you can run or walk along the Seawall.

MAP 4: 1253 Johnston St., 604/683-7373 or 800/663-1840, www.granvilleislandhotel.com

Kitsilano

Map 5

Corkscrew Inn $$

Glass artist Sal Robinson has outfitted the Corkscrew Inn, the B&B that she co-owns with her husband, Wayne Meadows, in a 1912 Craftsman-style Kitsilano home, with her original art deco-inspired wine-themed stained glass. You'll see her work in the sitting areas, dining room, and the five guest rooms, which also have custom-designed baths; one features tiles that Robinson designed to depict the Empire State Building. The inn also takes its name from Meadows's collection of antique corkscrews, which he displays in a tiny "museum" on the lower level. Rates include a family-style hot breakfast, which might feature a wild salmon frittata or lemon ricotta pancakes.

MAP 5: 2735 W. 2nd Ave., 604/733-7276 or 877/737-7276, www.corkscrewinn.com

UBC and Point Grey

Map 5

West Coast Suites at UBC $$

On the University of British Columbia campus, West Coast Suites at UBC are modern one-bedroom apartment-style suites. Units have a king bed in the bedroom, a living room with a small dining table and a sofa bed, and a full kitchen. Other amenities include flat-screen TVs, Wi-Fi, and U.S. and Canadian phone calls. Open year-round, the suites are located a short walk from the UBC bus loop.

MAP 5: 5959 Student Union Blvd., 604/822-1000 or 888/822-1030, http://suitesatubc.com

HI-Vancouver Jericho Beach $

Fancy a cheap sleep by the beach? Hostelling International runs this seasonal hostel in a former military barracks, a short walk from the shore in Point Grey. The dorms remain true to their origins, with each room sleeping 14 to 18 people in curtained-off four-person "quads," each with two

195

bunk beds. Updated private rooms, with shared baths down the hall, accommodate two to four. There's also a private room with a queen bed and an en suite bath, as well as two family rooms, each sleeping 2-4 and sharing a kitchen and bath.

The hostel has a kitchen for guests' use, complimentary Wi-Fi, laundry facilities, bike rentals, and a small café. The nearest commercial district, with a grocery store, liquor store, and several restaurants, is along West 4th Avenue near Alma Street, about a 15- to 20-minute walk from the hostel. Buses run along West 4th Avenue toward downtown (20-25 minutes) and the UBC campus (10 minutes).

MAP 5: 1515 Discovery St., 604/224-3208 or 778/328-2220, www.hihostels.ca; May-mid-Sept.

Pacific Spirit Hostel $

More student dormitory than classic travelers' hostel, Pacific Spirit Hostel offers summer-only budget accommodations in Place Vanier Residence, a UBC residence hall. Sleeping options include basic private single or double rooms; you get a bed, a desk, and a storage cabinet, but not much else. There are shared baths and a TV lounge on each floor. Although complimentary Wi-Fi is available, you can access it only in the lobby, not in the rooms.

The hostel is open only during the university's summer break, May through mid-August. From the UBC bus loop, walk west on University Boulevard and turn right onto Lower Mall; it's about a 10-minute walk.

MAP 5: 1935 Lower Mall, 604/822-1000 or 888/822-1030, http://suitesatubc.com; May-mid-Aug.

Richmond

Map 8

Fairmont Vancouver Airport Hotel $$$

You can't stay closer to the departure gates than at this luxury lodging inside the terminal at Vancouver International Airport. At the Fairmont Vancouver Airport Hotel, the lobby sits above the U.S. departures hall, yet despite the bustle below, this contemporary property feels surprisingly quiet. The floor-to-ceiling windows in the 392 guest rooms, many of which overlook the runways, are triple-glazed to keep out the airplane noise; pillow-top mattresses and white duvets cover the king or queen beds. To unwind before or after your travels, swim in the lap pool, work out in the fitness

facility, or book a treatment at the spa.

Even if you're not staying at the hotel, head for the Jetside Bar (11am-1am Mon.-Sat., 11am-midnight Sun.) for refreshments. You can watch the planes come and go over drinks and light meals while waiting for your flight.

MAP 8: 3111 Grant McConachie Way, subway: YVR Airport, 604/207-5200 or 866/540-4441, www.fairmont.com

River Rock Casino Resort $$

This Richmond entertainment complex houses B.C.'s largest casino, a 1,000-seat theater, a free-form indoor saltwater pool with a 70-foot (21-meter) waterslide, and two hotels.

The main hotel, River Rock Casino Resort, has 203 spacious and contemporary one- or two-bedroom suites with separate sleeping and sitting areas. West-facing units look out to the Fraser River. Across the street, the Hotel at River Rock has smaller, less expensive, but still comfortable rooms. In the hotel building, the Sea Harbour Seafood Restaurant (8888 River Rd., Richmond, 604/232-0816, www.seaharbour.com; 10:30am-3pm and 5pm-10pm Mon.-Fri., 10am-3pm and 5pm-10pm Sat.-Sun.) serves excellent dim sum.

MAP 8: 8811 River Rd., subway: Bridgeport, 604/247-8900 or 866/748-3718, www.riverrock.com

The North Shore

Map 9

Pinnacle Hotel at the Pier

Pinnacle Hotel at the Pier $$

Convenient to mountain activities, eight-story Pinnacle Hotel at the Pier has panoramic views across the water to the Vancouver skyline. Of the 106 modern guest rooms, with Wi-Fi included, those on the harbor side have small step-out balconies, and if you open the bath blinds, you can take in the vistas while you soak in the tub. City-side rooms glimpse the mountains. In the health club, you can enjoy the seascape from the cardio and weight machines, waterside sundeck, or indoor Olympic-size pool. The hotel is a five-minute walk from Lonsdale Quay and a 12-minute ride on the SeaBus to downtown Vancouver.

MAP 9: 138 Victory Ship Way, North Vancouver, 604/986-7437 or 877/986-7437, http://pinnaclepierhotel.com

VICTORIA AND VANCOUVER ISLAND

British Columbia's capital city mixes historic and hip, while the island's Pacific coast lures ocean lovers with surf, sand, and rainforest trails.

Fairmont Empress, Victoria

Vancouver Island offers lots of ways to relax, from enjoying a cup of tea or a glass of wine to snorkeling with seals, watching whales, and catching waves.

British Columbia's capital city, Victoria, is located at the southern tip of Vancouver Island, across the Strait of Georgia from the city of Vancouver. You can easily spend a day or more taking in the sights along the Inner Harbour, venturing offshore for whale-watching, or enjoying traditional afternoon tea. A boom in contemporary restaurants, craft breweries, and cool cocktail bars means that you'll eat and drink well, too. Just outside of Victoria, the Cowichan Valley is a growing wine region, where you can sip and sample what's new at the winery tasting rooms.

North of Victoria, Nanaimo is an alternate ferry port between Vancouver and the island; it's the most convenient route between Vancouver and Tofino on the island's west coast. Besides an attractive waterfront and historic sites, Nanaimo is worth a stop for a unique adventure: snorkeling with a colony of seals who live near the city's harbor. Be sure to sample a sweet Nanaimo bar, too.

Vancouver Island's striking west coast is the region's ocean playground. You can explore the beaches and rainforest trails in the Pacific Rim National Park Reserve and unwind in the sand-and-surf communities of Tofino and Ucluelet. Day-trip to remote hot springs, kayak to a First Nations island, or go on a whale- or bear-watching excursion. Oceanfront resorts and fine casual restaurants (seafood is a specialty) keep you comfortable when you come in from the sea.

HIGHLIGHTS

☆ **VICTORIA'S INNER HARBOUR:** Buskers, ferries, floatplanes, and travelers all converge on Victoria's waterfront, where the city's major sights are located (page 200).

☆ **ROYAL BRITISH COLUMBIA MUSEUM:** Trace British Columbia's roots at this museum of cultural and natural history (page 201).

☆ **BUTCHART GARDENS:** Elaborate floral displays and holiday lights make these gardens one of Vancouver Island's most popular year-round attractions (page 213).

☆ **WHALE-WATCHING:** You may spot orcas, humpbacks, or gray whales from the whale-watching boats that depart from Victoria (page 217).

☆ **SNORKELING WITH SEALS:** Suit up and snorkel up close with harbor seals on this unique half-day adventure from Nanaimo (page 228).

☆ **PACIFIC RIM NATIONAL PARK RESERVE:** Explore the rainforest and beaches in this lush oceanfront national park (page 232).

☆ **TOFINO:** This funky town on Vancouver Island's far west coast has beautiful beaches, great restaurants, and a chill surfer vibe, plus lots of on-the-water excursions (page 235).

Victoria's Inner Harbour

Victoria

The British Empire lived long and prospered in British Columbia's capital city, Victoria. British explorer James Cook became the first non-aboriginal person to set foot in what is now British Columbia, when he landed on Vancouver Island's west coast in 1778. Sixty-five years later, the Hudson's Bay Company established a trading post on the island's southeastern corner, naming it Fort Victoria, after the British queen.

Victoria is still known for its British traditions, particularly elegant afternoon tea, and as Canada's warmest region, Victoria has been a popular destination for retirees. These days, though, Victoria has shed its reputation as a destination for "the newly wed and the nearly dead." It's an increasingly modern, multicultural community that's drawing entrepreneurs, passionate foodies, and other independent types, with cultural attractions, vibrant restaurants, and plenty to do in the mild outdoors.

SIGHTS
DOWNTOWN
✪ Victoria's Inner Harbour

Victoria's harbor is the center of activity downtown, with ferries and floatplanes coming and going, buskers busking, and plenty of tourists soaking up the scene and the sun. Many companies offering whale-watching tours and other water-based excursions have their offices along the waterside promenade, and Tourism Victoria (812 Wharf St., 250/953-2033, www.tourismvictoria.com; 9am-5pm daily) runs a visitor information center here, with public restrooms.

Victoria Harbour Ferry (250/708-0201, www.victoriaharbourferry.com) operates a water taxi (11am-5pm daily Mar. and Oct., 11am-7pm daily Apr.-mid-May, 10am-9pm daily mid-May-mid-Sept.) around the Inner Harbour in cute colorful boats, with stops at Fisherman's Wharf, the Delta Victoria Ocean Pointe Resort, and many other waterside points. Fares vary by distance; a basic one-zone trip, which includes many Inner Harbour points, is $6 per person. They also offer 45-minute harbor tours (10am-5pm daily Mar.-Oct.; adults $26, seniors and students $24, under age 13 $14), departing every 30 minutes from the Causeway Marina in front of the Fairmont Empress.

Fairmont Empress

A landmark on the Inner Harbour, the Fairmont Empress (721 Government St., 250/384-8111, www.fairmont.com) has cast its grand ivy-covered visage across Victoria's waterfront since 1908. Architect Francis M. Rattenbury designed and built the hotel as one of the Canadian Pacific Railway's majestic château-style lodgings. British royals have slept here, including Prince Charles and Camilla in 2009, as have U.S. presidents and numerous celebrities, including Katharine Hepburn, Bob Hope, John Travolta, Harrison Ford, and Barbra Streisand.

Even if you're not staying at the Empress, you can walk through its public spaces, dine in its restaurants and lounges, or take afternoon tea (a Victoria tradition). On the front lawn, check out the beehives where Fairmont staff harvest honey to use in the property's kitchen.

totem pole, Royal British Columbia Museum

⚙ Royal British Columbia Museum

Tracing British Columbia's cultural and natural history, the Royal British Columbia Museum (675 Belleville St., 250/356-7226, http://royalbcmuseum.bc.ca; 10am-5pm daily late Sept.-late May, 10am-5pm Sun.-Thurs., 10am-10pm Fri.-Sat. late May-late Sept.; adults $24, seniors, students, and ages 6-18 $17) was founded in 1886. A highlight is the First Peoples Gallery, with totem poles, masks, regalia, and other indigenous objects, along with exhibits that illuminate the lives of Canada's first inhabitants.

You can take a one-hour guided tour (included with museum admission); check the calendar on the museum's website or in the lobby for tour times and topics. To spread out your museum meanderings over two consecutive days, buy a discounted two-day ticket (adults $36, seniors, students, and ages 6-18 $25.50).

The museum has an IMAX Theatre (IMAX only adults $11.95, seniors and ages 6-18 $9.75, students $10.75, with museum admission adults $34, seniors and ages 6-18 $27, students $28), showing a changing selection of movies on the big screen.

Adjacent to the museum, several totem poles stand in Thunderbird Park. Also outside is the 1852 Helmcken House, the oldest public building in B.C. still on its original site; the Hudson's Bay Company built the cabin for Dr. John Sebastian Helmcken and his wife, Cecilia Douglas. A physician and politician, Helmcken helped bring B.C. into the Canadian Confederation, though he allegedly once said that Canada would eventually be absorbed into the United States.

B.C. Parliament Building

Although Vancouver, on the mainland, is a much larger city, Victoria has been the provincial capital since British Columbia joined the Canadian Confederation in 1871. The seat of the provincial government is the B.C. Legislative Assembly, which convenes in the stately 1897 Parliament Building (501 Belleville St., 250/387-8669, tour information 250/387-3046, www.leg.bc.ca; tours 9am-5pm daily mid-May-early Sept., 9am-5pm Mon.-Fri. early-Sept.-mid-May; free), overlooking the Inner Harbour.

Thousands of twinkling white lights illuminate the Parliament Building, making the copper-roofed stone structure even more photogenic at night than it is during the day. British-born architect Francis M. Rattenbury (1867-1935) designed the building, winning a design competition and his first major commission less than a year after he arrived in B.C. from England at age 25.

On 30- to 45-minute tours of the grand building, you'll learn more about the province's history and

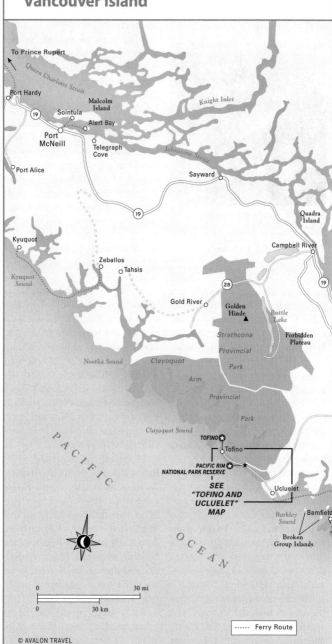

Vancouver Island

To Prince Rupert

Queen Charlotte Strait

Knight Inlet

Port Hardy

Malcolm Island

Sointula

Alert Bay

Port McNeill

Telegraph Cove

Johnstone Strait

Port Alice

Sayward

Quadra Island

Kyuquot

Campbell River

Kyuquot Sound

Zeballos

Tahsis

Gold River

Golden Hinde ▲

Buttle Lake

Strathcona

Provincial

Forbidden Plateau

Nootka Sound

Clayoquot

Park

Arm

Provincial

Park

Clayoquot Sound

TOFINO

Tofino

PACIFIC RIM NATIONAL PARK RESERVE ★

SEE "TOFINO AND UCLUELET" MAP

Ucluelet

PACIFIC

Barkley Sound

Bamfield

OCEAN

Broken Group Islands

0   30 mi

0   30 km

...... Ferry Route

© AVALON TRAVEL

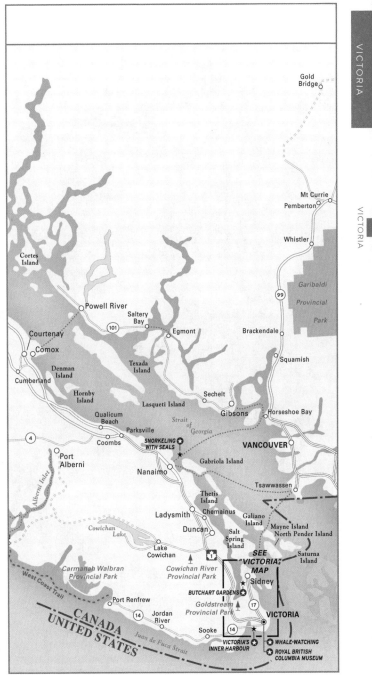

Gold Bridge

Mt Currie
Pemberton

Whistler

Cortes Island

Garibaldi Provincial Park

Powell River
Saltery Bay
Egmont

99

Courtenay
Comox

Brackendale

Denman Island

Squamish

Cumberland

Texada Island

Hornby Island

Sechelt

Lasqueti Island

Qualicum Beach
Parksville

Strait of Georgia

Gibsons

Horseshoe Bay

4

Coombs

SNORKELING WITH SEALS ★

VANCOUVER

Port Alberni

Nanaimo

Gabriola Island

Tsawwassen

Albert Inlet

Thetis Island

Ladysmith
Chemainus

Galiano Island

Cowichan Lake

Duncan

Salt Spring Island

Mayne Island
North Pender Island

Lake Cowichan

1

SEE "VICTORIA" MAP

Carmanah Walbran Provincial Park

Cowichan River Provincial Park

Saturna Island

West Coast Trail

Sidney

Port Renfrew

BUTCHART GARDENS ★
Goldstream Provincial Park

17

CANADA
UNITED STATES

Jordan River

14

Sooke

14

VICTORIA

Juan de Fuca Strait

VICTORIA'S INNER HARBOUR ★   ★ **WHALE-WATCHING**
★ **ROYAL BRITISH COLUMBIA MUSEUM**

203

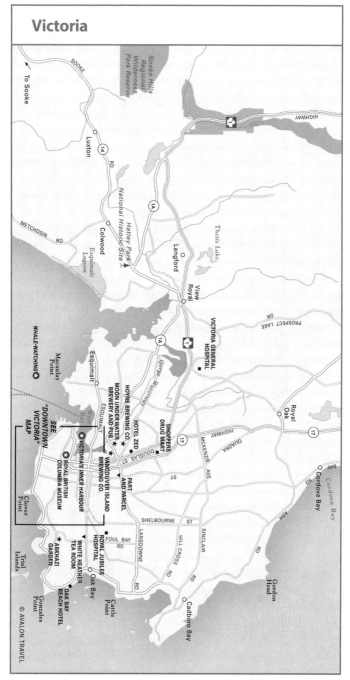

Victoria

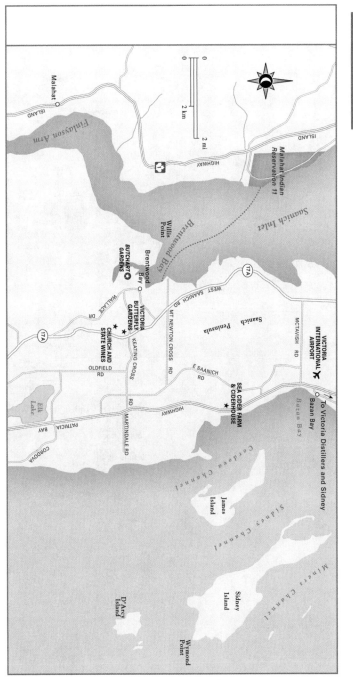

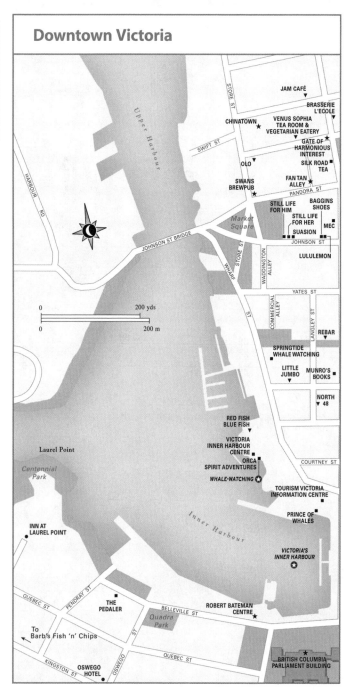

Downtown Victoria

VICTORIA

VICTORIA

Upper Harbour

STORE ST

JAM CAFÉ

BRASSERIE
L'ECOLE

CHINATOWN ★   VENUS SOPHIA
TEA ROOM &
VEGETARIAN EATERY

SWIFT ST

GATE OF
HARMONIOUS
INTEREST ★

OLO ▼   SILK ROAD
TEA

SWANS
BREWPUB ★   FAN TAN
ALLEY ★

PANDORA ST

STILL LIFE   BAGGINS
FOR HIM   SHOES

STILL LIFE
FOR HER

Market
Square   SUASION   MEC

JOHNSON ST

JOHNSON ST BRIDGE   LULULEMON

HARBOUR RD

STORE ST

WHARF ST

WADDINGTON ALLEY

YATES ST

0   200 yds

COMMERCIAL ALLEY

LANGLEY ST

REBAR

0   200 m   SPRINGTIDE
WHALE WATCHING

LITTLE
JUMBO ▼   MUNRO'S
BOOKS

NORTH
▼ 48

RED FISH
BLUE FISH ▼

VICTORIA
INNER HARBOUR
CENTRE

ORCA
SPIRIT ADVENTURES

WHALE-WATCHING ✪   COURTNEY ST

TOURISM VICTORIA
INFORMATION CENTRE

Laurel Point

Centennial
Park   Inner Harbour   PRINCE OF
WHALES

INN AT
LAUREL POINT ●   VICTORIA'S
INNER HARBOUR ✪

QUEBEC ST

PENDRAY ST

THE
PEDALER

BELLEVILLE ST   ROBERT BATEMAN
CENTRE ★

To
Barb's Fish 'n' Chips   Quadra
Park

OSWEGO ST

QUEBEC ST

KINGSTON ST   OSWEGO
HOTEL ●   BRITISH COLUMBIA ★
PARLIAMENT BUILDING

206

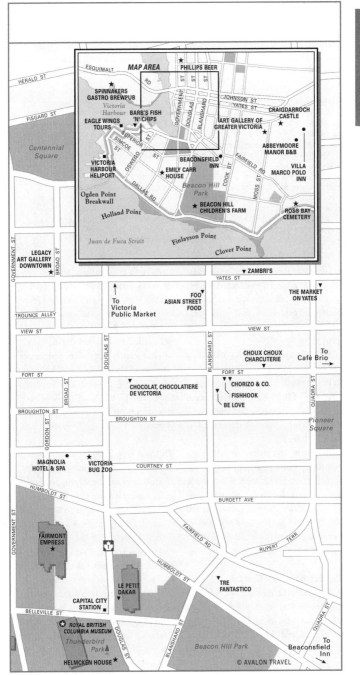

MAP AREA

ESQUIMALT

★ PHILLIPS BEER

HERALD ST

FISGARD ST

★ SPINNAKERS
GASTRO BREWPUB

Victoria
Harbour

■ BARB'S FISH
'N' CHIPS

EAGLE WINGS
TOURS

Centennial
Square

GOVERNMENT ST

DOUGLAS ST

BLANSHARD

JOHNSON ST

YATES ST

★ CRAIGDARROCH
CASTLE

▲ ART GALLERY OF
GREATER VICTORIA

FAIRFIELD RD

● ABBEYMOORE
MANOR B&B

SIMCOE ST

OSWEGO ST

★ VICTORIA
HARBOUR HELIPORT

Ogden Point
Breakwall

DALLAS RD

★ BEACONSFIELD
INN

★ EMILY CARR
HOUSE

Beacon Hill
Park

COOK ST

MOSS ST

● VILLA
MARCO POLO INN

Holland Point

★ BEACON HILL
CHILDREN'S FARM

★ ROSS BAY
CEMETERY

Juan de Fuca Strait

Finlayson Point

Clover Point

GOVERNMENT ST

BROAD ST

★ LEGACY
ART GALLERY
DOWNTOWN

▼ ZAMBRI'S

YATES ST

↑ To
Victoria
Public Market

FOO ▼
ASIAN STREET
FOOD

BLANSHARD ST

▼ THE MARKET
ON YATES

TROUNCE ALLEY

VIEW ST

VIEW ST

DOUGLAS ST

CHOUX CHOUX ▼
CHARCUTERIE

To →
Café Brio

FORT ST

BROAD ST

FORT ST

▼ CHOCOLAT, CHOCOLATIERE
DE VICTORIA

▼▼ CHORIZO & CO.
▼ FISHHOOK

BROUGHTON ST

GORDON ST

BROUGHTON ST

■ BE LOVE

QUADRA ST

Pioneer
Square

● MAGNOLIA
HOTEL & SPA

★ VICTORIA
BUG ZOO

COURTNEY ST

BURDETT AVE

HUMBOLDT ST

FAIRFIELD RD

RUPERT TERR.

GOVERNMENT ST

★ FAIRMONT
EMPRESS

🄸

HUMBOLDT ST

▼ TRE
FANTASTICO

■ LE PETIT
DAKAR

BELLEVILLE ST

■ CAPITAL CITY
STATION

QUADRA ST

To →
Beaconsfield
Inn

✪ ROYAL BRITISH
COLUMBIA MUSEUM

Thunderbird
Park

DOUGLAS ST

BLANSHARD ST

Beacon Hill Park

★ HELMCKEN HOUSE

© AVALON TRAVEL

207

ONE DAY IN VICTORIA

Catch an early-morning ferry from Vancouver to Swartz Bay and head straight for **Butchart Gardens** to wander the blossom-lined paths. When you've had your fill of flowers, drive to downtown Victoria and get oriented with a quick stroll around the **Inner Harbour.** Continue up Government Street to the narrow lanes of **Chinatown,** then browse the boutiques along Lower Johnson Street.

Wander into the grand **Fairmont Empress** for a glimpse of the city's Victorian past; for the full Empress experience, book **afternoon tea** in the hotel's elegant tearoom. Or if you'd rather a more contemporary lunch, **Zambri's** serves fine Italian fare.

After lunch, visit the **Royal British Columbia Museum** to learn more about the region's cultural and natural history, take a short tour of the **Parliament Building,** or stop into the **Robert Bateman Centre** to explore the work of this noted B.C. artist. If you'd prefer an outdoor adventure, go **whale-watching;** plenty of tour boats depart from the Inner Harbour.

Unwind over drinks in one of Victoria's lounges, or do a beer crawl to sample the city's **craft breweries.** Then enjoy dinner at **Brasserie L'Ecole** if you're in the mood for a French bistro experience or **OLO** if you prefer more adventurous cuisine paired with creative cocktails.

After dinner, settle into your hotel or take the late ferry back to Vancouver, after your very full Victoria day.

governmental operations. In the legislative chambers, for example, desks are set two sword-lengths apart so that no one would get injured during the years when members of parliament carried swords.

Other notable features include a cedar canoe in the rotunda that Steven L. Point, the first aboriginal lieutenant governor of British Columbia, carved in 2010, and stained-glass work commemorating Queen Victoria's diamond jubilee.

Tours are free, but reservations are required. Book your tour at the tour information kiosk, which is outside the building during the summer season and inside the main entrance fall through spring. On weekdays, visitors can also explore the building on their own (9am-5pm Mon.-Fri.).

Robert Bateman Centre

Artist and naturalist Robert Bateman is a notable Canadian wildlife painter. Born in Ontario in 1930, he made an epic round-the-world journey in a Land Rover before returning to Canada to teach and paint, eventually relocating to B.C.'s Salt Spring Island. View his paintings and learn more about his interesting life at the Robert Bateman Centre (470 Belleville St., 250/940-3630, http://batemancentre.org; 10am-9pm daily June-Sept., 10am-5pm daily Oct.-May; adult $12.50, seniors and students $8.50, ages 6-18 $6), in the 1924 beaux arts Steamship Terminal on the Inner Harbour.

Victoria Bug Zoo

If you're not afraid of ants, tarantulas, and other crawling, flying, or wriggling insects, visit this fascinating little museum devoted to the world of bugs. The Victoria Bug Zoo (631 Courtney St., 250/384-2847, www.victoriabugzoo.ca; 10am-5pm Mon.-Thurs., 10am-6pm Fri.-Sun.; adults $12, seniors, students, and ages 5-17 $8) houses more than 40 insect species, as well as Canada's largest ant colony, which you can view through a clear wall. Guides are on hand to share fun bug facts.

Fisherman's Wharf

Fisherman's Wharf

Can you imagine yourself living on the water? With your house *in* the water? The residents of the 30 compact floating houses in the Float Home Village at Fisherman's Wharf (1 Dallas Rd., www.fishermanswharfvictoria.com) do just that. Wander the docks and envision life in this colorful waterfront community; these are private homes, though, so do respect residents' privacy.

Fisherman's Wharf has several outdoor eateries, including ever-popular Barb's Fish 'n' Chips, touristy shops, and kayak rentals. From the Inner Harbour, it's a lovely walk along the waterfront on the David Foster Harbour Pathway, or you can catch a Victoria Harbour Ferry (www.victoriaharbourferry.com).

Emily Carr House

Known for her paintings of British Columbia's landscape and its native people, artist Emily Carr (1871-1945) is considered one of Canada's most important early-20th-century painters. Unusually for a woman of her era, she made several solo trips to remote First Nations communities, where she wanted to document what she believed was the disappearing indigenous culture. She didn't begin seeing commercial success until late in her life, after a 1927 National Gallery of Canada exhibit featured some of her work; the now-famous artist managed a Victoria apartment building for 15 years to support herself.

Set in a Victorian home in Victoria's James Bay neighborhood where she was born and spent her childhood, Emily Carr House (207 Government St., 250/383-5843, www.emilycarr. com; 11am-4pm Tues.-Sat. May-Sept.; adults $6.75, seniors and students $5.75, ages 6-18 $4.50) is a museum about her life and work and about B.C. society during her era.

Beacon Hill Park

Established in 1882, the 200-acre (81-hectare) Beacon Hill Park (bounded by Douglas, Southgate, and Cook Streets and the Dallas Road waterfront, www.beaconhillpark.ca; free) is Victoria's urban green space, with flower gardens, walking paths, and several attractions, including one of the world's tallest totem poles, measuring nearly 128 feet (39 meters) tall, and the Mile 0 marker, in the park's southwest corner, which denotes the start of the 5,000-mile (8,000-kilometer) Trans-Canada Highway.

Near the center of the park, Beacon Hill Children's Farm (Circle Dr., 250/381-2532, www.beaconhillchildrensfarm.ca; 10am-4pm daily Mar.-Apr. and early Sept.-mid-Oct., 10am-5pm daily May-early Sept.; free) has wandering peacocks, furry alpacas, and a petting zoo. A highlight is the daily goat stampede (10:10am and 5:10pm daily summer, 10:10am and 4:10pm daily spring and fall), when the farm's goats race between their sleeping barn and the petting area. It's one of those things you just have to see!

TWO SCANDALS AND A MURDER

Architect Francis Mawson Rattenbury became one of British Columbia's most notable architects at the turn of the 20th century, designing Victoria's Parliament Building, the Empress Hotel, and the Vancouver Court House, which now houses the Vancouver Art Gallery. Yet Rattenbury became enmeshed in two marital scandals that tarnished his reputation and eventually led to his grisly murder.

In 1898, not long after he completed work on the Parliament Building, Rattenbury married Florence Nunn, and they had two children. However, as his professional stature grew, his personal life deteriorated, and by the early 1920s, he and Florence were living in different sections of their Oak Bay home, communicating only through their daughter.

At a reception at the Empress Hotel in 1923, Rattenbury met a young musician, Alma Pakenham, nearly 30 years his junior, and they began a very public affair. Florence initially refused Rattenbury's request for a divorce, agreeing only after he moved Alma into their home, where Florence still lived.

Rattenbury's indiscreet behavior scandalized Victoria society. Even after he and Alma married in 1925, they were never accepted in the community.

In 1929, they moved to England to start fresh. Instead, they became embroiled in another scandal. Rattenbury had begun drinking, and when they settled in England, his alcoholism worsened, triggering depression and, reportedly, impotence. After they hired 18-year-old George Stoner as a chauffeur, Alma began an affair with the teenager.

Apparently jealous that Alma had any relationship at all with her husband, Stoner attacked Rattenbury in their home, hitting him repeatedly on the head with a mallet. When Rattenbury died not long after the attack, both Alma and Stoner were charged with murder.

After a public trial at London's Old Bailey that mesmerized the city, Alma was found innocent and Stoner guilty, sentenced to die by hanging. Four days later, apparently distraught by the scandal and by her lover's sentence, Alma committed suicide by stabbing herself to death.

Despite the trial's verdict, Alma became the villain in the court of public opinion, accused of corrupting an innocent boy. Stoner's death sentence was commuted to life in prison.

For the murder of the eminent B.C. architect whose life deteriorated into scandal, George Stoner served only seven years in jail.

The **Cameron Bandshell**, near Arbutus and Bridge Ways, hosts summertime **Concerts in the Park** (250/361-0500, www.victoria.ca; 1:30pm Fri.-Sun. mid-June-mid-Sept.; free), with performances ranging from classical to swing to jazz and blues.

Legacy Art Gallery

The **Legacy Art Gallery Downtown** (630 Yates St., 250/721-6562, http:// uvac.uvic.ca; 10am-4pm Wed.-Sat.; free), a small satellite of the University of Victoria's art collections, has changing shows that typically feature contemporary artists with British Columbia connections.

Chinatown

Settled in the 1850s, Victoria's Chinatown (Fisgard St. at Government St.) is the oldest in Canada. Although it has now shrunk to a couple of blocks around Fisgard Street, where the neighborhood's gateway, the **Gate of Harmonious Interest**, stands, the district was once Canada's largest Chinese settlement.

After B.C.'s gold rush drew the first Chinese immigrants, the community really began to grow as Chinese workers arrived in Victoria on their way to jobs on the Canadian Pacific Railway. More than 17,000 Chinese immigrants came to Canada between 1881 and 1884.

Gate of Harmonious Interest, Chinatown

Today, you'll find a few Chinese-run shops and restaurants and many non-Asian boutiques and eateries. One remaining landmark is narrow Fan Tan Alley (between Fisgard St. and Pandora Ave.), a lane just three to six feet (1 to 2 meters) wide, where, somehow, several shops have managed to squeeze in.

Breweries

Victoria's craft beer scene has bubbled up in recent years, with a cluster of breweries in an industrial district north of the downtown core, and other microbreweries and brewpubs scattered around the city. Here's where to find the suds:

- Swans Brewpub (506 Pandora Ave., 250/361-3310, http://swanshotel.com; 11am-1am Mon.-Fri., 9am-1am Sat., 9am-midnight Sun.)
- Phillips Beer (2010 Government St., 250/380-1912, www.phillips-beer.com; store 10am-5pm Mon., 10am-6pm Tues.-Thurs. and Sat., 10am-7pm Fri.; tours 4pm Tues.-Thurs., 2pm Fri.-Sat.; $6, reservations recommended)
- Vancouver Island Brewing Co. (2330 Government St., 250/361-0005, http://vanislandbrewery.com; store 11am-6pm Tues.-Sat., tours 4pm Fri.-Sat.; $7)
- Moon Under Water Brewery and Pub (350 Bay St., 250/380-0706, www.moonunderwater.ca; 11:30am-11pm Mon.-Thurs. and Sat., 11:30am-midnight Fri., 11:30am-8pm Sun.)
- Hoyne Brewing Co. (2740 Bridge St., 250/590-5758, http://hoyne-brewing.ca; noon-6pm Mon.-Fri., 11am-6pm Sat.)
- Spinnakers Gastro Brewpub (308 Catherine St., 250/386-2739, www.spinnakers.com; 11:30am-11pm daily)

EAST OF DOWNTOWN
Abkhazi Garden

The story of this manicured garden is a love story between a British woman born in Shanghai and an erstwhile prince from the Republic of Georgia. Marjorie Pemberton-Carter, known as Peggy, first met Prince Nicholas Abkhazi in Paris in the 1920s. Although they wrote to each other over the years, circumstances kept them apart; during World War II, each spent time in prisoner of war camps—Nicholas in Germany and Peggy in Shanghai.

En route from China to Britain in 1945, Peggy stopped to see friends in Victoria. Her visit turned more permanent when she purchased an overgrown lot and decided to build a summer home. Peggy had lost contact with Nicholas, but he wrote to her in early 1946; they met later that year in New York, and by November, they had returned to Victoria and married.

The home and garden that the newlyweds built on Peggy's property, and where they lived for more than 40 years, became the Abkhazi Garden (1964 Fairfield Rd., 778/265-6466, http://conservancy.bc.ca; 11am-5pm daily Apr.-Sept., 11am-5pm Wed.-Sun. Oct.-Mar., last admission 1 hour before closing; $10 donation). The compact garden, just over one acre (0.4 hectares), features a rhododendron woodland with large Garry oak trees, a winding path known as the Yangtze River, and a variety of other plantings around the site's natural rock formations.

Peggy's 1947 summer home is now The Teahouse at Abkhazi Garden (778/265-6466, www.abkhazite-ahouse.com; 11am-5pm daily May-Sept., 11am-5pm Wed.-Sun. Oct.-Apr.; $11-18), which serves soups, salads, and light meals as well as traditional afternoon tea ($30).

From downtown Victoria, take B.C. Transit bus 7 for UVIC (one-way $2.50) from Douglas and View Streets and get off on Fairfield Road at Foul Bay Road, opposite the garden.

Craigdarroch Castle

Like any good British-inspired city, Victoria has a castle, a grand stone Romanesque revival structure, complete with turrets, stained glass, and Victorian-era artifacts.

Robert Dunsmuir, a Scottish immigrant who made his fortune mining coal on Vancouver Island, built the 39-room mansion, known as Craigdarroch Castle (1050 Joan Crescent, 250/592-5323, www.the-castle.ca; 9am-7pm daily mid-June-early Sept., 10am-4:30pm daily early Sept.-mid-June; adults $13.95, seniors $12.95, students $8.95, ages 6-12 $5), in the late 1880s. Sadly, Dunsmuir died before the castle was finished. His wife Joan lived here with three of her unmarried daughters (the Dunsmuirs

had 10 children) from the castle's completion in 1890 until she died in 1908.

With more than 20,000 square feet (1,880 square meters) of floor space, the castle, now a national historic site, is decorated as it would have been in the Dunsmuirs' time, with lavish Victorian appointments, including sculptures, paintings, books, and period furnishings.

From downtown Victoria, any of the Fort Street buses (one-way $2.50), including B.C. Transit bus 14 for UVIC, bus 15 for UVIC, or bus 22 for Hillside Mall, will drop you near the castle. On foot, allow 30 to 35 minutes from the Inner Harbour.

Art Gallery of Greater Victoria

Built around an 1899 Victorian mansion that now houses the museum shop, the Art Gallery of Greater Victoria (1040 Moss St., 250/384-4171, www.aggv.ca; 10am-5pm Mon.-Sat., noon-5pm Sun. mid-May-mid-Sept., 10am-5pm Tues.-Sun. mid-Sept.-mid-May; adults $13, seniors and students $11, ages 6-17 $2.50) has a significant collection of work by Victoria-born painter Emily Carr and one of Canada's most extensive Asian art holdings. The gallery's changing exhibitions typically showcase Canadian or Asian works.

The Art Gallery is 1.5 miles (2.3 kilometers) east of the Inner Harbour. B.C. Transit bus 15 for UVIC (one-way $2.50), which runs along Fort Street, will drop you at the corner of Fort Street and Fernwood Road, around the corner from the gallery. You can easily combine visits to the Art Gallery and nearby Craigdarroch Castle.

Ross Bay Cemetery

Many notable Victorians are buried in the historic Ross Bay Cemetery

(Fairfield Rd. at Stannard Ave.; dawn-dusk daily; free), which stretches between Fairfield Road and the Dallas Road waterfront. The Victorian-era cemetery's most visited grave is that of artist Emily Carr (1871-1945), near the intersection of Fairfield Road and Arnold Avenue. The cemetery is also the final resting place of Sir James Douglas, who served as British Columbia's first governor from 1858 to 1864, and Robert Dunsmuir, who built Craigdarroch Castle. The cemetery includes sections for different Christian denominations, with separate areas for First Nations and Chinese people, and a potter's field, where the poor were buried.

Cemetery maps are available online from the Old Cemeteries Society of Victoria (250/598-8870, www.oldcem. bc.ca). The society offers tours ($5) focusing on different aspects of the cemetery's history. In July and August, tours are offered every Sunday at 2pm, while September through June, tours generally run on the first and third Sundays; check their website for a schedule.

From Douglas Street in downtown Victoria, B.C. Transit bus 3 or 7 (one-way $2.50) will take you along Fairfield Road to the cemetery. It's a 35- to 40-minute walk from the Inner Harbour.

THE SAANICH PENINSULA

The Saanich Peninsula extends north of downtown Victoria to the communities of Saanich, North Saanich, Sidney, and Brentwood Bay. Partly suburban and partly a rural landscape of farms, forests, and fields, the peninsula is worth exploring for one major attraction—the popular Butchart Gardens—and for several smaller sights; it's also home to

several wineries and distilleries. The Swartz Bay Ferry Terminal, with boats to Vancouver and several of the Gulf Islands, is at the northern tip of the Saanich Peninsula.

Butchart Gardens

✪ Butchart Gardens

How did a cement factory and limestone quarry become one of Vancouver Island's most popular garden attractions? Jennie Butchart and her husband, Robert, moved to the island from Ontario in the early 1900s, where Robert established a quarry and cement business, and Jennie became the company's chemist. The Butcharts built a large manor nearby and began planting flowers around it.

The Butcharts named their estate Benvenuto, Italian for "welcome," and by the 1920s, more than 50,000 people were visiting their gardens every year. Now, nearly one million visitors annually come to ogle the floral displays at the 55-acre (22-hectare) Butchart Gardens (800 Benvenuto Ave., Brentwood Bay, 250/652-5256, www. butchartgardens.com; 9am-10pm daily mid-June-early Sept., 9am-5pm daily early-late Sept. and Apr.-mid.-June, 9am-4pm daily Oct. and Mar., 9am-3:30pm daily Nov. and, 9am-9pm daily Dec.-early Jan.; mid-June-Sept. adults $32.60, students 13-17 $16.30, ages 5-12 $3, reduced rates in other seasons).

When the company limestone quarry was exhausted, Jennie had the former pit transformed into what is now known as the Sunken Garden. Other highlights include the Rose Garden, the Italian Garden, and the serene Japanese Garden. On summer Saturday nights (July-early Sept.), fireworks shows are choreographed to music. During the winter holidays, the pathways twinkle with thousands of lights.

The Butchart Gardens are 14 miles (23 kilometers) north of Victoria and 12.5 miles (20 kilometers) south of the Swartz Bay Ferry Terminal. From downtown Victoria, B.C. Transit bus 75 (one-way $2.50) can take you to the gardens in about 45 minutes.

Victoria Butterfly Gardens

Don't be surprised if a common Mormon or a blue morpho lands on your head inside this tropical greenhouse. More than 3,000 butterflies dart and flutter around the palm trees and exotic plants at the family-friendly Victoria Butterfly Gardens (1461 Benvenuto Ave., Brentwood Bay, 250/652-3822 or 877/722-0272, www.butterflygardens.com; 10am-5pm daily early Mar.-Oct., 10am-4pm daily Nov.-early Mar., extended hours Dec., last admission 1 hour before closing; adults $16.50, seniors and students $11, ages 5-12 $6), which houses about 75 different species from around the world.

The Butterfly Gardens are 12 miles (20 kilometers) north of Victoria and 11 miles (18 kilometers) south of the Swartz Bay Ferry Terminal, near the Butchart Gardens. B.C. Transit bus 75 (one-way $2.50) can take you from downtown Victoria in about 40 minutes.

Shaw Ocean Discovery Centre

A small modern aquarium on the waterfront in the town of Sidney, the Shaw Ocean Discovery Centre (9811 Seaport Pl., Sidney, 250/665-7511, www.oceandiscovery.ca; 10am-5pm daily July-early Sept., 10am-4:30pm daily early Sept.-June, last admission 30 minutes before closing; adults $15, seniors $12, ages 13-18 $8, ages 4-12 $7.50) focuses on the marinelife of the Salish Sea, the waters surrounding southern Vancouver Island. More than 3,500 creatures, representing 150 different species, are typically on view. On Saturday and Sunday, marine-themed games, crafts, and other special activities add to the fun for kids.

Along Highway 17, the aquarium is 17 miles (28 kilometers) north of downtown Victoria and four miles (6.5 kilometers) south of the Swartz Bay Ferry Terminal. B.C. Transit buses 70 and 72 (one-way $2.50) stop in Sidney en route between Victoria and the ferry terminal. Get off at 5th Street and Beacon Avenue, and walk down Beacon to the aquarium.

Wineries and Distilleries

You don't have to go far from Victoria to go wine-tasting, with several wineries and distilleries across the Saanich Peninsula.

One of the region's more established wineries, Church and State Wines (1445 Benvenuto Ave., Central Saanich, 250/652-2671, www.churchandstatewines.com; 11am-6pm Fri.-Sun. mid-late Apr., 11am-6pm daily May-Oct., 11am-5pm Thurs.-Sun. Nov.-Dec.) launched with just 10 acres (4 hectares) on the island and now has a winery and vineyards in the Okanagan Valley as well. Try their wines at the tasting bar or with lunch in the Bistro (11am-3pm Wed.-Sun. June-Oct., 11am-3pm Thurs.-Sun. Nov.-Dec., $17-21).

On a 10-acre (4-hectare) farm with more than 1,300 apple trees, Sea Cider Farm & Ciderhouse (2487 Mt. St. Michael Rd., Saanichton, 250/544-4824, www.seacider.ca; 11am-4pm daily May-Sept., 11am-4pm Wed.-Sun. Oct.-Apr.) produces traditional fermented artisanal ciders.

The master distillers at the craft distillery Victoria Distillers (9891 Seaport Pl., Sidney, distillery 250/544-8218, lounge and tour bookings 250/544-8217, http://victoriadistillers.com; lounge 2pm-7pm Sun.-Wed., 2pm-9pm Thurs.-Sun., reduced hours in winter; tastings and tours 2pm-5pm Thurs.-Sat.; tours $7) infuse their signature Victoria Gin with a custom blend of botanicals. They make an aged Oaken Gin and an unusual hemp vodka, too. The 45-minute tours of the facility include tastings; you can reserve tour spots in advance, although reservations are not required.

WEST OF DOWNTOWN

Wend your way through the suburbs west of the city center to reach another of Victoria's famous castles.

Hatley Park National Historic Site

Given that his father, Robert, built Craigdarroch Castle, perhaps it's no surprise that James Dunsmuir (1851-1920) and his wife, Laura, wanted a castle of their own, particularly as the parents of 12 children. The 1908 Edwardian stone manor that they constructed, now known as Hatley Castle at the Hatley Park National Historic Site (2005 Sooke Rd., 250/391-2511, www.royalroads.ca; 10:15am-3pm daily; adults $18.50, seniors $16, ages 6-17 $11), has 40 rooms, including 22 bedrooms and eight baths.

You can visit the castle, on the campus of Royal Roads University, on a one-hour guided castle tour (11:45am and 2:45pm Sat.-Sun. May-early Sept.) that takes you through the main-floor rooms and offers up details about the Dunsmuir family's history. The castle's upper floors, used as university offices, aren't part of the tour. Another option is the one-hour guided estate tour (10:30am, 11:45am, 1:30pm, and 2:45pm Mon.-Fri., 10:30am and 1:30pm Sat.-Sun. May-early Sept.), which focuses on the castle's exterior and gardens, along with the family's story.

If you don't have time for a tour, or if you're in town outside the summer season, visit just the manicured gardens (adults $5, seniors $4, ages 6-17 $3.50) or the small museum (free) about the Dunsmuir family.

Hatley Park is 7.5 miles (12 kilometers) west of the Inner Harbour. While it's possible to get here by public transit, it's much faster to come by car.

FESTIVALS AND EVENTS

Honoring Victoria's namesake queen, the city's Victoria Day festivities (www.tourismvictoria.com, May) include a parade downtown.

Aboriginal dancers, singers, and musicians perform at Victoria's three-day Aboriginal Cultural Festival (www.aboriginalbc.com, June), which also showcases works by First Nations artists.

It's not just mimes aping visitors at the annual Victoria International Buskers Festival (http://victoriabuskers.com, July). Professional street performers from around the world, including magicians, jugglers, flame throwers, acrobats, and more, show their stuff on stages around the city.

Food and wine lovers celebrate Vancouver Island's bounty at Taste: Victoria's Festival of Food and Wine (www.victoriataste.com, July), a weekend of wine-tastings, seminars, and dinners.

The annual Victoria Symphony Splash (www.victoriasymphony.ca, Aug.) includes a live performance by the Victoria Symphony from a floating stage moored in the Inner Harbour.

The Victoria Fringe Fest (http://victoriafringe.com, Aug.) is an 11-day festival of weird and often wonderful theater, comedy, and storytelling performances.

The Victoria Classic Boat Festival (www.classicboatfestival.ca, Sept.) celebrates the island's maritime heritage with boat parades, races, and other events.

SHOPPING

Shops line Government Street, stretching north from the Inner Harbour, many selling T-shirts, Canadian flag patches, and other souvenirs. Lower Johnson Street in Chinatown has more distinctive local clothing, jewelry, and shoes.

CLOTHING AND ACCESSORIES

In Chinatown, Lower Johnson Street between Government and Wharf is a mix of trend-conscious chains like yoga-wear maker Lululemon (584 Johnson St., 250/383-1313, www.lululemon.com; 10am-7pm Sun.-Wed.

and Sat., 10am-8pm Thurs.-Fri.) and locally run boutiques, including Still Life for Her (550 Johnson St., 250/386-5658, http://stilllifeboutique.com; 10:30am-6pm Mon.-Sat., 11am-5pm Sun.) and its companion store Still Life for Him (560 Johnson St., 250/386-5655, http://stilllifeboutique.com; 10:30am-6pm Mon.-Sat., 11am-5pm Sun.), and Suasion (552 Johnson St., 250/995-0133, http://shopsuasion.com; 10:30am-6pm Mon.-Sat., 11am-5pm Sun.).

Sneaker fans run into Baggins Shoes (580 Johnson St., 250/388-7022, http://bagginsshoes.com; 10am-6pm Mon.-Fri., 11am-5pm Sun.), which has one of the world's largest selections of Converse styles. In the Atrium Building, Head Over Heels (1323 Blanshard St., 250/590-5154, www.headoverheelsvictoria.ca; 10:30am-5:30pm Mon.-Sat., noon-4pm Sun.) sells fashion-forward shoes.

BOOKS

Nobel prize-winning author Alice Munro and her former husband Jim opened Munro's Books (1108 Government St., 250/382-2464, www.munrobooks.com; 9am-6pm Mon.-Wed. and Sat., 9am-9pm Thurs.-Fri., 9:30am-6pm Sun.) in 1963. Although the writer is no longer involved in its management, this well-stocked old-school bookstore in a grand 1909 former bank carries titles by Canadian authors and other books of local interest.

GOURMET FOOD AND DRINK

Stocking a mind-boggling variety of teas, with helpful labels about their ingredients, flavors, and caffeine content, Silk Road Tea (1624 Government St., 250/704-2688, www.silkroadteastore.com; 10am-6pm Mon.-Sat.,

11am-5pm Sun.) also carries tea-related products and cosmetics. Take a seat at their tea bar to rest your shopping-weary feet over a freshly brewed cup, or book a massage in their on-site spa. They have a second location in the Victoria Public Market (1701 Douglas St., 778/433-9838; 10am-6pm Mon.-Sat., 11am-5pm Sun.).

OUTDOOR GEAR

If you need clothing or supplies for outdoor adventures, head for the Victoria location of MEC (Mountain Equipment Co-op, 1450 Government St., 250/386-2667, www.mec.ca; 10am-7pm Mon.-Wed., 10am-9pm Thurs.-Fri., 9am-6pm Sat., 11am-5pm Sun.), Canada's largest retailer of outdoor wear and sports gear.

whale-watching boats leave from Victoria's Inner Harbour

SPORTS AND RECREATION
✪ WHALE-WATCHING

The waters off Vancouver Island, the Gulf Islands, and Washington's San Juan Islands are home to several pods of resident orcas (also known as killer whales), particularly during the summer. Pods of transient orcas, as well as Pacific gray whales, humpback whales,

and minke whales, migrate through the region.

Numerous Victoria-based companies offer three- to five-hour whale-watching tours from April through October, though summer (July and August) is peak season for both whales and travelers. Some operators use inflatable Zodiacs, which give you a rougher but more exhilarating ride. Others use larger boats for a calmer trip and more shelter from the weather, a better choice on rainy days or choppy seas. Victoria's whale-watching tour companies include:

- Orca Spirit Adventures (250/383-8411 or 888/672-6722, www.orcaspirit.com; adults $115, ages 13-17 $85, ages 3-12 $75), with departures from two Inner Harbour locations: 950 Wharf Street, at the Harbour Air Terminal, or 146 Kingston Street, at the Coast Harbourside Hotel
- Prince of Whales (812 Wharf St., 250/383-4884 or 888/383-4884, www.princeofwhales.com; adults $105-120, ages 13-17 $95, ages 5-12 $85)
- Eagle Wing Tours (Fisherman's Wharf, 12 Erie St., 250/384-8008 or 800/708-9488, www.eaglewingtours.com; adults $135, ages 13-17 $105, ages 3-12 $85)
- SpringTide Whale Watching (1119 Wharf St., 250/384-4444 or 800/470-3474, www.victoriawhalewatching.com; adults $115, seniors $105, ages 13-18 $95, ages 2-12 $85)

FOOD
AFTERNOON TEA

The Fairmont Empress (721 Government St., 250/384-8111, www.fairmont.com; 11:30am-5:30pm daily, reservations recommended; adults

afternoon tea at the Fairmont Empress

the Big Muckle Giant Tea For Two ($60 for 2, each additional person $30).

For a less formal (and meat-free) tea, visit **Venus Sophia Tea Room & Vegetarian Eatery** (540 Fisgard St., 250/590-3953, www.venussophia.com; afternoon tea 11am-4:30pm daily; adults $34, ages 12 and under $24), a pretty-in-pink Chinatown storefront. Choose among their signature teas to pair with a seasonally changing assortment of sandwiches, baked goods, and sweets.

$75, ages 12 and under $37.50) has been offering afternoon tea since the hotel opened in 1908. Upholding that tradition, the regal tea lounge still serves an estimated 500,000 cups of tea every year, along with tiered trays of finger sandwiches, scones with jam and clotted cream, and assorted pastries.

The **Dining Room at Butchart Gardens** (800 Benvenuto Ave., Brentwood Bay, 250/652-8222, www.butchartgardens.com; noon-3pm daily Apr.-Sept.; adults $35, ages 11 and under $20) serves traditional afternoon tea in spring and summer, with a mix of sweet and savory items. From October through March, the Gardens offer high tea (adults $36, ages 11 and under $120), adding warm dishes like quiche and Cornish pasty to the menu of sandwiches and desserts. Vegetarian versions of both afternoon tea and high tea are available.

In the traditionally British neighborhood of Oak Bay, the **White Heather Tea Room** (1885 Oak Bay Ave., 250/595-8020, www.whiteheather-tearoom.com; 11:15am-5pm Tues.-Sat., last seating 3:45pm) offers a traditionally British afternoon tea in several sizes, from the Wee Tea ($20.50 pp) to the Not-So-Wee Tea ($26.50 to

GROCERIES AND MARKETS

In a historic building that once housed the Hudson's Bay department store, the **Victoria Public Market** (1701 Douglas St., 778/433-2787, http://victoriapublicmarket.com; 10am-6pm Mon.-Sat., 11am-5pm Sun.) draws foodies with stalls selling cheeses, chocolate, tea, olive oil, pie, and other goodies, plus a seasonal **farmers market** (11am-3pm Wed. and Sat. Mar.-Nov.).

Another snacking destination is Fort Street, where upscale food shops include **Chorizo & Co** (807 Fort St., 250/590-6393; 8:30am-5pm Mon.-Tues., 8:30am-10pm Wed.-Fri., 11am-10pm Sat.), a Spanish deli and tapas bar; **Choux Choux Charcuterie** (830 Fort St., 205/382-7572, www.chouxchouxcharc.com; 10am-5:30pm Mon.-Fri., 10am-5pm Sat.) for cured meats and artisanal cheese; and **Chocolat, Chocolatiere de Victoria** (703 Fort St., 250/381-0131, www.chocolatvictoria.ca; 9:30am-6pm Mon.-Sat.) for handmade chocolates.

To buy groceries close to downtown, head for **The Market on Yates** (903 Yates St., 250/381-6000, www.themarketstores.com; 7am-11pm daily), a well-stocked local food store.

VICTORIA'S CHOCOLATE PROJECT

David Mincey is passionate about chocolate. The owner and resident chocolate obsessive at the **Chocolate Project** (Victoria Public Market, 1701 Douglas St., www. chocolateproject.ca) is on a mission to improve the chocolate that is produced around the world and that we eat closer to home.

In his stall in Victoria's Public Market, Mincey carries single origin, sustainably produced chocolate from many different countries. If you stop to chat, he'll tell you about the horrors of conventional chocolate production; he says that most commercial chocolate comes from West African plantations where enslaved people provide the labor, which is how companies can produce chocolate bars selling for $3 or less. He can tell you about the small businesses and individual growers across the globe who produce the chocolate he sells, many of whom he has visited personally.

chocolate from the Chocolate Project

You can find Mincey at his stand most Fridays, Saturdays, and Sundays during Public Market hours (10am-6pm Mon.-Sat., 11am-5pm Sun.), offering tastings, running impromptu workshops, and generally preaching the chocolate gospel. His chocolate bars start around $10 each, and he'll convince you that they're worth it.

MODERN CANADIAN

Taking its name from a Chinook word meaning "hungry," ✪ **OLO** (509 Fisgard St., 250/590-8795, www. olorestaurant.com; 5pm-10pm Mon.-Thurs., 5pm-11pm Fri., 10am-2pm and 5pm-11pm Sat., 10am-2pm and 5pm-10pm Sun.; $18-46) doesn't just satisfy your hunger. This fashionably relaxed Chinatown restaurant, decorated with woven wooden light fixtures that dangle from the ceiling like outsized birds' nests, delights guests with its innovative seasonal fare, from alder smoked salmon with beets and rye crackers to lamb with potato gnocchi and squash to the popular burger garnished with greens and garlic mayo. If you're feeling adventurous, order the "family meal" for your table and let the kitchen prepare a multicourse feast.

✪ **Little Jumbo** (506 Fort St., 778/433-5535, www.littlejumbo. ca; 5pm-11pm Mon., 5pm-midnight Tues.-Thurs. and Sun., 5pm-1am Fri.-Sat.; $21-32) feels like a secret speakeasy, set at the end of a narrow hallway. In the cozy narrow room with exposed brick walls and green lights illuminating the banquettes, the well-stocked bar and hardworking bartenders draw cocktail connoisseurs (they'll make you delicious "mocktails," too, if you're keeping with the Prohibition theme), but the kitchen is serious as well. Even simple dishes, like fresh green salads or an antipasto platter, are thoughtfully prepared, and you might find innovations like hoisin-glazed duck with Sichuan-braised mushrooms.

You'll want to eat your vegetables when they're as delicious as the fried brussels sprouts salad at **North 48** (1005 Langley St., 250/381-2428, www. northfortyeight.com; 11:30am-2pm and 4pm-9pm Tues.-Thurs., 11:30am-2pm and 4pm-10pm Fri.-Sat., 4pm-10pm Sun.; $12-26), a downtown restaurant and lounge, where the menu mixes comfort foods such as mussels and clams in a broth of bacon and local beer with cool creations like octopus tacos. Tiki cocktails and even nonalcoholic drinks like the house-made ginger beer add to the fun.

Café Brio (944 Fort St., 250/383-0009 or 866/270-5461, www.cafe-brio.com; 5:30pm-late Tues.-Sat.; $15-33) is an old favorite with a modern Mediterranean menu. Look for dishes like grilled albacore with spinach in a red wine broth, braised beef short ribs with roasted root vegetables, or spaghetti with fresh tomatoes. Note to grazers, or those with small appetites: You can order most dishes in full or half portions. The wine list is strong on B.C. labels.

An unassuming order-at-the-counter eatery, Part and Parcel (2656 Quadra St., 778/406-0888, www.partandparcel.ca; 11:30am-9pm Tues.-Sat.; $7-13) surprises with the first-rate quality of its straightforward but innovative dishes. On the changing menu that leans heavily on salads and sandwiches, super-fresh greens might be topped with spring rhubarb, fresh tuna might come sandwiched with pickled green beans, and pillowy gnocchi might sport a creamy sesame sauce. In the Quadra Village neighborhood, not quite two miles (3 kilometers) north of the Inner Harbour, this local joint is an easy pit stop on the way to or from the Swartz Bay ferry.

SEAFOOD

It's a little hard to find, but that hasn't stopped the hordes from lining up at the wharf-side shipping container housing Red Fish Blue Fish (1006 Wharf St., 250/298-6877, www.redfish-bluefish.com; 11am-9pm daily mid-Feb.-Oct.; $10-23), a busy seafood

takeaway at the foot of Broughton Street. Choose tempura-battered Pacific cod, wild salmon, B.C. halibut, or oysters for your fish-and-chips. The hand-rolled fish tacos and salmon sandwich with pickled cucumbers are other popular picks.

Reel in a quick bite at Fishhook (805 Fort St., 250/477-0470, www.fishhookvic.com; 11am-9pm daily; $6-13), which specializes in seafood *tartines,* open-faced sandwiches topped with cured, broiled, or smoked fish. Try the sablefish with kale and housemade pickles or the tuna melt with cheddar and caramelized broccoli. This casual café also makes an array of fish curries.

A Victoria institution on Fisherman's Wharf, Barb's Fish 'n' Chips (1 Dallas Rd., 250/384-6515, http://barbsfishandchips.com; 11am-dark daily mid-Mar.-Oct.; $6-19) has been serving up seafood since 1984. It's one mile (1.6 kilometers) west of downtown; you can also get here on the Victoria Harbour Ferry (250/708-0201, www.victoriaharbourferry.com).

ASIAN

For a quick bite with flavors from across Asia, pop into Foo Asian Street Food (769 Yates St., 250/383-3111, www.foofood.ca; 11:30am-10pm Mon.-Sat., 11:30am-9pm Sun.; $9-15) for a short rib *bánh mì,* pork fried rice, butter chicken, and other crowd-pleasing dishes that take cues from Vietnam, China, India, Japan, and Thailand. They don't have many seats, but they do have local beer on tap.

FRENCH

A long-standing French bistro on the edge of Chinatown, ✪ Brasserie L'Ecole (1715 Government St., 250/475-6260, www.lecole.ca;

5:30pm-11pm Tues.-Sat.; $19-34) continues to charm with its warm welcome and its just-classic-enough menu. You might find local trout paired with lentil fritters and squash puree, bratwurst with tomato-braised coco beans and fried kale, or *steak frites*. They stock a long list of Belgian beers and French wines. No reservations.

ITALIAN

The modern Italian fare at ✪ Zambri's (820 Yates St., 250/360-1171, www.zambris.ca; 11:30am-3pm and 5pm-9pm Mon.-Thurs., 11:30am-3pm and 5pm-10pm Fri.-Sat, 10:30am-2pm and 5pm-9pm Sun.; $17-32), in the equally modern Atrium Building, makes one of Victoria's best meals, Italian or otherwise. The pastas, like penne with gorgonzola and peas or orecchiette with house-made sausages and rapini, are always good choices, as are the pizzas, or you can try more elaborate mains like tuna *alla livornese* (sauced with onions, tomatoes, olives, and wine) or beef tenderloin paired with polenta. Save room for desserts like panna cotta or chocolate *pot de crème*.

VEGETARIAN

You can order a local craft beer or a "superfood" cocktail (perhaps the Coastal Gin & Tonic made with spirulina and bull kelp) at cool, laid-back Be Love (1019 Blanshard St., 778/433-7181, http://beloverestaurant.ca; 11am-9:30pm Sun.-Thurs., 11am-10pm Fri.-Sat.; $14-21), a bright vegetarian café where veggie-friendly doesn't mean ascetic. Try a salad like arugula and melon with shaved fennel and pumpkin seeds or the Bibimbap Bowl, a mix of house-made kimchi, seaweed, sautéed veggies, pickled shiitakes, and grilled tempeh on brown rice. Want a

booze-free beverage? Note the big vats of kombucha above the bar.

An old favorite among plant-eaters and their omnivorous dining companions, Rebar (50 Bastion Square, 250/361-9223, www.rebarmodernfood.com; 11:30am-9pm Mon.-Fri., 8:30am-9pm Sat., 8:30am-8pm Sun.; $11-22) serves vegetarian comfort food like curries, enchiladas, and stir-fries, along with a few seafood dishes. Their almond burger is a classic. Save room for a sweet, like a homey ginger molasses cookie or gooey carrot cake.

DINERS

A favorite joint for breakfast or brunch is funky Jam Café (542 Herald St., 778/440-4489, www.jamcafevictoria.com; 8am-3pm daily; $8-16), where the hip takes on diner classics include fried oatmeal, red velvet pancakes, and chicken and waffles. Come hungry, and be prepared to line up; they don't take reservations.

BAKERIES AND CAFÉS

Well-prepared coffee, baked goods, and light meals such as salads, charcuterie, and pastas draw locals and visitors to the sunny patio or cozy interior at Tre Fantastico (810 Humboldt St., 250/590-8014, www.caffefantastico.com; 7am-10pm daily), a café set a short stroll from the Inner Harbour.

For a quick exotic meal, stop into Le Petit Dakar (711 Douglas St., 250/380-3705, www.lepetitdakarbc.ca; 11am-5pm Mon.-Fri.; $7-11), a tiny Senegalese takeaway. The personable chef-owner will guide you through the small menu where you might dig into *mafe* (a meat stew enriched with peanut butter), black-eyed bean ragout, or chicken curry.

Canada isn't known as a barbecue nation, but Pig BBQ Joint (1325

Blanshard St., 250/590-5193, www.pig-bbqjoint.com; 11am-10pm daily; $8-18) does a fine job with its pulled pork, smoked chicken, and beef brisket. In this casual downtown joint, expect big flavors, but don't expect niceties like utensils or plates.

ACCOMMODATIONS

Victoria's hotels are clustered around the Inner Harbour. In some surrounding neighborhoods, you'll find B&Bs and other good-value lodgings.

UNDER $150

An old motel given new life as a funky retro lodging, Hotel Zed (3110 Douglas St., 250/388-4345 or 800/997-6797, www.hotelzed.com; $99-209 d), decorated in vibrant oranges, turquoises, fuchsias, and purples, is Victoria's most fun place to stay. The 63 rooms have rotary phones (with free local calls), comic books in the baths, and complimentary Wi-Fi. The indoor-outdoor pool has a bubblegum-pink waterslide. A hip diner-style restaurant, The Ruby (250/507-1325, http://therubyvictoria.com; 8am-8pm Sun.-Thurs., 8am-9pm Fri.-Sat.; $13-18), cooks big breakfasts and roasts free-range chicken; downstairs, there's a Ping-Pong lounge. It's two miles (3 kilometers) north of the Inner Harbour, but the hotel runs a free shuttle downtown in their vintage VW bus.

$150-250

In a 1912 Victorian home in the residential Rockland neighborhood, ✪ Abbeymoore Manor B&B (1470 Rockland Ave., 250/370-1470 or 888/801-1811, www.abbeymoore.com; $159-299 d) looks formal, with polished woodwork, oriental rugs, and period furnishings, but the longtime owners keep things comfortable with help-yourself coffee, tea, soft drinks, and snacks, a book- and game-filled guest library, and hearty morning meals. The five guest rooms are all traditionally appointed, while the three suites (two on the garden level and one on the top floor) are more modern. Wi-Fi and local calls are included; no kids under 14.

To capture Victoria's traditional ambience, stay at the Beaconsfield Inn (998 Humboldt St., 250/384-4044 or 888/884-4044, www.beaconsfield-inn.com; $169-279 d), a nine-room B&B in a 1905 Edwardian manor furnished with antiques, stained-glass windows, and chandeliers. Most guest rooms have fireplaces and whirlpool tubs; all have down comforters and Wi-Fi. Rates include full breakfast, afternoon tea and cookies, and evening sherry. No kids under 12.

Noted Canadian architect Arthur Erickson designed one wing of the Inn at Laurel Point (680 Montreal St., 250/386-8721 or 800/663-7667, www.laurelpoint.com; $149-323 d, parking $17), where most of the contemporary suites are angled to take advantage of the property's waterfront views. The Laurel Wing units are more conventional, but the harbor vistas from these rooms aren't bad either. With a quiet setting a short walk from the busy Inner Harbour, the Pacific Rim-style lodging has an indoor pool and a sundeck facing a Japanese garden. The well-regarded Aura Restaurant (250/414-6739, www.aurarestaurant.ca) is open for breakfast, lunch, and dinner. Wi-Fi is included.

OVER $250

A bit removed from the Inner Harbour's fray, but still an easy stroll from the sights, the condo-style

Oswego Hotel (500 Oswego St., 250/294-7500 or 877/767-9346, www.oswegohotelvictoria.com; $190-310 d, 2-bedroom unit $350-595, parking $15-20) has 80 stylish, urban studio, one-bedroom, and two-bedroom units. All have kitchen facilities with granite counters, stainless-steel appliances, and French-press coffeemakers, as well as large baths with soaker tubs. The upper-floor suites have expansive city views. Wi-Fi is included.

A landmark on the Inner Harbour, the ✪ Fairmont Empress (721 Government St., 250/384-8111 or 800/441-1414, www.fairmont.com; $449-749, parking $30) charms with its polished staff and stately public spaces. The guest rooms, updated in 2017 with a blend of classic and contemporary furnishings, vary from petite to grand, but you're here for the heritage and gracious service as much as the physical space. An indoor pool and well-equipped health club keep you busy, while the Willow Stream Spa keeps you pampered. Q at the Empress serves contemporary fare with produce from the rooftop garden and around the island, paired with B.C. wines and local craft beers; the Empress is famous for its traditional afternoon tea. Join Fairmont's complimentary President's Club to get Wi-Fi access; otherwise, it's $15 per day.

✪ Magnolia Hotel & Spa (623 Courtney St., 250/381-0999 or 877/624-6654, www.magnoliahotel.com; $239-419 d, parking $24), a well-managed boutique lodging two blocks from the Inner Harbour, caters to both business and leisure travelers. The 64 rooms are decorated in soothing grays and creams, with mini-fridges, single-cup coffeemakers, complimentary Wi-Fi, and flat-screen TVs.

The best rooms are on the sixth and seventh floors above the surrounding buildings; from the corner units, you can see the Parliament Building, illuminated at night. Work out in the compact gym or borrow a complimentary bike to go touring. The staff are quick with a greeting or to offer assistance, from directions to restaurant recommendations.

Oak Bay Beach Hotel

A stay at the ✪ Oak Bay Beach Hotel (1175 Beach Dr., 250/598-4556 or 800/668-7758, www.oakbaybeachhotel.com; $188-568 d) feels like an escape to a seaside resort, particularly when you swim or soak in the heated mineral pools that front the ocean. The 100 generously sized suites have electric fireplaces, flatscreen TVs, kitchen facilities, and deluxe baths. The panoramic vistas from the water-facing rooms are spectacular. Rates include Wi-Fi, local calls, and parking. The Snug, a British-style pub, serves classics like fish-and-chips and bangers and mash with a cold pint; Kate's Café keeps guests and locals supplied with coffee and pastries. The hotel is in the residential Oak Bay district, east of downtown.

To stay in an upscale Italian

Renaissance manor, book a room at the deluxe Villa Marco Polo Inn (1524 Shasta Pl., 250/370-1524, www.villamarcopolo.com; $239-339 d), built in 1923 in the Rockland district. The four romantic guest suites entice with European linens, Persian carpets, fireplaces, and a plush Silk Road style. Breakfasts feature homemade muffins, organic produce, and locally made charcuterie, with a sweet or savory entrée. Lounge in the garden or the wood-paneled library, checking your email if you must (Wi-Fi and local calls are included), but if you laze with your beloved in your double soaker tub instead, your messages can surely wait.

INFORMATION AND SERVICES
VISITOR INFORMATION

Tourism Victoria (812 Wharf St., 250/953-2033, www.tourismvictoria.com; 9am-5pm daily) runs a year-round information center on the Inner Harbour, with helpful staff who can assist you in booking tours and accommodations. The building has public restrooms, too.

Tourism Vancouver Island (www.vancouverisland.travel) publishes a guide to things to do across the island, available online and in print from area visitors centers.

MEDICAL SERVICES

Victoria General Hospital (1 Hospital Way, 250/727-4212 or 877/370-8699, www.viha.ca) and Royal Jubilee Hospital (1952 Bay St., 250/370-8000 or 877/370-8699, www.viha.ca) provide emergency medical services. The pharmacy at Shoppers Drug Mart (3511 Blanshard St., 250/475-7572, www.shoppersdrugmart.ca) is open 24 hours daily.

GETTING THERE
AIR

The fastest way to travel between Vancouver and Victoria is by floatplane or helicopter. Both take off and land from the city centers, making this option convenient for a car-free day trip. It's more expensive than taking the ferry, but the scenery over the Gulf Islands and Strait of Georgia is impressive.

Harbour Air (604/274-1277 or 800/665-0212, www.harbourair.com; 35 minutes; one-way adults $139-242) flies frequently throughout the day between the Vancouver Harbour Flight Centre (1055 Canada Pl., behind the Vancouver Convention Centre, 604/274-1277) and the Victoria Inner Harbour Centre (1000 Wharf St., 250/384-2215).

Helijet (800/665-4354, www.helijet.com; 35 minutes; one-way adults $179-285, seniors $215) departs frequently throughout the day between Vancouver Harbour Heliport (455 Waterfront Rd., near Waterfront Station, 604/688-4646) and Victoria Harbour Heliport (79 Dallas Rd., 250/386-7676), between the Ogden Point Cruise Ship Terminal and Fisherman's Wharf. One child (ages 2-12) flies free with each adult; additional one-way children's fares are $79.

If you're coming from farther away, you can fly to Victoria International Airport (YYJ, 1640 Electra Blvd., Sidney, 250/953-7533, www.victoriaairport.com), which is north of downtown, from a number of U.S. and Canadian cities. Air Canada (www.aircanada.com) flies between Victoria and Vancouver, Calgary, Toronto, or San Francisco. WestJet (www.westjet.com) has flights between Victoria and Calgary, Edmonton, Kelowna (B.C.), Las Vegas, and Phoenix. Alaska Air (www.alaskaair.com) makes the quick hop between Victoria and Seattle.

CAR AND FERRY

BC Ferries (888/223-3779, www.bc-ferries.com) provides frequent service between the Vancouver metropolitan area on the mainland and Vancouver Island. Ferries transport foot passengers, bicycles, cars, trucks, and recreational vehicles. Reservations ($15 at least 7 days in advance, $18.50 1-6 days in advance, $22 same-day travel) are recommended for vehicles, particularly if you're traveling on summer weekends or during holiday periods. Reservations are not available for walk-on passengers or bicycles.

Metropolitan Vancouver has two ferry docks, which are both outside the city center. The Tsawwassen Terminal (1 Ferry Causeway, Delta), 24 miles (38 kilometers) south of Vancouver, is the departure point for ferries to Victoria. The Tsawwassen-Swartz Bay Ferry (one-way adults $17.20, ages 5-11 $8.60, cars $56.45, bikes $2) takes you between the mainland and Victoria in one hour and 35 minutes.

To drive from Vancouver to Tsawwassen, head south on Oak Street, following the signs for Highway 99 south, and cross the Oak Street Bridge into Richmond. Stay on Highway 99 through the George Massey Tunnel. Exit onto Highway 17 south toward the Tsawwassen ferry terminal. Allow about 45 minutes to drive from downtown Vancouver to Tsawwassen, with extra time during the morning and evening rush hours.

From late June through early September, ferries between Tsawwassen and Swartz Bay generally run every hour between 7am and 9pm daily, and every two hours the rest of the year; however, there are frequent variations, so check the B.C. Ferries website (www.bcferries.com) for the schedule before you travel.

The Swartz Bay Terminal (Highway 17) is 20 miles (32 kilometers) north of Victoria at the end of Highway 17, about a 30-minute drive. After you exit the ferry at Swartz Bay, follow Highway 17 south, which goes directly into downtown Victoria, where it becomes Blanshard Street.

DIRECT BUS AND FERRY

To travel between Vancouver to Victoria without your own car (and without splurging on a flight), the easiest option is to take a direct bus service that picks up passengers at several points downtown, takes you onto the ferry, and continues into downtown Victoria.

BC Ferries Connector (604/428-9474 or 888/788-8840, www.bcfconnector.com; one-way bus adults $47.50, seniors or B.C. resident adults $35.60, students $28.50, ages 5-11 $23.75), operated by Wilson's Transportation, transports passengers between downtown Vancouver and downtown Victoria. The bus takes you to the Tsawwassen Ferry Terminal and drives onto the ferry. At Swartz Bay, you reboard the bus and travel to downtown Victoria. Trips depart several times daily in each direction, and reservations are required; the entire trip takes about four hours.

In Vancouver, the BC Ferries Connector bus originates at Pacific Central Station (1150 Station St.). For a slightly higher fare (one-way bus adults $52.50, seniors or B.C. resident adults $39.40, students $31.50, ages 5-11 $26.25), you can schedule a pickup from many downtown Vancouver hotels. In Victoria, the coach takes you to the Capital City

Station (721 Douglas St.), behind the Fairmont Empress Hotel, one block from the Inner Harbour.

The BC Ferries Connector fare does not include a ferry ticket (one-way adults $17.20, ages 5-11 $8.60), which you must purchase in addition to your bus ticket.

DIRECT FERRY

As this book went to press, V2V Vacations was slated to begin operating a direct ferry service between downtown Vancouver and downtown Victoria. Launching in 2017, the *V2V Empress* (250/590-9154 or 855/554-4679, www.v2vvacations.com, one-way adults $120, ages 12 and under $60), a high-speed, 300-passenger catamaran, will make one daily trip in each direction between the Vancouver Harbour Flight Centre (1055 Canada Pl., behind the Vancouver Centre) and the Victoria Steamship Terminal (470 Belleville St.) on the Inner Harbour. Travel time is 3.5 hours.

PUBLIC TRANSIT

If you don't have a lot of luggage, it's possible to take public transit between downtown Vancouver and the Tsawwassen Ferry Terminal and from the Swartz Bay Ferry Terminal to downtown Victoria. It's much cheaper than the BC Ferries Connector option, but it takes a little longer.

In Vancouver, take the Canada Line to Bridgeport Station, where you change to bus 620 for Tsawwassen Ferry (www.translink.ca; one-way adults $5.60, seniors, students, and ages 5-13 $3.80). The total trip takes about an hour.

After taking the Tsawwassen-Swartz Bay Ferry (www.bcferries. com; 1 hour and 35 minutes; one-way adults $17.20, ages 5-11 $8.60), catch

B.C. Transit bus 70 for Swartz Bay/Downtown Express (www.bctransit.com/victoria; 50 minutes; one-way $2.50 pp) to downtown Victoria.

GETTING AROUND

Victoria's Inner Harbour is compact and walkable, easy to navigate without a car. It's possible to reach sights outside the city center on the region's public buses, although to explore farther afield on Vancouver Island, having your own vehicle is more convenient.

BUS

B.C. Transit (250/382-6161, http://bctransit.com/victoria; one-way $2.50) runs buses around Victoria, to Butchart Gardens, and to the Swartz Bay Ferry Terminal. Hours vary by bus route, but major routes typically begin service between 6am and 7am and stop service between 11pm and midnight. Service to the Swartz Bay ferry begins at 5:30am Monday through Saturday and 6:30am on Sunday.

FERRY

Victoria Harbour Ferry (250/708-0201, www.victoriaharbourferry.com; 11am-5pm daily Mar. and Oct., 11am-7pm daily Apr.-mid-May, 10am-9pm daily mid-May-mid-Sept.) can take you around the Inner Harbour in their cute colorful boats, stopping at Fisherman's Wharf, the Delta Victoria Ocean Pointe Resort, and many other waterside points. Fares vary by distance; a basic one-zone trip is $6 per person.

TAXI

You can usually find taxis near the Inner Harbour and the Fairmont Empress Hotel. Victoria taxi rates start at $3.30, plus $1.93 per kilometer. Local cab companies include Bluebird

Cabs (250/382-2222, www.taxicab.com) and Yellow Cab of Victoria (250/381-2222, www.yellowcabvictoria.com).

CAR

Victoria's downtown sights are all clustered around the Inner Harbour, so if you've driven downtown, park your car and do your exploring on foot. Having a car is handy to visit attractions outside downtown or on the Saanich Peninsula.

Parking

Pay for downtown on-street parking (Mon.-Sat. 9am-6pm $1.50-3 per hour) at the nearby pay stations with coins or credit cards. Parking is free in the evenings and on Sunday.

The city has five centrally located public parking garages (first hour free, subsequent hours $2 per hour, $12 per day, $14 per day at Bastion Square) open 24 hours daily: Bastion Square Parkade (575 Yates St.), Broughton Street Parkade (745 Broughton St., below the Central Library), Centennial Square Parkade (645 Fisgard St.), Johnson Street Parkade (750 Johnson St.), and View Street Parkade (743 View St.). Rates are in effect 8am-6pm Monday-Saturday; parking is free in the evenings and on Sunday.

You can also park in these city-run surface lots ($2.25 per hour, $13.50 per day): 900 Wharf Street (near the Harbour Air terminal) and 820 Courtney Street. There's no free parking in these lots; pay rates are in effect 24 hours daily.

Car Rentals

Avis (800/879-2847, www.avis.ca), Budget (250/953-5300 or 800/668-9833, www.budget.ca), Hertz (800/263-0600, www.hertz.ca), and National (250/656-2541 or 800/227-7368, www.nationalcar.ca) have rental desks at Victoria International Airport. Enterprise (250/655-7368, www.enterprise.com) has a nearby off-airport location. Both Budget and National also have rental offices downtown, near the Inner Harbour.

BICYCLE

Victoria is a bike-friendly city. Among the scenic routes for visitors on bikes are Dallas Road, which skirts the seashore on the city's southern edge, and Fairfield Road, which passes Ross Bay Cemetery.

Running along a former rail line, the 35-mile (55-kilometer) Galloping Goose Trail takes you from Victoria west to the town of Sooke. You can follow the 18-mile (29-kilometer) Lochside Regional Trail, another rail trail, between Swartz Bay and Victoria.

The Pedaler rents bikes and runs cycling tours.

The Pedaler (321 Belleville St., 778/265-7433, http://thepedaler.ca; 9am-6pm daily May-Sept., call for off-season hours) has a fleet of modern bikes for rent (1 hour $10, 2 hours $16, full-day $30). They also run fun guided cycling tours, including the two-hour **Castles, Hoods & Legends** (adults $49, youth $45), a short tour of Victoria's major sights; the four-hour **Eat.Drink.Pedal** ($109), which takes you through several Victoria neighborhoods with stops for pizza, ice cream, and other treats; and the three-hour **Hoppy Hour Ride** ($89), sampling Victoria's craft breweries.

Nanaimo

This city of 85,000 on Vancouver Island's east coast, 70 miles (110 kilometers) north of Victoria, is an alternate ferry port between the city of Vancouver and the island, convenient if you're traveling to Tofino on the island's west coast. British Columbia's third oldest city, Nanaimo is worth a stop for its pretty waterfront, historic sites, and a unique adventure: snorkeling with a colony of seals who live near the harbor. Be sure to sample a Nanaimo bar, the local signature sweet.

SIGHTS AND RECREATION
NANAIMO MUSEUM

The modern **Nanaimo Museum** (100 Museum Way, 250/753-1821, www.nanaimomuseum.ca; 10am-5pm daily mid-May-early Sept., 10am-5pm Mon.-Sat. early Sept.-mid-May; adults $2, seniors and students $1.75, ages 5-12 $0.75) tells the stories of the city's development, from its First Nations communities to its days as a mining hub, when the Hudson's Bay Company established a coal mine nearby. Other exhibits focus on the city's quirkier traditions, like its annual summer bathtub race.

THE BASTION
Built in 1853 by the Hudson's Bay Company, **The Bastion** (95 Front St.), on the Nanaimo waterfront, is the city's oldest structure and North America's only original wooden bastion (fortified tower). The first-floor exhibit area talks about the Hudson's Bay Company and its trading activities; the upper floors illustrate the building's military uses.

Outside the Bastion, stop to watch the midday **cannon firing ceremony** (noon daily mid-May-early Sept.), with a local bagpiper and a really big bang.

✪ SNORKELING WITH SEALS
Looking for a unique adventure? A colony of harbor seals lives around Snake Island, a rock outcropping located 15 minutes by boat from Nanaimo harbor. **Sundown Diving** (22 Esplanade Rd., 250/753-1880, www.sundowndiving.com) runs half-day tours ($100 pp) to the island, where you can **snorkel with the seals.**

The tour starts at the company's downtown shop, where you're outfitted with a wetsuit, hood, booties, gloves, and snorkeling gear. Your guide will take you to the harbor, where you board the motorboat to Snake Island. Scoot into the water to swim alongside these marine creatures, which are surprisingly graceful as they glide through the sea.

Bring a bathing suit, towel, and water bottle. You don't need snorkeling

ON THE NANAIMO BAR TRAIL

The city of Nanaimo has its own namesake dessert: the **Nanaimo bar.** This sweet treat, which became popular in the 1950s, has three layers: a nutty base of coconut, cocoa, and graham cracker crumbs, with a custard filling and a thick dark chocolate coating on top. You can find Nanaimo bars at bakeries all around town.

You can get more adventurous with your Nanaimo bars, too, if you follow the city's **Nanaimo bar trail.** At more than 30 stops, you can sample numerous variations on the Nanaimo bar theme. There's a rich, creamy vegan version at **Powerhouse Living Foods** (200 Commercial St., 250/571-7873, www.powerhouseliving. ca) and a whipped cream-slathered deep-fried wonder at **Pirate Chips** (1-75 Front St., 250/753-2447). Several watering holes, including the **Modern Café** (221 Commercial St., 250/754-5022, www.themoderncafe.ca), even serve a Nanaimo bar martini.

deep-fried Nanaimo bars at Pirate Chips

Get a guide to the Nanaimo bar trail on the website of **Tourism Nanaimo** (www.tourismnanaimo.com) or pick up a copy at the **Nanaimo Visitor Centre.**

---

experience, but you should be comfortable swimming in deep water.

FOOD

Start your day with pastries and coffee from **Mon Petit Choux** (120 Commercial St., 250/753-6002, www. monpetitchoux.ca; 8am-5pm Mon.-Sat., 9am-5pm Sun.; $6-11), a sunny French-style café downtown. Beyond the sweets, they serve breakfasts (including scrambled eggs with smoked salmon or a *croque-madame* on house-made brioche) and light lunches, from quiche to sandwiches on their own baguettes.

Despite its name, the **Modern Café** (221 Commercial St., 250/754-5022, www.themoderncafe.ca; 11am-11pm Mon.-Wed., 11am-midnight Thurs.-Sat., 10am-11pm Sun.; $14-28) is one of Nanaimo's oldest restaurants, serving food and drinks in its pub-style space downtown since 1946. Burgers, sandwiches, salads, and several types of macaroni and cheese are

the lunchtime draws, while the dinner menu adds heartier plates like maple-glazed ribs or grilled steak. To drink? A Nanaimo bar martini!

The wood-burning oven takes center stage at **La Stella Trattoria** (321 Wesley St., 778/441-4668, www.lastellatrattoria.com; 5pm-9:30pm Wed.-Sun.; $14-18) in Nanaimo's Old City Quarter, 0.5 mile (800 meters) up the hill from the harbor, turning out crisp-crust pizzas topped with fresh ingredients like arugula, prosciutto, and locally produced *bocconcini*. Handmade pastas and Italian salads give you options beyond the pies.

When you pull up to the Westwood Tennis Club, a 15-minute drive west of downtown, you'd never guess that behind the courts is a fine lakeside bistro. **Christina's on the Lake** (2367 Arbot Rd., 250/753-2866, www. christinasonthelake.com; 11:30am-2:30pm and 5:30pm-8:30pm Tues.-Sat.; reduced off-season hours; $22-29) serves comfortably creative dishes, like pan-seared salmon with wild mushroom risotto or steak in a red wine *jus*, in a lovely dining room and patio overlooking peaceful Westwood Lake. Before or after your meal, loop the lake on the 3.5-mile (5.5-kilometer) walking trail.

ACCOMMODATIONS

If you're going to stay over in Nanaimo, the friendly Buccaneer Inn (1577 Stewart Ave., 250/753-1246 or 877/282-6337, www.buccaneerinn. com; $75-200 d) is the closest place to sleep near the Departure Bay ferry terminal. In this basic but well-maintained family-run motel, many of the nautical-themed rooms and suites have kitchens. Rates include parking, Wi-Fi, and local phone calls. The inn is on a busy road, although traffic typically quiets at night.

The modern 15-story Coast Bastion Hotel (11 Bastion St., 250/753-6601 or 800/716-6199, www. coasthotels.com; $145-290 d) overlooks the harbor downtown, with water vistas from its upper floors; request a corner unit for prime views. The 179 rooms have all the expected amenities, including white linens with colorful accents, air-conditioning, coffeemakers, flat-screen TVs, safes, and included Wi-Fi and local calls. The hotel has a fitness room and spa. Park in the nearby city parkade ($8.50 for 24 hours) or let the hotel valet deal with your car for an additional $8.

Oh, the views! At MGM Seashore B&B (4950 Fillinger Crescent, 250/729-7249, www.mgmbandb.com; $199-299 d), with three guest rooms in a residential neighborhood north of town, the panoramas stretch across the water, particularly out on the mammoth deck, where you can soak in the hot tub. Owners Marilyn and Glenn McKnight start guests' stays with a welcome Nanaimo bar, serve a full breakfast, and stock a guest lounge with espresso, tea, books, and movies. The Honeymoon Suite has a whirlpool tub positioned toward the ocean vistas, while the Sunset Room, with a round king bed, opens to the deck. The more basic King Room could accommodate a family, with a king bed and two singles.

INFORMATION AND SERVICES

Tourism Nanaimo (www.tourismnanaimo.com) runs the year-round Nanaimo Visitor Centre (2450 Northfield Rd., 250/751-1556 or 800/663-7337; 9am-6pm daily May-mid.-Sept., 9am-5pm Mon.-Sat. mid-Sept.-Apr.), off Highway 19 northwest of the city center, and provides lots of information about the area.

GETTING THERE
AIR

Harbour Air (604/274-1277 or 800/665-0212, www.harbourair.com; 20 minutes; one-way adults $76-129) flies regularly between the Vancouver Harbour Flight Centre (1055 Canada Pl., 604/274-1277) and Nanaimo's Pioneer Waterfront Plaza (90 Front St., 250/714-0900).

Helijet (800/665-4354, www.helijet.com; 20 minutes; one-way adults $109-139, seniors $97) buzzes across the water Monday through Friday between Vancouver Harbour Heliport (455 Waterfront Rd., near Waterfront Station, 604/688-4646) and Nanaimo Harbour Heliport (Port of Nanaimo Welcome Centre, 100 Port Dr.). One child (ages 2-12) flies free with each adult; additional one-way children's fares are $79.

THE ISLAND'S BIGGEST TREES

Heading west from Nanaimo toward Vancouver Island's west coast, you'll pass through a section of old-growth rainforest, with massive trees that began their lives more than 800 years ago.

In **Cathedral Grove,** which is part of **MacMillan Provincial Park** (Hwy. 4, 250/474-1336, www.env.gov.bc.ca; dawn-dusk daily; free), you can follow two short trails through these forests of giants.

The biggest trees—colossal Douglas firs—are on the south side of the highway. The largest measures more than 30 feet (9 meters) around. On the north side of the road, the trail passes through groves of ancient western red cedars and along the shore of Cameron Lake.

Cathedral Grove is 40 miles (65 kilometers) west of Nanaimo and 10 miles (16 kilometers) east of Port Alberni. Highway 4 runs directly through the park; there's a parking lot near the big trees.

Cathedral Grove

CAR

Via Horseshoe Bay

BC Ferries' **Horseshoe Bay Terminal** (6750 Keith Rd., West Vancouver), where the most direct ferries leave for Nanaimo, is on the North Shore, 12 miles (20 kilometers) northwest of downtown Vancouver. The **Horseshoe Bay-Departure Bay Ferry** (one-way adults $17.20, ages 5-11 $8.60, cars $56.45, bikes $2) takes one hour and 40 minutes.

From downtown **Vancouver to Horseshoe Bay,** take **West Georgia Street** to the **Lions Gate Bridge.** Watch the signs carefully as you approach Stanley Park en route to the bridge to stay in the proper lane. The center lane on the three-lane bridge reverses its travel direction at different times of the day, typically creating two travel lanes into the city in the morning and two travel lanes toward the North Shore during the afternoon rush hour.

After you cross the Lions Gate Bridge, bear left toward Marine Drive

west/Highway 1/Highway 99. Enter **Marine Drive** and stay in the far right lane to take the first right onto **Taylor Way** (the sign says "Whistler"). Follow Taylor Way up the hill, and exit left onto **Highway 1** west. Continue on Highway 1 to the ferry terminal. The drive from downtown to Horseshoe Bay generally takes about 30 minutes, but allow extra time during the morning and afternoon commute times.

From late June through early September, ferries between Horseshoe Bay and Departure Bay generally make eight or nine trips daily, with six or seven daily runs the rest of the year; check the **BC Ferries website** (www.bcferries.com) for the seasonal schedule.

The **Departure Bay Terminal** (680 Trans-Canada Hwy., Nanaimo) is two miles (3 kilometers) north of downtown Nanaimo.

Via Tsawwassen

Another route between the mainland and Nanaimo is the

Tsawwassen-Duke Point Ferry (one-way adults $17.20, ages 5-11 $8.60, cars $56.45, bikes $2). The ferry ride is two hours. Ferries run 6-8 times per day. Consider this route if you are traveling to the Nanaimo area from points south of Vancouver.

The Duke Point Terminal (400 Duke Point Hwy., Nanaimo) is off Highway 1, nine miles (16 kilometers) south of downtown Nanaimo.

PUBLIC TRANSIT

From downtown Vancouver, bus 257 for Horseshoe Bay Express (www.translink.ca; 45 minutes; one-way adults $4.10, seniors, students, and ages 5-13 $2.80) runs to the Horseshoe Bay Ferry Terminal from several stops along West Georgia Street. The slightly slower bus 250 for Horseshoe Bay (www.translink.ca; 55 minutes; one-way adults $4.10, seniors, students, and ages 5-13 $2.80) follows a similar route. Alternatively, Greyhound (800/661-8747, www.greyhound.ca) operates several buses daily to the Horseshoe Bay Ferry Terminal from Pacific Central Station (1150 Station St.; 45 minutes; adults $5.05-15.20).

After taking the Horseshoe Bay-Departure Bay Ferry (www.bcferries.com; 1 hour and 40 minutes; one-way adults $17.20, ages 5-11 $8.60), catch B.C. Transit bus 2 (www.bctransit.com/nanaimo; 20 minutes; one-way adults $2.50, seniors, students, and ages 5-11 $2.25) from the Departure Bay Ferry Terminal to downtown Nanaimo.

The West Coast

Vancouver Island's west coast can feel like the edge of the world. After you climb the winding road up and over the spines of mountains in the center of the island, you finally reach the west shore, where the Pacific waves crash along the beach. Here are the ocean sands and peaceful coastal rainforests of the island's first national park, along with two easygoing west coast towns, larger Tofino to the north and Ucluelet to the south. These peninsula communities have whale-watching tours, First Nations canoe trips, and plenty of other outdoor adventures, as well as good restaurants and beachfront lodges.

The weather on the west coast can be cooler, damper, and more changeable than elsewhere on the island. Bring layers, rain gear, and shoes or boots that can get wet.

Whatever the weather, the west coast is a laid-back region where local surfers carry their boards on their bikes, and cocktail hour can seem like a sacred ritual. And it's hugely popular with travelers: Tofino's population of 2,000 can swell to more than 20,000 on weekends in July and August.

Don't worry, though. Even in midsummer, there's plenty of room here at the edge of the world.

✪ PACIFIC RIM NATIONAL PARK RESERVE

With 14 miles (22 kilometers) of sandy beaches and dunes backed by coastal rainforest, the reserve protects a wide swath of Vancouver Island's west coast. Established in 1970, it was the island's first national park.

Tofino and Ucluelet

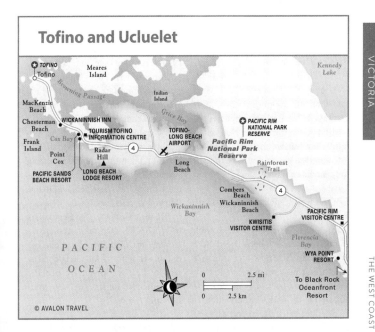

TOFINO
Tofino
Meares Island
Browning Passage
Indian Island
Kennedy Lake
MacKenzie Beach
Chesterman Beach
WICKANINNISH INN
Grice Bay
PACIFIC RIM NATIONAL PARK RESERVE
Frank Island
Cox Bay
TOURISM TOFINO INFORMATION CENTRE
TOFINO-LONG BEACH AIRPORT
Pacific Rim National Park Reserve
Point Cox
Radar Hill
4
Long Beach
Rainforest Trail
4
PACIFIC SANDS BEACH RESORT
LONG BEACH LODGE RESORT
Combers Beach
Wickaninnish Beach
PACIFIC RIM VISITOR CENTRE
Wickaninnish Bay
KWISITIS VISITOR CENTRE
Florencia Bay
PACIFIC OCEAN
WYA POINT RESORT
0   2.5 mi
0   2.5 km
To Black Rock Oceanfront Resort
© AVALON TRAVEL

VISITING THE PARK

The **Pacific Rim National Park Reserve** has three geographically separate components. Most visitors head directly to the park's **Long Beach Unit** (Pacific Rim Hwy., 250/726-3500, www.pc.gc.ca), north of the Tofino-Ucluelet junction. The park visitors center is here, as is the longest beach on the island's west coast. You can camp, too, although you can easily day-trip to the park from Tofino or Ucluelet.

You can reach the park's **Broken Islands Group,** offshore in Barkley Sound, only by boat. Check the park website for recommended tour operators who organize guided kayaking or sailing tours to the islands.

Also part of the park is the 47-mile (75-kilometer) **West Coast Trail** (May-Sept.), a rugged backpacking route.

Park Passes and Fees

Purchase a **day pass** (adults $7.80, seniors $6.80, ages 6-16 $3.90) for the Pacific Rim National Park Reserve at the **Pacific Rim Visitor Centre** (2791 Pacific Rim Hwy., Ucluelet), at the park's **Kwisitis Visitor Centre** (Wick Beach, off Pacific Rim Hwy.), or from vending machines at parking lots within the park.

Buying a Parks Canada **annual discovery pass** (adults $67.70, seniors $57.90, ages 6-16 $33.30, families $136.40), valid for a year, is a good deal if you're spending at least a week in one or more parks. It's good at more than 100 national parks and national historic sites across Canada. Buy annual passes online from Parks Canada or at any park visitors center.

For both day and annual passes, family passes cover up to seven people in a single vehicle.

Visitors Center

Start your park visit at the Kwisitis Visitor Centre (485 Wick Rd., off Pacific Rim Hwy., 250/726-3524, www.pc.gc.ca; 10am-5pm daily May-mid-Oct., 10am-5pm Fri.-Sun. mid-Oct.-May). The park encompasses the traditional territory of the Nuu-chah-nulth First Nation, and you can get an introduction to their culture though the center's exhibits.

SPORTS AND RECREATION
Beaches

Confusingly, Wickaninnish Beach is not the beach where the deluxe Wickaninnish Inn is located; that hotel is on Chesterman Beach. Rather, the wide dune-backed Wick Beach is adjacent to the park visitors center.

North of Wick Beach and adjacent to old-growth forest, Long Beach creates the longest sand dune on Vancouver Island; it's more than nine miles (16 kilometers) long.

Hiking

Several gentle hiking trails start from the park's Kwisitis Visitor Centre. The Nuu-chah-nulth Trail, 1.5 miles (2.5 kilometers) each way, has interpretive panels about First Nations culture. You can branch from this trail onto the 0.5-mile (800-meter) South Beach Trail, which leads to a pebble beach with often spectacular waves; don't swim here, though, due to the strong currents. The gentle Shorepine Bog Trail, a 0.5-mile (800-meter) loop, takes you through an old-growth temperate rainforest.

CAMPING

Above the beach, 7.5 miles (12 kilometers) north of the Tofino-Ucluelet junction, Green Point Campground (www.pc.gc.ca; May-early Oct.; $23.50-32.30) has 94 drive-in sites and 20 forested walk-in sites with flush toilets and running water but no showers.

The walk-in sites include five equipped camping sites ($70), which are handy if you're not traveling with your own camping gear. The equipped sites come with a tent that sleeps 4 to 6 people, sleeping pads, a tarp shelter, stove, and lantern. You need to bring sleeping bags or bedding, cooking supplies, food, and other personal items. Remember your flashlights.

Make campsite reservations (877/737-3783, www.reservation.parks-canada.gc.ca) online or by phone, beginning in January for the upcoming season. Reservations are especially recommended for stays between mid-June and August.

GETTING THERE

Pacific Rim National Park Reserve's Long Beach Unit is located off Highway 4, 19 miles (30 kilometers) south of Tofino and 10 miles (16 kilometers) north of Ucluelet.

By car and ferry from Vancouver, the 165-mile (260-kilometer) trip across the Strait of Georgia and then across Vancouver Island takes about six hours. Drive northwest from Vancouver to the Horseshoe Bay Ferry Terminal and take the Horseshoe Bay-Departure Bay Ferry (www.bcferries.com; 1 hour and 40 minutes; one-way adults $17.20, ages 5-11 $8.60) to Nanaimo. When you leave the Departure Bay ferry terminal, follow the signs to Highway 19/Parksville. Just past Parksville, exit onto Highway 4 westbound toward Port Alberni. Check your gas gauge; there are no gas stations between Port Alberni and the Pacific coast.

Highway 4 comes to a T at the Tofino-Ucluelet junction. Turn right

REST STOP: SPROAT LAKE

Sproat Lake

When you're driving to or from Vancouver Island's west coast, there are few places to stop as you cross the mountains between Port Alberni and Tofino. For a break or some good food, stop at **Sproat Lake Landing** (10695 Lakeshore Rd., Port Alberni, 250/723-2722, www.sproatlakelanding.com), where **Drinkwaters Social House** (11am-11pm Mon.-Fri., 9am-11pm Sat.-Sun.) serves farm-to-table meals overlooking the 15-mile (25-kilometer) lake. If you have time, take a 90-minute cruise on the *Drinkwater IV tugboat* (10am and 2pm daily spring-fall, $45). Book one of the seven modern guest rooms ($140-250) if you want a longer rest; the best have lake views.

(north) onto the Pacific Rim Highway toward Tofino. The park's Kwisitis Visitor Centre is five miles (eight kilometers) north of the junction.

⭐ TOFINO

Like all of the west coast, the Tofino area was First Nations territory where generations of fishers and hunters lived and foraged, both on the mainland and on the islands offshore. Spanish explorers first ventured to the region in the late 1700s, followed quickly by British expeditions, but it wasn't until 1909 that the town of Tofino was officially established, when fishing, logging, and mining were the main occupations along the coast. Tofino's nickname comes from these hardscrabble jobs and the region's stormy winters: Tough City.

While surfers and other nature-

seekers began arriving in the 1960s, the creation of the Pacific Rim National Park Reserve in 1970 and the paving of Highway 4 to the coast in 1972 launched the modern tourist era.

Today, laid-back, surfer-friendly Tofino has a small village around its scenic harbor, where fishing vessels set off to sea, whale-watching and other tour boats dock, and floatplanes come and go. The beaches and oceanfront lodges are on the peninsula, south of town.

SIGHTS

The **Tofino Botanical Gardens** (1084 Pacific Rim Hwy., 250/725-1220, www.tbgf.org; 9am-dusk daily; adults $12, seniors $10, students $8), two miles (3 kilometers) south of town, offer a refuge from the wilderness of Vancouver Island's wild west coast,

235

Tofino Botanical Gardens

with cultivated plants, old-growth rainforest, and works by local artists. Many plants are local, including a tree that's roughly 800 years old, while others include Chilean rainforest vegetation, Himalayan lilies (the world's largest), and other varieties that grow in climates similar to that of British Columbia's coastal regions. Examine the traditional dugout canoe, handmade by First Nations carver Joe Martin, displayed with photos of his family and commentary from his children. Kids may appreciate the chickens and goats that wander the garden's grounds. Named for Charles Darwin and stocked with "books full of dangerous ideas," Darwin's Café (hours vary) serves coffee, homemade pastries, and light breakfasts and lunches.

The Whale Centre (411 Campbell St., 250/725-2132, www.tofinowhalecentre.com; 9am-5pm daily May-June and Sept.-Oct., 8am-8pm daily July-Aug., hours vary Nov.-Apr.; free) has a little museum with a gray whale skeleton and information about local marinelife.

TOURS AND EXCURSIONS

To really experience the west coast, get offshore to explore the coastline and nearby islands, and look for the wildlife that populates the region. Most tours operate from March or April through October or November, although trips can be postponed or canceled if the seas get too rough.

The following companies are among those offering tours in the Tofino area:

- **Remote Passages Marine Excursions** (51 Wharf St., 250/725-3330 or 800/666-9833, www.remote-passages.com)
- **Ocean Outfitters** (368 Main St., 250/725-2866 or 877/906-2326, www.oceanoutfitters.bc.ca)
- **T'ashii Paddle School** (250/266-3787 or 855/883-3787, www.tofino-paddle.com)
- **The Whale Centre** (411 Campbell St., 250/725-2132 or 888/474-2288, www.tofinowhalecentre.com)

Hot Springs Cove/Maquinna Marine Provincial Park

A full-day trip to these remote hot springs is a highlight for many Tofino visitors. Located 27 nautical miles (50 kilometers) northwest of Tofino, Hot Springs Cove, in Maquinna Marine Provincial Park at the north end of Clayoquot Sound, is accessible only by boat (adults $125-130, under age 13 $89-105) or floatplane (adults $199, under age 13 $179-185).

Traveling by boat (1.5 to 2 hours each way), you may spot whales, sea lions, and even bears or other wildlife, so you might consider this trip an alternative to a separate whale-watching tour. With the floatplane option, you save a little time, traveling one-way by boat, the other on a scenic 20-minute flight.

Once you arrive at the dock, it's a one-mile (1.6-kilometer) walk on a boardwalk through the rainforest to the natural hot springs. Climb

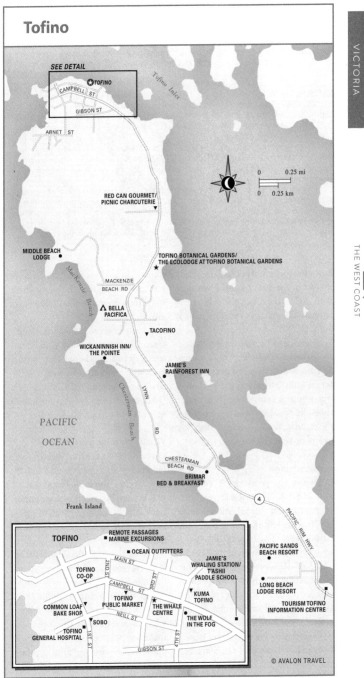

Tofino

SEE DETAIL

TOFINO

CAMPBELL ST

GIBSON ST

ARNET ST

Tofino Inlet

0   0.25 mi
0   0.25 km

RED CAN GOURMET/
PICNIC CHARCUTERIE

MIDDLE BEACH
LODGE

TOFINO BOTANICAL GARDENS/
THE ECOLODGE AT TOFINO BOTANICAL GARDENS

MACKENZIE
BEACH RD

Mackenzie Beach

BELLA
PACIFICA

TACOFINO

WICKANINNISH INN/
THE POINTE

JAMIE'S
RAINFOREST INN

LYNN RD

Chesterman Beach

PACIFIC
OCEAN

CHESTERMAN
BEACH RD

BRIMAR
BED & BREAKFAST

4

Frank Island

PACIFIC RIM HWY

PACIFIC SANDS
BEACH RESORT

LONG BEACH
LODGE RESORT

TOURISM TOFINO
INFORMATION CENTRE

TOFINO

REMOTE PASSAGES
MARINE EXCURSIONS

OCEAN OUTFITTERS

MAIN ST

2ND ST

TOFINO
CO-OP

CAMPBELL ST

3RD ST

JAMIE'S
WHALING STATION/
T'ASHII PADDLE SCHOOL

KUMA
TOFINO

COMMON LOAF
BAKE SHOP

TOFINO
PUBLIC MARKET

NEILL ST

THE WHALE
CENTRE

4TH ST

THE WOLF
IN THE FOG

SOBO

TOFINO
GENERAL HOSPITAL

1ST ST

GIBSON ST

© AVALON TRAVEL

TWO DAYS ON VANCOUVER ISLAND'S WEST COAST

Start your day with a morning stroll along the beach; **Chesterman Beach** is one of the area's most beautiful. Then wander through the **Tofino Botanical Gardens** to explore the old-growth rainforest, stopping at the garden's **Darwin's Café** when it's time for a coffee break.

Have lunch at the orange food truck, **Tacofino.** Then head for **Pacific Rim National Park Reserve** to check out the displays in the **Kwisitis Visitor Centre** and hike near the shore. Later, take a **surfing lesson,** go swimming, or book a **First Nations Dugout Canoe Tour** with the excellent guides at T'ashii Paddle School. Have dinner at **The Wolf in the Fog,** where the don't-miss appetizer is the potato-crusted oyster, and any local seafood is bound to be stellar.

The next morning, pick up coffee and a ginger scone at **Common Loaf Bake Shop,** before heading for the waterfront for an offshore excursion. Take a full-day trip to **Hot Springs Cove,** a kayak excursion to **Meares Island,** or a shorter **whale-watching** or **bear-watching tour.**

After your tour, clean up and drive to the **Wickaninnish Inn** for a cocktail in their window-lined lounge facing the sea. If your budget allows, stay for a special dinner at **The Pointe,** or if you'd rather have a more casual meal, head into town for a restorative bowl of ramen at **Kuma Tofino** or the wild salmon chowder at **SoBo.** Either way, stop to take a few sunset photos over the harbor to remember your west coast adventures.

down the rocks and take a natural hot shower in the gushing sulfur springs, then soak in the rock pools. The water temperature averages a soothing 110°F (43°C).

There's a rustic shelter with change rooms and a pit toilet above the springs and a restroom near the docks. Don't forget your bathing suit, towel, and water bottle. Sports sandals or water shoes will protect your feet from the rocks. Bring snacks or a picnic to enjoy before or after you soak.

Meares Island

Declared a park by the Tla-o-qui-aht and Ahousaht First Nations, **Meares Island**—its traditional name is Wanachis-Hilthhoois—is across the harbor from the village of Tofino.

A popular way to get to the island is on a half-day **kayak excursion** ($79). Some companies also run **water shuttles** (adults $25-30, under age 12 $15-20) to the island. Tour companies also collect a $3-5 park pass fee.

Once you arrive on Meares Island, you can hike through the rainforest on the moderate 1.9-mile (3 kilometer) round-trip **Big Tree Trail,** which takes you into an old-growth forest, where some trees are more than 1,000 years old.

For experienced hikers, the island's steep, challenging **Lone Cone Trail** leads up to a 2,395-foot (730-meter) peak with panoramic views across the island and the sound. It's only 0.6 mile (1 kilometer) in each direction, but it's essentially a vertical trail.

Whale-Watching

On **whale-watching excursions** (adults $89-109, under age 13 $69-79) from Tofino, you'll likely spot Pacific gray whales. You might also see humpback whales, bald eagles, sea lions, harbor seals, and occasionally orcas or porpoises.

As on the trips that depart from Victoria, you can choose from a tour in an inflatable Zodiac, which gives you a choppier but more thrilling ride, or on a larger, more sheltered boat, which would be more comfortable in inclement weather. On either type of craft, whale-watching tours typically last two to three hours.

Bear-Watching

From Tofino, you can take a boat through Clayoquot Sound to several spots where it's possible to observe the area's resident population of black bears. On these bear-watching excursions (adults $89-99, under age 13 $69-79), the tour boats dock offshore, where, if you're lucky, you'll spot bears foraging along the rocky beaches or in the tidal pools.

You stay on the boat throughout these two- to three-hour tours. Bring a camera with a telephoto lens for the best photos, since the boats must remain a safe distance away from the animals.

First Nations Dugout Canoe Tours

First Nations-owned T'ashii Paddle School (250/266-3787 or 855/883-3787, www.tofinopaddle.com) offers several excellent paddling tours in hand-carved dugout canoes, where you'll learn about local indigenous communities and their traditional culture.

Departing from Jamie's Whaling Station (606 Campbell St.), excursions include a two-hour Harbour Canoe Tour (late May-mid-Oct.; $65 pp), which is especially lovely at sunset; a Meares Island Canoe Tour (Mar.-Oct.; $89 pp), a four-hour paddling and hiking excursion; and a full-day Lemmens Inlet Canoe Tour (Mar.-Oct., by request only; $130 pp). Check the website for specific departure times.

SPORTS AND RECREATION
Beaches

Sandy beaches line the peninsula that stretches south from Tofino to Ucluelet. All are along the Pacific Rim Highway, listed here from north to south.

Sheltered MacKenzie Beach is closest to Tofino, with several resorts and campgrounds.

Beginning surfers hone their skills on the south end of 1.7-mile (2.7-kilometer) Chesterman Beach, one of Tofino's most scenic and popular stretches of sand. Toward the beach's north side, you can explore the tidepools at low tide.

Home to several resorts, including Pacific Sands and Long Beach Lodge, Cox Bay Beach has a popular surf break. At the bay's northern tip, you can explore several tidal caves, accessible only at low tide. The Wickaninnish Inn is on North Chesterman Beach.

Continuing south, you'll reach the beaches in Pacific Rim National Park Reserve, including Long Beach and Wickaninnish Beach.

Surfing

Tofino is western Canada's surfing capital (yes, Canada really has a surfing capital), with plenty of places to take lessons or catch the waves. While you can surf year-round, hardcore surfers come in winter when the waves are biggest; if you're just getting started, summertime is warmest, with the gentlest surf.

With a crew of women as instructors, Surf Sister Surf School (250/725-4456, www.surfsister.com) specializes in teaching women to surf, although they offer lessons for both men and women.

The Surf Club Adventure Centre (250/725-2442, www.longbeachlodgeresort.com) at the Long Beach Lodge Resort is another highly regarded surf school, teaching group and private lessons.

Schooner Cove Trail

Hiking

The **Rainforest Education Society** (250/725-2560, www.raincoasteducation.org) offers free one-hour interpretive walks in July and August that explore the tidepools and rainforest along Cox Bay. Check the website for the schedule and other details.

Guides from the First Nations-owned **T'ashii Paddle School** (250/266-3787 or 855/883-3787, www.tofinopaddle.com) lead winter **Cultural Walks on the Schooner Cove Trail** (11am daily mid-Dec.-Mar.; $80 pp) in Pacific Rim National Park Reserve that combine a gentle hike through the old-growth rainforest with information about local First Nations culture. Book in advance on their website.

FESTIVALS AND EVENTS

In early spring, gray whales begin returning to the waters off Vancouver Island's west coast. During the weeklong **Pacific Rim Whale Festival** (www.pacificrimwhalefestival.com, Mar.), you can learn more about these creatures with presentations, documentary films, guided walks, whale-watching tours, and other events.

The **Tofino Food and Wine Festival** (www.tofinofoodandwinefestival.com, June) is a weekend of dining, sipping, and toe-tapping to live music, on the grounds of the Tofino Botanical Gardens.

Celebrating local bivalves, the **Clayoquot Oyster Festival** (www.oystergala.com, Nov.) brings seafood lovers to town for oyster farm tours, restaurant events, a gala party, and plenty of oyster eating.

FOOD

For a small community, Tofino has a significant food culture, emphasizing innovative uses of local seafood and produce. Outside the summer months, many restaurants have reduced hours, so call to confirm before you set out. Except for The Pointe at the Wickaninnish Inn, Tofino's eating places are casual; patrons often look like they've wandered directly off a boat because, most likely, they have.

Groceries and Markets

The area's largest grocery store is Tofino Co-op (140 First St., 250/725-3226, www.tofinocoop.com; 8:30am-9pm daily summer, call for off-season hours). South of town, tiny but well-stocked Beaches Grocery (1184 Pacific Rim Hwy., 250/725-2237) carries fruits and vegetables, baked goods, and other food items, from chips to Asian chili sauce.

Find local produce, prepared foods, and crafts at the Tofino Public Market (Tofino Village Green, 3rd St. and Campbell St., www.tofino-market.com; 10am-2pm Sat. late May-mid-Oct.).

Modern Canadian

Oysters in a potato web? Corn-fried cod cheeks with pickled peppers? Some of the west coast's most imaginative dishes come out of the open kitchen at ✪ The Wolf in the Fog (150 4th St., 250/725-9653, www.wolfinthefog.com; 5pm-midnight daily; $16-32), where the second-floor dining room sparkles with polished wood and the big windows look out toward the harbor. While there's some serious technique and respect for local ingredients here, the chefs don't take themselves too seriously; the menu includes an option to "add foie gras to anything." To drink, try a cocktail like The Angler, with smoked salmon-infused vodka, maple, ginger, and fresh orange, or a Cedar Sour, with cedar-infused rye. The bottom line? Good food, good drinks, good fun.

Though the name is short for "sophisticated bohemian," airy SoBo (311 Neil St., 250/725-2341, www.sobo.ca; 11:30am-9pm daily; $16-35), with sunny yellow walls and floor-to-ceiling windows, is more refined than hippie, serving modern world-beat fare at lunch and dinner. Noon-hour dishes roam from Asian salad to huevos rancheros to pizza, while in the evening, you might try cedar-planked salmon, whiskey-braised beef brisket, or seafood stew. SoBo is justifiably famous for its smoked wild fish chowder.

Tofino's special-occasion restaurant, ✪ The Pointe at the Wickaninnish Inn (500 Osprey Ln., 250/725-3106, www.wickinn.com; 8am-2pm and 5pm-9pm daily; $28-48) emphasizes local seafood, foraged ingredients, and regional products. The polished staff and walls of curved windows wrapping the ocean panoramas around you don't hurt either. You might start with ginger-cured foie gras or with a Pacific Harvest of mussel custard, kelp, clams, and pickled sea asparagus, as a prelude to snapper and shrimp paired with prawn dumplings and grilled cucumber or roast duck in a hemlock *jus*. There are sweets, of course, from a platter of petit fours to fancy s'mores. Can't decide (or ready to splurge)? Choose a four- to six-course tasting menu ($85-100 pp) with optional wine pairings.

Asian

When you crave a restorative bowl of ramen, head for Kuma Tofino (101-120 4th St., 250/725-2215, www.kumatofino.com; 4pm-11pm daily; $10-14), a modern Japanese eatery. Sake and local craft beer stand up to sharing plates like crispy chicken *karaage,* fresh tuna *tataki,* and bright house-made pickles.

Mexican

Before it became a Mexican mini-chain with branches in Vancouver and Victoria, Tacofino (1184 Pacific Rim Hwy., 250/726-8288, www.taco-fino.com; 11am-8pm daily spring-fall, 11am-5pm daily winter; $4-14) was a taco truck in Tofino ("Taco-fino," get it?). This orange truck parked behind a surf shop south of town channels a surfer vibe with tacos (try the tuna with seaweed and ginger), burritos, and slushie drinks like tangy lime-mint "freshies." Park at one of the long outdoor tables, or take yours to the beach.

Bakeries and Cafés

From local hippies to texting teens to travelers, everyone stops into the red house that's home to long-standing Common Loaf Bake Shop (180 1st St., 250/725-3915; 8am-6pm daily) for de-lectable cinnamon buns, ginger scones, breads, and muffins. They make soup, sandwiches, and pizza, too.

In an industrial building on the town's south side, Red Can Gourmet (700 Industrial Way, 250/725-2525, www.redcangourmet.com; 7:30am-7pm Wed.-Thurs. and Sun., 7:30am-8pm Fri.-Sat.; $17-25) cooks gourmet takeout fare, from sandwiches and sal-ads midday to more substantial din-ner plates, such as seafood curry with smoked tofu or beef tenderloin, as well as pizza.

Tiny Picnic Charcuterie (Industrial Way, behind Red Can Gourmet, 250/889-5738, www.pic-niccharcuterie.com; 10am-5pm Mon.-Sat., 11am-5pm Sun. Apr.-Sept., 10am-5pm Wed.-Sat., 11am-5pm Sun. Oct.-Mar.) sells their own cured and smoked meats, with a selection of local and imported cheeses.

ACCOMMODATIONS
Tofino's nicest accommodations are south of town, along the peninsula

beaches. Book in advance for summer high season (mid-June-mid-Sept.). In winter, many lodgings offer storm-watching packages, when the big win-ter surf and rain rolls in.

$150-250
Once a field station for research groups, The Ecolodge at Tofino Botanical Gardens (1084 Pacific Rim Hwy., 250/725-1220, www.tbgf.org; $159-239 d) is a simple comfort-able lodge in the midst of the gar-dens. Guests gather in the great room for a continental breakfast or just to relax; you can use the kitchen to prep meals or browse the lodge's nature library. Eight basic, colorfully deco-rated rooms share two large baths. Two additional suites, with private baths, have family-friendly nooks with bunk beds. There are no TVs, but Wi-Fi is included, as is garden admission.

At Jamie's Rainforest Inn (1258 Pacific Rim Hwy., 250/725-2323 or 855/433-2323, www.tofinorainfor-estinn.com; $229-269 d), a well-kept motel facing the woods on the inlet side of the highway, the 38 rooms have microwaves, minifridges, cof-feemakers, and included Wi-Fi. The king-bed rooms have gas fireplaces, and the larger units include kitchen-ettes with cooktops. Ask about dis-counts on whale-watching and other tours from their affiliated adventure company, Jamie's Whaling Station (www.jamies.com).

Overlooking two beaches and the offshore islands, Middle Beach Lodge (400 MacKenzie Beach Rd., 250/725-2900 or 866/725-2900, www.middlebeach.com; $155-465 d) offers a variety of accommodations. The original lodge has tiny, no-frills rooms with no TVs or closets, but the nicest of these economical units have ocean views. In the main lodge, rooms are slightly larger with wooden floors and flat-screen TVs; choose an end unit upstairs for the best water vistas. Also on the forested property are roomy cabins with kitchen facilities; some have sleeping lofts, fireplaces, or hot tubs. Your room almost doesn't matter when you take in the panoramic views from the overstuffed chairs in the wood-beamed great room, where a deluxe continental breakfast buffet (included in the rates) is served.

overlooking Chesterman's Beach from BriMar Bed & Breakfast

Over $250

The three gold-and-burgundy guest rooms at the cedar-shingled ✪ **BriMar Bed & Breakfast** (1375 Chesterman Beach Rd., 250/725-3410, www.brimarbb.com; $279-339 d) look right onto Chesterman Beach, close enough to hear the surf. On the second floor, the spacious Moonrise Room has an equally spacious private bath, while the slightly smaller Sunset Room has a private bath across the hall. The secluded Loft Unit, under the eaves, runs the whole length of the top floor. Rates include Wi-Fi and an ample breakfast, with fruit, granola, yogurt, baked goods, and a hot dish like eggs Benedict or baked french toast. Guests ca[n] themselves to coffee and tea hours and store snacks in the way fridge.

Even if you're not staying at the **Long Beach Lodge Resort** (1441 Pacific Rim Hwy., 250/725-2442, www.longbeachlodgeresort.com; $199-439 d, cottages $449-589), have a drink or a meal in the resort's inviting **Great Room,** with walls of windows facing the ocean. The lodge has a highly regarded surf club, where both kids and adults can learn to ride the waves. When it's time to sleep, choose from 41 studio units in the main lodge, with sturdy Douglas fir furnishings, or from 20 two-bedroom cottages in the forest, set back from the beach. Solo travelers: In the off-season, the resort regularly offers excellent discounts for individual guests.

Opened in 1972 on the beach at Cox Bay, **Pacific Sands Beach Resort** (1421 Pacific Rim Hwy., 250/725-3322, www.pacificsands. com; $235-365 d, 2-bedroom unit $490-850) has grown to encompass a variety of units in several buildings. Most of the modern condo-style beach houses have two bedrooms and views across the lawn to the waterfront. In other buildings, the studio to two-bedroom units are smaller but still feel airy and beachy. All suites have full kitchens, handy since there's no restaurant on-site, though the lobby coffee bar sells drinks, snacks, and quick meals. Rent beach cruiser bikes to go cycling or gather the gang in the gazebo to roast marshmallows.

The most deluxe lodging on Vancouver Island's west coast is the ✪ **Wickaninnish Inn** (500 Osprey Ln., 250/725-3100 or 800/333-4604, www.wickinn.com; $310-900 d), which nestles into 100 acres (40 hectares) of old-growth rainforest on Chesterman Beach. Behind the unassuming gray exteriors, the inn is filled with aboriginal art and 75 rustic yet elegant accommodations with earth-tone furnishings, gas fireplaces, flat-screen TVs hidden in cabinets that open by remote control, soaker tubs, and heated bath floors. Wi-Fi and bicycles are complimentary. The Ancient Cedars Spa has seven treatment rooms, including one set dramatically above the rocks; guests can join daily yoga classes. Local musicians perform at the Driftwood Café (named for its bar made of driftwood), which serves coffee, pastries, and light meals. The Pointe, the inn's premier restaurant, is among the region's finest.

INFORMATION AND SERVICES

The Pacific Rim Visitor Centre (2791 Pacific Rim Hwy., Ucluelet, 250/726-4600, www.pacificrimvisitor.ca; 8am-7pm daily June-early Sept., 10am-5pm daily May and early-Sept.-mid-Oct., 9am-5pm Tues.-Sat. mid-Oct.-Apr.), at the Tofino-Ucluelet junction, where Highway 4 meets the Pacific Rim Highway, provides information about the region. Parks Canada staff are on hand to offer visitor services for Pacific Rim National Park Reserve May through October.

Tofino Tourism (www.tourismto-fino.com) has a detailed website with useful trip-planning tips. They run the Tofino Information Centre (1426 Pacific Rim Hwy., Tofino, 250/725-3414 or 888/720-3414, www.tourismtofino.com; 9am-7pm daily mid-June-early Sept., 10am-5pm daily early-Sept.-mid-June), 4.5 miles (7 kilometers) south of downtown Tofino

and 15.5 miles (25 kilometers) north of the Tofino-Ucluelet junction.

Small Tofino General Hospital (261 Neill St., 250/725-4010, www.viha.ca) offers 24-hour emergency services.

GETTING THERE
Air

The Tofino-Long Beach Airport (YAZ, Pacific Rim Highway, www.tofinoairport.com) is seven miles (11 kilometers) southeast of the town of Tofino and 18 miles (30 kilometers) northeast of Ucluelet.

Orca Airways (888/359-6722, www.flyorcaair.com) has regular flights to Tofino from the South Terminal at Vancouver International Airport (5220 Airport Rd. S., Richmond, www.yvr.ca; year-round, one hour; one-way adults $175-220) and from the Victoria International Airport (1640 Electra Blvd., Sidney, 250/953-7533, www.victoriaairport.com; mid-May-mid-Oct., one hour; one-way adults $225-270).

KD Air (800/665-4244, www.kdair.com; one-way adults $175-225) also flies between Vancouver's South Terminal and Tofino.

Car

A road trip from Vancouver to Tofino involves taking a ferry from the mainland to Nanaimo, and then driving west across the island; allow six hours to make the journey.

From Vancouver, drive northwest to the Horseshoe Bay Ferry Terminal and take the Horseshoe Bay-Departure Bay Ferry (www.bcferries.com; 1 hour and 40 minutes; one-way adults $17.20, ages 5-11 $8.60) to Nanaimo.

Although the drive from Nanaimo to Tofino is just 130 miles (210 kilometers), it takes at least three hours, longer if you stop to sightsee en route. When you exit the Departure Bay ferry terminal, follow the signs to Highway 19/Parksville. Just past Parksville, exit onto Highway 4 westbound toward Port Alberni. Check your gas; there are no gas stations between Port Alberni and the Pacific coast.

Highway 4 winds its way across the island, over and around the mountains that form the island's spine. At several points, the road becomes quite narrow and curvy; don't be in a rush to make this trip. If you find that a line of impatient drivers is forming behind you, use one of the pullouts to move over and allow them to pass.

Highway 4 comes to a T at the Tofino-Ucluelet junction. Turn right (north) onto the Pacific Rim Highway toward Tofino; it's 20 miles (32 kilometers) from the junction into town.

Bus

Tofino Bus (250/725-2871 or 866/986-3466, www.tofinobus.com) can take you to Tofino starting from Vancouver's Pacific Central Station (1150 Station St.; 7.5 hours; adults $62, seniors and students $56, ages 2-11 $46). This route runs in partnership with Greyhound, which provides bus service from Vancouver to Horseshoe Bay, where you board the Horseshoe Bay-Departure Bay Ferry to Nanaimo. After arriving at the Nanaimo ferry terminal, you transfer to the Tofino Bus to the west coast. You must purchase a ferry ticket in addition to the bus fare.

Tofino Bus can also take you to Tofino from Nanaimo's Departure Bay Ferry Terminal (4 hours; adults $46, seniors and students $42, ages 2-11 $23) and from downtown Victoria (6.5 hours; adults $69, seniors and students $62, ages 2-11 $36).

GETTING AROUND

Easy to explore on foot, the town of Tofino is just a few blocks square, with most shops and restaurants along Campbell or Main Streets, between 1st and 4th Streets. To travel between town and the beaches, it's easiest to have your own car, although it's possible to cycle or take a bus.

Car

From its junction with Highway 4, the Pacific Rim Highway runs 20 miles (32 kilometers) up the peninsula to the town of Tofino, passing Pacific Rim National Park Reserve and beaches along the way. In town, the highway becomes Campbell Street.

If you arrive in Tofino without a car, you can rent one from Budget (188 Airport Rd., 250/725-2060, www.bcbudget.com) at the Tofino airport.

Bus

The free Tofino Transit shuttle bus (www.tofinobus.com; 11am-8pm daily late June-early Sept.) runs during the summer between town and Cox Bay, with stops near several beaches. Buses leave about once an hour in each direction, so check the schedule online before setting out.

Bike

Cycling is a good way to travel between the village of Tofino and the beaches. Ride along the 3.75-mile (6-kilometer) Multi-Use Path, locally known as the MUP, a fairly flat, paved trail that parallels Highway 4 from town to Cox Bay. TOF Cycles (660 Sharp Rd., 250/725-2453, www.tofcycles.com) and Tofino Bikes (1180 Pacific Rim Hwy., 250/725-2722, http://tofinobike.com), both located between MacKenzie and Chesterman Beaches, rent bikes.

UCLUELET

Once considered the workaday counterpart to more upscale Tofino, 25 miles (40 kilometers) to the north, Ucluelet (population 1,600) is coming into its own as a holiday destination. While it's close enough to the Pacific Rim National Park Reserve to explore the trails and beaches, you can also enjoy the sand and hiking routes in and around town.

SIGHTS AND RECREATION

Ucluelet Aquarium (180 Main St., 250/726-2782, www.uclueletaquarium. org; 10am-5pm daily mid-Mar.-Nov.; adults $14, seniors and students $10, ages 4-17 $7) has a rare "catch and release" philosophy. In the spring, staff bring in sealife from the local waters of Clayoquot and Barkley Sounds to populate the kids'-eye-level tanks, releasing them in the autumn back to the wild. The "please touch" displays are fun for youngsters and not-so-youngsters alike.

For hikers, the **Wild Pacific Trail** (www.wildpacifictrail.com) has several moderate options at the foot of the Ucluelet peninsula. The 1.6-mile (2.6-kilometer) **Lighthouse Loop** starts and ends on Coast Guard Road south of Terrace Beach. The hillier **Artist Loop** takes you 1.7 miles (2.8 kilometers) along the cliffs starting from either Brown's Beach or Big Beach Park near Black Rock Oceanfront Resort. Get a map on the trail website or from the Pacific Rim Visitor Centre.

FOOD

Stop into **Zoë's Bakery and Café** (250 Main St., 250/726-2253; 7:30am-4pm Tues.-Fri., 8am-4pm Sat.-Sun.; $5-10) for pastries, soups, quiche, sandwiches, and other baked goods.

Try the Savory Breakfast Egg Bake Thingy, a delicious mash-up of sourdough bread cubes and bacon, topped with an egg. Zoë's is also known for its carrot cake.

ACCOMMODATIONS AND CAMPING

The Ucluelet First Nation runs the unique ✪ **Wya Point Resort** (2695 Tofino-Ucluelet Hwy., 250/726-2625 or 844/352-6188, www.wyapoint.com), which has several lodging options on a remote section of coast. Nine wood-frame **lodges** ($289 one-bedroom, $389 two-bedroom), decorated with works by First Nations carvers, are upscale cabins, each sleeping four to six, with solid hand-built bed frames, living rooms with sleep sofas, full kitchens, and spacious decks above Ucluth Beach. Fifteen heated **yurts** ($150-175) made of thick canvas offer more rustic accommodations. You can cook outside on the barbecue and sleep inside on the sofa bed; some yurts also have bunk beds for the kids. Shared washrooms are nearby. The third option is the **campground** (early-Mar.-mid-Oct., $35-60), where some sites overlook the ocean and others sit in the forest near the beach.

along the Wild Pacific Trail, Ucluelet

Family-friendly 133-room **Black Rock Oceanfront Resort** (596 Marine

Dr., 250/726-4800 or 877/762-5011, www.blackrockresort.com; $169-379 d) has everything you need for a beach getaway. Modern studios and one-bedroom suites in the main lodge, decorated in earthy greens and blacks, have kitchen facilities, spacious baths with heated floors and soaker tubs, and free Wi-Fi. Choose a fourth-floor room for the best views. Surrounded by trees in separate buildings, the Trail Suites range from studios to two-bedroom units. On the sea-facing deck is a plunge pool and two hot tubs; inside is a small fitness room and spa. Borrow a complimentary bicycle to go exploring. When you get hungry, Fetch Restaurant, specializing in seafood, cooks up breakfast, lunch, and dinner; Float Lounge serves drinks and light meals.

INFORMATION AND SERVICES

Get local information at the Pacific Rim Visitor Centre (2791 Pacific Rim Hwy., Ucluelet, 250/726-4600, www.pacificrimvisitor.ca; 8am-7pm daily June-early Sept., 10am-5pm daily May and early-Sept.-mid-Oct., 9a 5pm Tues.-Sat. mid-Oct.-Apr.) at tne Tofino-Ucluelet junction.

GETTING THERE

By car and ferry from Vancouver to Ucluelet, the 165-mile (260-kilometer) trip across the Strait of Georgia and then across Vancouver Island takes about six hours. Drive northwest from Vancouver to the Horseshoe Bay Ferry Terminal and take the Horseshoe Bay-Departure Bay Ferry (www. bcferries.com; 1 hour and 40 minutes; one-way adults $17.20, ages 5-11 $8.60) to Nanaimo. When you leave the Departure Bay ferry terminal, follow the signs to Highway 19/Parksville. Just past Parksville, exit onto Highway 4 westbound toward Port Alberni. Check your gas; there are no gas stations between Port Alberni and the Pacific coast.

Highway 4 comes to a T at the Tofino-Ucluelet junction. Turn left (south) onto the Pacific Rim Highway; Ucluelet is five miles (9 kilometers) south of the junction.

WHISTLER AND THE SEA-TO-SKY-HIGHWAY

The Sea-to-Sky Highway, one of western Canada's most stunning roadways, connects Vancouver to the year-round outdoor mecca of Whistler.

totem pole at the Squamish Lil'wat Cultural Centre

Just a two-hour drive, it's perfect for a day trip or as part of a longer exploration. Whistler offers not just North America's largest snow sports resort but also plenty of opportunities for hiking, biking, paddling the glacier-fed lakes, and exploring the region's First Nations heritage.

Between Whistler and Vancouver, the town of Squamish is a hot spot for outdoor activities, including excellent hiking and the region's best white-water rafting. For those looking for gentler adventures, Squamish's Sea-to-Sky Gondola delivers stellar mountain views and access to mountain-top hiking trails.

HIGHLIGHTS

✪ **SEA-TO-SKY GONDOLA:** A 10-minute ride up this 2,790-foot (850-meter) Squamish peak gives you expansive views of Howe Sound and the surrounding mountains. There's a suspension bridge, lots of hiking trails, and a great patio at the top (page 253).

✪ **BRACKENDALE EAGLES PROVINCIAL PARK:** One of North America's largest populations of bald eagles spends the winter months in this park near Squamish (page 255).

✪ **STAWAMUS CHIEF PROVINCIAL PARK:** For strong hikers, a day hike up the rocky summit known as the Chief is a popular adventure (page 255).

✪ **WHISTLER-BLACKCOMB:** From skiing and snowboarding to hiking, canoeing, rock climbing, and zip-lining, if it's an outdoor adventure, you can do it at this mountain resort (page 259).

✪ **SQUAMISH LIL'WAT CULTURAL CENTRE:** Learn about the Whistler region's First Nations communities at this modern museum and cultural facility (page 262).

✪ **SCANDINAVE SPA:** After your Whistler adventures, ease your sore muscles into the hot and cold pools at this Scandinavian-style soaking spa (page 264).

skiing at Whistler-Blackcomb

Squamish

Located midway between Vancouver and Whistler along the Sea-to-Sky Highway (Hwy. 99), Squamish is perched between the Coast Mountains and Howe Sound. Cafés, local eateries, and a few shops populate the town's sleepy downtown, while along Highway 99, strip malls and fast-food joints give Squamish a mountain-suburban feel. The real action in Squamish, though, is outdoors.

It's a popular destination for all manner of outdoor adventures, including hiking, rock climbing, and whitewater rafting. You can see the area's most famous peak, the Stawamus Chief, from the highway, or tackle the Chief on a day hike.

Squamish takes its name from the Squamish First Nation, the people whose traditional territory encompasses the modern-day town. In more recent times, mining was an important contributor to the local economy; a historic mine is now a visitor attraction. Another Squamish attraction, if you're passing through between December and February, is seeing bald eagles; one of North America's largest populations of eagles spends the winter months near Squamish.

Squamish makes an easy day trip from Vancouver or a stopover between Vancouver and Whistler. It's 40 miles (65 kilometers) from Vancouver to Squamish, a one-hour drive, and 37 miles (60 kilometers) between Squamish and Whistler, which takes 45 minutes.

SIGHTS AND ACTIVITIES

BRITANNIA MINE MUSEUM

Beginning in 1904 and continuing through much of the 20th century, the Britannia Beach area south of Squamish was copper mining territory. During its heyday, the Britannia Mine produced more copper than any other mine in the British Empire. Workers from more than 50 countries settled here, living in barracks by the water or in a company town high in the surrounding hills.

While the Britannia Mine provided valuable resources and jobs for decades, it also created environmental havoc, particularly on the local water supply. After the mine closed in 1974, its environmental impacts took years to remediate.

The mine site is now the Britannia Mine Museum (1 Forbes Way, Britannia Beach, 604/896-2233 or 800/896-4044, www.britanniaminemuseum.ca; 9:30am-5:30pm daily; adults $29, seniors $26.50, ages 13-18 $23, ages 5-12 $18.50), where you can explore the mine's complicated history and get a glimpse of what it was like to work in the 130-mile (210-kilometer) network of tunnels underground.

Britannia Mine Museum

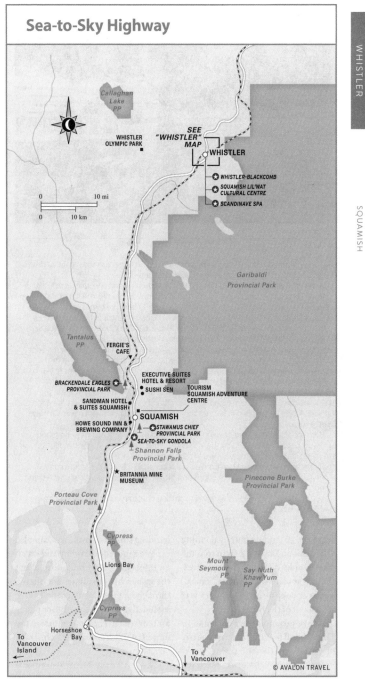

Sea-to-Sky Highway

Callaghan Lake PP

WHISTLER OLYMPIC PARK

SEE "WHISTLER" MAP

WHISTLER

WHISTLER-BLACKCOMB

SQUAMISH LIL'WAT CULTURAL CENTRE

SCANDINAVE SPA

0   10 mi
0   10 km

Garibaldi Provincial Park

Tantalus PP

FERGIE'S CAFE

BRACKENDALE EAGLES PROVINCIAL PARK

EXECUTIVE SUITES HOTEL & RESORT

SUSHI SEN

TOURISM SQUAMISH ADVENTURE CENTRE

SANDMAN HOTEL & SUITES SQUAMISH

HOWE SOUND INN & BREWING COMPANY

SQUAMISH

STAWAMUS CHIEF PROVINCIAL PARK

SEA-TO-SKY GONDOLA

Shannon Falls Provincial Park

BRITANNIA MINE MUSEUM

Pinecone Burke Provincial Park

Porteau Cove Provincial Park

Cypress PP

Lions Bay

Cypress PP

Mount Seymour PP

Say Nuth Khaw Yum PP

Horseshoe Bay

To Vancouver Island

To Vancouver

© AVALON TRAVEL

251

SCENIC DRIVE: THE SEA-TO-SKY HIGHWAY

Horseshoe Bay

Highway 99, the Sea-to-Sky Highway, is one of western Canada's most beautiful drives. And in a region full of beautiful drives, that's high praise.

At its southern end, the winding road that leads from West Vancouver to Whistler hugs the shores of Howe Sound, where the Gulf Islands rise from the water. You can stop at **Horseshoe Bay** (http://horseshoebayvillage.com), where the ferries depart for Vancouver Island and B.C.'s Sunshine Coast, to stroll the harbor and admire the vistas.

Another stopping point is **Porteau Cove Provincial Park** (www.env.gov.bc.ca), which has a small pebbly beach along a scenic stretch of coastline.

In **Squamish** (www.exploresquamish.com), you have views both of the waterfront and the mountains, particularly the iconic Stawamus Chief that looms above the highway. As you continue toward **Whistler** (www.whistler.com), the road begins to climb, and both forests and peaks surround you.

Keep your camera handy, but pull off at one of the many turnouts to take in the views. At several viewpoints, informational kiosks explore the region's First Nations heritage, a "Cultural Journey" designed in partnership with Whistler's **Squamish Lil'wat Cultural Centre** (www.slcc.ca).

With rock faces plunging down to the roadway and forested islands just offshore, you can easily become distracted by the scenery, so drive carefully. Watch your speed, too, as the speed limit changes frequently, as do the number of travel lanes.

From October through March, drivers are required to have winter tires or carry (and know how to use) chains, since sections of Highway 99 can become snow-covered and slippery.

Yet, whatever the season, this drive is a striking one, so pack up the car, and hit the road from sea to sky.

Begin the 45-minute tour by donning a hard hat and riding a train into the mine. Guides demonstrate explosives, drilling tools, and how the "muck" (rocks sparkling with copper) was hauled out of the tunnels.

Above ground, tours continue in the 1923 mill building that rises nearly 20 stories into the hill; inside, workers had to climb 375 steps to reach the building's highest level. You can also explore a museum building and watch an interesting 15-minute film about the mine's history. Tours are offered throughout the day, but schedules vary seasonally; check the website or phone for tour times. The temperature in the mine (54°F/12°C) can feel chilly, so bring a sweater.

The Britannia Mine Museum is

32 miles (52 kilometers) north of Vancouver and 7.5 miles (12 kilometers) south of Squamish, along Highway 99.

SHANNON FALLS PROVINCIAL PARK

Pull off the highway between Britannia Beach and Squamish for a short stroll to B.C.'s third highest waterfall. At Shannon Falls Provincial Park (Hwy. 99, 604/986-9371, www.env.gov.bc.ca; dawn-dusk daily; free), the falls descend 1,100 feet (335 meters) in a narrow, rushing gush. An easy 0.25-mile (400-meter) walking trail leads through the forest to the falls.

Beyond the falls, up a short steep trail (there are stairs), you can hike to another viewpoint for a closer look at the cascading waters.

Shannon Falls is 36 miles (58 kilometers) north of Vancouver and 1.25 miles (2 kilometers) south of Squamish. The park has a snack bar and restrooms with flush toilets (snack bar and restrooms open mid-May to mid-Oct.).

✪ SEA-TO-SKY GONDOLA

For spectacular views of Howe Sound, the Chief, and the surrounding mountains, take a ride up the Sea-to-Sky Gondola (36800 Hwy. 99, 604/892-2550, www.seatoskygondola.com; 10am-6pm Sun.-Thurs., 10am-8pm Fri.-Sat. mid-May-mid-Sept., 10am-5pm daily mid-Sept.-mid-May; adults $40, seniors $38, ages 13-18 $24, ages 6-12 $14). A 10-minute trip in the eight-passenger gondola whisks you up to the 2,790-foot (850-meter) summit, where you can enjoy the vistas, have lunch on the deck at the Summit Lodge, and access a network of hiking trails. Purchase your gondola tickets

online at least 24 hours before your visit to save a few dollars.

Once you've taken the gondola to the summit, a highlight is the Sky Pilot Suspension Bridge, a 330-foot (100-meter) span that crosses from the Summit Lodge to a viewing platform with expansive views. If you're afraid of heights, don't worry; you don't have to cross the bridge to reach most of the hiking trails.

Sky Pilot Suspension Bridge, Sea-to-Sky Gondola

Another adventure that begins from the gondola summit is the Via Ferrata (604/892-2550, www.seatoskygondola.com; daily May-Oct., tour times vary; over age 7 $109). This "iron way" gives you the experience of rock climbing without needing any special climbing skills or experience. With a guide, you take a short hike down from the Summit Lodge. From there, you clip into a safety cable, cross bridges and a catwalk, and climb a series of steel rungs up the rock face. You'll have beautiful views as you climb, but skip this activity if you're acrophobic. The tour is 1.5 hours. You have to purchase a gondola ticket in addition to the Via

Ferrata tour fee. Kids under eight are not allowed on the Via Ferrata.

Hiking

A number of hiking trails start at the gondola summit. Two are easy walking paths: the 0.25-mile (400-meter) Spirit Trail, a flat loop trail with interpretive panels about the region's First Nations, and the Panorama Trail, a one-mile (1.6-kilometer) loop that takes you to a lookout with excellent views of the Stawamus Chief.

Also starting from the summit is the moderate Wonderland Trail. This forested one-mile (1.6-kilometer) loop has a couple of slightly steeper segments, before flattening out as it circles small Wonderland Lake.

Experienced hikers can pick from several challenging trails that begin at the gondola summit, including the intermediate Shannon Basin Loop Trail (6 miles/9.7 kilometers) and the more difficult Al's Habrich Ridge Trail (7.5 miles/12 kilometers) and Skyline Ridge Trail (15 miles/24 kilometers). Check with gondola staff for trail conditions before attempting these longer hikes, and be sure you have water, snacks, warm clothing, and a rain-resistant jacket, even if it's sunny and warm when you set out; the mountain weather here can change quickly.

Want a workout? You can hike *up* to the gondola summit on the Sea-to-Summit Trail and then ride the gondola (one-way $15) back down. It's a 4.5-mile (7.5-kilometer) steady climb; average hikers should allow three to five hours.

Winter Activities

The Sea-to-Sky Gondola is open year-round. From December through April, weather permitting, trails are open for winter walking and snowshoeing, and there's also a tube park where kids can slide down a hill on inner tubes. Before planning a winter visit, phone for trail conditions and current operating hours.

Food

The small Basecamp Café (9am-3pm daily) at the gondola base sells coffee, drinks, trail mix, pastries, and a few sandwiches, but it's worth waiting till you get to the Summit Restaurant and Edge Bar (10am-5:30pm daily; $9-14), in the lodge at the top of the gondola, for a meal with a view. The kitchen cooks up burgers, sandwiches, salads, and baked goods, and serves beer from Squamish's own Howe Sound Brewing Company. If you prefer to picnic, you can bring your own food.

Parking

Although you can park for free in the lot at the gondola base, stays in this lot are limited to three hours. If you're planning to do a longer hike or linger at the top (or if this parking area is full), park in the free lot at Darrell Bay, on Highway 99 opposite Shannon Falls Provincial Park, 0.3 mile (500 meters) south of the gondola.

To walk from the Darrell Bay parking area to the gondola base, carefully cross Highway 99 toward Shannon Falls and follow the Shannon Falls Connector Trail, which has signs directing you toward to the Sea-to-Sky Gondola.

SHUTTLE

To visit the gondola for the day from Vancouver, you can also take the Sea To Sky Gondola shuttle (hours vary seasonally; round-trip, including lift tickets, adults $69, seniors $59, ages 6-18 $49, under 6 $25). It picks up passengers in the morning from several points in downtown Vancouver, including the Hyatt Hotel on Burrard Street, Library Square, and Canada Place, and will return you to the city in the late afternoon.

✪ BRACKENDALE EAGLES PROVINCIAL PARK

From late November through mid-February, hundreds of bald eagles come to winter north of Squamish in the now-protected 1,865-acre (755-hectare) environs of Brackendale Eagles Provincial Park (www.env.gov.bc.ca; dawn-dusk daily Apr.-Sept.). It's one of the most significant winter eagle populations in North America. In a recent peak year, volunteers counted more than 3,700 eagles in the vicinity.

You can't actually enter the park during the eagle season; it's closed to visitors between October and March to provide a protected habitat for the birds. However, you can watch the eagles from across the river. Eagle Run Park (Government Rd.; dawn-dusk daily), along the municipal dyke, has several viewing points where you can spot the birds. Bring binoculars if you have them. In December and January on the weekends, volunteer interpreters staff the Eagle Run viewing area (9:30am-3:30pm Sat.-Sun.) and can tell you more about the eagles and their migration patterns.

Coming from Vancouver or points south, follow Highway 99 past downtown Squamish, turn left (west) onto Mamquam Road, and then go right (north) on Government Road toward Brackendale.

FESTIVALS AND EVENTS

Wondering how lumberjacks get their jollies? At the Squamish Days Loggers Sports Festival (www.squamishdays.ca, July-Aug.), a weekend of family fun, you can watch competitions in ax-throwing, tree-climbing, birling (also known as log rolling), and other events, and enjoy pancake breakfasts, bed races, barbecues, and more.

SPORTS AND RECREATION
HIKING
✪ Stawamus Chief Provincial Park

Looming above Highway 99 just north of the Sea-to-Sky Gondola, the rocky cliff known as the Chief has long been a must-do climb for experienced hikers and rock climbers. A challenging but popular day hike takes you from the Chief's base to the top of the cliffs in the Stawamus Chief Provincial Park (Hwy. 99, 604/986-9371, www.env.gov.bc.ca or http://seatoskyparks.com; dawn-dusk daily).

The Chief actually has three summits, and you can choose to hike one or all. First Peak, at 2,000 feet (610 meters), draws the most hikers; from the summit, you have great views of Howe Sound. From the parking lot to the First Peak summit is just 2.5 miles (4 kilometers) round-trip. However, because the trail is quite steep, most hikers allow two to three hours.

Second Peak, at 2,150 feet (655 meters), has lots of viewpoints from its summit, looking across Howe Sound, the town of Squamish, and the mountains in nearby Garibaldi Provincial Park. From the parking lots, it's three miles (5 kilometers) round-trip to the Second Peak. Allow four to five hours.

Third Peak is the tallest of the three summits, rising 2,300 feet (702 meters). You can hike to Third Peak directly from the base or continue from the Second Peak trail. Either route is 4.5 miles (7 kilometers) round-trip; allow five to seven hours.

The hikes up The Chief are considered intermediate-level adventures. Note, though, that on the routes to First and Second Peaks, there are sections where you need to climb ladders or grab onto chains to help you reach the top. For all these hikes, bring water, snacks, a rain jacket, and warm layers. Get an early start and, especially in the summer, hike on a weekday if you want to avoid congestion on these often-busy trails.

Garibaldi Provincial Park

The region's largest provincial park, the 750-square-mile (1,942-square-kilometer) Garibaldi Provincial Park (www.env.gov.bc.ca) extends from Squamish north to Whistler and beyond. Hikers have a lot of territory to explore in this vast park, with more than 55 miles (90 kilometers) of hiking trails.

The southernmost section of the park, Diamond Head, is closest to Squamish and includes the park's namesake, the 8,786-foot (2,678-meter) Mount Garibaldi. For experienced day hikers, a scenic trail in the Diamond Head area leads up to Elfin Lakes (7 miles/11 kilometers, each way); allow three to five hours one-way. To find the trailhead, turn east off Highway 99 onto Mamquam Road, 2.5 miles (4 kilometers) north of Squamish. Follow the paved road past the Squamish Golf and Country Club, and take the gravel road just after the Mashiter Creek Bridge. In 3.7 miles (6 kilometers), turn left onto the Garibaldi Park road, which will take you to the parking lot. It's 10 miles (16 kilometers) from the highway to the parking area.

Farther north, you can do several day hikes in the park's Black Tusk/Garibaldi Lake sector. It's a six-mile (9-kilometer) climb to Garibaldi Lake. Allow three to four hours each way; the trail has an elevation change of nearly 2,800 feet (850 meters). From the same starting point, you can hike to Taylor Meadows. This 4.75-mile (7.5-kilometer) route follows the Garibaldi Lake trail for the first 3.75 miles (6 kilometers) before heading up into the alpine meadows. Allow three to four hours each way; the trail also has an elevation change of about 2,800 feet (850 meters). The Garibaldi Lake parking lot is 23 miles (37 kilometers) north of Squamish or 12 miles (19 kilometers) south of Whistler, along Highway 99.

At the park's higher elevations, snow is usually on the ground from October until June or July. Check the trail conditions report on the park website before you set out.

RAFTING

Two rivers in the Squamish area offer white-water rafting adventures. Trips on the Cheakamus River are gentler, with class I and II rapids, good for family excursions. The faster Elaho-Squamish River, with class III and IV rapids, will give you more of a thrill. For the Elaho trips, kids generally need to be at least 12 years old and weigh at least 90 pounds (40 kilograms).

SunWolf Rafting (70002 Squamish Valley Rd., 604/898-1537 or 877/806-8046, www.sunwolf.net) offers full-day Elaho River trips (June-Sept.; adults $169, ages 12-16 $155) that include a barbecue lunch. They also run half-day Cheakamus River family trips (June-Sept.; adults $99, ages 5-12 $69). In winter, when hundreds of eagles

GO SEA-TO-SKY IN A FERRARI

Have you always fantasized about whizzing along a serpentine highway in a Ferrari or Lamborghini? Then Scenic Rush (5775 Marine Dr., West Vancouver, 604/926-5777 or 855/926-5777, http://scenicrush.com) lets you live out your exotic car dream.

This unique tour company, based in West Vancouver, offers several experiences that enable you to drive the stunning Sea-to-Sky Highway in a Ferrari F430 Spider, Lamborghini Gallardo, Nissan GT-R, or Audi R8.

Book the 2.5-hour Sea to Sky Experience (Apr.-Oct.; adults $595, passenger or second driver $75), and you'll have a chance to try all four vehicles along the 50-mile (80-kilometer) oceanfront route to and from the town of Squamish. If that's not a sufficient thrill, consider the 7-hour Whistler Experience (May-Sept.; adults $1,495, passenger or second driver $195), where you not only get to drive all these cool cars for 140 miles (225 kilometers) to Whistler and back, you'll also have time to explore Whistler Village and sit down for lunch.

Scenic Rush also offers the one-hour Porteau Cove Experience (mid-Mar.-mid-Nov.; adults $395, passenger $35), which lets you try out two of the cars as you drive the scenic 30 miles (48 kilometers) between West Vancouver and Porteau Cove.

Note that for any of these experiences, the driver must be at least 24 years old and have a valid driver's license and a minimum of seven years' driving experience.

Whichever option you choose, keep your camera handy. Not only are the views pretty spectacular, but you'll surely need to share that selfie behind the wheel of the Ferrari.

nest at Brackendale Eagles Provincial Park, SunWolf operates guided Eagle Float Tours (Dec.-mid-Feb.; adults $110, ages 5-12 $75) that enable you to view the eagles from the river, closer than you can see them from the shore. Canadian Outback Rafting (40900 Tantalus Rd., 866/565-8735, www.canadianoutbackrafting.com) runs Elaho River trips (May-Sept.; adults $154, ages 13-16 $140) and Cheakamus River float trips (May-Sept.; adults $95, ages 5-16 $66). Whistler-based Wedge Rafting (211-4293 Mountain Square, Whistler, 604/932-7171 or 888/932-5899, http://wedgerafting.com) operates Elaho (May-Sept.; adults $169, ages 12-16 $155) and Cheakamus (May-Sept.; adults $99, ages 6-16 $69) trips as well.

FOOD AND ACCOMMODATIONS

Howe Sound Inn & Brewing Company (37801 Cleveland Ave., 604/892-2603, www.howesound.com) is a brewery, a restaurant, and a place to stay. Rates at the 20-room inn ($89-129 d) include Wi-Fi and a brewery tour. The brewpub (11am-midnight Mon.-Thurs., 11am-1am Fri., 8am-1am Sat., 8am-midnight Sun.; $11-18) serves pizzas, salads, burgers, and other pub fare to pair with the craft beer. Free brewery tours are offered daily at 1pm.

A popular spot for breakfast, Fergie's Café (70002 Squamish Valley Rd., Brackendale, 604/898-1537 or 877/806-8046, www.sunwolf.net; 8am-3pm daily; $12-15) serves homestyle classics with local ingredients, like eggs Benedict, pulled pork hash, Nutella french toast, and burgers.

Locals recommend Sushi Sen (40382 Tantalus Way, Garibaldi Highlands, 604/898-8235, www.sushisensquamish.com; lunch 11:30am-2pm Tues.-Fri., dinner 5pm-9pm Tues.-Thurs., 5pm-9:30pm Fri., 4pm-9:30pm Sat., 4pm-9pm Sun.; $8-21) when they need a *maki* or *nigiri* fix. While the menu emphasizes sushi, you can choose a few other Japanese standards, including chicken teriyaki or tempura.

If you want to stay overnight in Squamish, the town has several mid-range chain hotels off Highway 99, including the **Executive Suites Hotel and Resort** (40900 Tantalus Rd., Garibaldi Highlands, 604/815-0048 or 877/815-0048, www.executivesuitessquamish.com; $125-229 d) and the **Sandman Hotel & Suites Squamish** (39400 Discovery Way, 604/848-6000 or 800/726-3626, www.sandmanhotels.ca; $149-199).

GETTING THERE AND AROUND
CAR

It's a one-hour, 40-mile (65-kilometer) drive from Vancouver to Squamish via Highway 1 and the Sea-to-Sky Highway.

From downtown Vancouver, take West Georgia Street to the Lions Gate Bridge. After crossing the bridge, bear left toward Marine Drive west/Highway 1/Highway 99. Enter Marine Drive and stay in the far right lane to take the first right onto Taylor Way, following signs for "Whistler." Follow Taylor Way up the hill, and exit left onto Highway 1 west. Continue on Highway 1 until it merges with Highway 99, the Sea-to-Sky Highway, which will take you to Squamish.

BUS

While it's easiest to explore Squamish if you have a car, it's possible to get from Vancouver to Squamish on the bus.

Greyhound (800/661-8747, www.greyhound.ca; 1 hour and 20 min.; one-way adults $11-23) runs several buses a day between Vancouver's Pacific Central Station (1150 Station St.) and their Squamish depot (40446 Government Rd., Squamish, 604/898-3914). While designed for commuters, the **Squamish Connector** (604/802-2119, www.squamishconnector.com; one-way adults $25) can take you between the Squamish Adventure Centre (38551 Loggers Ln.) and downtown Vancouver if your travel times fit with their bus schedule. **Perimeter Transportation** (604/717-6600 or 888/717-6606, http://www.perimeterbus.com) operates buses between the Squamish Adventure Centre and either YVR airport (one-way adults $75) or downtown Vancouver (one-way adults $55), although their fares are much higher.

Once you've arrived in Squamish, you can take local buses that **B.C. Transit** (604/892-5559, https://bctransit.com/squamish/home) operates. Use the trip planner on their website to map your in-town routes.

INFORMATION AND SERVICES

At the Squamish Adventure Centre, just off Highway 99, **Tourism Squamish** (38551 Loggers Ln., 604/815-4994 or 877/815-5084, www.tourismsquamish.com; 8am-5pm daily) provides lots of information about the region, including details about hiking trails. The building has a café and restrooms, handy for a Sea-to-Sky pit stop.

Whistler

More than two million visitors every year make their way to this mountain town that has a permanent population of only 10,000. The core of the village is an alpine-style pedestrian plaza, where restaurants, pubs, and shops line the walkways, and all paths lead, sooner or later, to the ski lifts. Most visitors come to get outdoors—to ski or snowboard in winter, and to hike, cycle, canoe, kayak, rock climb, or zip-line in the warmer months. Others simply want to stroll through the pedestrian village and perhaps ride the gondola to gaze across the mountains.

Just a two-hour drive from Vancouver, Whistler is close enough for a day trip. If you enjoy outdoor adventures, though, you might want to spend two days or more. There's plenty to do!

Whistler has several neighborhoods stretching along Highway 99, with the main Whistler Village about midway through the area. Creekside, where there's a separate base village with its own lifts, and Function Junction, a more industrial area with some of the town's services, are south of Whistler Village. The Upper Village and the Blackcomb base areas are just north of Whistler Village.

SIGHTS AND ACTIVITIES
✪ WHISTLER-BLACKCOMB

From more than 200 trails for skiing and snowboarding to mountain biking, gondola rides, hiking, zip-lining, and much more, the two-mountain Whistler-Blackcomb Resort (604/967-8950 or 800/766-0449, www.

whistlerblackcomb.com) has scads of outdoor things to do all year long.

Whistler's PEAK 2 PEAK Gondola

PEAK 2 PEAK Gondola

Whistler's PEAK 2 PEAK Gondola (10:15am-5pm daily late May-late Sept., 10:15am-5pm Sat.-Sun. late Sept.-mid-Oct.; adults $54-59, seniors and ages 13-18 $47-52, ages 7-12 $27-30) runs 2.73 miles (4.4 kilometers) between Whistler and Blackcomb Mountains. It holds the world's record for the longest unsupported span (that is, the straight-line distance between two towers) at 1.88 miles (3,024 meters) and for the highest lift of its kind, rising 1,427 feet (436 meters) above the valley floor. It transports skiers and snowboarders between the two mountains in winter, and from spring through fall, it's open to sightseers to enjoy the peaks' panoramas.

Allow about two hours for a sightseeing trip on the PEAK 2 PEAK Gondola. The PEAK 2 PEAK ride itself takes about 20 minutes, but to reach the gondola station, you need to take either the Whistler Village Gondola or chairlifts on Blackcomb Mountain,

Whistler

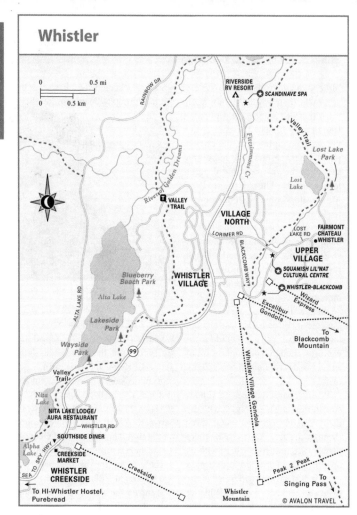

which add another 25 minutes each way. If you plan to go hiking, allow additional time.

Gondola tickets are typically cheaper if you buy them online in advance, but check the weather forecast first. The views are obviously best on a sunny, clear day.

Via Ferrata

Do you want to try rock climbing but don't have any training or experience?

Consider Whistler's **Via Ferrata** (604/938-9242, www.mountainskillsacademy.com; 4 hours; adults $139, ages 14-18 $119), a guided climbing route that's open to anyone who's reasonably fit, even if you've never done any climbing. The name comes from the Italian for "iron way," and the Via Ferrata route includes a series of iron rungs built into the mountain, which provide hand grips and footholds as you ascend the rock face. You clip on

ONE DAY IN WHISTLER

If you've come to North America's largest winter sports resort during the ski season, you'll likely spend your day out on the snow. But if you're at Whistler before the snow falls, here's how to organize a great one-day trip.

Whistler is located on the traditional territory of two First Nations, so start your day with a visit to the modern **Squamish Lil'wat Cultural Centre,** where you can learn about the history and present-day culture of these two communities. The excellent **Audain Art Museum** has noteworthy collections of Northwest Coast native masks, works by contemporary Vancouver photographers, and paintings by B.C.'s Emily Carr. If you want to know more about how Whistler became the outdoor resort it is today, wander over to the informative **Whistler Museum,** which tells the stories of many area entrepreneurs.

rest stop on Whistler's Via Ferrata

Then you want to get outdoors, whether you head up the mountain for a ride on the **PEAK 2 PEAK Gondola,** which wings you between Whistler and Blackcomb Mountains; challenge yourself with a climb on the **Via Ferrata;** go **zip-lining** or **mountain biking,** or simply **take a hike.** The biggest challenge might be seeing how many activities you can fit into your single day.

When you've had your fill of outdoor adventure, unwind at the forested **Scandinave Spa Whistler,** a Scandinavian-style bath experience where you alternate between hot soaks and cold plunges.

Then choose one of Whistler's top dining rooms, perhaps **Araxi** or the **Bearfoot Bistro,** for a leisurely evening meal. At Bearfoot Bistro, you can even have a nightcap in their **Ketel One Ice Room,** the coldest vodka tasting room in the world—a unique way to cap off your active Whistler day.

to a series of safety cables during your climb, which you do in small groups with a guide. Your guide will give you tips as you ascend and talk you through some of the more challenging sections.

The Via Ferrata route starts with a short hike up from the Whistler Roundhouse (at the top of the Whistler Gondola) across a boulder field or a snowy slope or both, depending on the season, to the start of the climbing route. After your climb, you hike or take the chairlift back to your starting point. Wear sturdy hiking shoes, and bring a rainproof jacket and a small backpack with water and snacks.

You need to purchase a PEAK 2 PEAK Gondola ticket in addition to

the Via Ferrata tour ticket. Via Ferrata tours are seasonal, generally beginning in late May or June and continuing until early October; tours typically start at 9am or 1pm, but call or check the website to confirm.

Lift-Accessed Hiking

Whistler-Blackcomb has lots of hiking trails, from short easy strolls to all-day adventures, that you can access from the lifts or gondolas.

From the top of the Whistler Gondola or the Whistler side of the PEAK 2 PEAK Gondola near the Roundhouse Lodge, you can access the moderate **Harmony Lake Trail and Loop,** a 1.6-mile (2.5-kilometer) round-trip circuit through the forest to pretty Harmony Lake. You can extend this hike on the steeper 0.7-mile (1.1-kilometer) Harmony Meadows Trail, which connects to the Harmony Lake route.

For a more challenging hike with panoramic views, take the Peak Express chair (a short walk from the Roundhouse Lodge) to the start of the 5.8-mile (9.4-kilometer) High Note Trail. This trail follows the mountain ridges, with great views of the Black Tusk peak in Garibaldi Provincial Park and Cheakamus Lake far below. You can circle back on the trail and ride the lift down, or for an all-day adventure, hike back down to the village; the latter route is about 14 miles (22 kilometers).

Pick up a trail map showing these and other hiking routes at the Whistler Visitor Centre (4230 Gateway Dr.) or get one online at the website of Whistler-Blackcomb (www.whistlerblackcomb.com).

Lift-Accessed Mountain Biking

Have you seen those cyclists, suited up in knee pads, elbow pads, helmets, and other protective gear, flying down the mountain trails? At Whistler-Blackcomb, you can join them, whether you're learning to mountain bike or whizzing down those trails yourself at North America's largest mountain bike park.

From mid-May through mid-October, 70 trails across three different areas are open to mountain bikers, who take their bikes up the lifts.

You can choose a package including lift tickets and lessons (one-day $129-149) or, if you know what you're doing, buy a lift ticket (one-day adults $69) and hit the trails on your own. Bike rentals are available at shops around the village.

Winter Sports

In winter, Whistler-Blackcomb has 37 lifts providing access to more than 200 trails across 8,171 acres (3,300 hectares), so you can ski or snowboard here for days and still discover new terrain.

Whistler Village is at an elevation of 2,214 feet (675 meters), while the highest lift takes you up to nearly 7,500 feet (2,284 meters), so the weather can be very different at the base than it is in the alpine regions. Even when there's no snow in the village, the mountains are typically covered in the white stuff from late November into April.

Lift tickets (one-day adults $129) are most expensive when you walk up to the ticket window and purchase a single-day, same-day ticket. Discounts are available when you buy tickets online in advance, purchase multiday tickets or passes, or sometimes when you buy your tickets as part of a package with your lodging. The Edge Card program offers discounts to residents of British Columbia, Washington State, and Oregon, with larger savings for advance purchases. Explore all the pricing options and details at Whistler-Blackcomb (604/967-8950 or 800/766-0449, www.whistlerblackcomb.com).

✪ SQUAMISH LIL'WAT CULTURAL CENTRE

For centuries before Whistler was an outdoor holiday destination, aboriginal communities called the region home. Discover this heritage at the Squamish Lil'wat Cultural Centre (4584 Blackcomb Way, 604/964-0999 or 866/441-7522, www.slcc.ca; 10am-5pm Tues.-Sun.; adults $18, seniors and ages 13-18 $13.50, ages 6-12 $8), a fascinating multimedia exploration of the two First Nations whose

Squamish Lil'wat Cultural Centre

traditional territory encompasses the Whistler region.

After rhythmic beats of a drum and a traditional First Nations welcome song greet you, watch a short film about the history and present-day culture of these two communities. Then check out the exhibits, from hand-carved canoes to woven baskets to information about aboriginal languages. You can often try out a native craft or chat with "cultural ambassadors," museum staff who come from the Squamish or Lil'wat communities. The center's Thunderbird Café uses local ingredients in dishes like Squamish salmon chowder, Lil'wat venison chili, and bannock (a biscuit-like bread), and the gift shop sells locally made crafts.

WHISTLER MUSEUM

Like many ski "villages" with their alpine facades and purpose-built pedestrian strolls, Whistler can seem like a manufactured community. The Whistler Museum (4333 Main St., 604/932-2019, www.whistler-museum.org; 11am-5pm Fri.-Wed.,

11am-9pm Thurs.; suggested donation $5) tells the history of how the present-day Whistler-Blackcomb resort came to be and the stories of the entrepreneurs and innovators who made it happen.

Another way to learn more about the town and its heritage is to take the museum's one-hour Valley of Dreams Walking Tour (1pm daily June-Aug.; donations accepted), starting at the Whistler Visitor Centre (4230 Gateway Dr.). You'll hear tales of the community's entrepreneurial women, the year of the naked skiers, and much more.

WHISTLER OLYMPIC PLAZA

Whistler joined Vancouver in hosting the 2010 Winter Olympic Games. One legacy of the Games is now a popular photo stop: in front of the colorful Olympic rings that adorn Whistler Olympic Plaza in the village. Also in the plaza is an outdoor amphitheater, where concerts, festivals, and other special events take place.

AUDAIN ART MUSEUM

Whistler scored an art-world coup when Vancouver businessman and philanthropist Michael Audain decided to build a 56,000-square-foot (5,200-square-meter) gallery in this mountain town to house much of his extensive art collection. Focusing on British Columbia artists from the region's earliest eras to the present, the Audain Art Museum (4350 Blackcomb Way, www.audainartmuseum.com; 10am-5pm Wed.-Mon.; adults $18, ages 16 and under free) has one of Canada's largest collections of work by early-20th-century artist Emily Carr; other highlights include 19th-century Northwest Coast masks and Vancouver photography.

WHISTLER ON A BUDGET

Whistler is one of those destinations where there are more things to do than you could pack into a summer-long stay, but many of those activities can be budget-blowing adventures. If you're watching your loonies but still want to enjoy the best of what Whistler has to offer, follow these tips for organizing your Whistler stay.

- **Come off-season.** If you can schedule your Whistler visit for the spring (May-early June) or fall (Sept.-Oct.), you'll often find lower rates for accommodations and occasional deals for tours and activities.

- **Look for free or low-cost activities.** You can hike or cycle many trails around Whistler without purchasing a lift ticket to go up on the mountain. Go for a swim in area lakes or visit the Whistler Museum (by donation). Window-shopping in the village and walking the Valley Trail are both free, too.

- **Maximize your spending.** If you do buy a lift ticket for sightseeing or hiking, get an early start and spend as much time as you'd like up on the mountain. You can stay on the mountain all day on your single ticket.

- **Pack a lunch.** Look for accommodations with kitchen facilities, so you can prepare some of your own meals, even if it's just fruit and yogurt for breakfast or a sandwich for the trail. Another option is to have your big meal out at lunch when restaurant prices are a little lower than in the evenings.

- **Go easy on the booze.** Many of Whistler's bars and après-ski hangouts have free live music for the price of a drink. But you don't have to spend the money for *several* drinks to enjoy the tunes.

SCANDINAVE SPA

To unwind after a day on the mountains, head for **Scandinave Spa Whistler** (8010 Mons Rd., 604/935-2424 or 888/935-2423, www.scandinave.com; 10am-9pm daily; adults $65, minimum age 19), a Scandinavian-style bath experience set among the trees. You alternate between heat—in a series of hot pools, saunas, and steam baths—and brief cold plunges in a chilled pool or shower, following each sequence with a period of relaxation in the lounges or in a hammock in the forest. To make the experience even more tranquil, the spa has a "silence" policy; you can't talk in the bath area.

Bring your own bathing suit. The spa provides towels and lockers. Several types of massage treatments are available for an additional fee.

Scandinave Spa is located two miles (3.5 kilometers) north of Whistler Village, along Highway 99.

TRAIN WRECK SITE AND SUSPENSION BRIDGE

After a freight train derailed near Whistler in 1956, a logging company towed the mangled railcars into the woods nearby, where they were abandoned. Over the years, local graffiti artists began using the train cars as their canvas, and today, Whistler's **train wreck site** (off Jane Lakes Rd., www.whistler.ca; dawn-dusk; free), located south of town near Cheakamus Crossing, is an unusual outdoor art gallery, with the train cars tagged and retagged with vivid designs.

In 2016, the town of Whistler built a new **suspension bridge** over the Cheakamus River, making it easier to access the train wreck site. From Jane Lakes Road, you can follow a section of the Sea-to-Sky Trail that leads to the bridge and the train site. It's about a 30-minute walk through the woods.

ENTERTAINMENT AND EVENTS

NIGHTLIFE

One of Whistler's most popular pastimes is "après" (aka après-ski, literally "after skiing"), and what do you do after a day in the mountains but hit the pub? Here are several places where the party starts when the lifts close.

Merlin's Bar and Grill (4553 Blackcomb Way, 604/938-7700; 11am-1am daily), located at the Blackcomb Mountain base, often has live music, as does the Garibaldi Lift Company Bar & Grill (4165 Springs Ln., 604/905-2220; 11am-1am daily), at the base of the Whistler Gondola. In the Creekside area, Dusty's Bar & BBQ (2040 London Ln., 604/905-2171; 11am-1am daily) has been pouring pints since the 1960s.

The laid-back Dubh Linn Gate Irish Pub (Pan Pacific Whistler Mountainside, 4320 Sundial Crescent, 604/905-4047, www.dubhlinngate.com; 8am-1am daily), steps from the Whistler Village lifts, keeps 25 varieties of beer on tap and offers a long list of single-malt scotch. They serve an authentic Irish breakfast and varied pub fare throughout the day.

Bearfoot Bistro (4121 Village Green, 604/932-3433, http://bearfootbistro.com; 6pm-late daily) is among Whistler's best restaurants, but it's also a destination for drinkers: Their Ketel One Ice Room is the coldest vodka tasting room in the world. Don a heavy parka (which the restaurant provides) and venture into the frosty tasting room, with its carved ice walls and year-round temperature of -25°F (-32°C). Choose a tasting flight ($48) from their selection of 50 different vodkas, made in destinations as diverse as Poland, the Ukraine, and Pemberton, B.C.

Several Whistler hotels have more sedate drinking scenes, more upscale lounge than rowdy party, including the Mallard Lounge at the Fairmont Chateau Whistler (4599 Chateau Blvd., 604/938-8000, www.fairmont.com; 11am-midnight Sun.-Thurs., 11am-1am Fri.-Sat.), known for its martinis and creative seasonal cocktails, and the Sidecut Bar at the Four Seasons Whistler (4591 Blackcomb Way, 604/935-3400, www.fourseasons.com; 11am-late daily). Cure Lounge at Nita Lake Lodge (2131 Lake Placid Rd., 604/966-5700, www.nitalakelodge.com; 11:30am-late daily), in the Creekside area, has a great patio overlooking the lake.

What about a private wine-tasting at your hotel or condo? Taste Whistler (604/902-9463 or 844/470-9463, www.tastewhistler.com; from $79-99 pp) creates customized wine-tastings for groups of friends, families, or corporate events, from a Wine 101 sampler to a B.C. wine or champagne tasting, and they'll come to you.

THE ARTS

The Whistler Arts Council (604/935-8410, www.artswhistler.com) hosts concerts, films, and other productions as part of their Performance Series at Maury Young Arts Centre (4335 Blackcomb Way).

For something a little different, see what's happening at The Point Artist-Run Centre (5678 Alta Lake Rd., www.thepointartists.com), which presents live music during July and August in the Saturdays at the Point events, as well as occasional music, film, theater, and dance performances throughout the year. The facility is south of the village on the west side of Alta Lake.

FESTIVALS AND EVENTS
Spring to Summer

Plenty of special events bring visitors to Whistler in the spring and summer. There's something on the calendar most weekends from late May through Canadian Thanksgiving in mid-October.

Bring the kids to the annual Whistler Children's Festival (www.whistlerchildrensfestival.com, July), a weekend of family-friendly arts, crafts, and entertainment ranging from African dancing to First Nations drumming.

A "celebration of mindful living," Wanderlust Whistler (www.wanderlust.com, July-Aug.) includes several days of yoga classes, meditation workshops, concerts, lectures, guided hikes, and local food.

Crankworx Freeride Mountain Bike Festival (www.crankworx.com, Aug.) draws wild and crazy mountain bikers to town for a week of downhill and cross-country cycling, stunt riding, and plenty more two-wheeled fun.

One of Whistler's top restaurants hosts the Araxi Longtable Series (www.araxi.com, Aug.-Sept.), lavish alfresco dinners highlighting the region's late-summer bounty.

Fall to Winter

Whistler isn't only about sports. The town shows its artistic side during the annual Whistler Writers Festival (www.whistlerwritersfest.com, Oct.), when Canadian and international authors conduct readings, teach seminars, participate on panels, and mingle with guests to discuss their work.

Why come to Whistler in November, when it's chilly for hiking and cycling but too early to ski? Because that's when Whistler hosts a bang-up food and wine festival. The annual Cornucopia Festival (www.whistlercornucopia.com, Nov.) draws food and wine lovers from far and wide for two weeks of wine-tastings and seminars, guest chef events, special dinners, and lots of parties.

Whistler Film Festival (www.whistlerfilmfestival.com, Dec.) screens up to 90 movies, including world premieres, features, documentaries, and shorts during this five-day international competition. At least 50 percent of the films are Canadian. You might even spot a celebrity or two.

Whistler hosts one of North America's largest gay and lesbian ski weeks, the Whistler Pride and Ski Festival (www.gaywhistler.com, Jan.). It's eight days of LGBTQ-friendly snow sports, après-ski events, parties, concerts, and more.

SPORTS AND RECREATION
HIKING AND BIKING

Winding 25 miles (40 kilometers) through the Whistler area, the paved Valley Trail (www.whistler.ca) is open to both walkers and cyclists. You can follow short stretches of the trail, for example, between the Blackcomb base area and Whistler Village, or head north to Green Lake or south to the Creekside area and beyond.

Close to Whistler Village (you can follow the Valley Trail), Lost Lake Park has several easy hiking and cycling trails. Walkers can circle the lake on the Lost Lake Loop trail, while mountain bikers can follow several single-track routes through the park.

Whistler has several areas of old-growth forest with massive trees. A moderate five-mile (8-kilometer) loop hike takes you through one of these forests along the Ancient Cedars Trail, where the trees are up to 1,000 years old. The trailhead is north of the village; take Highway 99 north past Green Lake and turn left onto 16-Mile Forest Service Road. It's three miles (5 kilometers) from the highway to the parking area. Bring mosquito repellent, since this area can be buggy.

Get trail maps showing these and other trails from the Whistler Visitor Centre (4230 Gateway Dr.) or online from the Whistler municipality website (www.whistler.ca) or from www.whistler.com.

ZIP-LINING

Fancy a ride on the longest zip line in Canada or the United States? Ziptrek Ecotours (604/935-0001 or 866/935-0001, www.ziptrek.com) offers several different zip-line options, including The Sasquatch (daily May-mid-Oct., 1.5 hours; adults $119, seniors and ages 10-14 $99), which runs more than 7,000 feet (2 kilometers), starting on Blackcomb Mountain and zipping down to the Whistler side.

Ziptrek also offers The Eagle (daily year-round, 2.5-3 hours; adults $139, seniors and ages 6-14 $119), which takes you down five zip lines and across four treetop bridges. If zip-lining is your passion, you can combine the Sasquatch and Eagle tours (4.5 hours; adults $209, seniors and ages 10-14 $189). Newcomers to zip-lining, or younger kids, may prefer The Bear (year-round, 2.5-3 hours; adults $119, seniors and ages 6-14 $99), a slightly gentler combination of zip lines and bridges. Hours vary seasonally, so call or check the website for details.

Superfly Ziplines (211-4293 Mountain Square, 604/932-0647, www.superflyziplines.com; 9am-5pm daily, 3 hours, adults $129-149, ages 7-13 $99) has a zip-line tour that includes a 0.6-mile (1 kilometer) line that's more than 500 feet (150 meters) high.

TREETOP ADVENTURES

If you're looking for an activity that's gentler than zip-lining but still gets you high in the trees, consider a two-hour TreeTrek Canopy Walk (604/935-0001 or 866/935-0001, www.ziptrek.com; daily year-round, call or check the website for tour times; adults $39, seniors and ages 6-14 $29), which follows a series of bridges suspended among the old-growth forest on Blackcomb Mountain. The highest of the eight viewing platforms rises nearly 200 feet (60 meters) above the forest floor; the oldest trees in the area are about 800 years old. On this excursion offered by Ziptrek Ecotours, your guide will introduce you to the local ecology as you explore the woods.

Want more of a challenge? Superfly's Treetop Adventure Course (211-4293 Mountain Square, 604/932-0647, www.superflyziplines.com; 9am-5pm daily; $59) takes you through the treetops on a ropes course, where you navigate swaying bridges, rope swings, tightropes, and zip lines. Kids not tall enough to reach 71 inches (180 centimeters) can try the Kids Treetop Adventure Course ($29), designed for youngsters ages 7-14 who can reach to 55 inches (140 centimeters).

BOBSLED AND SKELETON

During the 2010 Winter Olympic Games, the Whistler Sliding Centre (4910 Glacier Ln., 604/964-0040, www.whistlersportlegacies.com) hosted the bobsled, skeleton, and luge competitions. You can live out your almost-Olympic dreams with rides down the same slippery track that the Olympic athletes used.

In summer, whiz down the track in the Rolling Thunder (Thurs.-Mon. late June-early Sept., advance reservations required; $99 pp), a bobsled on wheels. A pilot steers your sled, which holds up to four passengers and can reach speeds of 50 mph (80 km/h). Kids must be at least 12 to ride (12- and 13-year-olds must have an adult accompany them; those ages 14 to 18 need a parent or guardian present to sign a waiver). Participants must also be between 4 foot 6 and 6 foot 5 (137 to 196 centimeters) and weigh between 85 and 285 pounds (39 to 129 kilograms).

In winter, the Thunder on Ice (daily early Dec.-late Mar., advance reservations required; $179 pp) bobsled experience sends you down the ice at even faster speeds: up to 75 mph (120 km/h). The sled holds a pilot and one or two guests. For this experience, you must be between ages 14 and 75; youth ages 14 to 16 must ride with a parent or guardian, and those ages 17 and 18 must have a responsible adult sign a waiver. All participants must be between 4 foot 6 and 6 foot 8 (137-203 centimeters) and weigh between 90 and 270 pounds (41-122 kilograms) with your winter clothing on.

If you're really adventurous, ride head-first on the skeleton down the icy track. Lightning on Ice (daily early Dec.-late Mar., advance reservations required; $179 pp) gives you two solo runs, where you may find yourself hurtling down the track at close to 60 mph (100 km/h). Minimum age for the skeleton is 16, and the maximum is 75. Parents or guardians must sign a waiver for youth under age 19, and all participants must be between 4 foot 6 and 6 foot 5 (137-198 centimeters) and weigh between 90 and 220

pounds (41-120 kilograms) with your winter clothing on.

To reach the Whistler Sliding Centre from Whistler Village, follow Blackcomb Way to Glacier Lane.

WATER SPORTS

One of Whistler's most peaceful outdoor experiences is a kayak or canoe tour along the River of Golden Dreams. Whistler Eco Tours (604/935-4900 or 877/988-4900, www.whistlerecotours.com) offers three-hour guided (adults $130, under age 13 $91) or self-guided (adults $90, under age 13 $60) paddles that start on Alta Lake, travel through a scenic wetlands area, and wrap up at beautiful Green Lake. On the guided tour, your guide will tell you about the area's ecology and give you paddling tips. Both the self-guided and guided options are family-friendly and include transportation back to the village.

Whistler Eco Tours also rents single kayaks ($30 per hour) and canoes, double kayaks, stand-up paddleboards, and pedal boats (all $35 per hour) from their base in Wayside Park on Alta Lake, between the village and Creekside.

You can swim in several Whistler-area lakes, although the water can be chilly. You'll find beaches at Alpha Lake near Creekside, Alta Lake between Creekside and the village, Lost Lake near the village, and Green Lake, a large glacier-fed lake north of the village.

Prefer to do your swimming indoors? Then visit the Meadow Park Sports Centre (8625 Hwy. 99, 604/935-7529, www.whistler.ca; adults $8.50, ages 13-18 $5, ages 4-12 $4.25), a public recreational facility with a 25-meter lap pool as well as a kids' pool with a lazy river. Located two miles (three kilometers) north of the village, the center and pool are generally open 6am-10pm daily, but call or check the website for seasonal variations.

WINTER SPORTS

As an alternative to skiing and snowboarding on Whistler-Blackcomb, go to the Whistler Olympic Park (5 Callaghan Valley Rd., 604/964-0060, www.whistlersportlegacies.com; late Nov.-early Apr., weather permitting) for cross-country skiing (adults $26, ages 7-18 $15), snowshoeing (adults $15.50, ages 7-18 $8.25), and tobogganing ($15 per vehicle). Gear rentals are available. The park is 15 miles (23 kilometers) from the village; follow Highway 99 south to Callaghan Valley Road.

FOOD

Like many resort towns, Whistler offers several splurge-worthy dining rooms. If you're watching your budget, you'll need to pick your dining spots carefully, but burgers, pizza, and diner-style meals can fuel you up at moderate prices. Another money-saving option, when you're staying in a condo or lodging with kitchen facilities, is to have one or more meals "at home" or pack a lunch for your outdoor adventures.

GROCERIES AND MARKETS

The Whistler Farmers Market (Upper Village Stroll, Blackcomb Village Base; 11am-4pm Sun. June-mid-Oct., 2pm-7pm Wed. July-Aug.) brings locally grown produce and other goodies to the village every weekend from late spring through fall, with an additional weekday market in midsummer.

Whistler Marketplace IGA (4330 Northlands Blvd., 604/938-2850, www.marketplaceiga.com; 9am-9pm daily) is the largest and most centrally located grocery store in the village.

Handy to pick up a snack or the toothpaste you forgot, the Whistler Grocery Store (4211 Village Square, 604/932-3628, www.whistlergrocery.com; 8am-11pm daily) keeps long hours and is the closest market to the slopes. If you're staying in the Creekside area, your go-to grocery is Whistler's Creekside Market (305-2071 Lake Placid Rd., 604/938-9301, www.creeksidemarket.com; 8am-10pm daily).

MODERN CANADIAN

Long considered one of Whistler's top restaurants, ✪ Araxi (4222 Village Square, 604/932-4540, www.araxi.com; 5pm-late Mon.-Fri, 10am-2pm and 5pm-late Sat.-Sun.; $30-53) emphasizes regional ingredients, whether it's fresh oysters (there is an oyster bar, with oyster happy hour 3pm-5pm daily) or produce grown on local farms. The menu might include chorizo-crusted B.C. halibut with roasted tomato fondue or pan-roasted duck breast with parmesan-mushroom polenta and caramelized pears. Sate your sweet tooth with the warm Valrhona chocolate fondant or the refreshing lemon tart.

With more than 20,000 bottles, ✪ Bearfoot Bistro (4121 Village Green, 604/932-3433, http://bearfootbistro.com; 6pm-late daily; prix fixe $78-108 pp) has one of the largest wine cellars in western Canada, the better to pair with their modern Canadian cuisine. Accompanied by live jazz, dinners are multicourse prix fixe affairs that might start with an heirloom tomato salad with ricotta *salata* or scallop ceviche with pickled watermelon rind, and continue with arctic char paired with artichoke *agnolotti,* beef striploin with roasted bone marrow and oyster mushrooms, or *za'atar*-rubbed grilled quail. Of course, there are sweets, including ice cream that they whip up tableside, mixing cream with liquid nitrogen. If you prefer a lighter meal, perhaps oysters and champagne, a game burger, or duck confit with a chili-honey glaze, take a seat in their less formal champagne lounge (from 4pm Mon.-Fri., from 3pm Sat.-Sun.; $12-22), which is open from après-ski until late evening.

Overlooking the village and up 21 steps from the street, 21 Steps Kitchen + Bar (4433 Sundial Place, 604/966-2121, www.21steps.ca; 5:30pm-midnight daily; $15-36) serves crowd-pleasing comfort food, from roast chicken, pork schnitzel, and bison steak to pasta. You can also stop in for cocktails and small plates, like

orange-soy braised pork ribs or cheesy baked mushroom caps.

Popular for breakfast, casual Elements Urban Tapas Parlour (102B-4359 Main St., 604/932-5569, www.elementswhistler.com; 8am-2pm and 5pm-10pm Sun.-Thurs., 8am-2pm and 5pm-11pm Fri.-Sat.; $9-26) serves plates to share later in the day, from a wild salmon combo plate (offering the fish cured, maple-smoked, and raw) or mini venison burgers topped with gruyère to bison short ribs paired with pineapple salsa. The restaurant is located in the Summit Hotel building.

✪ Aura Restaurant (2131 Lake Placid Rd., 604/966-5715, www.ni-talakelodge.com; 7am-11:30am and 5:30pm-9pm Mon.-Sat., 7am-2pm and 5:30pm-9pm Sun., off-season hours vary; $20-30) at Creekside's Nita Lake Lodge is worth a visit even if you're not staying at this lakefront hotel, both for its fine contemporary fare and for

tuna crudo, Aura Restaurant

the lovely lakeside setting. You might begin with a seasonal salad or tuna *crudo* dressed with citrus vinaigrette, accompanied by a watermelon martini or a Violaceus Fizz (a blend of lavender-infused gin and lemon soda). For your main course, you could try seared scallops with sweet pea puree, fresh B.C. salmon, or cider-brined pork chops with a side of grilled asparagus, cauliflower gratin, or a shareable platter of garden veggies.

JAPANESE

A longtime favorite for Japanese fare, upscale Sushi Village (11-4340 Sundial Crescent, 604/932-3330, http://sushivillage.com; 5:30pm-10pm Mon.-Thurs., noon-2:30pm and 5:30pm-10pm Fri.-Sun.; $16-38) has been keeping Whistler in *nigiri, maki,* teriyaki, and tempura since the 1980s. Another popular spot for Japanese meals is Sushi Sachi (106-4359 Main St., 604/935-5649, www.sachisushi.com; noon-2pm and 5pm-late Tues.-Fri., 5pm-late Sat.-Sun.; $13-30) at the Summit Lodge.

Part grocery store and part quick-serve Japanese eatery, Fuji Market (205-4000 Whistler Way, 604/962-6251, www.fujimarket.ca; 11am-9pm daily; $5-12) stocks ready-made sushi and cooks up ramen, tempura, and other inexpensive Japanese bites. You can pick up wasabi peas, jars of kimchi, and other Asian ingredients. It's in a strip mall on the edge of the village, near the Whistler Conference Centre.

ITALIAN AND PIZZA

A life raft of good value in a sea of expensive eateries, family-friendly Pasta Lupino (121-4368 Main St., 604/905-0400, www.pastalupino.com; 11am-9pm daily; $14-18) serves a small menu of Italian classics, including spaghetti and meatballs, lasagna, and chicken parmigiana. In the evenings, pasta dinners come with soup or salad, plus homemade focaccia.

The wood-fired oven turns out traditional Neapolitan-style pizzas at Pizzeria Antico (101-4369 Main St., 604/962-9226, www.pizzeriaantico.ca; 11am-10pm Sun.-Wed., 11am-11pm Thurs.-Sat.; $13-20), like the Prosciutto con Ruccola, topped with arugula, prosciutto, tomato, and mozzarella, or the Funghi, sauced with porcini cream and layered with roasted mushrooms and onions. Several fresh salads, grilled *paninis* (at lunch), and pastas (at dinner) round out the menu.

SPANISH

Under the same ownership as Araxi, cozy Bar Oso (150-4222 Village Sq., 604/962-4540, http://baroso.ca; 11:30am-late daily; $8-25) serves up Spanish-style tapas with a B.C. twist. You might nibble wild scallop *crudo* with olives and oranges, a salad of roasted beets with buffalo mozzarella, or a platter of house-made charcuterie. To sip, there are local beers, sangrias, and interesting cocktails.

BURGERS

Like burgers? Splitz Grill (4369 Main St., 604/938-9300, www.splitzgrill.com; 11am-9pm daily; $5-13) has 'em, and they're not just traditional beef patties. You can get lamb, bison, lentil, even salmon. Line up at the counter, order your burger, and choose from a large selection of toppings. *Poutine*, fries, and beer are the favored accompaniments.

DINERS

For fuel-me-up breakfasts and hearty meals served with friendly sass, head for the Southside Diner (2102 Lake Placid Rd., Creekside, 604/966-0668, www.southsidediner.ca; 7am-9pm Sun.-Thurs., 7am-10pm Fri.-Sat.; $10-16), off Highway 99 in the Creekside area. Morning menus get you going with breakfast *poutine* (home fries topped with poached eggs, sausage, cheese curds, and gravy), "big-ass pancakes" (yes, they're big), and the usual egg suspects. Later in the day, you can stuff yourself with burgers, sandwiches, meatloaf, or macaroni and cheese.

VEGETARIAN

You might walk away with a green mustache after slurping down a fresh juice or smoothie at The Green Moustache (122-4340 Lorimer Rd., 604/962-3727, http://greenmoustache-juice.com; 8am-6pm daily; $7-10), a tiny juice bar and vegetarian eatery. In the morning, they serve breakfast bowls, like muesli or chia pudding topped with nuts, berries, and house-made almond or cashew milk. Later, order a big salad or the Buddha Bowl, a blend of rice and quinoa piled high with fresh veggies.

BAKERIES AND CAFÉS

✪ Purebread (www.purebread.ca), Whistler's best bakery, offers an irresistible array of treats, from scones and croissants to lemon crumble bars, salted caramel bars, and oversized brownies. For a savory snack, opt for a Pudgie Pie, a portable pastry that might be stuffed with goat cheese, potatoes, or other veggies. If you're packing for a picnic, try the Dysfunction Ale bread, a hearty loaf made with spent grains from the Whistler Brewing Company. Purebread has two Whistler branches: a convenient Village location (Main St., Olympic

Plaza, 604/962-1182; 8:30am-5:30pm daily) and their original Function Junction shop (1-1040 Millar Creek Rd., 604/938-3013; 8:30am-5pm daily) on the south side of town.

ACCOMMODATIONS AND CAMPING

Whistler accommodations include a range of hotels and condominium buildings. Hotels provide more services, such as on-site restaurants, ski valets, and concierge staff; some, but not all, have kitchenettes or in-room fridges and microwaves. Renting a condo is often less expensive, particularly for a family, and you'll have a kitchen where you can prepare some meals. Many Whistler hotels charge for overnight parking, so factor that fee into your lodging budget.

Whistler has two "peak" seasons. The main high season is during the winter for skiing and snowboarding, which typically begins in late November and continues until April. There's also a "mini peak" during July and August, when visitors come for hiking, biking, and other summer activities. The most expensive time to stay at Whistler is during the Christmas-New Year holiday, when rates soar. The February-March school holiday weeks are also pricey. During the rest of the year, lodging rates are usually lowest midweek.

Check the Tourism Whistler website (www.whistler.com) for lodging deals, particularly if you're making last-minute plans. The Whistler-Blackcomb website (www.whistler-blackcomb.com) sometimes posts discounts on accommodations as well.

UNDER $150

Built as part of the Athletes Village for the 2010 Winter Olympics, the

HI-Whistler Hostel (1035 Legacy Way, 604/962-0025 or 866/762-4122, www.hihostels.ca; $33-38 dorm, $82-134 d) still feels new, offering dorm beds as well as good-value, basic, but modern private rooms with flat-screen TVs and en suite baths—worth considering even if you don't normally stay in a hostel. Dorms sleep eight in four bunk beds, each with reading lights, electrical outlets, lockers, and shared washrooms. Parking and Wi-Fi are free, and common areas include a café, a TV room, a lounge with a pool table, a big shared kitchen, and an outdoor terrace. Rates are highest December through February, when the hostel can have more of a ski-party atmosphere. Summer is typically quieter, when staff organize guided hikes, local brewery tours, and other activities. The hostel is five miles (8 kilometers) south of Whistler Village; at the Function Junction crossroads, turn east onto Cheakamus Lake Road. B.C. Transit buses to the village stop out front.

$150-250

Catering to skiers and snowboarders in winter, and to cyclists and other active guests in summer, the ✪ AAVA Whistler Hotel (4005 Whistler Way, 604/932-2522 or 800/663-5644, www.aavawhistlerhotel.com; $135-450 d, parking $19) will loan you a complimentary GoPro camera to record your day's adventures (neat, right?). While it's not upscale (hotel staff say, "We don't valet your car, but we do valet your bike"), this 192-room lodging feels sociable, with several lobby seating areas and a communal worktable with a charging station. There's space to lounge on the outdoor deck, too, around the compact pool and hot tub. Outfitted with one king, two queens,

or a queen plus a sofa bed, the guest rooms are crisp and modern, with minifridges, safes, and Keurig coffeemakers; the prime top-floor units have vaulted ceilings. Wi-Fi and local calls are free. You can walk to the Whistler base in about 10 minutes.

Feeling funky? The boutique 41-room Adara Hotel (4122 Village Green, 604/905-4009 or 866/502-3272, www.adarahotel.com; $119-329 d, parking $20) goes beyond typical ski-lodge style, starting from its lobby, furnished with curvaceous orange banquettes, a massive stone fireplace, and stylized antler sculptures; you can grab coffee and a breakfast bar here in the morning, or give the resident dog a pat. Out on the sundeck is a small hot tub and summer-only pool. Standard rooms have electric fireplaces, French press coffeemakers, minifridges, microwaves, and modern baths with rain showers, but the coolest units are the lofts, with a bedroom upstairs and a living area below. Wi-Fi is included.

The three-story Listel Hotel Whistler (4121 Village Green, 604/932-1133 or 800/663-5472, www.listelhotel.com; $139-369 d, parking $20) is simple but comfortable, with a quiet location off the Village Stroll yet close to the lifts at the Whistler base. Most of the 98 rooms are standard units with two queen beds, free Wi-Fi, coffeemakers, and minifridges. There's a hot tub (but no pool) on the outdoor patio. Rates include continental breakfast. The excellent Bearfoot Bistro (604/932-3433, http://bearfootbistro.com; 6pm-late daily; prix fixe $78-108 pp) is on the property.

At the serene boutique Summit Lodge and Spa (4359 Main St., 604/932-2778 or 888/913-8811, www.summitlodge.com; $130-479 d, parking $20), the 81 studio and one-bedrooms suites, with cherry furnishings, all have kitchenettes. Wi-Fi and local calls are included, and you can borrow a complimentary bike to cycle around town. The Asian-style Taman Sari Royal Heritage Spa (604/938-5982, www.tamansarispa.com) uses traditional Javanese herbs in many of its treatments. Other hotel amenities include a sauna, hot tub, and year-round outdoor pool. You're surrounded by lots of good restaurants, and it's a 10- to 15-minute walk to the lifts.

Most of the studio units at the 84-room Whistler Pinnacle Hotel (4319 Main St., 604/938-3218 or 888/999-8986, www.whistlerpinnacle.com; $149-349 d, parking $19), a quieter older property off the Village Stroll, have full kitchens (handy if you don't want to eat out for every meal), gas fireplaces, included Wi-Fi and local calls, and modern baths with whirlpool tubs to soak away any adventure-induced aches and pains. Units on the fourth floor feel larger, with vaulted ceilings. There's a guest laundry and a small outdoor lap pool. Quattro Italian Restaurant (604/905-4844, http://quattrorestaurants.com; 5:30pm-10pm daily; $24-48) and the modern French Alta Bistro (604/932-2582, www.altabistro.com; 5:30pm-late daily; $29-39) are the on-property dining options.

Though it's a chain hotel, family-friendly Hilton Whistler Resort & Spa (4050 Whistler Way, 604/932-1982 or 800/515-4050, www.hiltonwhistler.com; $141-450 d, parking $32-36) feels surprisingly local, with aboriginal art in the lobby and a great location just a five-minute walk from the lifts. The 287 guest rooms, in two towers, are among the largest in Whistler Village, ranging from standard units

and studios (with kitchenettes) up to three-bedroom suites. The outdoor pool is open year-round, as are the two hot tubs; in summer, you can play tennis on-site. Rates include Wi-Fi and local phone calls.

Four Seasons Whistler Hotel

OVER $250

With a solicitous staff and all sorts of amenities, ✪ Four Seasons Whistler Hotel (4591 Blackcomb Way, 604/935-3400, www.fourseasons.com; $399-539 d, $675-1,399 suite, parking $39) is among Whistler's top resort hotels. Decorated in ski-lodge earth tones, the 273 rooms and suites have gas fireplaces, big closets, minifridges, and flat-screen TVs; ask for an upper-floor unit for slope-side views. If you haven't gotten enough exercise on the mountain, you can work out in the 24-hour fitness room or swim in the heated outdoor pool. The three hot tubs and eucalyptus steam room are popular après-ski, as is the library-style Sidecut Bar. Located in Whistler's Upper Village, the Four Seasons isn't a ski-in, ski-out property, but the hotel offers a free ski concierge, so you can leave your gear slope-side. A complimentary car service can take you around town.

Like a grand mountain lodge, the ✪ **Fairmont Chateau Whistler** (4599 Chateau Blvd., off Blackcomb Way, 604/938-8000 or 800/606-8244, www.fairmont.com; $299-619 d, parking $35-39) keeps you comfortable, whether you're in your room, exploring the property, or out in the village. The 550 rooms and suites, some with views of the slopes, have down duvets, fluffy bathrobes, flat-screen TVs, and Keurig coffeemakers. The Fairmont charges a daily resort fee ($12 per room), which covers most of the things you'd want to do, including Internet access, use of the indoor and outdoor pools and the well-equipped health club, yoga classes, tennis, a shuttle to take you to various village destinations, and valet service for your skis, bikes, or golf clubs. The **Mallard Lounge** is popular for après-ski cocktails, and the hotel has several other dining outlets, including **The Grill Room** (6pm-9pm daily; $33-59) for steak and seafood and the more casual **Wildflower Restaurant** (7am-10:30am and 6pm-9pm Mon.-Fri., 7am-11am and 6pm-9pm Sat.-Sun.; $22-49).

You can't stay much closer to the lifts than at the 121-unit all-suite **Pan Pacific Whistler Mountainside** (4320 Sundial Crescent, 604/905-2999 or 888/905-9995, www.panpacific.com;

kayaks on the dock, Nita Lake Lodge

$279-689 d, parking $28-32), steps from Blackcomb's Excalibur gondola. Decorated with cherry-hued Craftsman-style furnishings, the studio, one-bedroom, and two-bedroom units all have full kitchens, gas fireplaces, flat-screen TVs, and DVD players. The studios nominally sleep four, with a queen-size Murphy bed and a sleep sofa, but the larger suites are more comfortable for families. Other amenities include a heated outdoor saltwater pool, two hot tubs, complimentary Wi-Fi, and free local phone calls. The **Dubh Linn Gate Irish Pub** (604/905-4047, www.dubhlinngate. com; 8am-1am daily; $14-25) is popular for drinks and pub fare, with more than 25 beers on tap and live music most nights.

Slightly farther from the gondolas than its sister property, the **Pan Pacific Whistler Village Centre** (4299 Blackcomb Way, 604/966-5500 or 888/966-5575, www.panpacific. com; $169-539 d, parking $28-32) has a more modern boutique feel, but similar amenities: suites ranging from studios to three bedrooms with full kitchens, a saltwater lap pool, two hot tubs, a sauna, and a fitness facility. Rates include breakfast, Wi-Fi, local calls, and a complimentary shuttle to get around the village. You can store your ski or snowboard gear at the Pan Pacific Mountainside.

Set on a lake in the Creekside area, ✪ **Nita Lake Lodge** (2131 Lake Placid Rd., 604/966-5700, www.nitalakelodge.com; $289-559 d, suites $409-849, parking $20-30) is a beautiful setting for a stay in any season. The 77 spacious contemporary suites—studio, one-, and two-bedroom units on four floors—have fireplaces, compact kitchenettes hidden in an armoire, and modern baths with rain showers and soaker tubs; the best units have lake views. You can choose all kinds of activities, from lounging in the rooftop hot tubs to kayaking, canoeing, or stand-up paddleboarding on the lake, or riding up the Valley Trail on the complimentary bicycles. There's a full-service spa, as well as three restaurants, including the more formal Aura Restaurant (7am-11:30am and 5:30pm-9pm Mon.-Sat., 7am-2pm and 5:30pm-9pm Sun., off-season hours vary; $20-30) overlooking the lake, Cure Lounge (11:30am-11pm Mon.-Sat., 10am-11pm Sun.; $13-25), and casual Fix Café (6:30am-3:30pm daily; $5-13), which serves pastries, coffee, and sandwiches, giving you plenty of dining options. The hotel offers a free shuttle to the village or the Creekside gondola.

CAMPING AND CABINS

The Riverside Resort (8018 Mons Rd., 604/905-5533, www.parkbridge. com) has several lodging options, including campsites for tents and RVs, yurts, and sturdy log cabins. It's located two miles (3.5 kilometers) north of the village.

The 14 family-friendly cabins ($210-250), with solid wood furnishings, have a living room, small kitchen, bedroom with a queen bed, and bath on the main level, plus a sleeping loft with two twin beds. They're equipped with electricity and even a flat-screen TV. The yurts ($105-145) are more rustic, but they still have electricity and heat. Sleeping up to five, most have a bunk bed with a single over a double bed, and either a futon couch or a separate single with a trundle bed. Washrooms with showers are a short walk away. RV campsites ($52-65) include both fully and partially serviced sites.

There's a quiet wooded walk-in tent campground ($23-40) with sites along the river.

The campground's main building has a small market and café; bicycle rentals are available. Other amenities include a guest laundry, a kids' playground, a volleyball court, and a putting course. The Valley Trail crosses the campground property, so you can follow it into town.

CONDO RENTALS

You can book many condo accommodations through the Tourism Whistler (www.whistler.com) and Whistler-Blackcomb (www.whistlerblackcomb. com) websites and through many of the standard online booking services for hotels. You can also find condos through Airbnb (www.airbnb.com).

Check locally based rental agencies, including alluraDirect (604/707-6700 or 866/425-5872, www.alluradirect. com), which sometimes offer deals that the larger booking services don't have.

INFORMATION AND SERVICES

VISITOR INFORMATION

Tourism Whistler (www.whistler. com) should be your starting point for information about the Whistler region. The website has lots of details about the area, both on and off the mountain, and they run the year-round Whistler Visitor Centre (4230 Gateway Dr., 604/935-3357 or 877/991-9988, www.whistler.com/whistler-visitor-centre) in the village, which supplies maps, answers questions, and books accommodations and activities. Hours vary seasonally, but the visitors center is open at least 8am-6pm daily; it stays open until 8pm or 10pm on busy weekends and holiday periods.

Whistler-Blackcomb (604/967-8950 or 800/766-0449, www.whistlerblackcomb.com) books lift tickets, equipment rentals, ski and snowboard lessons, and accommodations (reservations 604/296-5316 or 888/403-4727) and can provide information about other mountain activities in every season. Check the website for toll-free reservations numbers from many different countries.

MEDICAL SERVICES

The Whistler Health Care Centre (4380 Lorimer Rd., 604/932-4911, www.vch.ca; 8am-10pm daily) provides emergency medical services to both locals and visitors. Doctors are on-call after hours.

The Whistler area has several medical clinics that will see visitors for minor issues, including the Whistler Medical Clinic (4380 Lorimer Rd., 604/932-3977, www.whistlermedicalclinic.com) and Town Plaza Medical Clinic (40-4314 Main St., 604/905-7089, www.medicalclinicwhistler.com).

Rexall (103-4360 Lorimer Rd., 604/932-2303; 4212 Village Square, 604/932-4251, www.rexall.ca; 9am-7pm daily) has two Whistler pharmacies. Shoppers Drug Mart (121-4295 Blackcomb Way, 604/905-5666, www.shoppersdrugmart.ca; 9am-9pm daily) also provides pharmacy services.

GETTING THERE
CAR

Allow about two hours to make the 75-mile (120-kilometer) drive between Vancouver and Whistler along the spectacular Sea-to-Sky Highway.

From downtown Vancouver, take West Georgia Street to the Lions Gate Bridge. Watch the signs carefully as you approach Stanley Park en route to the bridge to stay in the proper lane.

The center lane on the three-lane bridge reverses its travel direction at different times of day, typically creating two travel lanes into the city in the morning and two travel lanes toward the North Shore during the afternoon rush hour.

After you cross the Lions Gate Bridge, bear left toward Marine Drive west/Highway 1/Highway 99. Enter Marine Drive and stay in the far right lane to take the first right onto Taylor Way (the sign says "Whistler"). Follow Taylor Way up the hill, and exit left onto Highway 1 west. Continue on Highway 1 until it merges with Highway 99 (the Sea-to-Sky Hwy.). Stay on Highway 99 through Squamish and into Whistler.

AIR

A dramatic way to travel between Vancouver and Whistler, if your budget allows, is by floatplane, which takes you above Howe Sound, the Gulf Islands, and the surrounding peaks.

Harbour Air (604/274-1277 or 800/665-0212, www.harbourair.com; 45 minutes; one-way adults $200) flies twice daily in each direction between the Vancouver Harbour Flight Centre (1055 Canada Pl., behind the Vancouver Convention Centre, 604/274-1277) and Green Lake (8069 Nicklaus North Blvd.), two miles (3 kilometers) north of Whistler Village. There's a free shuttle between the Green Lake terminal and the village. The shuttles operate in conjunction with the flight schedules.

BUS

To visit Whistler without a car, Greyhound (800/661-8747, www.greyhound.ca; about 2.5 hours; one-way adults $17-38) operates several buses a day between Vancouver and

Whistler and is the least expensive option. In Vancouver, the bus depot is at Pacific Central Station (1150 Station St.). In Whistler, the bus stops in Creekside (2029 London Ln.) and Whistler Village (4230 Gateway Dr.).

Pacific Coach Lines (604/662-7575 or 800/661-1725, www.pacific-coach.com; one-way adults $55, ages 5-11 $27.50) runs buses several times daily between downtown Vancouver and Whistler Village. The trip takes 2.5 hours. The downtown stops are on Burrard Street at Alberni Street outside the Fairmont Hotel Vancouver, and at Melville Street adjacent to the Hyatt Vancouver. You can also take their YVR Whistler SkyLynx bus (one-way adults $74, ages 5-11 $37) directly between Vancouver International Airport and Whistler, which takes three hours.

GETTING AROUND
CAR

Whistler Village is a pedestrian zone, so you have to leave your car outside the village proper. Whistler has several public parking lots where you can park all day.

Day lots 1 to 5, on Blackcomb Way near Lorimer Road, are closest to Whistler Village. Lots 4 and 5 are always free. Lots 1, 2, and 3, which are closer to the lifts, are paid lots ($2 per hour, $8 per day) until 5pm; they're free from 5pm to 3am. Closer to the Blackcomb base area, off Glacier Lane, day lots 6, 7, and 8 are also free. From November through March, you can't park overnight in any of the day lots; between April and October, you can park for up to 72 hours.

In the Creekside area, you can park free in the Creekside base underground garage. Follow London Lane off Highway 99.

Public paid parking is available at Whistler Conference Centre (4010 Whistler Way; per hour/day $1/$10, 24-hour maximum) and Whistler Public Library (4329 Main St.; per hour/day $1/$10, 24-hour maximum).

BUS

B.C. Transit (604/932-4020, http://bctransit.com/whistler; $2.50 pp) runs several bus routes through the Whistler area that are useful if you're staying outside of the central Whistler Village. The Whistler Creek route travels between the village and Creekside, and the Valley Connector links many of Whistler's residential neighborhoods with the Whistler Gondola Exchange, where you can board the mountain gondola.

Two bus routes are free during the winter season, including the Upper Village/Benchlands route that can take you to the village from condos in those neighborhoods, and the Marketplace Shuttle between the Whistler Gondola Exchange and the Marketplace shopping center.

The Valley Connector route operates 5:15am-3:30am daily. The other routes vary seasonally; call or check the website for hours.

TAXI

Whistler has two local taxi companies: Whistler Resort Cabs (604/938-1515, www.resortcabs.com) and Whistler Taxi (604/932-3333, www.whistler-taxi.com). Both operate 24 hours daily. Taxi fares average $5 within Whistler Village, $10 between the village and Creekside, and $15 between the village and other Whistler neighborhoods.

BACKGROUND

The Landscape

GEOGRAPHY

Canada is the world's second largest country, covering an immense area of 3,855,230 square miles (nearly 10 million square kilometers). Canadian land stretches from the Atlantic to the Pacific to the Arctic, and shares its long southern boundary, along the 49th parallel, with the United States.

Bordering the Pacific Ocean, British Columbia is the country's westernmost province and its third largest geographically, after Ontario and Quebec; it's about the size of Germany, France, and the Netherlands combined. To the south are the U.S. states of Washington, Idaho, and Montana; to the north are the Yukon and Alaska. More than 60 percent of B.C.'s population is clustered in the province's southwest corner, in and around the city of Vancouver, in the region known as the Lower Mainland.

Siwash Rock in Vancouver's Stanley Park

Vancouver is known for its dramatic natural setting, perched between the mountains and the sea. Water surrounds the downtown peninsula, where three bridges cross False Creek, connecting the city center to the rest of the metropolitan area. Two more bridges take you over the Burrard Inlet to the city's North Shore, where several mountains dominate the landscape, with three local ski areas and numerous parks. Continuing north, along the strikingly beautiful Sea-to-Sky Highway, you'll reach Whistler, North America's largest winter resort and a year-round outdoor playground; it's a two-hour drive from downtown Vancouver.

Vancouver is a particularly green city, not only for its environmental policies, but also for its rainforest setting, with tall trees dominating the region. Douglas fir, western cedar, Sitka spruce, and hemlock all grow in B.C.'s coastal regions, and many of these giants are the tallest in Canada. Even within the city of Vancouver, you can wander through the forests in Stanley Park, on the end of the downtown peninsula, and in Pacific Spirit Regional Park, near the University of British Columbia campus.

If you travel inland from Vancouver, into the province's vast interior, you'll cross several mountain ranges. The Coast Mountains, which extend from Washington State to the Yukon, rise to more than 9,800 feet (3,000 meters) in their southern sections. Driving over these mountains, you leave behind the coastal rainforests and descend into a sunnier, drier region known as the Okanagan. Located along a string of scenic lakes, this agricultural valley has become B.C.'s major wine-producing area and a popular holiday destination. It's also home to Canada's only desert.

Continuing east through southern British Columbia, you'll cross the Columbia Mountains in B.C.'s Kootenay region, and then nearing the provincial border with Alberta, you'll reach the Canadian Rockies. British Columbia has four beautiful national parks—Mount Revelstoke, Glacier,

Kootenay, and Yoho—in this mountain region.

Vancouver Island is west of the city of Vancouver, across the Strait of Georgia. It's a big island, measuring 285 miles (460 kilometers) from north to south; from east to west, it's between 30 and 75 miles (50 to 120 kilometers) across. British Columbia's capital city of Victoria is located on the southeast tip of Vancouver Island, a 90-minute ferry ride or 35-minute flight from mainland British Columbia.

A spine of mountains, including several approaching 7,000 feet (2,100 meters), runs along the center of Vancouver Island. Winding your way between these peaks will take you to the island's western shore, with lovely sandy beaches in the Pacific Rim National Park Reserve and in the nearby communities of Tofino and Ucluelet.

Because coastal British Columbia sits near the edge of two tectonic plates, the large North American plate and the smaller Juan de Fuca plate, it's located in an earthquake zone. Small earthquakes do occur with some regularity across the region, although few have been felt in the metropolitan areas; the last major earthquake shook the area back in 1700. However, researchers say that there's a 25 percent chance of another significant quake occurring in the next 50 years.

CLIMATE

Unlike the rest of Canada, coastal British Columbia has a temperate climate. In fact, Victoria has the mildest climate of any Canadian city. The weather in Vancouver and Victoria is similar, although Victoria is normally a degree or two warmer and slightly drier.

In both Vancouver and Victoria,

summers are sunny and mild, with daytime temperatures in July and August averaging 68-75°F (20-25°C). In January, the coldest month, expect average temperatures during the day of 41-43°F (5-6°C), dipping close to the freezing level at night. From November through March, it's not terribly cold, but it is rainy, frequently cloudy, and gray. While it can snow in the cities, it's relatively rare, and snow doesn't typically stick around for more than a couple of days. When it's raining in Vancouver, it's often snowing in the North Shore mountains and in Whistler.

Spring comes early to coastal B.C., with flowers beginning to bloom in late February or early March. By April, Vancouver's cherry trees blanket the city streets with their pink blossoms. It can still rain in the spring, but showers are shorter and temperatures milder than during the winter months. Early autumn (September and October) is another moderate season with comfortable temperatures and less frequent rain.

The region's numerous microclimates can cause surprising variations in weather, even across short distances. The North Shore, where it snows regularly at higher elevations, receives far more rain than downtown Vancouver. In contrast, it rains noticeably less in the suburb of Richmond, where Vancouver International Airport is located, than on the downtown peninsula. Within the city itself, there are variations, too. It can be snowing in Vancouver's Point Grey neighborhood or near Queen Elizabeth Park, when at lower elevations just down the hill, in Kitsilano, along False Creek, or downtown, it's raining.

ENVIRONMENTAL ISSUES

Vancouver is a green city, with parks throughout the metropolitan region, citywide recycling initiatives, and programs to encourage everything from environmentally friendly construction to car sharing. Farmers markets are helping to provide better access to locally grown food, though most operate only from May through October. The city is in the midst of a major initiative to make Vancouver even more bicycle-friendly; a bike-sharing program launched in the downtown core in 2016, and the city continues to build bike lanes on many urban streets.

As residential and commercial towers sprout up throughout metropolitan Vancouver, development has become a major issue. Recent city governments have worked to increase urban density—building up, rather than out—to try to reduce the environmental impact of commuting from the suburbs and, at least in theory, enable more people to live in the central city. In many districts, historic homes and other structures are being razed to make room for more expensive towers, and neighborhoods are changing in character as they become more densely populated.

History

ABORIGINAL ROOTS

Aboriginal people have lived in western Canada for more than 10,000 years. The southwestern corner of British Columbia, where Vancouver is located, is the traditional territory of several aboriginal groups, collectively known as the Coast Salish. Coast Salish territory extends across the Strait of Georgia to Vancouver Island, which is also home to the Nuu-chah-nulth and the Kwakwaka'wakw peoples.

The west coast's natural resources defined the early life of Canada's coastal people. Much of their food came from the sea, where salmon, crab, and other species were abundant. They used the region's large trees, particularly the western red cedar, to construct their homes and longhouses, to carve oceangoing dugout canoes, and to craft massive totem poles, which commemorated the events, histories, and people of these native communities. Although totems have come to be a symbol of many aboriginal peoples, only six west coast First Nations originally carved the poles.

EUROPEAN EXPLORATION

The earliest European explorers to reach North America's west coast were the Spanish, who traveled north from Mexico as early as the 1540s. However, it wasn't until the 1700s that extensive exploration of the region got underway, when Spanish, Russian, French, and British ships all traveled along the coast of what is now British Columbia.

The British left the most lasting legacies, beginning with an expedition in the 1770s that British explorer James Cook captained. Cook became the first non-aboriginal person to set foot in what is now British Columbia, when he landed on Vancouver Island's west coast in 1778. Cook's crew included a young sailor named George Vancouver, who had joined the Royal Navy in 1772 when he was just 13 years old.

In 1792, George Vancouver returned to the region as captain of another Pacific Northwest expedition, charged with mapping the coastal areas and negotiating with the Spanish. The mainland beach where Captain Vancouver met with two Spanish captains is known today as Spanish Banks.

In the early 1800s, explorers and fur traders traveled westward across North America. Explorer Simon Fraser, who came from eastern Canada, reached the Pacific after following the river that today bears his name. The Hudson's Bay Company established the first permanent European settlement in the Lower Mainland in 1827 at Fort Langley, east of present-day Vancouver. In 1843, the company set up a trading post on Vancouver Island, naming it Fort Victoria. That post, on the island's southeastern point, would become the city of Victoria.

THE GOLD RUSH

In 1858, nine years after the start of the California gold rush in the United States, miners found gold along British Columbia's Fraser River. Thousands of miners traveled from eastern Canada and from the United States to seek their fortunes. Many Chinese, too, joined the search for gold, coming either from California or directly from China, triggering a major wave of immigration.

Although the gold rush didn't last long, many of these settlers remained in B.C. and found work in the emerging fishing and lumber industries, businesses that would remain the backbone of the province's economy for years to come.

After two small sawmills began operation in the 1860s along the Burrard Inlet, the entrepreneurial Captain John Deighton opened a nearby saloon to quench the millworkers' thirst. Although the district where the saloon was located had officially been named "Granville," Deighton's nickname, "Gassy Jack"—for his habit of telling tall tales—gave the area its more enduring name: Gastown.

WHEN CANADA BECAME A COUNTRY

A milestone year in Canadian history is 1867, when the British Parliament passed the British North America Act, creating the Dominion of Canada as a stand-alone nation, independent of Great Britain. Ontario, Quebec, Nova Scotia, and New Brunswick became the country's first four provinces, joining together at Confederation on July 1, 1867. Canadians celebrate Confederation annually on July 1, now the Canada Day holiday.

British Columbia joined the Canadian Confederation in 1871 (following Manitoba and the Northwest Territories, which came on board in 1870). B.C.'s government signed up with the expectation that the cross-country railroad, under construction to link the east and west, would be completed. It took nearly 15 more years, including a major influx of workers from China, but the Canadian Pacific Railway (CPR) officially finished the 3,100-mile (5,000-kilometer) transcontinental railroad in 1885, when workers drove in the last spike at Craigellachie, B.C., in the mountains west of the town of Revelstoke.

IMMIGRATION

The railway opened up the west to rapid settlement and drew large numbers of migrants from eastern Canada, the United States, and Europe, especially from Italy, the Ukraine, Poland, Germany, and Hungary. Chinese immigration continued, and small numbers of Japanese began arriving in British Columbia around the same time, many of whom found work along the coast in the fishing industry on boats or in canneries.

At that point, the western terminus of the rail line reached only as far as Port Moody, on the Burrard Inlet 12 miles (20 kilometers) east of Vancouver. The CPR's decision to extend the railroad to the fledging settlement then known as Granville fueled Vancouver's development. Named for the British explorer, the city of Vancouver was officially incorporated in 1886, and the first transcontinental passenger train rolled into town in 1887.

Migrants continued settling in B.C. throughout the early 1900s. The University of British Columbia was established in 1908 and by the 1920s, Vancouver had become the third largest city in Canada, a position it retains today.

Canada didn't always welcome these immigrants, however. Despite the Chinese role in constructing the railroads, the federal government attempted to restrict further immigration from China. They imposed a "head tax" on every Chinese newcomer. In 1885, the tax was $50; by 1903, it had been raised to $500. In 1923, the Canadian Parliament passed the Chinese Immigration Act, an exclusionary measure that effectively prevented Chinese immigrants from entering Canada. The act was finally repealed in 1947 after World War II.

WORLD WAR II

During the Second World War, more than a million Canadians fought for the Allies, joining the United States, Britain, France, and Australia among the nations who battled the Axis coalition of Germany, Italy, and Japan.

At home, anti-Asian sentiment began to rise after the 1941 Japanese attack on Pearl Harbor, particularly in British Columbia, which by this time had a well-established Japanese Canadian population, most of whom lived in and around Vancouver. In January 1942, the B.C. government established a 100-mile (160-kilometer) "security zone" between the Pacific Ocean and the Coast Mountains, extending south to the U.S. border and north to the Yukon. They decreed that all male Japanese Canadians between the ages of 18 and 45 were prohibited from living in the area; they were separated from their families and sent to relocation camps in B.C.'s remote interior regions.

Less than two months later, the government extended the prohibition to all people of Japanese origin and began relocating women, children, and seniors. Overall, more than 22,000 people of Japanese heritage, three-quarters of whom were Canadian citizens, were forcibly relocated, and their land and other property were confiscated. Many spent the

war years in these rustic internment camps in British Columbia's Kootenay and eastern mountain regions.

After the war, most of the interned Japanese Canadians were given the choice of moving east of the Rockies or returning to Japan. The majority opted to relocate again, settling in the prairies or farther east in Ontario, although several thousand were sent to Japan. The Japanese were forbidden to return to the B.C. coast until 1949.

RESIDENTIAL SCHOOLS

Another dark period in Canada's history began in the 1880s, when the Canadian government began establishing residential schools for aboriginal children. Native students were required to attend these church-run boarding schools, where children were removed from their families. The schools' objective was to assimilate aboriginal youth into mainstream Canadian culture. In 1920, Parliament passed the Indian Act, which made it illegal for native children to attend any educational institution other than a residential school.

While some students' experiences at the schools were positive, the vast majority suffered through poor education, inadequate food, isolation from their families and culture, and in some cases, physical or sexual abuse. The last residential schools closed, or were turned over to aboriginal communities to operate, in the 1980s. However, the schools' negative legacy continues to affect many aboriginal people today, with high rates of alcoholism, drug abuse, domestic violence, and suicide plaguing many communities.

Canada's Assembly of First Nations filed a class action lawsuit against the Canadian government in 2005 for the ongoing trauma that the residential school system had caused. When the suit was settled, and both the federal government and the churches agreed to pay compensation to survivors of the schools, the 2006 Indian Residential Schools Settlement Agreement became the largest class action settlement in Canadian history. In 2008, Canada's House of Commons publicly apologized for the government's role in creating and maintaining the residential school system.

CONTEMPORARY TIMES

In recent years, several events triggered significant changes in and around Vancouver.

In 1986, Vancouver marked its centennial, hosting Expo '86, a World's Fair that focused on developments in transportation and communications. This international exposition took place on a formerly derelict site along False Creek that had been redeveloped to house more than 50 pavilions. Britain's Prince Charles and Princess Diana were among the first visitors, and more than 22 million people visited Expo '86 during its six-month run, with tourists continuing to arrive long after the event officially closed. Vancouver built the city's first SkyTrain line in anticipation of the Expo, and many other city landmarks, including Canada Place, Science World, B.C. Place, and the Cambie Bridge, were constructed during this era.

In the late 1980s and early 1990s, thousands of Hong Kong residents immigrated to Canada, and a large percentage settled in British Columbia. Many were afraid of how their country might change when the United Kingdom handed over Hong Kong to the Chinese government in 1997. This wave of immigration was the first of several that significantly increased Vancouver's Asian population; many more immigrants arrived from Taiwan and mainland China, beginning in the 1990s and continuing through the present day.

In 2010, Vancouver hosted the Olympic Winter Games, which again turned the world's attention to the region. The Olympics' legacy included a new subway line connecting the airport and downtown, as well as the candelabra-like Olympic Cauldron, which has become a waterfront landmark. The residential buildings along False Creek where athletes lived during the Games formed the basis for a new neighborhood, known as the Olympic Village.

Government and Economy

GOVERNMENT

Canada is divided into 10 provinces and three territories. The country has a three-tiered governmental structure, with federal, provincial (or territorial), and municipal governments.

FEDERAL GOVERNMENT

Headquartered in Ottawa, the nation's capital, the federal government is responsible for foreign policy, defense, immigration, and other national issues. Since the country is a constitutional monarchy with roots in the British Commonwealth, Canada's official head of state is the monarch of the United Kingdom. However, the king or queen's role in Canada is largely symbolic; the prime minister is the country's chief executive.

Parliament, the national legislature, has two bodies: the elected 338-member House of Commons and the appointed 105-member Senate. The major political parties, to which the House of Commons members belong, include the Liberal Party, Conservative Party, New Democratic Party (NDP), Bloc Québécois, and Green Party. Justin Trudeau, who was elected prime minister in 2015, is the leader of the Liberal Party.

By law, federal elections must now be held at least every four years. In practice, the ruling government has the power to call an election at any time. In addition, if the current government loses a confidence vote in the House of Commons, that vote brings down the government and triggers a new election. Canada's shortest Parliament session lasted just 66 days (in 1979) before the government was brought down. The longest-serving government, from 1911 through 1917, held power for 2,152 days.

PROVINCIAL AND LOCAL GOVERNMENTS

The provincial governments handle health care, education, policing, and highways, among other things. The governmental structure at the provincial level parallels that of the federal government. The head of each provincial government is the premier, a position analogous to a U.S. state governor. Each province and territory has its own legislature.

Although Vancouver is British Columbia's largest city, Victoria is the provincial capital. B.C.'s Legislative Assembly meets in the 1897 provincial Parliament Building, overlooking Victoria's Inner Harbour. The 85 provincial representatives are known as MLAs, members of the legislative assembly. In recent years, two parties have dominated provincial politics in B.C.: the Liberals and the NDP.

Local issues, such as zoning, city police and firefighting, snow removal, garbage, and recycling, are the municipal governments' purview. The local governments in Vancouver, Victoria, and other B.C. cities are each led by a mayor, who works with the local city council to determine local policy and regulations.

ECONOMY

Service industries dominate the economies of Vancouver and Victoria. Tourism, including hotels, restaurants, and all sorts of recreation-focused businesses, is a significant pillar of the economy, as are health care, education, financial services, trade (particularly with Pacific Rim countries), and, increasingly, technology. Due to recent changes in liquor laws, numerous craft breweries have opened in both cities.

A construction boom in both Vancouver and Victoria has kept job growth high in this industry. Outside the urban areas, other industries that contribute significantly to B.C.'s economy include agriculture, forestry (about 60 percent of the province's land is forested), mining, oil and gas extraction, and fishing.

Poverty, drug use, and homelessness are very visible issues on the streets of Vancouver (and to a lesser extent, in Victoria). It's common to see people sleeping in parks, hanging out on the sidewalks, or pushing their possessions in a shopping cart across Vancouver, especially in Gastown, Chinatown, and the east side of downtown. The extent of the problem can surprise visitors, particularly because you'll see people living on the streets, even when those streets are lined with cool restaurants and stylish shops.

While the Vancouver city government has been working on programs to reduce homelessness and increase the availability of affordable housing, those programs have not yet been particularly successful, in part because Vancouver continues to be Canada's most expensive housing market. In early 2017, the average purchase price of a single-family detached home was over a million dollars, and buying even a one-bedroom condo would set you back over $500,000.

Rental prices have been rising steadily, too. In 2016, the Canada Mortgage and Housing Corporation reported that the average monthly rent in the city of Vancouver was $1,268 for a one-bedroom apartment and $1,757 for a two-bedroom unit. If you want to live downtown, you'd pay an average of $1,425 for a one-bedroom and $2,167 for a two-bedroom place.

Local Culture

POPULATION

Stretching over a vast landmass, Canada has a population of 36 million (as of 2016). By contrast, the United States, its geographically smaller neighbor to the south, is almost 10 times larger in population, with more than 320 million inhabitants. Nearly three-quarters of all Canadians live within 100 miles (160 kilometers) of the U.S. border.

With 4.7 million residents, British Columbia is Canada's third most populous province, after Ontario (nearly 14 million) and Quebec (8.3 million).

Vancouver is Canada's third largest city, after Toronto and Montreal, and has approximately 2.5 million residents in the metropolitan region. Victoria is the second largest city in B.C., but with 365,000 people, it's significantly smaller than metro Vancouver.

DIVERSITY

Canada's major cities, including Toronto, Montreal, and Vancouver, are among the most multicultural on the planet. Nationwide, more than 20 percent of Canada's population was born outside of the country, but that figure is much higher in urban areas; in Vancouver, 40 percent of residents were born outside Canada. Though the majority of Canadians have their origins in Europe, more than half of the country's recent immigrants have come from Asia, with significant numbers arriving from the Philippines, China, and India. Other major immigrant populations include those coming from the United States, Pakistan, the United Kingdom, Iran, South Korea, Colombia, and Mexico.

In Vancouver, 70 percent of the region's recent immigrants have arrived from Asia, and overall, more than 40 percent of the population is of Asian descent, including a mix of people born in Canada and those born abroad. It's often called the most Asian major city outside of Asia, and you'll find Asian influences in everything from art and fashion to urban design and food.

While Victoria is becoming increasingly diverse, it's still a far more homogenous community than Vancouver. The majority of the city's citizens trace their roots to the United Kingdom and western Europe; 11 percent of Victoria's population is Asian.

INDIGENOUS CULTURES

Canada has three officially recognized aboriginal groups: the First Nations, the Inuit, and the Métis. The Inuit people live primarily in Canada's far north, while the Métis—descendants of French settlers and their First Nations spouses—have historically settled in the prairies and the west. First Nations, the largest indigenous group, is the term for aboriginal people who are neither Inuit nor Métis.

In British Columbia today,

approximately 5 percent of the population is of aboriginal heritage. Two-thirds are First Nations, representing 200 different communities; most of the rest are Métis.

Of these indigenous people, one in four lives in the Lower Mainland in and around Vancouver, where the largest of the 11 First Nations are the Musqueam, Squamish, and Tsleil-Waututh. Many public events in Vancouver now begin with a statement acknowledging that they're taking place on the traditional territory of these native communities.

Across the Strait of Georgia, Vancouver Island is home to 53 different First Nations, including the Esquimalt and Songhees near Victoria, the Saanich First Nations on the peninsula of the same name north of Victoria, and B.C.'s largest First Nation, the Cowichan, whose territory includes the present-day Cowichan Valley outside of Victoria.

FRENCH LANGUAGE AND CULTURE

Ever since European explorers first landed on Canada's shores, both English- and French-speaking colonists settled the country. As a result, Canada has two official languages: English and French. That means that any official federal government communications, from tax forms to airport signs to national park brochures, must be produced in both English and French, and products sold in Canada must contain information on their packaging in both languages.

The province of Quebec is Canada's major francophone region, and there are numerous French-speaking communities in other parts of the country. In British Columbia, although many people can speak some French and kids study the language in school, only about 70,000 people, or 1.5 percent of the population, have French as their mother tongue. In fact, you're more likely to hear Mandarin, Cantonese, Tagalog, or Punjabi on the streets of Vancouver than you are to hear people speaking French.

RELIGION

Christianity is the major religion in Canada. Nearly 40 percent of Canadians are Catholic, and about a quarter are Protestant. Conversely, recent census figures indicate that nearly 25 percent of Canadians claim no religious affiliation at all.

Canada's largest non-Christian religious group is Muslim, representing about 3 percent of the population nationwide. Other major religious groups in Canada include Hindus (1.5 percent of the population), Sikhs (1.4 percent), Buddhists (1.1 percent), and Jews (1 percent).

In British Columbia, these numbers differ somewhat from the nation's population overall. About 45 percent of B.C.'s residents are Christians, and more than 40 percent say that they have no religious affiliation. Five percent are Sikhs, 2 percent Buddhists, just under 2 percent Muslims, 1 percent Hindus, and less than 1 percent Jews.

THE ARTS
LITERATURE

Though she's more often associated with Ontario, where she was born (in 1931) and has lived much of her life, Canadian short-story writer and novelist Alice Munro spent the 1950s and '60s in Vancouver and Victoria. She and her then-husband Jim opened Munro's Books in Victoria in 1963, a classic bookstore that's still operating today. Her many books include *The Lives of Girls and Women* (1971), *Who Do You Think You Are?* (1978), *The View From Castle Rock* (2006), and *Dear Life* (2012). Munro became the first Canadian woman to win the Nobel Prize for Literature, when she received the award in 2013.

Many British Columbia authors have written about the region's Asian communities in both fiction and memoir. In his novel, *The Jade Peony* (1995), Wayson Choy, who was born in Vancouver in 1939, paints a portrait of life in Vancouver's Chinatown in the first half of the 20th century. He continued to explore similar themes in a follow-up work of fiction, *All That Matters,* and in his memoir, *Paper Shadows: A Chinatown Childhood.*

In her novel, *Obasan,* Vancouver-born Joy Kogawa writes about the forced relocation and internment of Japanese Canadians in western Canada during World War II, depicted through the eyes of a young Vancouver girl. It's based on her own experiences; Kogawa and her family were required to leave Vancouver and sent to Slocan, B.C., during the war.

Other contemporary B.C. writers include novelist and artist Douglas Coupland, who popularized the term for an entire generation with his 1991 novel, *Generation X: Tales for an Accelerated Culture*; fiction writer Caroline Adderson, who has set several of her novels, including *The Sky Is Falling* (2010), in and around Vancouver; and CBC radio and podcast host Grant Lawrence, who published the humorous B.C.-based *Adventures in Solitude: What Not to Wear to a Nude Potluck and Other Stories from Desolation Sound* in 2010.

VISUAL ARTS

The visual artist whose work is perhaps most closely associated with British Columbia is the Victoria-born painter Emily Carr (1871-1945), known for her paintings of B.C.'s landscape and its indigenous people. Unusually for a woman of her time, Carr traveled—on her own—to Haida Gwaii and other remote northern communities, where she painted scenes of First Nations' life. You can see Carr's work at the Vancouver Art Gallery (www.vanartgallery.bc.ca) and at Whistler's Audain Art Museum (www.audain-artmuseum.com).

While Carr had no aboriginal heritage herself, another well-known B.C. artist came from mixed European and First Nations ancestry. Bill Reid (1920-1998) created more than 1,500 sculptures, carvings, and other works, most of which explore the traditions of the Haida First Nation, to which his mother belonged. Vancouver's Bill Reid Gallery of Northwest Coast Art (www.billreidgallery.ca) is dedicated to Reid's work; you can also see his massive sculptures in the Vancouver International Airport and at the Museum of Anthropology (http://moa.ubc.ca) on the University of British Columbia campus.

Painter and naturalist Robert Bateman captured scenes of B.C.'s landscapes and wildlife, which you can view at the Robert Bateman Centre (http://batemancentre.org) in Victoria. In the 1950s and '60s, photographer Fred Herzog focused his lens on wildlife of a different sort, taking photos of Vancouver's downtown streets.

The city of Vancouver has a significant public art program that places art around the city. Look for works like *A-maze-ing Laughter,* opposite English Bay in the West End, by Beijing-based contemporary artist Yue Minjun, and *The Birds,* two 18-foot-tall (5.5-meter) sculptures in the Olympic Village, by Vancouver's Myfanwy MacLeod. Find a directory of local public art on the City of Vancouver's website (http://vancouver.ca).

MUSIC

Many musicians and performers with British Columbia connections have gone on to wider acclaim.

Though born in Ontario, rock singer-songwriter Bryan Adams launched his early career in Vancouver. Canadian crooner Michael Bublé was born and raised in the Vancouver suburb of Burnaby and still maintains homes in the area. Tegan and Sara, the powerhouse musical duo (and identical twins), reside at least part time in Vancouver.

Singer-songwriter Sarah McLachlan, who founded the Lilith Fair tours highlighting women musicians, established the Sarah McLachlan School of Music in Vancouver, which provides free music instruction to local at-risk youth.

Singer Nelly Furtado was born in Victoria, and jazz artist Diana Krall, who's married to fellow musician Elvis Costello, also has island roots; she hails from the city of Nanaimo.

FILM AND TV

Vancouver and Toronto vie for the title of Hollywood North, since both cities are popular filming locations for movies and TV series.

Recent movies shot in or around Vancouver include *Deadpool* (2015), starring Vancouver native Ryan Reynolds; *Tomorrowland* (2015), with George Clooney; *50 Shades of Grey*

(2014), based on the popular book of the same name; and *Big Eyes* (2014), directed by Tim Burton and starring Amy Adams.

Although the number of movies being made in Canada rises and falls with the relative strength of the U.S. and Canadian dollars (when the Canadian dollar is weaker compared to the U.S. currency, it's cheaper to make films north of the border), it's not unusual to stumble upon a film set as you wander around Vancouver. To increase your chances of spotting a celebrity when you're in town, check the Creative BC website (www.creativebc.com), which lists movies and TV shows currently filming in British Columbia.

FOOD AND DRINK

What should you eat in Vancouver? As in any major North American city, Vancouver restaurants span the globe, serving meals that take cues from Italy, France, Spain, China, Japan, and more.

Vancouver is known for seafood, particularly salmon, halibut, oysters, and spot prawns, caught in regional waters. The city's restaurants have embraced the eat local movement, so look for seasonal produce and locally raised meats. With a large Asian population, Vancouver has some of the best Chinese food in North America, as well as good Japanese and Korean fare, and many non-Asian restaurants incorporate Pacific Rim influences in their dishes.

British Columbia wines, from the Okanagan Valley or Vancouver Island, are good accompaniments to most Vancouver meals, as are regionally brewed craft beers. Plenty of bartenders have adopted a "drink local" philosophy, too, incorporating locally grown herbs, house-made bitters, and other fresh ingredients into creative cocktails and alcohol-free drinks.

ESSENTIALS

Getting There

hiking on Whistler Mountain

AIR

Vancouver International Airport (YVR, 3211 Grant McConachie Way, Richmond, 604/207-7077, www.yvr.ca) is a major international gateway with flights from across Canada, the United States, Mexico, Europe, Asia, and the Pacific. The airport is south of the city center in the suburb of Richmond. It's 25 minutes from the airport to downtown by public transit, taxi, or by car. All the major car rental companies have offices at the Vancouver airport.

To get to most Vancouver destinations from the airport by taxi, you'll pay a flat rate by zone ($31-37). The Canada Line branch of the SkyTrain subway network stops at the airport. One-way adult fares ($7.75-9) from the airport to downtown vary by time of day. Returning to the airport from downtown costs $2.75-4.

TRAIN

Pacific Central Station (1150 Station St.), near the intersection of Main and Terminal Streets on the edge of Chinatown, is Vancouver's main rail depot. It's also the city's long-distance bus station.

AMTRAK

Amtrak (800/872-7245, www.amtrak.com), the U.S. passenger rail carrier, runs trains to Vancouver from Seattle, Washington, and Portland, Oregon. You can make connections in either Seattle or Portland to U.S. points farther south or east. Trains from Seattle (5.5 hours) operate twice a day; the direct Portland-Vancouver train (8 hours) runs once a day in each direction. These trains have electrical outlets and free Wi-Fi in both standard economy and business classes; the latter seats give you additional legroom.

Tip for cyclists: You can walk your bike onto the Seattle or Portland trains for a fee of US$5.

VIA RAIL

Canada's national passenger rail carrier, VIA Rail (514/989-2626 or 888/842-7245, www.viarail.ca), runs cross-country trains to Vancouver from Toronto. The major stops along the Toronto-Vancouver route of *The Canadian,* VIA Rail's flagship train, are Winnipeg (Manitoba), Saskatoon (Saskatchewan), Edmonton and Jasper (Alberta), and Kamloops (British Columbia).

If you do the 2,775-mile (4,466-kilometer) Toronto-to-Vancouver rail trip nonstop, it's a four-night, three-day journey. *The Canadian* operates three times a week in each direction from May through mid-October, and twice a week from mid-October through April. It's possible to get off en route and continue your journey on a subsequent train. For example, you could take the train from Toronto to Jasper in the Canadian Rockies, get off the train for two or three days, and catch the next train onward to Vancouver.

VIA Rail offers several classes of service on *The Canadian.* In Economy class, the cheapest option, you have a reclining seat and access to a washroom (but no shower). Meals aren't included, although you can buy meals and snacks on the train or outside the train during a few brief stopovers.

A more comfortable alternative is Sleeper Plus class, which offers several choices of accommodations. The least expensive is a berth, which is a seat by day that converts into a bunk, shielded by a heavy curtain, at night; the bunks can be either a lower or upper unit. Berth passengers have access to men's and women's restrooms and private shower rooms in the corridor.

Another Sleeper Plus option is a cabin, which can sleep 1-4 people. Cabins have their own toilets and sinks, and passengers can use the shower rooms in the corridor. Note that in the one-person cabin, the bed folds down over the toilet, so if you need to use the facilities during the night, you have to fold up your bed or use the restroom in the hallway.

The top-end sleeper accommodations are in Prestige Sleeper class, which offers a more modern cabin with a private bathroom and shower. These units have an L-shaped leather couch by day with a Murphy bed for two that folds down at night.

All the Sleeper class fares include three meals a day in the dining car, nonalcoholic drinks, and access to a window-lined viewing car. You can also sit in the bar-snack car, with complimentary coffee, tea, fruit, and cookies.

Outside of the busy summer travel season, VIA Rail frequently offers discounts of up to 50 percent off their standard fares. Check their website or sign up for their newsletter to find out about seat sales. They also offer occasional last-minute travel deals, which are posted on the VIA Rail website (www.viarail.ca).

THE ROCKY MOUNTAINEER

The Rocky Mountaineer (1755 Cottrell St., at Terminal Ave., 604/606-7245 or 877/460-3200, www.rockymountaineer.com, mid-Apr.-mid-Oct.) is a privately run luxury train that offers rail trips between Vancouver, Banff, Lake Louise, Jasper, and Calgary. You can travel round-trip from Vancouver to the Canadian Rockies and back, or you can book a one-way journey through the Rockies from Vancouver to Calgary (or vice versa). Another route starts in Seattle and stops in Vancouver before continuing to the Rockies. Rocky Mountaineer trains travel during the day and stop overnight in Kamloops, where you stay in a hotel, en route to or from the Rockies.

Unlike a standard train trip, many Rocky Mountaineer packages include activities that range from gondola rides to helicopter tours, as well as accommodations along the way. It's also possible to book a Rocky Mountaineer holiday that covers rail fare and accommodations only; for example, they offer two-day train trips between Vancouver and Lake Louise, Banff, or Jasper. Rail packages start at $1,741 per person and depend on the destinations, number of travel days, and the level of service and accommodations.

Rocky Mountaineer trains do not use Vancouver's Pacific Central Station, where VIA Rail and Amtrak trains depart; they have a separate depot nearby.

BUS

Greyhound (800/661-8747, www.greyhound.ca) runs buses to Vancouver's Pacific Central Station (1150 Station St.) from across Canada and from many U.S. cities, including direct service from Seattle.

Between Seattle and Vancouver, other bus services include Bolt Bus (877/265-8287, www.boltbus.com) and Quick Shuttle (604/940-4428 or 800/665-2122, www.quickcoach.com). Bolt Bus arrives and departs from Pacific Central Station and often offers lower fares, while Quick Shuttle stops at Canada Place and will also pick up or drop off passengers at a number of downtown hotels, with advance reservations.

CAR

Coming from the United States, Interstate 5 takes you north from Seattle, Washington, to the U.S.-Canada border. When you pass through border control, you'll be on Highway 99 in British Columbia, which leads to metropolitan Vancouver.

The main east-west route across Canada is Highway 1, the Trans-Canada Highway. It's possible to follow Highway 1 from eastern Canada, Calgary, and the Canadian Rockies all the way to Vancouver; however, it's not the fastest route.

If you're coming from Calgary or Banff to Vancouver, follow Highway 1 west into British Columbia and continue west to the city of Kamloops. From Kamloops, take Highway 5, the Coquihalla Highway, southbound, toward Merritt and Hope. Highway 5 meets Highway 3, which you take westbound to rejoin Highway 1 at the town of Hope and continue west to Vancouver.

From Jasper to Vancouver, the shortest route is to follow Highway 16 west to Highway 5, where you turn south toward Kamloops. At Kamloops, continue south on Highway 5, to Highway 3 west, to Highway 1 west.

Getting Around

You don't need a car to get around downtown Vancouver. The downtown peninsula is easy to navigate on foot, cabs are readily available, and the city has a good public transportation system with its SkyTrain subway and comprehensive bus network. It can be faster to go by car to some places outside downtown, like the University of British Columbia or the North Shore, but these destinations are not difficult to reach by transit.

PUBLIC TRANSPORTATION

TransLink (604/953-3333, www.translink.ca) runs the city's public transportation system. Use the Trip Planner feature on the TransLink website to plot your route.

TRANSIT FARES AND PASSES

Vancouver transit fares (one-zone/two-zone/three-zone adults $2.85/$4.10/$5.60, seniors, students, and ages 5-13 $1.80/$2.80/$3.80) are divided into three zones, based on the distance you travel. Pay a basic one-zone fare if:

- your trip is entirely within the Vancouver city limits.

- you're traveling only by bus. All bus trips are one zone, regardless of distance.

- you're traveling anywhere after 6:30pm on weekdays or all day Saturday, Sunday, and holidays.

If you're taking the SkyTrain between downtown Vancouver and the airport Monday through Friday before 6:30pm, you need to pay a two-zone fare. During those hours, the SeaBus between Vancouver and North Vancouver is also a two-zone trip.

When you board the SkyTrain at the YVR Airport station, you pay a $5 surcharge in addition to the regular transit fare.

If you're going to be riding transit extensively, buy a day pass (adults $10, seniors, students, and ages 5-13 $7.75), which covers one day of unlimited travel on the SkyTrain, buses, and SeaBus across all zones.

How to Buy Tickets and Passes

At SkyTrain or SeaBus stations, buy a ticket or day pass from the vending machine, which accepts cash, credit cards, and debit cards.

On the bus, you can pay your fare in cash; you need exact change. If you've bought a ticket on the SkyTrain or SeaBus within the previous 90 minutes, you can use that same ticket on the bus.

For any mode of travel, you can also buy a Compass Card, an electronic stored-value card, which gives you a discounted fare (one-zone/two-zone/three-zone adults $2.20/$3.25/$4.30). Buy Compass Cards at station vending machines, online (www.compasscard.ca), or at London Drugs stores around the city.

When you purchase a Compass Card, you're charged a $6 card deposit. You can get your deposit back when you no longer need the card, either by returning your card in person to the Compass Customer Service Centre (Stadium-Chinatown Station) or to the West Coast Express Office (Waterfront Station), or by mailing in a refund request. See the TransLink website for mail-in refund instructions.

How to Use a Compass Card

Before boarding the SkyTrain or SeaBus, tap your Compass Card at the fare gates. After your trip, tap your card as you exit the station, so the system can calculate the correct fare and debit it from your card balance. Remember to tap out, or you'll be charged the maximum fare.

When you board a bus, tap your card on the card reader. You don't have to tap out when you get off the bus, since all bus trips are a one-zone fare.

SKYTRAIN

Vancouver's SkyTrain subway has two lines that converge downtown at Waterfront Station and a third line that travels to some of the city's eastern suburbs.

Traveling to or from Waterfront Station, the Canada Line (5am-1am daily) makes several downtown stops. Its two branches can take you between downtown and the airport (take the YVR branch) or other destinations in Richmond (the Richmond-Brighouse branch). If you're heading anywhere downtown or along the Cambie Corridor, you can take any Canada Line train; going south, the two branches diverge at Bridgeport Station.

The Expo Line (5am-1:30am Mon.-Fri., 6am-1:30am Sat., 7am-12:30pm Sun.) travels between downtown and the Vancouver suburbs of Burnaby, New Westminster, and Surrey, east of the city. Going east, the Expo Line splits into two branches, one terminating at King George Station in Surrey, and the other going to Production Way-University Station in Burnaby. Take either branch from downtown to Chinatown, Main Street (near Science World), or Commercial Drive.

The Millennium Line (5:30am-1:30am Mon.-Fri., 6:30am-1:30am Sat., 7:30am-12:30pm Sun.) serves Vancouver's northeastern suburbs, operating between VCC-Clark Station and Lafarge Lake-Douglas Station in Coquitlam. Transfer between the Millennium and Expo Lines at Commercial-Broadway, Production Way-University, and Lougheed Town Centre Stations.

BUS

The main bus routes in downtown Vancouver run along Granville, Burrard, Robson, Georgia, Pender, Hastings, and Davie Streets. Useful routes outside downtown travel along West 4th Avenue, Broadway, Oak, Cambie, and Main Streets, and along Commercial Drive.

At any bus stop, text the posted stop number and the bus route number to 33333 and you'll receive a reply listing the next two buses for that route scheduled to arrive at that stop. Or, from the TransLink website's Next Bus page (http://nb.translink.ca), enter the stop number to see when the next buses are coming to that stop; this service uses GPS tracking data to determine buses' current locations. Signs at every bus stop show the stop number.

Bus schedules vary by route, but regular service begins between 5am and 6pm and runs until 1am or 2am. Vancouver also has 12 Night Bus routes that provide limited service into the wee hours; get schedules on the TransLink website (www.translink.ca).

FERRIES
AQUABUS AND FALSE CREEK FERRIES

Two privately run ferry services shuttle passengers across False Creek between downtown, Granville Island, Science World, and several other points. Schedules vary seasonally, but in summer, service starts around 6:45am-7am and continues until after 10pm. These ferries aren't part of the TransLink system and require separate tickets.

The colorful Aquabus ferries (604/689-5858, www.theaquabus.com; adults $3.50-6, day pass $15, seniors and ages 4-12 $2-4, day pass $13) stop at the foot of Hornby Street, Granville Island, Yaletown's David Lam Park, Stamps Landing, Spyglass Place near the Cambie Bridge, the foot of Davie Street in Yaletown, Plaza of Nations, and Olympic Village. They operate 12-passenger miniferries, as well as 30-passenger boats that accommodate bicycles.

False Creek Ferries (604/684-7781, www.granvilleislandferries.bc.ca; adults $3.50-6, day pass $16, seniors and ages 4-12 $2.25-4, day pass $12) follow a similar route, stopping at the Vancouver Aquatic Centre in the West End, Granville Island, Vanier Park (near the Maritime Museum and Museum of Vancouver), David Lam Park, Stamps Landing, Spyglass Place, the foot of Davie Street, Plaza of Nations, and Olympic Village.

SEABUS

The SeaBus (604/953-3333, www.translink.ca) ferry is the fastest route between downtown's Waterfront Station and North Vancouver's Lonsdale Quay, taking just 12 minutes to cross the Burrard Inlet. TransLink bus and SkyTrain tickets are valid on the SeaBus.

TAXIS

In downtown Vancouver, you can usually hail taxis on the street or find cabs waiting at hotels, restaurants, bars, and transit stations.

You can also phone for a cab or book one online. Local taxi companies include Blacktop & Checker Cabs (604/731-1111, www.btccabs.ca), MacLure's Cabs (604/831-1111, www.maclurescabs.ca), Vancouver Taxi (604/871-1111, www.avancouvertaxi.com), and Yellow Cab (604/681-1111, www.yellowcabonline.com).

Vancouver taxis are metered, with a base fare of $3.20 plus $1.84 per kilometer, except for trips starting at Vancouver International Airport. From the airport, you'll pay a flat rate by zone ($31-37) to most Vancouver destinations. Cabs accept cash and credit cards.

DRIVING
PARKING

Vancouver's on-street parking meters ($1-6 per hour) operate 9am-10pm daily, including holidays. Rates vary by location. You can park at most metered spaces for up to two hours. Pay for parking using coins, credit cards, or the Pay by Phone app (604/909-7275, www.paybyphone.com).

Find locations and rates for the EasyPark city-run parking garages and lots online (www.easypark.ca), or look for their bright orange signs. EasyPark garages are usually less expensive than privately owned parking facilities.

CAR RENTAL

The major car rental companies have offices at Vancouver International Airport, including Alamo (604/231-1400 or 888/826-6893, www.alamo.ca), Avis (604/606-2847 or 800/230-4898, www.avis.ca), Budget (604/668-7000 or 800/268-8900, www.budget.ca), Discount (604/207-8140 or 800/263-2355, www.discountcar.com), Dollar (604/606-1656 or 800/800-6000, www.dollar.com), Enterprise (604/303-1117 or 800/261-7331, www.enterprise.com), Hertz (604/606-3700 or 800/654-3001, www.hertz.ca), National (604/273-6572 or 888/826-6890, www.nationalcar.ca), and Thrifty (604/207-7077 or 800/847-4389, www.thrifty.com). Most also have downtown locations.

Visas and Officialdom

For the most up-to-date requirements for visitors coming to Canada, visit Citizenship and Immigration Canada (www.cic.gc.ca).

Important note: If you have a criminal record, including misdemeanors or driving while impaired (DWI), no matter how long ago, you can be prohibited from entering Canada, unless you obtain a special waiver well in advance of your trip. Refer to the Citizenship and Immigration Canada website for additional information.

PASSPORTS AND VISAS
U.S. CITIZENS

The simple answer to the question of what documents U.S. citizens need to visit Canada is "a valid passport." If you are driving over the border, you can use a NEXUS card, issued as part of the U.S. government's Trusted Travel Program, as your entry document. See the U.S. Customs and Border Protection website (www.cbp.gov) for NEXUS details.

If you're driving, a valid U.S. Passport Card can also be used instead of a passport. Get more information about U.S. Passport Cards, which cannot be used for air travel, from the U.S. State Department (www.travel.state.gov).

Several U.S. states and Canadian provinces issue Enhanced Drivers Licenses that can be used as an alternative to a passport or passport card when you're crossing a land border; they're not valid for air travel. The U.S. Customs and Border Protection website (www.cbp.gov) has details about Enhanced Drivers Licenses.

Citizens of the United States do not need a visa to visit Canada for stays of less than six months.

CITIZENS OF OTHER COUNTRIES

All other foreign visitors to Canada must have a valid passport, and depending on your nationality, you may also need either a visitor visa or an Electronic Travel Authorization (eTA). Check with Citizenship and Immigration Canada (www.cic.gc.ca) to confirm what documents you require.

British, Australian, and New

Zealand citizens don't require a visa, nor do citizens of many European nations. However, in 2016, Canada introduced the Electronic Travel Authorization (eTA), which is required for visa-exempt visitors who are traveling to Canada by air. For example, a British citizen who is driving into Canada from the U.S. would not require a visa or an eTA but would need the eTA to fly into Canada. If you need an eTA, apply for this document online on the Citizenship and Immigration Canada website (www.cic.gc.ca).

EMBASSIES AND CONSULATES

American citizens in Vancouver, Victoria, or other parts of western Canada can get assistance from the U.S. Consulate General-Vancouver (1075 W. Pender St., Vancouver, 604/685-4311, www.vancouver.us-consulate.gov).

British nationals needing consular assistance can contact the British Consulate General-Vancouver (1111 Melville St., Ste. 800, Vancouver, 604/683-4421, www.gov.uk).

The Australian Consulate and Trade Commission, Vancouver (1075 W. Georgia St., Ste. 2050, Vancouver, 604/694-6160, www.canada.embassy.gov.au) provides consular assistance to Australian citizens in western Canada, while the New Zealand Consulate General, Vancouver (1050 W. Pender St., Ste. 2250, Vancouver, 604/684-7388, www.nzembassy.com/canada) can assist citizens of New Zealand.

CUSTOMS

Visitors to Canada can bring a reasonable amount of personal baggage, including clothing, camping and sports equipment, cameras, and computers for personal use.

Travelers must declare all food, plants, or animals they bring into Canada. In general, you're allowed to bring food for personal use, although there are restrictions on fresh fruits, vegetables, meats, and dairy products. Get the latest information from the Canadian Food Inspection Agency (www.inspection.gc.ca).

As long as you're of legal drinking age (19 in B.C.), you can bring a small amount of alcohol into Canada duty-and tax-free. You're allowed to bring *one* of the following: two bottles of wine (up to 53 fluid ounces or 1.5 liters), one standard bottle of other alcohol (40 ounces or 1.14 liters), or 24 cans or bottles of beer or ale (up to a total of 287 ounces or 8.5 liters). Visitors are also allowed to bring in up to 200 cigarettes or 50 cigars.

In general, visitors cannot bring weapons into Canada. Check the detailed requirements with the Canada Border Services Agency (www.cbsa.gc.ca).

Note that when you're flying to Canada from the United States or other international destinations, you clear immigration and customs at the Canadian airport after you land in Canada. However, if you're flying to the United States from Vancouver, Calgary, or other major Canadian cities, you clear U.S. immigration and customs at the Canadian airport *before* you board your flight. For example, if you were traveling from Vancouver to Los Angeles, you would clear U.S. immigration and customs at the Vancouver airport. Allow extra time for these immigration and customs procedures, in addition to the time it takes for standard airport passenger screening.

WORKING IN VANCOUVER

To work in Vancouver, Victoria, Whistler, or elsewhere in Canada, you must apply for and receive a work permit *before* you enter the country. The government agency responsible for work permits is Citizenship and Immigration Canada (www.cic.gc.ca). In general, you must have a job offer from a Canadian company in order to apply for a work permit.

However, if you're between the ages of 18 and 30-35, you might qualify for the International Experience Canada program, which enables young people to come to Canada on a working holiday (combining short-term work and travel), for an internship, or to work temporarily to gain international experience in your chosen profession. The options vary, depending on what country you're from, but the International Experience Canada program is available to citizens of 32 countries, including the UK, Australia, New Zealand, many European nations, Mexico, Chile, Hong Kong, Japan, South Korea, and Taiwan. Use the planning tool on the Citizenship and Immigration Canada website to determine if you're eligible for the program and what options you might have.

The International Experience Canada program is not available to U.S. citizens. However, you may be able to work with an organization that helps arrange short-term work programs in Canada. Read more about applying through one of these "Recognized Organizations" on the Citizenship and Immigration Canada website.

STUDYING IN VANCOUVER

To go to school in Canada, you must apply for and receive a study permit *before* you enter the country. Citizenship and Immigration Canada (www.cic.gc.ca) is the government agency responsible for study permits.

Vancouver is a popular destination for people who want to study English. The city has numerous language schools catering to foreign students. Languages Canada (www.languagescanada.ca) has more information about language study in Vancouver and elsewhere in Canada.

Health and Safety

Vancouver and Victoria are generally safe destinations, with no significant health issues for visitors. Travelers should use caution and be aware of their surroundings, especially at night. In Vancouver, avoid walking or running alone through the interior of Stanley Park or Pacific Spirit Regional Park, as many trails are quite remote; however, the Seawall path around Stanley Park is well traveled from dawn to dusk.

EMERGENCY AND MEDICAL SERVICES

Call 911 for assistance in an emergency.

In British Columbia, to speak with a nurse for medical information 24 hours a day, call 811 to reach the HealthLink BC service (www.healthlinkbc.ca). You can also phone HealthLink BC at 604/215-8110.

HOSPITALS

Vancouver General Hospital (920 W. 10th Ave., 604/875-4111, www.vch.ca) has a 24-hour emergency room, which will assist patients ages 17 and older. If children under 17 need emergency medical attention, take them to B.C. Children's Hospital (4480 Oak St., 604/875-2345 or 888/300-3088, www.bcchildrens.ca).

Downtown, you can get 24-hour emergency care at St. Paul's Hospital (1081 Burrard St., 604/682-2344, www.providencehealthcare.org). On the University of British Columbia campus, the UBC Urgent Care Clinic (UBC Hospital, Koerner Pavilion, 2211 Wesbrook Mall, 604/822-7121, www.vch.ca, 8am-10pm daily) is a good choice for X-rays and nonemergency medical issues.

Check the website Emergency Wait Times (www.edwaittimes.ca) for the estimated waiting time at local emergency rooms.

PHARMACIES

Several locations of Shoppers Drug Mart (www.shoppersdrugmart.ca) have 24-hour pharmacies, including branches in the West End (1125 Davie St., 604/669-2424), on Broadway near Vancouver General Hospital (885 W. Broadway, 604/708-1135), and in Kitsilano (2302 W. 4th Ave., 604/738-3138). Other centrally located branches have extended hours, including Robson and Burrard downtown (748 Burrard St., 778/330-4711, 8am-midnight daily) and Yaletown (1006 Homer St., 604/669-0330, 8am-midnight Mon.-Sat., 9am-midnight Sun.).

London Drugs (www.londondrugs.com), another Canadian pharmacy chain, has several downtown locations that are open late, including 710 Granville Street (604/448-4802, 8am-10pm Mon.-Fri., 9am-10pm Sat., 10am-8pm Sun.) and 1187 Robson Street (604/448-4819, 9am-10pm Mon.-Sat., 10am-10pm Sun.).

HEALTH INSURANCE

If you become ill or injured while traveling in British Columbia, go to the nearest hospital emergency room or walk-in health clinic.

If you're a resident of another Canadian province, your provincial health plan may not provide health

301

coverage while you're out of your home province. If the plan does provide coverage, it may pay only the amount it would pay for the service in your home province, not what you might be billed in British Columbia. Either way, before your trip, it's a good idea to purchase supplemental travel health insurance to cover any unexpected medical costs while you're on the road.

If you live outside Canada, make sure that you have health insurance that will cover you and your family in Canada. You normally have to pay for medical services provided in Canada and then file a claim with your health insurance provider after you return home.

CRIME

Compared to many cities around the world, Vancouver is relatively safe. The most prevalent crimes are property crimes. Bicycle thefts are a particular problem, and car break-ins happen more frequently than anyone would like. Don't leave valuables in your car, and always lock your bike.

Vancouver has a significant homeless population, many of whom congregate on the streets of Gastown and Chinatown, particularly along sections of Hastings Street, near Main Street. While that isn't a reason to avoid the area, use caution as you would in any urban neighborhood. Hop on the bus or take a cab if you're in this part of the city late at night.

Travel Tips

WHAT TO PACK

In casual Vancouver, decent slacks and a blouse or collared shirt would be appropriate attire almost anywhere. You can dress up a bit when you're eating out, and many people bring out their finery if they're attending the opera, the symphony, or a dance club.

Bring comfortable walking or hiking shoes, and clothes for the outdoors. In summer, bring a jacket or sweater for the cool evenings; even during the day, temperatures rarely rise much above 75°F (24°C).

If you're visiting between October and May, pack rain gear; a good rain jacket and an umbrella will protect you from the inevitable drizzle and frequent downpours. Temperatures typically don't drop below freezing in the city, but it can be cool enough that

you'd want a hat and gloves between November and March.

ACCESS FOR TRAVELERS WITH DISABILITIES

Many of western Canada's attractions, hotels, restaurants, entertainment venues, and transportation options are accessible to travelers with disabilities. A useful general resource about accessible travel to and around Canada is the government's Access to Travel website (www.accesstotravel.gc.ca). It includes details about transportation between and around B.C. cities and towns, as well as general tips and travel advice.

Most national and provincial parks offer accessible facilities. Many picnic areas, campsites, and park washrooms, as well as some trails, can accommodate wheelchairs and other mobility aids. Get details on facilities in specific parks from Parks Canada (www.pc.gc.ca) or B.C. Parks (www.env.gov.bc.ca).

TRAVELING WITH CHILDREN

Western Canada is an extremely family-friendly destination. Not only are there tons of fun things for families to do, but plenty of resources also help support traveling families or make travel more affordable.

Many museums, attractions, and recreational facilities offer free admission for kids under a certain age (often 5 or 6, but sometimes 11 or 12). Many offer discounted family admission rates, which generally include two adults and at least two children. Ask about family discounts when you're buying tickets.

Kids stay free at many major hotels. Other good lodging options for traveling families, besides the typical chain motels, include suite hotels (in cities) and cabins or cottages (in more rural areas), which often provide more space for the money, as well as kitchen facilities where you can prepare your own food. Some bed-and-breakfasts don't accept kids, so always ask.

Many restaurants in Canada offer children's menus with a few kid-approved food selections. Encourage your kids to try new things, though, since they may surprise you with their newfound love for bison burgers, handmade noodles, or sushi.

When you're visiting a national park or national historic site with kids, ask for a free Parks Canada Xplorer booklet, which has child-friendly activities to help them explore that destination. At most parks, Parks Canada staff offer interpretive programs, from wildlife talks to guided hikes, that are designed for kids or suitable for families; ask at the park visitors center or check the Parks Canada website (www.pc.gc.ca) for details and schedules.

Note that if only one parent is traveling with his or her children, the Canadian government recommends that the parent carry a written letter of permission from the other parent. Divorced parents who share custody should also travel with a copy of their legal custody documents. If you are traveling with a child who isn't your own (or for whom you're not the legal guardian), you should carry written permission from the parents or guardians indicating that you're allowed to travel with the child. You may be asked to present these letters at the border when you enter Canada. For a sample letter of consent, see the Travel and Tourism section of the Government of Canada's website (www.travel.gc.ca).

SENIOR TRAVELERS

The good thing about getting older is that you can often get discounts. Many B.C. attractions, lodgings, and transportation providers offer discounts for seniors. Normally, you need to be 65 to qualify for a senior discount, although occasionally these discounts are extended to travelers at age 60 or 62.

Parks Canada offers discounts at the country's national parks and national historic sites, with reduced rates for single-day admissions and annual passes.

GAY AND LESBIAN TRAVELERS

Canada is far more welcoming to gay and lesbian travelers than many other destinations. Marriage equality is the law in Canada.

Vancouver has a large LGBTQ community. The hub of the community is along Davie Street in the city's West End, with another popular area along Commercial Drive in East Vancouver, although accommodations, restaurants, and other facilities across the city (and indeed across B.C.) welcome gay and lesbian travelers. Tourism Vancouver (www.tourismvancouver.com) publishes a quarterly LGBTQ newsletter, *Out in Vancouver*. Gayvan Travel Marketing (www.gayvan.com) can tell you more about the local community, events, and resources.

Other resources for gay and lesbian travel to Canada include Travel Gay Canada (www.travelgaycanada.com), the country's gay and lesbian tourism association, and TAG Approved (www.tagapproved.com), which highlights gay-friendly hotels and attractions.

MONEY

Canada's currency is the dollar, and like its U.S. counterpart, it's divided into 100 cents. Canadian bills include $5, $10, $20, $50, and $100 denominations. Coins include five, 10, and 25 cents, and one and two dollars. The gold-colored one-dollar coin is called the "loonie," for the picture of the loon on its back side. The two-dollar coin is nicknamed the "toonie" (since it's equal to two loonies). Throughout this book, prices are listed in Canadian dollars (unless otherwise specified).

Major credit cards, including Visa, MasterCard, and American Express, are accepted throughout British Columbia, although some smaller establishments may take payment in cash only. You'll find automated teller machines (ATMs)—which Canadian banks call automated banking machines, or ABMs—in almost every town. Debit cards are also widely accepted through the region.

Bank of Canada (www.bankofcanada.ca), the Canadian central bank, publishes the official exchange rate between Canadian dollars and other currencies. You can exchange U.S. dollars, euros, British pounds, Australian dollars, and other major currencies for Canadian dollars at banks across B.C. or at currency exchange dealers in Vancouver, Victoria, and Whistler. Some B.C. businesses will accept U.S. dollars, although the exchange rate is usually worse than the official rate, and you'll get change back in Canadian funds. You're nearly always better off paying in Canadian currency or using a credit card.

TAXES

Purchases in Canada are subject both to a Federal Goods and Services Tax (G.S.T.) and, in most provinces, to an additional provincial sales tax (P.S.T.). The G.S.T. is currently 5 percent, and in British Columbia, the P.S.T. will add 7 percent to your purchases. Not every item you buy is subject to both types of sales tax; basic groceries and prepared food, books, newspapers, magazines, and children's clothing are all exempt from B.C.'s sales tax.

However, on accommodations, you'll pay an 8 percent P.S.T., plus an additional municipal and regional district tax of up to 3 percent. British Columbia charges a 10 percent tax on liquor.

WEIGHTS AND MEASURES

Canada officially uses the metric system. Distances and speed limits are marked in kilometers, gasoline and bottled beverages are sold by the liter, and weights are given in grams or kilograms.

Electrical service in Canada is 120 volts, the same as in the United States, with the same types of plugs.

British Columbia has two time zones. Most of the province, including Vancouver, Victoria, and Whistler, is in the Pacific time zone. The easternmost part of the province, on the Alberta border, is in the mountain time zone; Cranbrook, Golden, and Invermere are among the B.C. communities that follow mountain time.

British Columbia observes daylight savings time. Clocks move forward one hour on the second Sunday in March and turn back one hour on the first Sunday of November.

TOURIST INFORMATION

Near Canada Place, the Tourism Vancouver Visitor Centre (200 Burrard St., plaza level, 604/683-2000, www.tourismvancouver.com, 9am-5pm daily) provides helpful information about the city. Inside the visitors center, Tickets Tonight (604/684-2787, www.ticketstonight.ca, 9am-5pm daily) sells half-price same-day theater and event tickets.

Tourism Vancouver's Inside Vancouver blog (www.insidevancouver.ca) details goings-on around town and provides event listings. Destination BC (www.hellobc.com), the provincial tourism agency, has a useful website with information about

Vancouver and destinations across the province. The City of Vancouver website (http://vancouver.ca) provides details about city-run parks, theaters, and transportation. TransLink (www.translink.ca), the city's public transit system, has an online trip-planning function that can help you get around town.

COMMUNICATIONS AND MEDIA

The city's local daily newspapers include the Vancouver Sun (www.vancouversun.com) and Vancouver Province (www.theprovince.com). The daily Toronto-based Globe and Mail (www.theglobeandmail.com) covers news across Canada, including Vancouver, as does the CBC (www.cbc.ca), Canada's public television and radio outlet.

The Georgia Straight (www.straight.com) provides arts and entertainment listings, restaurant reviews, and area news. Other community news outlets include the Vancouver Courier (www.vancourier.com) and the WestEnder (www.westender.com). Vancouver Magazine (http://vanmag.com), a glossy monthly also available online, covers city news, restaurants, and events.

The online Scout Magazine (http://scoutmagazine.ca) features Vancouver restaurant and food stories. Miss 604 (www.miss604.com) and Vancouver Is Awesome (http://vancouverisawesome.com) are established local blogs.

Recreation

NATIONAL, PROVINCIAL, AND REGIONAL PARKS

NATIONAL PARKS

Throughout 2017, in honor of Canada's 150th anniversary, admission to all of the country's national parks is free.

Parks Canada (888/773-8888, www.pc.gc.ca) is the agency responsible for the country's national parks. You can purchase an annual Parks Canada Discovery Pass (adults $67.70, seniors $57.90, kids 6-16 $33.30, family/group $136.40), valid at more than 100 national parks, national marine conservation areas, and national historic sites across the country. The family/group pass is good for up to seven people arriving together at a particular site. If you're going to visit several parks and historic sites during your travels, a Discovery Pass can be a good value.

If you purchase your Discovery Pass at the beginning of a month, your pass will be valid for 13 months, rather than 12, since the pass expires on the last day of the month in which you bought it.

You can buy a Discovery Pass online or by phone from Parks Canada or in person at any national park or historic site. If you've already bought a day pass to a park or historic site within the past 30 days, you can credit the price of that ticket toward a Discovery Pass.

PROVINCIAL PARKS

British Columbia has more than 1,000 provincially managed parks and protected areas, run by B.C. Parks (www.env.gov.bc.ca). The B.C. Parks system is the second largest group of parks in Canada; only the country's national park system protects a larger area. The first provincial park in British Columbia, Strathcona Park on Vancouver Island, opened in 1911.

Among the most visited parks near Vancouver are Cypress Provincial Park (www.cypressmountain.com) on the North Shore, Shannon Falls Provincial Park (www.env.gov.bc.ca) and Stawamus Chief Provincial Park (http://seatoskyparks.com) in Squamish, and Garibaldi Provincial Park (www.env.gov.bc.ca), which extends from Squamish north to Whistler and beyond.

While there are fees to camp in B.C.'s provincial parks, day use at most B.C. parks is free.

REGIONAL AND URBAN PARKS

At the end of Vancouver's downtown peninsula, Stanley Park is the city's marquee park, with 1,000 acres (400 hectares) of rainforest, beaches, and walking trails. Near the University of British Columbia campus on Vancouver's West Side, Pacific Spirit Regional Park is even larger. This rainforest park measures more than 1,800 acres (760 hectares), with 40 miles (70 kilometers) of hiking paths. On the North Shore, West Vancouver's Lighthouse Park (www.lighthousepark.ca) rewards visitors with beautiful waterfront views.

HIKING

British Columbia has plenty of opportunities to hit the trail, whether you're looking to tromp around in the woods for an afternoon or set off on a multi-day hiking adventure. In Vancouver, you can hike in Stanley Park or Pacific Spirit Regional Park.

Just outside the city, there are numerous hiking routes on the North Shore, from the iconic Grouse Grind (www.grousemountain.com) to the trails in Cypress Provincial Park (www.cypressmountain.com). North Vancouver's Lynn Canyon Park (www.lynncanyon.ca) has a suspension bridge that's free to cross, as well as several easy-to-moderate hiking paths.

Within an hour's drive of Vancouver, the Squamish area is a popular hiking destination. Among the area's best hikes is the climb up "The Chief," the imposing rock cliff in Stawamus Chief Provincial Park (http://seatoskyparks.com). Hikers also gravitate to the 750-square-mile (1,942-square-kilometer) Garibaldi Provincial Park (www.env.gov.bc.ca) for its more than 55 miles (90 kilometers) of hiking trails.

Whistler has several hiking trails in or near the village, including the 25-mile (40-kilometer) Valley Trail (www.whistler.ca) that's open to both walkers and cyclists. Up on the mountain, Whistler-Blackcomb (www.whistlerblackcomb.com) has numerous hiking trails of all levels that you can access from the lifts or gondolas.

BIKING

Mountain bikers head for the North Shore, particularly the trails near the three local ski hills, Grouse (www.grousemountain.com), Cypress (www.cypressmountain.com), and Mount Seymour (www.mountseymour.com). Whistler-Blackcomb (www.whistlerblackcomb.com) is a mecca for mountain bikers, with more than 70 trails open from mid-May through mid-October.

In bike-friendly Victoria, you can cycle around the city or pedal a longer rail trail. The 35-mile (55-kilometer) Galloping Goose Trail runs along a former rail line from Victoria west to the town of Sooke, and the 18-mile (29-kilometer) Lochside Regional Trail connects Victoria and Swartz Bay, where the ferries from Vancouver dock.

WATER SPORTS

You can go swimming at Vancouver's many oceanfront beaches, including English Bay and Sunset Beaches in the West End, Second and Third Beaches in Stanley Park, and Kitsilano, Jericho, Locarno, and Spanish Banks Beaches on the West Side. Even in summer, though, the water temperature is rarely above 21°C (70°F).

Vancouver's several large public pools, particularly Kitsilano Pool and Stanley Park's Second Beach Pool, are warmer alternatives. You can swim indoors at the Vancouver Aquatic Centre (1050 Beach Ave.) in the West End.

You don't have to leave downtown Vancouver to go kayaking or stand-up paddleboarding either. Ecomarine Paddlesports Centre (www.ecomarine.com) rents kayaks and stand-up paddleboards at English Bay Beach and Granville Island, and they have kayaks for rent at Jericho Beach as well. You can also rent kayaks and stand-up paddleboards from Creekside Kayaks (www.creeksidekayaks.ca) on False Creek and from Vancouver Water Adventures (www.vancouverwateradventures.com), which has outlets at Granville Island and Kitsilano Beach.

Another destination for kayaking is Deep Cove (www.deepcovekayak.com) on Vancouver's North Shore, where you can paddle for an hour or two (or many more) through the scenic waters of the Indian Arm fjord.

For white-water rafting, head for Squamish, north of Vancouver, where several outfitters offer trips on the gentle Cheakamus River and the faster Elaho-Squamish River.

Western Canada's top surfing spot is Tofino, on Vancouver Island's west coast. Hard-core surfers suit up and hit the waves in the winter, when the surf is largest. Summer brings gentler waves and somewhat warmer temperatures.

WINTER SPORTS

In winter, you can ice-skate at a public rink in Robson Square downtown (www.robsonsquare.com) or at the Richmond Olympic Oval (http://richmondoval.ca). Grouse Mountain (www.grousemountain.com) also has a mountaintop skating rink.

On Vancouver's North Shore, less than 45 minutes from downtown, three local mountains, Grouse (www.grousemountain.com), Cypress (www.cypressmountain.com), and Mount Seymour (www.mountseymour.com), offer downhill skiing and snowboarding. The ski season on the North Shore typically runs from December through March. You can go snowshoeing at all three mountains, and Cypress offers cross-country skiing, too.

North America's largest snow sports resort is just a two-hour drive from downtown Vancouver. Whistler-Blackcomb (www.whistlerblackcomb.com) has more than 200 trails for skiing and snowboarding. The mountain usually opens in November and remains open until April. Weather permitting, you can even go glacier skiing on Blackcomb Mountain in the summer.

WHALE-WATCHING

Whale-watching trips depart regularly from downtown Vancouver, from the village of Steveston in Richmond south of Vancouver, and from the Inner Harbour in Victoria. These trips typically take you either among the Gulf Islands or south to Washington's San Juan Islands, depending on where whales have been spotted. Whale-watching season runs April through October.

On Vancouver Island's west coast, the Tofino area is another prime spot for whale-watching trips. A number of operators run whale-watching cruises from Tofino harbor from March or April through October or November.

GENERAL INFORMATION

Citizenship and Immigration Canada. *Welcome to Canada: What You Should Know.* Ottawa: Government Services Canada, 2013. http://www.cic.gc.ca/english/resources/publications/welcome/index.asp. A government publication that provides a useful overview of the Canadian immigration process and of life in Canada.

Ferguson, Will. *Canadian History for Dummies.* Toronto: John Wiley & Sons (Canada), 2005. The essentials of Canadian history distilled into an easy-to-read guide.

HISTORY AND CULTURE

Adderson, Caroline. *Vancouver Vanishes: Narratives of Demolition and Revival.* Vancouver: Anvil Press: 2015. A collection of essays and photographs chronicling how Vancouver is changing, as an increasing number of homes built in the 1920s, '30s, and '40s are torn down to make way for newer structures.

Coupland, Douglas. *Souvenir of Canada.* Vancouver: Douglas & McIntyre, 2002. A Vancouver-based artist and author dissects Canadian culture in a series of quirky essays and photos.

Davis, Chuck. *The Chuck Davis History of Metropolitan Vancouver.* Vancouver: Harbour Publishing, 2011. Running nearly 600 pages, this timeline of the city's history from the 1750s to modern times is packed with facts and local trivia.

Herzog, Fred. *Fred Herzog: Photographs.* Vancouver: Douglas & McIntyre, 2011. Vivid color photos of life on Vancouver's streets, primarily in the 1950s and '60s, by a noted local photographer.

Johnson, Pauline. *Legends of Vancouver.* Vancouver: Douglas & McIntyre, 1971. Born to a Mohawk father and English mother, Johnson published this title in 1911. She shares Coast Salish narratives about the Vancouver region that she learned from conversations with a Squamish First Nations chief, Joseph Capilano. Johnson's ashes are buried in Vancouver's Stanley Park.

FOOD

Dhalwala, Meeru and Vikram Vij. *Vij's: Elegant and Inspired Indian Cuisine.* Vancouver: Douglas & McIntyre, 2006. Recipes from Vancouver's most famous Indian restaurant.

Mundy, Jane. *The Ocean Wise Cookbook 2: More Seafood Recipes that are Good for the Planet*. Vancouver: Whitecap Books Ltd., 2015. In partnership with the Vancouver Aquarium, a Vancouver-based food and travel writer has compiled more than 100 recipes for sustainable seafood from leading Canadian chefs.

Yuen, Stephanie. *East Meets West: Traditional and Contemporary Asian Dishes from Acclaimed Vancouver Restaurants*. Vancouver: Douglas & McIntyre, 2012. A look at Vancouver's Asian cuisine through recipes adapted from local chefs.

FICTION

Adderson, Caroline. *The Sky Is Falling*. Toronto: Thomas Allen Publishers, 2010. Following a group of student idealists who share a Vancouver house, this novel is set in both 1984 and 2004, when the end of the world seemed close at hand.

Choy, Wayson. *The Jade Peony*. Vancouver: Douglas & McIntyre, 1995. A portrait of life in Vancouver's Chinatown in the early 20th century.

Kogawa, Joy. *Obasan*. Toronto: Penguin Canada, 2003 (first published 1981). The internment and forced relocation of Japanese-Canadians in Western Canada during World War II, depicted through the eyes of a young girl living in Vancouver.

Lee, Jen Sookfong. *The Better Mother*. Toronto: Alfred A. Knopf, 2001. A local author weaves a tale of a young Chinese boy and a burlesque dancer who cross paths in Vancouver's Chinatown.

Taylor, Timothy. *Stanley Park*. Toronto: Vintage Canada, 2001. Locavore chefs, coffee magnates, and the homeless cross paths in this thriller set in and around Vancouver's largest green space.

Internet Resources

CANADA

Destination Canada
www.canada.travel
The government of Canada's official guide to travel across the country.

Parks Canada
www.pc.gc.ca
The federal government agency that manages national parks and national historic sites across Canada. The Parks Canada website has details about things to do, camping, hiking, and other activities in the parks in the West and throughout the country.

Parks Canada Reservation Service
www.reservation.pc.gc.ca
Reservations booking service for Canada's national park campgrounds.

Citizenship and Immigration Canada
www.cic.gc.ca
The federal government agency responsible for overseeing visitors and immigrants to Canada, including information about visitor visas, work permits, study permits, and applications for permanent residence.

Canada Border Services Agency
www.cbsa-asfc.gc.ca

The federal government agency that manages Canada's borders, including what items visitors can bring into Canada. Their website also shows wait times at highway border crossings.

Environment Canada
www.weather.gc.ca

Provides weather forecasts and historical weather data for locations across Canada.

BRITISH COLUMBIA
Destination British Columbia
www.hellobc.com

British Columbia's provincial tourism agency, which provides travel tips and information for the region and operates a network of visitors centers.

B.C. Parks
www.env.gov.bc.ca

The agency responsible for managing British Columbia's provincial parks. Their website includes listings for each park, with maps, fees, and other details.

British Columbia Wine Institute
www.winebc.com

Has a detailed website with information about wineries and wine-touring tips in the Okanagan, Vancouver Island, and elsewhere in British Columbia.

Tourism Vancouver
www.tourismvancouver.com

Vancouver's tourism agency provides event schedules, tips for getting around, neighborhood profiles, and other information about the city's sights, hotels, restaurants, shops, and experiences.

Tourism Vancouver Island
www.vancouverisland.travel

Their free guide to things to do across Vancouver Island is available online and in print from area visitors centers.

Tourism Victoria
www.tourismvictoria.com

Promoting tourism in the city of Victoria, this organization runs a year-round information center on Victoria's Inner Harbour and provides information about attractions and activities, events, accommodations, and restaurants.

Tourism Whistler
www.whistler.com

Representing the Whistler region, this tourism agency has information to help you plan a mountain trip in any season.

Index

Restaurants Index

Nightlife Index

Shops Index

Hotels Index

Photo Credits

Acknowledgments

I'd like to thank a number of individuals and organizations for assistance and support while I was researching and writing *Moon Vancouver*.

I'm grateful for the assistance and advice I received from Destination BC, Tourism Vancouver, and the Tourism Whistler team. On Vancouver Island, many thanks to Holly Lenk and Katie Dabbs, Tourism Victoria; Chelsea Barr, Tourism Nanaimo; Samantha Fyleris, Tourism Tofino; Ronette Nyhan, Magnolia Hotel and Spa; and Heather McEachen, Tourism Vancouver Island.

More thank-yous to Paula Amos at the Aboriginal Tourism Association of BC; Kate Rogers and Brian Cant at the Tartan Group; Morgan Sommerville and Laura Serena of Serena PR; Marisa Cuglietta and the staff at Hawksworth Communications; Samantha Geer, Tiffany Soper, and the Avenue PR crew; Wendy Underwood, Fever Pitch Communications; and Nancie Hall, Fairmont Hotels. Thanks, too, to all my Travel Media Association of Canada colleagues for the helpful ideas and contacts.

My appreciation to the great people at Avalon Travel, especially Senior Editor Leah Gordon, map wizard Kat Bennett, Publishing Technologies Manager Darren Alessi, Editorial Director Kevin McLain, and former Acquisitions Editor Elizabeth Hansen.

And as always, many thanks to my team at home: to Michaela for snorkeling with the seals, testing deep-fried Nanaimo bars, and coaxing me onto the Via Ferrata; to Talia for the dim sum, bubble tea, and night market excursions; and to Alan, for launching our magnificent Vancouver adventure.

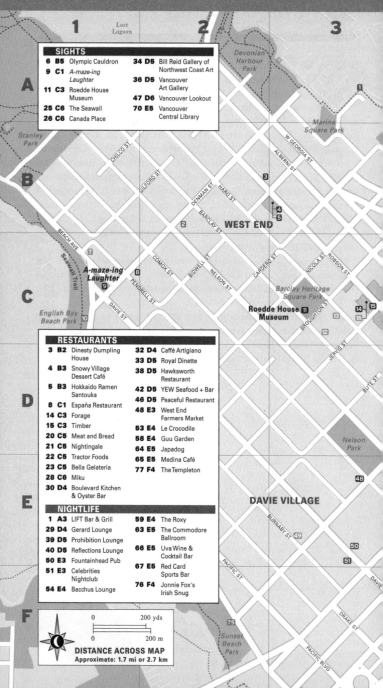

SIGHTS

6	**B5**	Olympic Cauldron	34	**D5**	Bill Reid Gallery of Northwest Coast Art
9	**C1**	A-maze-ing Laughter	36	**D5**	Vancouver Art Gallery
11	**C3**	Roedde House Museum	47	**D6**	Vancouver Lookout
25	**C6**	The Seawall	70	**E5**	Vancouver Central Library
26	**C6**	Canada Place			

RESTAURANTS

3	**B2**	Dinesty Dumpling House	32	**D4**	Caffè Artigiano
4	**B3**	Snowy Village Dessert Café	33	**D5**	Royal Dinette
5	**B3**	Hokkaido Ramen Santouka	38	**D5**	Hawksworth Restaurant
8	**C1**	España Restaurant	42	**D5**	YEW Seafood + Bar
14	**C3**	Forage	46	**D5**	Peaceful Restaurant
15	**C3**	Timber	48	**E3**	West End Farmers Market
20	**C5**	Meat and Bread	53	**E4**	Le Crocodile
21	**C5**	Nightingale	58	**E4**	Guu Garden
22	**C5**	Tractor Foods	64	**E5**	Japadog
23	**C5**	Bella Gelateria	65	**E5**	Medina Café
28	**C6**	Miku	77	**F4**	The Templeton
30	**D4**	Boulevard Kitchen & Oyster Bar			

NIGHTLIFE

1	**A3**	LIFT Bar & Grill	59	**E4**	The Roxy
29	**D4**	Gerard Lounge	63	**E5**	The Commodore Ballroom
39	**D5**	Prohibition Lounge	66	**E5**	Uva Wine & Cocktail Bar
40	**D5**	Reflections Lounge	67	**E5**	Red Card Sports Bar
50	**E3**	Fountainhead Pub	76	**F4**	Jonnie Fox's Irish Snug
51	**E3**	Celebrities Nightclub			
54	**E4**	Bacchus Lounge			

DISTANCE ACROSS MAP
Approximate: 1.7 mi or 2.7 km

0   200 yds
0   200 m

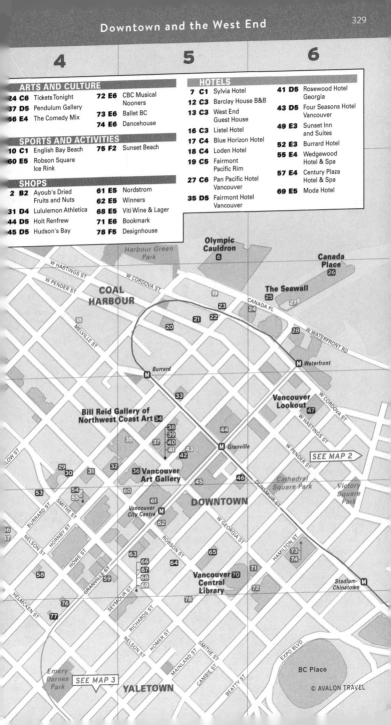

4   **5**   **6**

ARTS AND CULTURE

24 C6	Tickets Tonight	**72 E6**	CBC Musical Nooners
37 D5	Pendulum Gallery	**73 E6**	Ballet BC
56 E4	The Comedy Mix	**74 E6**	Dancehouse

SPORTS AND ACTIVITIES

10 C1	English Bay Beach	**75 F2**	Sunset Beach
60 E5	Robson Square Ice Rink		

SHOPS

2 B2	Ayoub's Dried Fruits and Nuts	**61 E5**	Nordstrom
31 D4	Lululemon Athletica	**62 E5**	Winners
44 D5	Holt Renfrew	**68 E5**	Viti Wine & Lager
45 D5	Hudson's Bay	**71 E6**	Bookmark
		78 F5	Designhouse

HOTELS

7 C1	Sylvia Hotel	**41 D5**	Rosewood Hotel Georgia
12 C3	Barclay House B&B	**43 D5**	Four Seasons Hotel Vancouver
13 C3	West End Guest House	**49 E3**	Sunset Inn and Suites
16 C3	Listel Hotel	**52 E3**	Burrard Hotel
17 C4	Blue Horizon Hotel	**55 E4**	Wedgewood Hotel & Spa
18 C4	Loden Hotel	**57 E4**	Century Plaza Hotel & Spa
19 C5	Fairmont Pacific Rim	**69 E5**	Moda Hotel
27 C6	Pan Pacific Hotel Vancouver		
35 D5	Fairmont Hotel Vancouver		

4 **5** **6**

SIGHTS

4	C2	Gastown Steam Clock	38	D5	Vancouver Police Museum
18	C3	Gassy Jack Statue	43	E3	Catfe
27	D2	Woodward's Building	44	E3	Dr. Sun Yat-Sen Classical Chinese Garden
34	D3	Millennium Gate			
36	D4	Rennie Collection at Wing Sang			

RESTAURANTS

10	C2	Revolver	40	D5	Kissa Tanto
19	C3	L'Abbatoir	41	E2	Chambar
23	C5	Ask for Luigi	42	E2	Jam Café
26	D2	Purebread	46	E4	Bao Bei Chinese Brasserie
28	D2	Tsuki Sushi Bar	47	E4	Juniper Kitchen & Bar
29	D2	Taishoken Ramen	48	E4	Juke
30	D3	Nelson the Seagull	49	F5	Crackle Crème
31	D3	Pidgin			

NIGHTLIFE

9	C2	The Pourhouse	17	C3	Six Acres
14	C3	Salt Tasting Room	20	C3	The Diamond
15	C3	Guilt & Company	22	C4	The Alibi Room
16	C3	Chill Winston	45	E4	The Keefer Bar

ARTS AND CULTURE

5	C2	Hill's Native Art	32	D3	Urban Aboriginal Fair Trade Gallery
7	C2	Coastal Peoples Fine Arts Gallery	37	D5	Movies in the Morgue
8	C2	Inuit Gallery of Vancouver	39	D5	Firehall Arts Centre

SHOPS

1	B2	Oak + Fort	13	C3	Örling & Wu
3	C2	One of a Few	21	C3	Lululemon Lab
6	C2	Kit and Ace	25	D1	The Paper Hound Bookshop
11	C3	Tees.ca	35	D3	Ming Wo
12	C3	John Fluevog			

HOTELS

| 2 | C1 | Delta Vancouver Suites | 24 | D1 | Victorian Hotel |
| | | | 33 | D3 | Skwachàys Lodge |

Crab Park

E WATERFRONT RD

ALEXANDER ST

POWELL ST

E CORDOVA ST

Vancouver Police Museum

E HASTINGS ST

ennie Collection at Wing Sang

CHINATOWN

E PENDER ST

KEEFER ST

E GEORGIA ST

UNION ST

STRATHCONA

DUNSMUIR VIADUCT

PRIOR ST

COLUMBIA ST

MAIN ST

GORE AVE

```
0        100 yds
0        100 m
```

DISTANCE ACROSS MAP
Approximate: 1.1 mi or 1.7 km

SEE MAP 7

© AVALON TRAVEL

SEE MAP 1

1   **2**   **3**

BURRARD ST

HORNBY ST

A

PACIFIC BLVD

HOWE ST

DAVIE ST

Emery Barnes Park

HOMER ST

SMITHE ST

GRANVILLE S

DRAKE ST

NELSON ST

CAMBIE ST

15 **Long Table Distillery**

SEYMOUR ST

RICHARDS ST

HELMCKEN ST

HAMILTON ST

MAINLAND ST

YALETOWN

B

Yaletown-Roundhouse

M

PACIFIC BLVD

Engine 374 Pavilion

MARINASIDE CRESCENT

GRANVILLE ST BRIDGE

George Wainborn Park

BEACH CRESCENT

David Lam Park

DRAKE ST

Seawall Trail

C

SEE MAP 4

False Creek

D

SIGHTS
15 **B1**	Long Table Distillery	**41** **C5**	Olympic Village
30 **B3**	Engine 374 Pavilion	**42** **C6**	Science World
32 **B4**	B.C. Place and the B.C. Sports Hall of Fame		

RESTAURANTS
2 **A1**	Giardino	**19** **B2**	Rodney's Oyster House
6 **A3**	The Buzz Café and Espresso Bar	**20** **B2**	La Pentola
7 **A3**	Homer Street Café and Bar	**23** **B3**	Small Victory Bakery
10 **A4**	Fanny Bay Oyster Bar	**24** **B3**	Blue Water Café
16 **B1**	Ancora Waterfront Dining and Patio	**25** **B3**	WildTale Coastal Grill
17 **B2**	Juno Sushi Bistro	**31** **B3**	Bella Gelateria Yaletown
18 **B2**	House Special	**39** **C5**	Terra Breads Bakery Café

NIGHTLIFE
9 **A4**	Central City Brew Pub	**37** **C5**	Tap & Barrel
13 **A4**	Frankie's Jazz Club	**47** **E5**	33 Acres Brewing
21 **B2**	Opus Bar	**48** **E6**	Brassneck Brewery
26 **B3**	Yaletown Brewing Company		

ARTS AND CULTURE
3 **A2**	Scotiabank Dance Centre	**44** **D6**	Winsor Gallery
5 **A3**	Contemporary Art Gallery	**45** **D6**	Equinox Galle
43 **D5**	Goldcorp Stage at the BMO Theatre Centre	**46** **D6**	Monte Clark Gal

SPORTS AND ACTIVITIES
1 **A1**	Bicycle Sports Pacific	**35** **C2**	David Lam Park
14 **A5**	Vancouver Canucks	**36** **C3**	Reckless Bike Stores
33 **B4**	B.C. Lions	**38** **C5**	Creekside Kayak
34 **B4**	Vancouver Whitecaps		

SHOPS
4 **A2**	My Sister's Closet	**29** **B3**	Global Atomic Designs
8 **A3**	Moulé	**40** **C5**	Legacy Liquor St
27 **B3**	Fine Finds Boutique		
28 **B3**	Woo To See You		

HOTELS
11 **A4**	YWCA Hotel Vancouver	**22** **B2**	Opus Hotel Vancouver
12 **A4**	Hotel BLU		

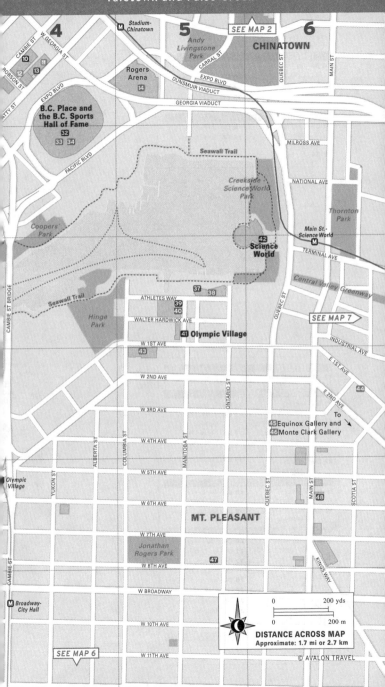

4

5

SEE MAP 2

6

Ⓜ Stadium-Chinatown

Andy Livingstone Park

CHINATOWN

CAMBIE ST

W GEORGIA ST

ROBSON ST

10
11
12
13

CARRAL ST

QUEBEC ST

MAIN ST

Rogers Arena

EXPO BLVD

EXPO BLVD

14

DUNSMUIR VIADUCT

BEATTY ST

B.C. Place and the B.C. Sports Hall of Fame

32

33 34

GEORGIA VIADUCT

MILROSS AVE

PACIFIC BLVD

Seawall Trail

Creekside Science World Park

NATIONAL AVE

Coopers Park

Thornton Park

Main St.-Science World
Ⓜ

CAMBIE ST BRIDGE

42
Science World

TERMINAL AVE

Seawall Trail

Central Valley Greenway

Hinge Park

ATHLETES WAY

37
38

QUEBEC ST

SEE MAP 7

39
40

WALTER HARDWICK AVE

41 **Olympic Village**

INDUSTRIAL AVE

W 1ST AVE

E 1ST AVE

43

W 2ND AVE

ONTARIO ST

E 2ND AVE

44

W 3RD AVE

To

45 Equinox Gallery and
46 Monte Clark Gallery

ALBERTA ST

COLUMBIA ST

MANITOBA ST

W 4TH AVE

W 5TH AVE

Ⓜ Olympic Village

YUKON ST

W 6TH AVE

QUEBEC ST

MAIN ST

SCOTIA ST

48

MT. PLEASANT

W 7TH AVE

Jonathan Rogers Park

47

W 8TH AVE

CAMBIE ST

KINGSWAY

W BROADWAY

Ⓜ Broadway-City Hall

0   200 yds

0   200 m

W 10TH AVE

DISTANCE ACROSS MAP
Approximate: 1.7 mi or 2.7 km

SEE MAP 6

W 11TH AVE

© AVALON TRAVEL

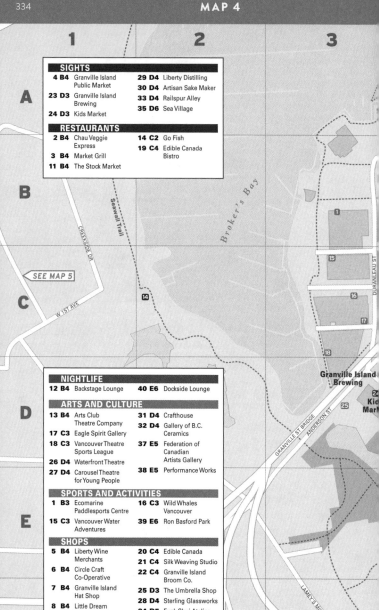

1 **2** **3**

SIGHTS
4 B4 Granville Island Public Market	**29 D4** Liberty Distilling
23 D3 Granville Island Brewing	**30 D4** Artisan Sake Maker
24 D3 Kids Market	**33 D4** Railspur Alley
	35 D6 Sea Village

RESTAURANTS
2 B4 Chau Veggie Express	**14 C2** Go Fish
3 B4 Market Grill	**19 C4** Edible Canada Bistro
11 B4 The Stock Market	

A

B

Seawall Trail

Broker's Bay

← SEE MAP 5

CREEKSIDE DR

W 1ST AVE

C

DURANLEAU ST

Granville Island Brewing

NIGHTLIFE
12 B4 Backstage Lounge	**40 E6** Dockside Lounge

ARTS AND CULTURE
13 B4 Arts Club Theatre Company	**31 D4** Crafthouse
17 C3 Eagle Spirit Gallery	**32 D4** Gallery of B.C. Ceramics
18 C3 Vancouver Theatre Sports League	**37 E5** Federation of Canadian Artists Gallery
26 D4 Waterfront Theatre	**38 E5** Performance Works
27 D4 Carousel Theatre for Young People	

SPORTS AND ACTIVITIES
1 B3 Ecomarine Paddlesports Centre	**16 C3** Wild Whales Vancouver
15 C3 Vancouver Water Adventures	**39 E6** Ron Basford Park

SHOPS
5 B4 Liberty Wine Merchants	**20 C4** Edible Canada
6 B4 Circle Craft Co-Operative	**21 C4** Silk Weaving Studio
7 B4 Granville Island Hat Shop	**22 C4** Granville Island Broom Co.
8 B4 Little Dream	**25 D3** The Umbrella Shop
9 B4 Net Loft	**28 D4** Sterling Glassworks
10 B4 Wickaninnish Gallery	**34 D5** Funk Shui Atelier
	36 E5 Ainsworth Custom Design

HOTELS
41 E6 Granville Island Hotel	

D

E

F

GRANVILLE ST BRIDGE

ANDERSON ST

Kids Market

LAMEY'S MILL RD

GRANVILLE BRIDGE

Granville Loop Park

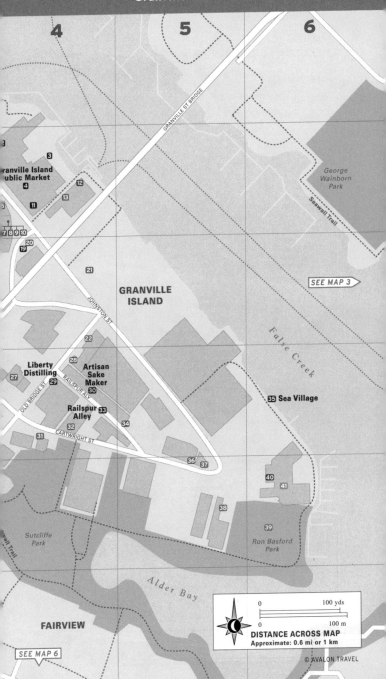

4
5
6

GRANVILLE ST BRIDGE

3
Granville Island
Public Market
4
12
13
11
7 8 9 10
20
19
21

JOHNSTON ST

GRANVILLE
ISLAND

George
Wainborn
Park

Seawall Trail

SEE MAP 3

False Creek

22

Liberty
Distilling
28
Artisan
Sake
Maker
27
29
RAILSPUR ALY
30
Railspur
Alley
33
34

OLD BRIDGE ST

35 Sea Village

32
31
CARTWRIGHT ST
36 37
40
41

38
39

Sutcliffe
Park
Ron Basford
Park

Seawall Trail

Alder Bay

FAIRVIEW

SEE MAP 6

0   100 yds
0   100 m
DISTANCE ACROSS MAP
Approximate: 0.6 mi or 1 km

© AVALON TRAVEL

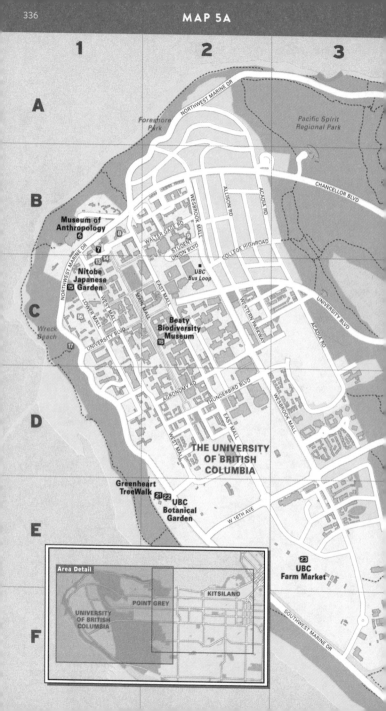

1

2

3

A

Foreshore
Park

Pacific Spirit
Regional Park

NORTHWEST MARINE DR

CHANCELLOR BLVD

B

**Museum of
Anthropology**
6

8

WALTER GAGE RD

WESBROOK MALL

ALLISON RD

ACADIA RD

STUDENT
UNION BLVD

9

COLLEGE HIGH ROAD

7

13 14

**Nitobe
Japanese
Garden**
15

NORTHWEST MARINE DR

EAST MALL

UBC
Bus Loop

UNIVERSITY BLVD

C

16

WEST MALL

MAIN MALL

LOWER MALL

UNIVERSITY BLVD

1

WESTERN PARKWAY

ACADIA RD

Wreck
Beach

17

**Beaty
Biodiversity
Museum**
18

D

AGRONOMY RD

THUNDERBIRD BLVD

WEST MALL

EAST MALL

WESBROOK MALL

**THE UNIVERSITY
OF BRITISH
COLUMBIA**

E

**Greenheart
TreeWalk**
21 22

**UBC
Botanical
Garden**

W 16TH AVE

23

**UBC
Farm Market**

F

Area Detail

**UNIVERSITY
OF BRITISH
COLUMBIA**

POINT GREY

KITSILAND

SOUTHWEST MARINE DR

4 **5** **6**

Spanish Banks
Beach

1

NORTHWEST MARINE DR

Locarno
Beach

2

3 **5**
4

11

Jericho
Beach

BELMONT AVE

10

Jericho
Beach Park

12

BLANCA ST
TOLMIE ST
SASAMAT ST
TRIMBLE ST

W 4TH AVE   W 4TH AVE

W 5TH AVE

W 6TH AVE

W 7TH AVE

Trimble
Park

SEE MAP 5B

W 8TH AVE   W 8TH AVE

University
Golf Club

W 9TH AVE

W 10TH AVE   W 10TH AVE

19

DISCOVERY ST
COURTENAY ST
CAMOSUN ST
CROWN ST

W 11TH AVE

W 12TH AVE

POINT GREY

W 13TH AVE

W 14TH AVE

W 15TH AVE

W 16TH AVE

20

Pacific Spirit
Regional Park

SIGHTS
6	**B1**	Museum of Anthropology	**21**	**E2**	Greenheart TreeWalk
15	**C1**	Nitobe Japanese Garden	**22**	**E2**	UBC Botanical Garden
18	**C2**	Beaty Biodiversity Museum	**23**	**E3**	UBC Farm Market

RESTAURANTS
3	**A6**	The Galley Patio and Grill	**7**	**B1**	Sage Bistro
			19	**C5**	Mix the Bakery

ARTS AND CULTURE
4	**A6**	Jericho Folk Club	**13**	**C1**	Frederic Wood Theatre
8	**B1**	Chan Centre for the Performing Arts	**14**	**C1**	Morris and Helen Belkin Art Gallery

SPORTS AND ACTIVITIES
1	**A5**	Spanish Banks Beach	**12**	**B6**	Jericho Beach
2	**A5**	Locarno Beach	**17**	**C1**	Wreck Beach
5	**A6**	Windsure	**20**	**D5**	Pacific Spirit Regional Park
11	**B6**	Ecomarine Paddlesports Centre			

HOTELS
9	**B2**	West Coast Suites at UBC	**16**	**C1**	Pacific Spirit Hostel
10	**B6**	HI-Vancouver Jericho Beach			

0   300 yds
0   300 m

DISTANCE ACROSS MAP
Approximate: 3.4 mi or 5.5 km

© AVALON TRAVEL

1

2

3

A

0   300 yds
0   300 m
DISTANCE ACROSS MAP
Approximate: 2.6 mi or 4.2 km

English
Bay

B

Jericho
Beach Park

POINT GREY RD

SEE MAP 5A

W 4TH AVE

C

Mcbride Park

HIGHBURY ST
ALMA ST
DUNBAR ST
COLLINGWOOD ST
WATERLOO ST
BLENHEIM ST
TRUTCH ST
BALACLAVA ST

W 10TH AVE

12 W BROADWAY

COURTENAY ST
CAMOSUN ST
CROWN ST
WALLACE ST

D

Almond Park

DUNBAR ST

POINT GREY

W 16TH AVE

E

Carnarvon Pa

Area Detail

KITSILANO

POINT GREY

UNIVERSITY OF BRITISH COLUMBIA

F

DUNBAR-SOUTHLANDS

© AVALON TRAVEL

SEE MAP 4

4 | **5** | **6**

Vancouver Maritime Museum ❶

Vanier Park

Kitsilano Beach

Museum of Vancouver ❷ ❸ ④

Kitsilano Beach Park

H. R. MacMillan Space Centre

MCNICOLL AVE

WHYTE AVE

CREELMAN AVE

❼

BURRARD ST

POINT GREY RD

CORNWALL AVE

❻

❿

YORK AVE

❽

W 1ST AVE

❾

⓫

KITSILANO

W 2ND AVE

㉗

W 3RD AVE

㉙

⓱ ⓳

W 4TH AVE

㉓

⓯ ⓲ ⓰

⑳ ㉑

㉒ ㉔ ㉕

㉖

㉘

㉚

W 5TH AVE

W 6TH AVE

W 7TH AVE

⓭

⓮

W 8TH AVE

W BROADWAY

㉛ ㉜

W 10TH AVE

Connaught Park

㉝

W 12TH AVE

W 13TH AVE

W 14TH AVE

W 15TH AVE

W 16TH AVE

W 18TH AVE

W 19TH AVE

ARBUTUS RIDGE

W 20TH AVE

W 21ST AVE

W 22ND AVE

W 23RD AVE

Trafalgar Park

MACDONALD ST · STEPHENS ST · TRAFALGAR ST · VINE ST · YEW ST · ARBUTUS ST · MAPLE ST · CYPRESS ST · BURRARD ST · PINE ST · FIR ST

atlow Park ⑤

VALLEY DR

OLIVER CRESCENT

W KING EDWARD AVE

SIGHTS

1	**A6**	Vancouver Maritime Museum	
2	**A6**	Museum of Vancouver	
3	**A6**	H. R. MacMillan Space Centre	

RESTAURANTS

9	**B5**	Café Zen	**25**	**C6**	Maenam
11	**B6**	AnnaLena	**26**	**C6**	Rain or Shine Ice Cream
15	**C5**	Culprit Coffee	**29**	**C6**	Chocolate Arts
16	**C5**	Au Comptoir	**30**	**C6**	Beaucoup Bakery & Café
18	**C5**	O5 Tea Bar	**32**	**D4**	Mr. Red Café
19	**C5**	Bishop's	**33**	**D4**	Kitsilano Farmers Market
21	**C5**	Mission			
24	**C6**	Fable			

NIGHTLIFE

8	**B5**	Local Public Eatery	**12**	**C2**	The Wolf and Hound
10	**B6**	Corduroy			

ARTS AND CULTURE

4	**A6**	Bard on the Beach

SPORTS AND ACTIVITIES

6	**B5**	Kitsilano Pool	**7**	**B5**	Kitsilano Beach

SHOPS

13	**C4**	The Travel Bug	**23**	**C6**	Wanderlust
14	**C4**	Kidsbooks	**27**	**C6**	Les Amis du Fromage
17	**C5**	Gravity Pope	**28**	**C6**	Comor Sports
20	**C5**	Silk Road Tea	**31**	**D4**	Pulp Fiction Books
22	**C6**	Two of Hearts			

HOTELS

5	**B4**	Corkscrew Inn

SEE MAP 4

W 8TH AVE
W BROADWAY
W 10TH AVE
W 11TH AVE
W 12TH AVE
W 13TH AVE
W 14TH AVE
W 15TH AVE
WOLFE AVE
W 16TH AVE

FIR ST
GRANVILLE ST
HEMLOCK ST
SPRUCE ST
OAK ST
LAUREL ST
WILLOW ST
HEATHER ST

FAIRVIEW

Heather Park
Douglas Park
SOUTH CAMBIE
Braemar Park

SIGHTS
32 **F2** VanDusen Botanical Garden
33 **F4** Queen Elizabeth Park

RESTAURANTS
1 **A1** Farmer's Apprentice
4 **A1** Rangoli
6 **A2** Tojo's
7 **A2** Salmon n' Bannock
8 **A3** Dynasty Seafood
9 **A3** Shao Lin Noodle House
13 **A5** Gene Coffee Bar
14 **A5** Chicha
16 **A5** Burdock & Co
17 **B1** West
20 **B4** Vij's
21 **B5** 49th Parallel Coffee Roasters
24 **C5** Liberty Bakery
28 **D5** The Acorn

NIGHTLIFE
15 **A5** The Cascade Room
29 **E5** The Shameful Tiki Room

ARTS AND CULTURE
2 **A1** Douglas Reynolds Gallery
5 **A1** Arts Club Theatre Company
12 **A5** The Sunday Service
18 **B1** Bau-Xi Gallery
19 **B4** Yuk Yuk's Vancouver Comedy Club
30 **E5** The Flame

SPORTS AND ACTIVITIES
31 **E5** Vancouver Canadians

SHOPS
3 **A1** Indigo
10 **A4** MEC
11 **A5** Sports Junkies
22 **C5** Vancouver Special
23 **C5** Twigg & Hottie
25 **C5** Barefoot Contessa
26 **D5** Front and Company
27 **D5** The Regional Assembly of Text

0   300 yds
0   300 m
DISTANCE ACROSS MAP
Approximate: 2.4 mi or 3.9 km

W 33RD AVE

OAK ST
WILLOW ST
HEATHER ST
CAMBIE ST

VanDusen Botanical Garden
VanDusen Botanical Garden 32
Oak Meadows Park
SEE MAP 8

To Farmer's Apprentice

A
B
C
D
E
F

1 2 3

1

2

3

A

Powell Street
Craft Brewery 1

POWELL ST

FRANKLIN ST

Callister 2
Brewing

EAST HASTINGS ST
7

JACKSON AVENUE

PRINCESS AVENUE

HEATLEY AVENUE

HAWKS AVENUE

CAMPBELL AVENUE

EAST PENDER ST

CLARK DR

FRANCES ST

Woodla
Park

B

MacLean
Park

E GEORGIA ST

SEE MAP 2

ADANAC ST

VENABLES ST

PARKER ST

Strathcona
Park

NAPIER ST

C

WILLIAM ST

CHARLES ST

GRANT ST

D 14

GRAVELEY ST

Central Valley Greenway

E 1ST AVE

E 2ND AVE

E 3RD AVE

E

E 4TH AVE

SEE MAP 3

Vcc-
Clark

M

Monument for 21
East Vancouver

CLARK DR

E 8TH AVE

F

E BROADWAY

© AVALON TRAVEL

Doan's Craft Brewing Company

Odd Society Spirits

Parallel 49 Brewing Company

Pandora Park

Templeton Park

Grandview Park

Victoria Park

McSpadden Park

Ⓜ Commercial Drive

Ⓜ Broadway

SIGHTS
1 A3	Powell Street Craft Brewery	**6 A5**	Parallel 49 Brewing Company
2 A3	Callister Brewing	**21 F3**	Monument for East Vancouver
3 A4	Odd Society Spirits		
4 A4	Doan's Craft Brewing Company		

RESTAURANTS
5 A4	The Pie Shoppe	**17 D4**	Merchant's Oyster Bar
9 B5	The Red Wagon	**19 E4**	La Grotta Del Formaggio
10 C4	Kin Kao Thai Kitchen	**20 E4**	Prado Café
15 D4	Turks Coffee House	**22 F4**	Jamjar

NIGHTLIFE
13 C4	Havana	**18 D4**	La Mezcaleria
16 D4	Storm Crow Tavern	**23 F4**	St. Augustine's

ARTS AND CULTURE
8 B4	York Theatre	**11 C4**	Vancouver East Cultural Centre

SPORTS AND ACTIVITIES
14 D1	Central Valley Greenway

SHOPS
7 B3	Gourmet Warehouse	**12 C4**	Still Fabulous

0	300 yds
0	300 m

DISTANCE ACROSS MAP
Approximate: 2.1 mi or 3.4 km

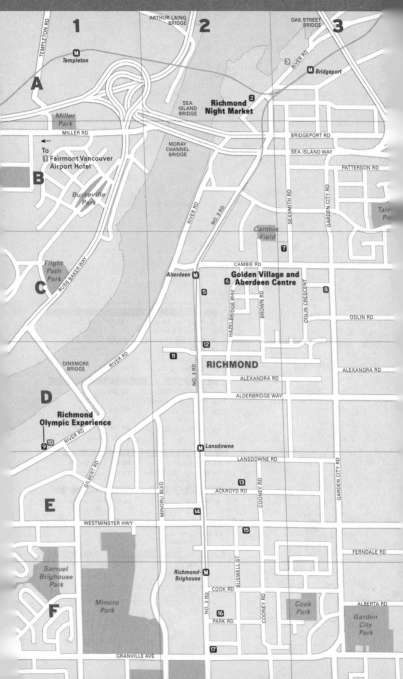

1

TEMPLETON RD

M Templeton

A

Miller Park

MILLER RD

To 1 Fairmont Vancouver Airport Hotel

B

Burkeville Park

RUSS BAKER WAY

Flight Path Park

C

DINSMORE BRIDGE

RIVER RD

D

Richmond Olympic Experience

9 10

RIVER RD

GILBERT RD

E

WESTMINSTER HWY

Samuel Brighouse Park

Minoru Park

F

GRANVILLE AVE

2

ARTHUR LAING BRIDGE

SEA ISLAND BRIDGE

2 Richmond Night Market

MORAY CHANNEL BRIDGE

RIVER RD

NO. 3 RD

Cambie Field

7

CAMBIE RD

Aberdeen M

5

HAZELBRIDGE WAY

BROWN RD

12

11

NO. 3 RD

RICHMOND

ALEXANDRA RD

ALDERBRIDGE WAY

M Lansdowne

LANSDOWNE RD

MINORU BLVD

13

ACKROYD RD

COONEY RD

14

15

Richmond-Brighouse M

BUSWELL ST

COOK RD

NO. 3 RD

16

COONEY RD

17

PARK RD

3

OAK STREET BRIDGE

RIVER RD

3

M Bridgeport

BRIDGEPORT RD

SEA ISLAND WAY

PATTERSON RD

SEXSMITH RD

GARDEN CITY RD

Talr Pe

Golden Village and Aberdeen Centre

ODLIN CRESCENT

8

ODLIN RD

ALEXANDRA RD

GARDEN CITY RD

FERNDALE RD

Cook Park

ALBERTA RD

Garden City Park

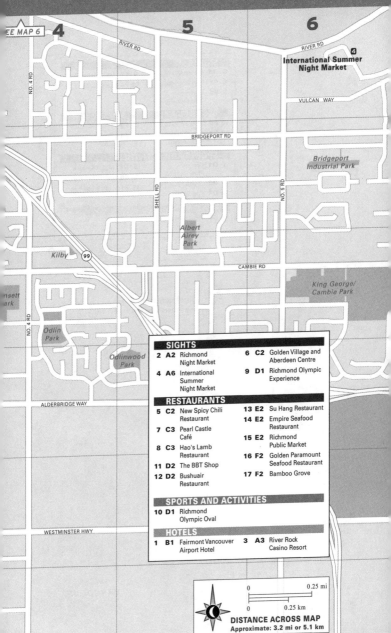

SEE MAP 6 **4** **5** **6**

RIVER RD

NO. 4 RD

RIVER RD

International Summer Night Market ④

VULCAN WAY

BRIDGEPORT RD

Bridgeport Industrial Park

SHELL RD

NO. 5 RD

Albert Airey Park

Kilby ⑨⑨

CAMBIE RD

King George/ Cambie Park

nsett ark

Odlin Park

NO. 4 RD

Odlinwood Park

ALDERBRIDGE WAY

SIGHTS

2	**A2**	Richmond Night Market		
4	**A6**	International Summer Night Market		
6	**C2**	Golden Village and Aberdeen Centre		
9	**D1**	Richmond Olympic Experience		

RESTAURANTS

5	**C2**	New Spicy Chili Restaurant
7	**C3**	Pearl Castle Café
8	**C3**	Hao's Lamb Restaurant
11	**D2**	The BBT Shop
12	**D2**	Bushuair Restaurant
13	**E2**	Su Hang Restaurant
14	**E2**	Empire Seafood Restaurant
15	**E2**	Richmond Public Market
16	**F2**	Golden Paramount Seafood Restaurant
17	**F2**	Bamboo Grove

SPORTS AND ACTIVITIES

10	**D1**	Richmond Olympic Oval

HOTELS

1	**B1**	Fairmont Vancouver Airport Hotel	**3**	**A3**	River Rock Casino Resort

WESTMINSTER HWY

0   0.25 mi
0   0.25 km

DISTANCE ACROSS MAP
Approximate: 3.2 mi or 5.1 km

© AVALON TRAVEL

GRANVILLE AVE

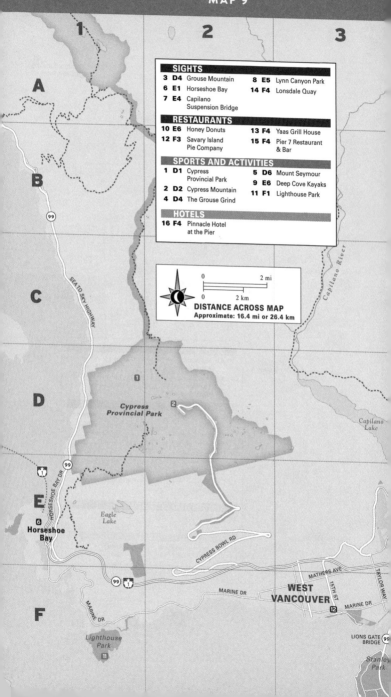

SIGHTS

- **3 D4** Grouse Mountain
- **6 E1** Horseshoe Bay
- **7 E4** Capilano Suspension Bridge
- **8 E5** Lynn Canyon Park
- **14 F4** Lonsdale Quay

RESTAURANTS

- **10 E6** Honey Donuts
- **12 F3** Savary Island Pie Company
- **13 F4** Yaas Grill House
- **15 F4** Pier 7 Restaurant & Bar

SPORTS AND ACTIVITIES

- **1 D1** Cypress Provincial Park
- **2 D2** Cypress Mountain
- **4 D4** The Grouse Grind
- **5 D6** Mount Seymour
- **9 E6** Deep Cove Kayaks
- **11 F1** Lighthouse Park

HOTELS

- **16 F4** Pinnacle Hotel at the Pier

0   2 mi
0   2 km

DISTANCE ACROSS MAP
Approximate: 16.4 mi or 26.4 km

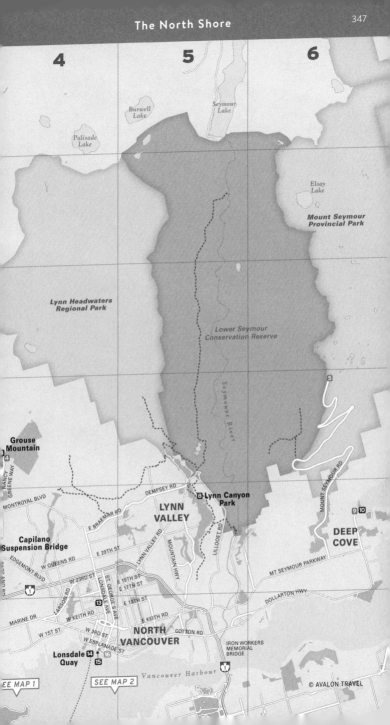

4

5

6

Burwell Lake

Seymour Lake

Palisade Lake

Elsay Lake

Mount Seymour Provincial Park

Lynn Headwaters Regional Park

Lower Seymour Conservation Reserve

Seymour River

5

Grouse Mountain

4

NANCY GREENE WAY

DEMPSEY RD

8 Lynn Canyon Park

MONTROYAL BLVD

LYNN VALLEY

E BRAEMAR RD

Capilano Suspension Bridge

E 29TH ST

EDGEMONT BLVD

W QUEENS RD

LYNN VALLEY RD

MOUNTAIN HWY

LILLOOET RD

MOUNT SEYMOUR RD

9 **10**

DEEP COVE

1

LARSON RD

W 23RD ST

E 19TH ST

LONSDALE AVE

ST GEORGES AVE

E 17TH ST

MT SEYMOUR PARKWAY

MARINE DR

W KEITH RD

E 13TH ST

13

E KEITH RD

DOLLARTON HWY

W 3RD ST

COTTON RD

NORTH VANCOUVER

W 1ST ST

W ESPLANADE ST

IRON WORKERS MEMORIAL BRIDGE

Lonsdale Quay **14**

15

16

Vancouver Harbour

1

SEE MAP 1

SEE MAP 2

© AVALON TRAVEL

Also Available

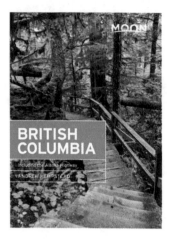

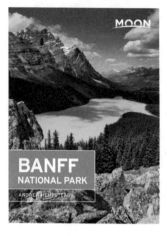

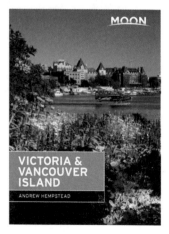

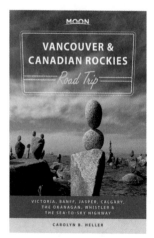